# RENEGADE
# SNARES

**RENEGADE SNARES**
**THE RESISTANCE AND RESILIENCE**
**OF DRUM & BASS**
**BEN MURPHY & CARL LOBEN**

A Jawbone book
Published in the UK and the USA
by Jawbone Press
Office G1
141–157 Acre Lane
London SW2 5UA
England
www.jawbonepress.com

ISBN 978-1-911036-79-1

Printed In The Czech Republic by PBtisk

1 2 3 4 5 25 24 23 22 21

# TABLE OF CONTENTS

**RENEGADE** An individual who rejects lawful or conventional behaviour.

**SNARES** A set of gut strings wound with wire fitted against the lower drumhead of a snare drum. Characteristics: bright, hard, clear, precise, metallic, shrill, noise-like, sharp, penetrating, rustling, hissing, shuffling, rattling, clattering, dry, cracking.

'**RENEGADE SNARES** works on another level. The whole movement of jungle/drum & bass was a kind of renegade movement. It was on the outside of the mainstream, totally independent, and like punk, years before it, it created a minor revolution with its back firmly turned on the establishment.'

**ROB HAIGH (OMNI TRIO)**

# Intro

It's July 2015. The buzz of the South Bank in London is a long way from the South Bronx in New York, where a quarter of a century previously, one Clifford Price was hanging with the TATS CRU of graffiti writers. Graffiti still adorns the skatepark underneath the concrete gables just along from the National Film Theatre, but Goldie's work today is taking place in rather more salubrious surroundings: the prestigious Royal Festival Hall.

It's the ultimate endgame for a style of music that Goldie played such a big part in shaping. In 1995, his *Timeless* album catapulted jungle/drum & bass into the mainstream, and Goldie with it. An aural masterwork that still stands up decades later, it's now being revisited by Goldie in a new form.

We're here for the second show of Goldie's full orchestral interpretation of *Timeless* with The Heritage Orchestra. It's the most powerful refutation imaginable for the haters who said drum & bass was too fast, ain't gonna last. 'Vindication,' Goldie would call it later. Drum & bass has been derided and overlooked, written off and ridiculed, but has grown from underground roots to now be perceived as high culture. It never needed this kind of affirmation, but it's still, finally, been embraced by the establishment. It's in the Royal-fucking-Festival Hall. It's transcended functionality.

Inside the venue, with its boxes up the walls straight out of a 70s sci-fi movie, there's a breathless expectation about the crowd. Despite the odd junglism T-shirt, many don't look like old ravers. It's a mixture of theatregoers and classical concert fans, mingling with a fair share of headz.

There's loads of kit onstage, and when The Heritage Orchestra emerge from the shadows, all wearing *Timeless* T-shirts with a twisted Metalheadz skull design on the front, clutching violins, cellos, and other instruments, they're greeted warmly. Goldie stands nonchalantly at the side of the stage before emerging right on cue.

There aren't many musicians in popular music who have the chutzpah to harness the immense power of a full orchestra and simultaneously rock the joint to its foundations like a sweaty rave. But Goldie is that man, and just one of the key players in the formation and evolution of modern music's last completely new language. This live performance tonight is elegant, fierce, explosive, reflective; exquisitely organised chaos, the paradoxical balance that defines jungle.

The crowd are on their feet; the two drummers smack the skins for all they're worth; the horn section conjures the vengeful spirit of darkcore rave synths. In the quieter moments, the musicality of *Timeless* unfurls through the massed string section. It's a stunning spectacle, and, in the eye of the storm, Goldie vacillates between meditative reflection and crazed concert conductor, egging on the players to ever-greater feats. His faith in the power of drum & bass is infectious. And, today, the influence of that genre is the most powerful it's been in many years.

## UNIQUE LANGUAGE

Taking root at the beginning of the 1990s from seeds sown in the previous decade (and even further back), drum & bass was the first completely original form of electronic dance music to develop in the UK. Though constructed from a motley assortment of pre-existing styles—hip-hop, reggae, hardcore, techno, house, jazz, soul, synth-pop—its rapid pace, mesh of samples, and black origins in London quickly developed into an unmistakable, unique language. As the music writer Simon Reynolds notes in his 1998 book *Energy Flash*, 'Jungle is where all the different musics of the African-American/Afro-Caribbean diaspora (the scattering caused by slavery and forced migration) reconverge. In jungle, all the most African elements (polyrhythmic percussion, sub-aural bass frequencies, repetition) from funk, dub reggae, electro, rap, acieed and ragga are welded into the ultimate tribal trance-dance.'

Thirty years since its beginnings, drum & bass is more influential than ever—and now on a worldwide scale. Though it's been mostly dismissed by the mainstream during its lifetime, this form of music has been able to achieve extraordinary things. In more recent times, drum & bass has not only filled London's enormous Wembley Arena (courtesy of DJ Andy C) but also topped the pop charts for the first time (thanks to Fresh and Sigma). It's inspired hugely popular dubstep acts like Skrillex in the USA; fostered homegrown scenes in

Brazil, The Netherlands, the Czech Republic, the USA, and Japan; and given rise to an increasing number of international festivals that see dedicated fans flying out to enjoy their favourite beats in the sunshine.

'Drum & bass has probably never reached those commercial zeniths that other genres have, because it can't get assimilated into 4/4—the tempo doesn't fit in with other genres,' says Andy C. 'We've had our popular moments, but we've always kept it real and kept it true on an underground level. When you're drum & bass, you really are—you get it. The BPM is unique, there's no other genre like it.'

Drum & bass is instantly recognisable in its mixture of elements. Hyperspeed drums that hover today around 170 beats per minute; bass tones designed to be felt as well as heard when played on a big soundsystem; electronic riffs or samples arranged in minimalist fashion. Yet within that definition, drum & bass and jungle are almost infinitely malleable and adaptable, and they can draw from such seemingly polarised genres as rowdy dancehall and blissed-out new-age ambient—sometimes in the space of a single track. The genre's cultural mix, flowing from predominantly black and working-class producers and DJs, has been inclusive from the beginning. It's open to input from all ethnicities and walks of life, as long as the music made or played is true to the genre's core ethos.

'The music's endured because it has been so multicultural for years,' says DJ Flight. 'Obviously it was inspired and took elements from all these other music styles that came from other countries, a lot of it from the States—jazz, hip-hop, soul—but it's a very British sound, and there's a lot of history in it.'

Drum & bass is partly a by-product of growing up in an imperfect, sometimes racist society. In its early days, seething polyrhythms offset with moments of beauty and soul were the epitome of the late-twentieth-century inner-city blues. 'A looking-glass of proud blues,' as Goldie surmised on his album *The Journey Man* in 2017.

Other styles of underground UK dance music influenced by drum & bass, like dubstep or two-step garage, have contributed to what has been described as the 'hardcore continuum', though it's the core sound of d&b that remains a rock-solid foundation. It continues to evolve, fracturing into multiple fragments, with a seemingly inexhaustible reserve of fresh ideas that some inventive new producer will dream up.

The fact that drum & bass has been able to achieve so much despite outright hostility from the establishment (Goldie at Royal Festival Hall notwithstanding) has helped to secure its underground legend—and renegade status. Its outlaw nature, in the face of radio regulators, a snobbish media, and racism, has made its DJs, producers, MCs, promoters, and fans stick together as a tight-knit crew who roll as a unit. Like a b-boy with a spray can writing his name on a subway train under cover of darkness in early 80s NYC, the renegades of d&b have indelibly inscribed their names on dance music, whether its cultural arbiters like it or not.

The unique background of jungle—where it came from, what it's been able to do—gives it one of the richest and most fascinating histories in any genre. And still, while it continues to be virtually ignored by most cool-hunting magazines and broadsheet newspapers, it has the power to fill arenas and bring a great cross-section of people together.

At this moment, when some countries are more divided than ever, drum & bass is testament to the power of music and culture being a way to bring people of different ethnicities and genders together, rather than driving them apart. It's been a potent agent of change, and the power of drum & bass exists in its community—a family united by its love of the sound and the rituals surrounding it. Though it's far from immune to the issues afflicting wider society—whitewashing and sexism being two examples—and at the time of writing has been stricken by the ongoing COVID-19 epidemic, it remains one of the UK's most vital cultural contributions, and its history confirms the music's transformative effect on popular culture and social cohesion.

# 01 Roots: Windrush, Soundsystems, and Black British Culture

On June 22, 1948, the *Empire Windrush* docked at Tilbury, near London, carrying several hundred passengers from Jamaica in the Caribbean, as well as from a number of other countries. An advert had been placed in a Jamaican newspaper offering cheap transport to the UK for anyone who wanted to go to live and work there, and just under five hundred people took up the offer. The British Nationality Act of 1948 had just been passed, giving citizenship to 'British subjects' from Commonwealth countries (former British colonies) and a number of black servicemen who had fought for the Allies in World War II also decided to make the journey to the 'mother country'.

The British government encouraged immigration from Commonwealth countries because post-war labour shortages meant that they needed people to work in the newly created National Health Service, on the rebooted transport networks, and so on. This influx of newly nationalised black men and women who followed from the Caribbean in the subsequent years became known in the UK as the Windrush generation. And some of the 'Children of Windrush' played a crucial part in building the UK's jungle/drum & bass scene.

The backbone of the scene from its inception were black guys whose parents migrated to the UK in the 1950s and 60s. Goldie's dad, Clement Price, arrived in the UK from Trinidad and met his (white) singer mum in a Midlands pub; the parents of Randall, Bryan Gee, Brockie, Congo Natty, and many others are all of Caribbean origin. There's also Ray Keith, whose parents are Mauritian, DJ Rap from Singapore, plus a load of white British youth who contributed to the early days of jungle—testimony to the multicultural make-up of assorted English cities.

'My dad came over in '56, and then he sent for my mum,' says Bristolian junglist Roni Size. 'They were together already but couldn't afford to come at the same time.' Roni's immediate family randomly ended up in Bristol, his mum working in the local hospital and his dad in the local Cadbury's factory and as a builder, but he remembers as a kid his extended family coming from Nottingham, Birmingham, and London for family gatherings.

'Both our parents are from Jamaica and arrived in the UK in the 1960s,' say drum & bass pioneers Fabio & Grooverider. 'Both of our parents worked in the transport industry and were brought over to help rebuild the country.'

'My mum and dad are both from Guyana originally, which is considered part of the Caribbean due to strong cultural links,' says jungle stalwart Jumpin Jack Frost (real name: Nigel Thompson) down the phone line. 'When did they arrive in the UK? Let me just put my mum on the phone, one second...'

Frost's mum, Ingrid, comes on the line. 'I arrived in June 1961,' she begins, explaining how she ended up living in Brixton. 'I think Nigel's dad came the year before. Did I experience racism in my early days here? Oh, yes, yes. There were situations where you'd see a job advertised, you go for the job, and when they actually see who you are then suddenly the job's gone. That sort of thing.

'And at school there was a lot of name-calling,' Ingrid continues. 'The way the children got treated at school was also an issue—because they were black, they were treated in a certain way, put into certain streams. But later on, I found that people whose children had been told *You will never make this, you will never do that*, have turned out to be doctors and lawyers and all this sort of thing.'

The Windrush generation had been invited to the UK from the Caribbean to help rebuild the country, and they could scarcely have anticipated the appalling level of racism they would experience on arrival. The 1950s was an era when signs saying things like 'No coloureds' or 'No Irish, no blacks, no dogs' frequently appeared in the windows of properties to let.

In late-1950s London, white working-class teddy boys would frequently racially abuse black West Indian migrants to Britain. Fuelled by the scapegoating rhetoric of far-right groups like Oswald Mosley's Union Movement, peddling claptrap like 'Keep Britain White', there was a number of violent attacks on black people in west London in late August 1958, leaving at least five black men unconscious. After an incident in which some teddy boys assaulted a mixed-race couple (Raymond Morrison and his white Swedish partner, Majbritt), approximately three hundred teddy boys began rampaging through Notting Hill, armed with iron bars, knives, and belts, breaking into homes and attacking any West Indian they could find. The shocked black community was forced to fight back in self-defence.

These 'racial riots', as the press called them at the time, continued for several days over the August Bank Holiday weekend. Senior police officers tried to dismiss the riots as 'the work of ruffians, both coloured and white' hellbent on hooliganism, but secret police papers released forty-four years later stated that they were overwhelmingly the work of a white working-class mob out to get members of the black community.

In response to the west London riots, a Caribbean Carnival was held early the following year to celebrate West Indian culture—the precursor to the annual Notting Hill Carnival, whose parade of floats and soundsystems would subsequently go on to attract over a million revellers to the streets of west London every August Bank Holiday weekend.

The black migrants who came to the UK from the Caribbean in the 50s and 60s brought with them a rich cultural heritage—especially new music. Lively family celebrations—contrasting with the starchy, reserved tone of many English affairs—would involve wiring up extra speakers to the radiogram for a dance, aunties and uncles bringing records over, and so on.

'Everyone had a gramophone in their house, you'd stack up all the seven-inches on it and they just came on one after another,' says Roni Size, recalling tracks like the rocksteady-heavy monster sound of *Monkey Spanner* by Dave & Ansel Collins and calypso cut *Shame & Scandal In The Family* on the Dansette. 'Our families brought culture, which is inbred now in the fabric of British society. The swagger, the language, the mindset . . . the thing about the musical influence was, my parents listened to Elvis as well. And Pat Boone, but then they'd also listen to The Mighty Diamonds. It was more the celebration—like with Carnival. The main thing that the Windrush generation brought here was the Jamaican spirit. And white rum.'

Jumpin Jack Frost talks about growing up around his uncles who were into a lot of funk and soul, and then experiencing the Jah Shaka Soundsystem—'skanking, being really heavily into it'—before becoming a box boy for Frontline International, 'helping to lift the [speaker] boxes and the wires into parties'. His autobiography *Big Bad & Heavy*, published in 2017, goes into fascinating detail about his trials and tribulations growing up around the music scene in London.

Soundsystem culture originated in Jamaica in the 1950s, when DJs would load up a truck with a generator, turntables, and huge speakers and set up street parties. It was actually the 'DJ' who would rap over the tunes while the 'selector' picked the tracks; as time went on, crews began cutting dubplates so that they'd have exclusive original sounds. This was a precursor to how drum & bass would operate several decades later.

With the continued migration of Caribbean people to the UK in the 1960s and 70s, a plethora of soundsystems emerged in most major cities in the UK where there was a black community. Basements were commandeered, and illicit blues parties would provide these systems with a homegrown DIY dance space to play styles like ska and reggae. Segueing with the growth of discotheques into nightclubs, soundsystems were crucial to the development of UK dance music.

Enoch Powell delivered his inflammatory 'Rivers Of Blood' speech in 1968, but on dancefloors and at gigs, black and white people were uniting through music. Disco and punk were the predominant sounds of the late 1970s, although punk—unlike disco—was pretty white in the main. Don Letts, whose parents were originally from Jamaica, was the hugely influential DJ at punk haunt the Roxy, playing dub reggae in between the punk bands. His sounds unwittingly spawned a 'punky reggae party' whereby subsequent post-punk bands filled their sound with more space, and acts like Big Audio Dynamite—who Letts featured in, alongside Mick Jones from The Clash—set out exploring a dub-wise beats sound. Reggae, of course, became huge in the 70s and 80s among black communities in Britain and beyond.

The ska-tinged 2-Tone sound was the principal band-centred UK youth music movement after punk. The two black guys who flanked deadpan singer Terry Hall in The Specials—Neville Staple and Lyndal Golding—were Jamaica-born, and the multiracial nature to 2-Tone (bands like The Beat and The Selecter) helped change a lot of previously racist attitudes among white working-class youth—as had Rock Against Racism a couple of years earlier.

In the 80s, these various cultural and musical roots would collide with the DIY sampling and electronics of black America, helping to truly kickstart a UK dance music phenomenon. 'The reggae scene, 2-Tone, they all played a part,' Marc Mac from 4hero later told welovejungle.com. '2-Tone was good because it was one of the first genres that made black and white people want to rave together. So the whole *rainbow people* thing was building.'

# 02 Rave: Elements Of Life

## HIP-HOP, RARE GROOVE, REGGAE

'Ultramagnetic MCs, Big Daddy Kane, James Brown,' listed jungle pioneer Dillinja, talking to *Melody Maker* in the mid-90s about his influences. 'If it wasn't for those geezers creating those breaks, our music wouldn't even be here.'

In the early 1980s, something new arrived in Britain from the USA that would go on to be one of the building blocks of UK dance music. Hip-hop was an irresistibly American and gritty inner-city sound that had sprung from the mean streets of New York borough the Bronx in the early 70s, later leaping the Atlantic.

DJ Kool Herc, who'd emigrated with his family from Jamaica to NYC when he was twelve, is credited with being the founding father of hip-hop. As early as 1973, he was renowned for cutting up instrumental funk breaks on two turntables so the drums would play in continuous loops for the pleasure of dancers. He was also known for his syncopated speaking on the mic—something he imported from Jamaican soundsystem culture. By the early 80s, hip-hop had evolved into its own distinct musical form, replete with rappers and original music that either replayed or sampled the drum-heavy sounds Kool Herc and Afrika Bambaataa would spin at New York block parties.

Hip-hop got huge in the USA first, thanks in part to tunes like Sugar Hill Gang's pop hit *Rapper's Delight*, then internationally. Its impact on the youth in the UK was massive, capturing the imaginations of teens in cities and towns across England especially. It was rebellious, countercultural, DIY, and it sounded like the future. Like punk, you could in theory do it yourself, but you didn't need a band, and its working-class, African-American origins made it exciting yet relatable to black Britons and white inner-city kids alike.

The drum-machine quakes of rap's embryonic 80s period were robotic yet funky; urban dwellers could appreciate the street reportage and harsh realities, despite the Stateside subject matter; and it was danceable, giving rise to body-poppers and breakdancers, decked out in Adidas and Puma trainers, writing graffiti on trains and walls, and attempting to replicate their American inspirations. Tunes like Run-DMC's *Sucker MCs* or LL Cool J's *My Radio* suggested a bold, minimalist direction for music. On the other hand, electro—a sound initially twinned with hip-hop—was even more futuristic, with its synth-generated cybernetic rhythms and spine-snapping bass shudders. Electro tunes like *Planet Rock* by Afrika Bambaataa and Hashim's *Al Naafiysh* made a sizeable impact in the UK.

As the 1980s progressed, the sound of the underground club scene in Britain was classified as 'rare groove': scarce or rediscovered funk, disco, and boogie tracks that had lain dormant but were now played on London pirate radio stations such as Kiss, Invicta, or JFM, and in clubs like the Wag and, later, the Soul II Soul night at the Africa Centre in Covent Garden. Soul II Soul was also a soundsystem to begin with, and its dances would later provide a bridge from soul, funk, hip-hop, and reggae into house music. Soul II Soul was fronted by funki dred Jazzie B, whose parents originally came from Antigua in the Caribbean, and their multiracial party nights helped set the London dance scene up to be a welcoming place for all races.

DJs on the rare-groove circuit—including Barrie Sharpe, Norman Jay, Gilles Peterson, Judge Jules (before his trance days), and the late Paul 'Trouble' Anderson—drew from tracks by James Brown & The J.B.'s, Cymande, and Roy Ayers, plus contemporary electronic funk tracks such as David Joseph's *You Can't Hide (Your Love From Me)*.

In parallel, after 1985, hip-hop began to get more sophisticated. Rap producers started to loop the breakbeats that were the bread and butter of the earliest days of hip-hop DJ sets in NYC in their own creations, as hardware samplers and sampling itself became more affordable. Sampling was initially the preserve of wealthy pop artists who could afford the enormous and prohibitively expensive sample-based synthesizer of the day, the Fairlight; but then, smaller, purpose-made sample boxes, manufactured by E-mu, Roland, and Akai, became available at considerably lower cost.

Though initially crudely produced, these sampled breakbeats were to become the bedrock of a more cut-and-paste, funk-loaded form of rap that mixed well with the rare groove prevalent in UK clubs. American groups from Stetsasonic to Public Enemy, backed by production whiz-kids Prince Paul and The Bomb Squad, respectively, began to twist these sampled drums and funk loops into unfamiliar and thrilling shapes. Public Enemy's pivotal 1987 track *Rebel Without A Pause* took an impossibly syncopated drum break from James Brown's *Funky Drummer* and dropped an atonal horn snippet from the J.B.'s' *The Grunt* over the top. Tied to Chuck D's reality-bomb rhymes, this was something shockingly new—avant-garde yet funky, with an appealing message of resistance at its core. Public Enemy especially are progenitors of what became hardcore and jungle, using multiple samples for noise and texture, not simply for melody or rhythm, and having an enormous influence on producers in the UK who grew up with hip-hop.

Reggae already had a strong black British following, and it had mainstream pop success beyond artists like Bob Marley thanks to tunes by Althea & Donna and UK singer Janet Kay, plus Sugar Minott and Smiley Culture. The 2-Tone record label and scene, with its ethnically mixed bands, had already brought a strand of punk-influenced ska and reggae into the public consciousness. Pirate station Dread Broadcasting Corporation—the first black-owned broadcaster in the UK—had DJs such as Ranking Miss P pumping roots and dub into homes across London for a time, and the increasingly prevalent Jamaican sound of digital dancehall—a modern form of reggae that harnessed electronics in much the same way as the rest of the music scene was doing in the 1980s—became a mainstay of local soundsystems in London, Leeds, Birmingham, Bristol, and other cities.

These multiple musical strands each had their own affiliations. Rare groove, in a presentiment of what was to come, was a style often played in warehouse spaces, and was the most open-minded to other forms of music being added to its dancefloor mix. Empty properties across London, which were plentiful then, would be commandeered for events such as Norman Jay's Shake 'n' Fingerpop party. The form of funk played was anti-establishment in its lyrical content, concerned with black empowerment, and in stark opposition to Margaret Thatcher's ruinous Conservative government, which had precipitated a massive rise in inequality and youth unemployment that decade, the latter rising to 17 percent in 1984.

'There was a general air of dissidence, often reflected in a playlist that included Gil Scott-Heron's anti-Reagan song *B-Movie*, Junior Murvin's *Police & Thieves*, or Brother D With The Collective Effort's *How We Gonna Make*

*The Black Nation Rise?*,' Bill Brewster and Terry Farley have said, discussing the staple sounds of rare-groove parties in their overview of this pre-acid-house era for Red Bull Music Academy. This outlaw sound looks uncannily prophetic now, in its anticipation of the rave scene's anti-authority stance.

## HOUSE MUSIC ALL NIGHT LONG

What would have arguably the biggest impact on a musical and social level was the dawn of house music in the UK. This style of electronic dance music—born in the black and gay communities of Chicago, before spreading to New York, Detroit, and the UK and Europe—was more DIY than any style that had come before. House producers could do everything themselves, like another musical hero of the time, Prince: they could be the bass player, drummer, orchestra, all with a few metal boxes and some imagination. Records by Jesse Saunders, Frankie Knuckles, Marshall Jefferson, and Jamie Principle in Chicago, and Todd Terry in NYC, were tentatively embraced in Britain, but it took time for them to get popular. First captured on wax in 1983 with Jesse Saunders's *On And On*, Jamie Principle's *Your Love*, and Chip E's *Time To Jack*, it was several years before house caught on in the UK, and some DJs within the rare-groove or hip-hop scene were initially resistant to it, distrusting its robotic backbeat, or—later—bemused by the abstract weirdness of tracks such as Phuture's *Acid Tracks*.

Still, some clicked with the sound and recognised its affinity with existing forms early on. Blues parties—unlicensed all-night clubs in the backrooms of people's houses, which had first arisen among the UK's Caribbean communities in the 1950s as social hubs where black people could congregate and avoid the pervasive racism elsewhere—became a place where house music sometimes manifested itself in the DJ's playlists. In Leeds, Mark Millington was a regular DJ at blues parties and events at community centres, and, with his Ital Rockers soundsystem, assisted by local musician Homer Harriott, he started to cross-pollinate the more typical reggae or soul sounds that were heard at these events with the emerging electronic dance style from the USA.

'When house came in from Chicago, Mark started buying those records,' Harriott would tell Matt Anniss, author of the book *Join The Future*. 'Before we played as Ital Rockers at the community centre, it had just been reggae…but we changed that.'

Seeing the style as a new manifestation of dub, Millington and Harriott began to create their own dubplate productions: special one-off records designed only to be played in their DJ sets, and based on popular house tracks of the time, with re-done, topical lyrics. In 1987, Ital Rockers would even have a soundclash—a DJ battle imported from reggae soundsystem culture—with another local DJ crew, Unique 3. Here, though, they incorporated house beats. Both Ital Rockers and Unique 3 would later go on to make their own tunes that emphasised the bass weight of soundsystems and combined it with electronic beats, anticipating the mix of hardcore and especially jungle.

House clubs sprang up in London and Manchester in the late 80s, with the Pyramid night at gay club Heaven in the capital leading the way. Clink Street was a venue in a former prison in south London, where, for a spell in 1988, the RIP (Revolution In Progress) nights reverberated to a heavy Chicago house soundtrack of 4/4 drums, and DJs such as Mr C, 'Evil' Eddie Richards, and Kid Bachelor regaled a mixed crowd of black clubbers, football casuals, and hedonists. Danny Rampling's Shoom took root initially nearby in Southwark, attracting a sizeable, fanatical following; there was Spectrum, another of the famous acid-house parties, run by Paul Oakenfold at Heaven; or The Trip, which occupied the now-demolished Astoria on Charing Cross Road.

In Manchester, the Hacienda, running since 1982, was one of the first clubs to embrace the incipient house-music movement at its Nude club night, with Mike Pickering adding it to a blend of soul and funk, before the tide turned decisively towards electronic dance music.

Something was happening to the music played at these events. While initially, all the records played at UK house clubs, and later raves, were American imports or tracks licensed for the UK market, British producers now started to experiment with their own version of house. In a similar way that Brit-funk bands such as Atmosfear or Cymande had drawn on their multicultural backgrounds to make dub-dipped jazz and funk, and Broken Glass had produced a UK response to the electro sound that had flooded the UK via the *Street Sounds* compilations, black British producers started to make a distinctly omnivorous version of house. Tunes like Ability II's *Pressure*, especially in its dub mix, had a stripped-down, reggae-influenced 'drum and bass' attitude, fixated with pushing the low-end higher in the mix, and dropping in soundsystem-influenced blips and bleeps. Tony Addis's Warriors Dance label, an extension of his Addis Ababa studio, foregrounded a black British style in its pioneering house music, influenced by African and Caribbean sounds, and delivered one of the earliest breakbeat rave tracks in Addis Posse's 1989 tune *Let The Warriors Dance*.

'Looking at the sound now, you can see it was the early template for jungle and drum & bass,' Tony Addis told Joe Roberts, in an article for Red Bull Music. 'But it's all an evolution of funk and black music reinventing itself and incorporating elements in its creative process.'

An early mutation of house in Britain was bleep & bass, a UK form of dance music that combines heavy soundsystem low-end with the electronic beats of the American sound plus stripped back, abstract noises. Labels like the influential Chill Records would put out tunes like Original Clique's *Come To Papa*, which sounded like an eight-bit computer game soundtrack with its weighty b-line and stripped-down vibe, and later released the proto-jungle *Rocking Down The House* by MI7, with its Apache breakbeat, reggae samples, and house bass. Several DJs who would later go on to become founders of jungle and drum & bass, such as Fabio & Grooverider, Nicky Blackmarket, and Ray Keith, first became active on the DJ circuit playing house.

If the new house club nights were an indication of the changing nature of British youth culture, it was the outdoor raves in the countryside and in warehouses in cities, both legal and illegal, that would cause a truly seismic shift. Massive outlaw events held outside the northern city of Blackburn, Lancashire, or enormous shindigs such as the legal mega-production Apocalypse Now at Wembley Studios, London, attracted huge numbers of revellers. In the wake of the original mega-raves Sunrise, Biology, and World Dance, promotions such as Fantazia, Dreamscape, Helter Skelter, and Raindance packed out warehouses, aircraft hangars, and fields with thousands of dancers. These raves were a temporary nirvana in which, for a brief time, clubbers could lose themselves and the boundaries of society could be dissolved.

Whereas in the past raves were powered by house and an eclectic blend of dancefloor genres, these large-scale events were increasingly driven by breakbeat hardcore. The music itself was evolving to suit its new setting, with producers and DJs eager to outdo each other with their futurist beats.

Quickly, rave culture reached a tipping point. These events brought out an ethnically diverse crowd; and, despite scepticism from house-music purists, they created something magical and unifying on a scale that was gobsmacking. The multicultural nature of key English cities was crucial to its development.

'It was the culture thing,' says jungle pioneer DJ SS, who started out in hip-hop before discovering acid-house raves. 'The unity—black, white, Asian, everybody mixing together. We'd never seen it before. It was full of football hooligans—in the afternoon they were fighting each other, but in the evening at the rave they were hugging each other. I said, I've got to be part of this. I got drawn into it by that.'

'Acid house was a multicultural explosion, it was a time of change,' says Jumpin Jack Frost. 'We had people from all backgrounds and cultures coming together and becoming friends.'

Raves became commonplace across the country, from Somerset to Essex, London to Staffordshire, and hippies mingled with b-boys and b-girls, brought together by music, an alternative lifestyle, and opposition to a hostile government. 'It was an amazing time where everything was brand new—nothing like this had happened before,' says Mark Archer of Altern 8 and Nexus 21. 'There was a true feeling of togetherness that wasn't just because of drugs.'

House became mainstream, and despite (or maybe partly because of) tabloid scare stories about drugs and the evils of rave culture, the sound and attitude continued to spread. 'The whole dance phenomenon was being oppressed to a level which branded party promoters and people who attended *evil acid party promoters*,' said Wayne Anthony of mega-rave event Biology, as quoted by Hillegonda Rietveld in her essay *Repetitive Beats: Free Parties And The Politics Of Contemporary DIY Dance Culture In Britain*.

As rave commentator Sarah Thornton writes in her book *Club Cultures*, 'Media-led moral panics provided the parties with increased "subcultural capital", which attracted a huge youth leisure market.'

Rave was painted as an alien and dangerous subculture by tabloid newspapers like *The Sun*, which generated absurd scare stories about events where youngsters 'high on ecstasy and cannabis' beheaded pigeons and scattered drug wraps all over warehouse floors. Behind it all was a lack of understanding and fear of the collective power of large groups communing in ways that couldn't be easily financially exploited in capitalistic fashion.

'I think, back then, it did seem like a bit of a threat,' says Warlock, a DJ who played multiple raves and clubs through the hardcore era, from Helter Skelter to Labyrinth, DJed on pirate station Pulse FM, and also wrote for the fanzine *Ravescene* at the time. 'They could see a lot of people assembling in large numbers, which they had little control over, and it was unregulated. Not controlled by the powers that be, whether it be for tax purposes or monetary gain. There were health and safety concerns. People didn't understand what it was. There was obviously the issue of drug taking, which you can't deny was at the heart of it. Looking back, it was a new frontier, and people didn't know what that might mean. We'd grown up in the 70s and 80s with all these scare stories, like, *Do this thing, and it's a gateway to being a heroin addict.* All that press at the time did was turn even more people on to this wave of music and partying. It gave it more exposure.'

'Initially, a lot of people looked down on raving in a field in a T-shirt, because it came from such a working-class thing,' Storm told *DJ Mag* in 1999. 'It was scaring the government that there was such a big black following. They didn't want it.'

## BREAKBEAT PRESSURE

During this wave of popularity, there were house hits in the charts, but some producers and DJs in the UK were looking beyond this predominantly American sound, thinking of ways to inject their own personality into the music. One method was through the bleep-techno sound of acts like Ital Rockers and Chill Records; another was hip-hop, something that house heads had grown up with and still loved, but which seemed incompatible with the new sound. Britain, of course, had its own hip-hop groups, and some of their late-80s records flirted with the electronic sounds and up-tempo beats that house had ushered in. Groups inspired by the breakbeat onslaught and noise blizzards of Public Enemy, also cognisant of the creeping electronic wave, produced speedy tracks that resulted in 'Britcore'—just one of the roots of what was to become hardcore.

Hijack's *Hold No Hostage*, Hardnoise's *Untitled*, Silver Bullet's *Bring Forth The Guillotine*, and Gunshot's *Battle Creek Brawl (Apocalypse Bass)* indicated the UK's appetite for steamrolling drum loops and heavy bass, while around the same time in 1989, Leeds group Unique 3 released *The Theme*, which combined warm sub-bass booms with a guest MC, a house beat, mystical synth eddies, and computer game bleeps. Hackney's Shut Up & Dance debuted a sampladelic cut-and-paste hip-hop cut with *5, 6, 7, 8*, before heading in a more explicitly electronic direction with the acid-squiggling and house breakbeat combo of *£10 To Get In*. The Criminal Minds, who were later to make a big mark on hardcore with their classic *Baptised By Dub*, were creating reggae-sampling, bass-heavy, and drum-smacking tracks such as 1990's *Urban Warfare*. DJ Mink's *Hey Hey Can You Relate* was a fast rap, funk-sample-propelled track released on Warp Records that got play—like American tracks by Young MC—by house DJs.

Hip-hop was in the water, but it flowed in a different way, and its breakbeats began to filter into the sets of house DJs at raves. 'In 1989, '90, the different genres played at raves went way beyond just house and techno, with fast-paced hip-hop, the odd Miami bass track, hip-house, and new beat, alongside slower tracks like *Afro Dizzi Act* by Cry Sisco,' says Mark Archer.

Just as imported US hip-hop culture caught imaginations in the UK at the beginning of the 80s, it took an American to fundamentally shift the direction of house into a distinctively British form. Brooklyn DJ Frankie Bones treated electronic music with the same kleptomaniacal glee as a rap producer hunting for samples, taking all the bits he liked and arranging them into beat tools that sounded exciting and fresh. His series of *Bonesbreaks* EPs proved immensely influential on a new breed of DJs who gravitated to funkier sounds, and listeners who recognised something culturally familiar in the samples of James Brown, KC & The Sunshine Band, and The Incredible Bongo Band laid over squidges of Roland TB-303 acid, as on *At My House*.

'That fusion of hip-hop, electro, and house, I'd say 100 percent that was born in the UK,' says Simon Colebrooke of 2 Bad Mice. 'The only other person that I know who was doing it outside the UK that got near it was Frankie Bones, 'cause the stuff he was doing sounded very UK anyway.

'The timing was right,' he continues. 'I'm from a hip-hop background, and I got into it from about the age of twelve. There was a massive hip-hop explosion in the early to mid 80s over here [in the UK], when you had people coming over and doing the Def Jam tour, with Eric B & Rakim, LL Cool J, and Public Enemy. So it was a bit of a natural progression to move from electro and hip-hop into this kind of house thing and fuse the genres together.'

Intriguingly, though there were a few examples of the fusion extant in the short-lived hip-house scene, typified by The Jungle Brothers' Todd Terry-produced *I'll House You* or tracks by KC Flightt and Tyree, America didn't really take to the mixture in any meaningful way, and Frankie Bones enjoyed his greatest success in the UK, where he was booked to play at raves open to his fusion of sounds.

Records like *Bonesbreaks* helped to bridge the gap between different musical worlds and became popular with some DJs who favoured a breakbeat rhythm added into the mix—particularly Fabio & Grooverider at London night Rage. Initially, records like Frankie Bones's beat tools were the only ones of their kind, and they would be played in the background of house tracks to pep them up, in addition to pitched-up rap instrumentals by Public Enemy or other artists produced by the Bomb Squad, such as Ice Cube.

### THEM'S THE BREAKS

By the start of the 90s, the sampler had become a standalone instrument. It would completely transform the musical landscape. Producers of hardcore and embryonic jungle would take machines made by Roland, Akai, and E-mu far beyond their intended use and harness them like virtuosos to construct impossible symphonies: combinations of music and abstract sound that would be unachievable by human hand alone.

What artists like Shut Up & Dance, A Guy Called Gerald, and 4hero did was to take the principles laid out by hip-hop producers—digging for beats, basslines, and musical phrases to use in their tracks—but push the technology in outlandish directions, messing with rhythms and tempos and transposing sounds from the real world into cybernetic forms. This was a futuristic version of the *musique concrète* pioneered by the likes of Pierre Henry and Luc Ferrari, painstakingly piecing sound together into new mutant assemblages.

Records like Shut Up & Dance's *Hooligan 69* or 4hero's *Mr Kirk's Nightmare* mark the dawn of a halcyon era of sampling. Sections from a variety of completely unconnected records could be combined to render something entirely new, and, as samples could be pitch-shifted or transposed, they could all play in key. This opened up possibilities for people to make tunes in their bedrooms or in rudimentary studios, using just a sampler or tracker software and a computer (usually an Atari ST or Commodore Amiga) to put together their beats. The idea of making music was no longer just the preserve of the live band; now it could be made by just one person—and that person didn't even need to be musically literate.

'Samplers were the only affordable way for home producers to get their hands on the sounds they wanted,' Mark Archer says, 'and they also allowed people who weren't musically trained a way to put together tracks without being very knowledgeable about music theory. Producers were also getting samplers to perform functions that they weren't designed to (at least correctly), and so brand-new production techniques were being formed purely from the use of samplers.'

Because hardcore, and acid house before it, placed more emphasis on the quality of danceable rhythms involved and the ear-catching sounds within, rather than harmonic sophistication, keen beginners could piece together their own magpie masterpieces from existing noises. Bits and pieces of the previous thirty years (or more) of recorded sound could be reassembled into patchwork creations, sometimes with additional synth work or drum machines added on top. Drawing from an established pool of influences—drum breaks from funk, rap samples, techno synths, house pianos, reggae basslines—makers of hardcore and what was quickly to become jungle rapidly fashioned a specific framework around which the sound could evolve. Soon, those influences and elements solidified into something tangible yet malleable and recognisably a musical language of its own.

Though by 1991 the sound was in full flow—and about to be taken into the pop charts and commercialised for novelty hits—the underground hardcore scene was a secret laboratory of innovations. Certain recurring musical ingredients kept cropping up, and the most crucial ingredient of them all was the breakbeat. A plethora of these breaks—drum solos sampled from other records, prized for their polyrhythmic funk—were made use of by UK producers, but there were a core number of beats that would continue to surface again and again thanks to their popularity, adaptability, and the way in which they summoned up the 'ghosts' of what was being sampled.

Perhaps the most famous breakbeat of all is the Amen break. An especially fierce drum solo that sounds like Satan himself smacking the skins with demonic relish, it was actually part of a gospel/soul record, *Amen, Brother* by The Winstons, a once-obscure 1960s American group. Drummer G.C. Coleman's inspired percussion solo remained mostly unknown until, in the 1980s, the record (an instrumental cover of *Amen* by Jester Hairston) was unearthed by hip-hop DJs and drum aficionados Breakbeat Lou and Lenny Roberts, who included it on one of the volumes of their long-standing series of rare (and now not so rare) tracks containing killer drum sections, *Ultimate Breaks And Beats*.

Devised more for hip-hop DJs to power their continuous drum mixes in order for b-boys and b-girls to dance, the sampler grew in popularity and came down in price, and the Amen break became ripe for exploitation in original records. It cropped up first in *Desire* by pioneering female rap group Salt-N-Pepa, and in the sample extravaganza *King Of The Beats* by Mantronix, a producer of electro and hip-hop pushing the new sampling technology as far as it could go. With its air-raid sirens and rudimentary editing of the beat, plus its sprinkling of funky flute, *King Of The Beats* and the way it used the breakbeat would prove to be a huge influence on rave production in general. Yet even more influential was when NWA jacked The Winstons' gospel favourite for their barnstorming gangsta-rap cut *Straight Outta Compton*. The roughneck street reportage of the track matched the fire and fury of the percussion hits, and this noisy, tough, and aggressive funk would go on to inform various hardcore and—much more so— jungle tracks to come. The most ubiquitous breakbeat in history, it also forms the backdrop of the *Futurama* TV theme, and has been used by Oasis, Björk, and countless pop acts.

Nowadays, the story of the Amen break is fairly well known, but few in the late 80s or early 90s knew where it came from. Its obscurity and quality made it doubly attractive as a sample. As a sample in hardcore, it filtered in via Atlanta rap group Success N Effect's 1989 track *Roll It Up (Bass Kickin Beats)*, a hip-house tune powered by that ten-tonne heavy break, furious scratching, and 4/4 percussion that showed the beat could work in a rave context. Carl Cox, a DJ now better known for his club-filling sets in Ibiza and across the world, originally played hardcore, and his 1991 tune *Let The Bass Kick* sampled Success N Effect's tune wholesale. Later, Cox's more recognisably hardcore track *I Want You Forever* surfaced on Paul Oakenfold's Perfecto label, with a monstrous Amen of its own. Shut Up & Dance also used the Amen in '91 on the sparse and eerie *Derek Went Mad*, combining it with unearthly synth and subterranean bass in what would be a crucial building block of jungle.

Yet the most momentous use of the Amen was about to land heavily with Lennie De Ice's dub-wise proto-jungle classic *We Are I.E.* The first release on i.e. Records, the tune was the concoction of Lenworth Green, and here, with his choice of musical elements, the foundations for an entire genre were laid down. With its house beat and euphoric pads at the start, listeners could be forgiven for thinking they were about to hear an acid track. But the heavy digital dub bassline sounded like a prime Channel One production, while the peppering of gunshots and a sample of an Algerian singer (the 'We Are I.E.' bit) suggested it was something completely new. A little way in, the Amen break drops, with the stop/start second snare on the offbeat structure that would become a jungle signature. This was the beginning of the Amen being used in a more creative way, rather than being simply rolled out—and in the minimalist structure of *We Are I.E.*, listeners were compelled to focus in on the heaviness of the drums and the bass, rather than the distractions of melodies, stabs, or synth riffs.

Key to the track's appeal, the Amen would become the ultimate jungle break after appearing in what many agree is one of the first proto-jungle tracks.

'The Amen has always been my fave break, not just 'cause of the choppage,' says Amen break surgeon Remarc. 'You can loop an Amen straight and it sounds like a full tune already to me. Vibe, energy, excitement—there's just everything in Amen to me.'

'The beauty of it, the way it can be manipulated, it's limitless,' says Mantra. 'There's so much scope and possibility within it.'

Second only to the Amen break—and possibly used even more frequently through hardcore, and especially jungle—is the Think break. It is derived from American singer Lyn Collins's classic *Think (About It)*, an early funk staple that saw James Brown's unparalleled rhythm section meet Collins's soulful vocals with explosive results. *Think* is unusual in that it contains four individual break sections plus a tambourine part, each one of which has been plundered extensively for breakbeat samples. The syncopated beat, accredited to the J.B.'s' then-drummer, John Morgan; the funky shouts of 'woo yeah' or 'you're bad, Hank' (a reference to the guitar playing of band member Hank Ballard); even just the sound of the record's tambourine, have made their way into hip-hop, pop, house, and, most of all, hardcore and jungle.

Widely popularised by the rap hit *It Takes Two* by Rob Base and DJ E-Z Rock, a track that had considerable chart success as well as becoming a dancefloor staple, Think later cropped up in hip-house tracks before its true potential was realised in rave music. Not only did Think have multiple sections—more than any other widely used break—it could be cut-and-pasted into endless funky drum hit configurations, making it a prime tool for the more adventurous hardcore producers. 2 Bad Mice, with production whiz Rob Playford, layered a rolling and cut-up Think break with two other breaks on the pioneering *Hold It Down*, while the thundering synth terror of T99's *Anasthasia* marries the stumbling, chopped break with the titanic weight of its central riff and a thumping 4/4 techno beat. Think would later become a regular feature of jungle, whose most creative producers would twist it into forms so alien it was almost unrecognisable from the source material.

'You can put that Lyn Collins shaker over anything,' says Sean O'Keeffe from 2 Bad Mice, 'and it elevates it, but without sounding to most people like it's on there. It's got the full monty. It's versatile—there's loads of different ways to EQ it. If you give Think to someone like Photek, he can take it to outer space.'

Another break that has powered jungle and drum & bass since the start is the one from *Apache* by Michael Viner's Incredible Bongo Band. It's an especially weird one as the funk instrumental is a cover of a tune by middle-of-the-road 1960 rock'n'roll staple *Apache* by Hank Marvin and The Shadows, originally written by Brit composer Jerry Lordan and inspired by watching an American cowboy film. The Incredible Bongo Band's version milks the sense of atmosphere conjured by the original's twanging guitar solos, adding huge horns and an irresistibly danceable mid-section, in which the percussion the band prided themselves upon comes to the fore. The Incredible Bongo Band had in fact been thrown together by in-house MGM record producer Michael Viner, but featured the remarkable talents of drummer Jim Gordon and, vitally, Bahamian percussionist King Errisson. Their version of *Apache* was a favourite of the earliest hip-hop DJ in New York City, DJ Kool Herc, who became famous for his pioneering use of two copies of a record to extend a break.

*Apache* became a staple of hip-hop, endlessly replayed and referenced, turning up in Sugar Hill Gang's own version, *Apache (Jump On It)*, in 1981, and also appearing on *Ultimate Breaks And Beats*. In the UK, it was popularised anew by Young MC's 1989 hip-hop hit *Know How*, a track that was played alongside house and early breakbeat tracks in raves and clubs, and which would directly inspire The Stone Roses to make their indie-dance track *Fool's Gold*.

Though the Apache break was used by American house DJ/producers Frankie Bones and Todd Terry, it was to later power early UK house/rave cuts such as MI7's *Rocking Down The House* and Rebel MC's *Better World*, while hardcore tracks by DMS, Mark One, and SL2 would also press the infinitely adaptable beat into service. Like Think, the Apache break would really come into its own in the jungle era, when King Errisson's cascade of drum slaps would be genetically altered and pushed through a robot filter, sounding more like the work of a funky cyborg than a human player.

'I've always had a soft spot for the Apache,' says DJ Flight. 'I think 'cause it sounds very warm and round. As soon as I hear that in a tune, my ears prick up straight away.'

Though myriad other drum solos—from James Brown's *Funky Drummer* through MFSB's *Get Down With The Philly Sound* to Kurtis Blow's *Do The Do*—would be used regularly as samples, these three original breakbeats would become the core ingredients in the sample wheelhouse of the UK's new breed of bedroom producers. Empowered by the new technology of sampling and home computers like the Atari ST and Commodore Amiga, plus tracker programs like OctaMED, producers making hardcore were beginning to push at the sound's boundaries, cleverly working around the limitations of the machines to imagine new ways of generating excitement in clubs or raves.

# 03 Sounds Of The Future: Musical Breakthroughs And Early Pioneers

**HARDCORE KNOWS THE SCORE**

The very first true UK hardcore breakbeat records arrived between 1989 and '90, emanating from London and the nearby counties of Essex and Hertfordshire. These were the sample-based creations of DJs and producers who had been bewitched by the rich musical mixture of American hip-hop, funk, and later house that captivated the UK's club scene, plus the more entrenched sounds of Jamaican reggae and dub. They sought to fuse these sounds together in rickety though riotous, party-starting tracks that, in the process of combining existing elements, became a deadly new compound.

Artists like Blapps Posse and Shut Up & Dance were beginning to make their own fusion records that didn't have a name yet but became a staple at raves especially. Shut Up & Dance, the Hackney duo of PJ & Smiley (Carlton Hyman and Philip Johnson), who went to school with DJ Hype, started out as more of a hip-hop collective, though they quickly adapted their beats and the releases on their Shut Up & Dance Records label to the incipient UK sound. 'We're not a rave group, we're a fast hip-hop group,' they claimed initially. 'We knew the rave scene was going on, but we were too busy trying to be Hackney's answer to Public Enemy,' Smiley later told the *Guardian*. 'Then that scene began playing our music, and we were thrown into it.'

Shut Up & Dance were especially important in bridging the gap between rap, reggae, and rave sounds through the releases on their label, including tracks released under the name Rum & Black, and through their productions for other artists like Ragga Twins, Peter Bouncer, and Nicolette. Their era-defining production for Ragga Twins, *Hooligan 69* (1990), is an exhilarating mesh of breakbeats, bleeps, pop-culture snippets, and early Detroit techno samples, plus the ragga chat of Deman Rocker and Flinty Bad Man, aka the Ragga Twins.

Ragga Twins had been part of the Unity soundsystem, and their move in this electronic direction was an early marker of the crucial reggae foundation of this evolving genre. Though *Hooligan 69* is sparse in its lyrical content, with the MCs there more in a party-hyping capacity, the line 'we no want no hooligan to get up and fight' summed up the euphoric mood of early hardcore, emphasising the way that ecstasy had transformed some aggressive football casuals into loved-up ravers—if only for the duration of the trip. Warehouses, dancefloors, and muddy fields could become empathic places where hugging rather than fighting occurred, and where rave drugs rather than alcohol were more likely to be ingested.

'I grew up around Wembley and Harrow, where I got chased home by skinheads,' Marc Mac of 4hero told *Clash* magazine in 2007. 'But you'd see proper football hooligans get into rave and drop their attitude. It was all getting mixed up.'

'The way I see it, hardcore was like our hip-hop,' says Warlock. 'In terms of sampling culture, hip-hop gave birth to sampling. You can find examples of early UK or Brit-hop from the late 80s and early 90s which are brilliant, but that wave of stuff, you can tell it's still trying to be an American kind of music. Once hardcore came along, it was like, This is our own thing, it's not trying to be anything else.'

'It was like that 'cause we classed it as our own,' adds Flinty Badman of Ragga Twins. 'Hip-hop, Americans classed as their music; we classed jungle as our own music, so it had a similarity. It was a group of people, and then everyone jumped on it and did their thing.'

Into this volatile mixture were added the heavier European synths of Belgian new beat and hardcore techno, typified by releases on R&S Records, in addition to oddities such as the dank, sulphuric-acid bleeps and sinister murmurs of 'ecstasy, ecstasy' in NYC producer Joey Beltram's *Energy Flash*. As dance drugs—mostly E and speed—became entrenched in the rave experience, dancers demanded more intense sounds, whether they were abstract blasts of machine noise or the overblown and hyper-emotional piano riffs of Italian house. The music started to get faster, with DJs pitching records up to meet the expectations of the up-for-it audience. The conditions were right for a new kind of music.

'Probably as early as 1990,' Mark Archer says, 'the term *only for the headstrong* was being used by MCs for the harder sounds and the ravers who stayed at raves until the end. A lot of the tracks were more breakbeat based with hard stab sounds/patterns.'

'Having been around since the very beginning of the scene, especially at Rage, I was influenced by the mishmash of Belgian, Italian house, and techno being mixed with US hip-house,' adds d&b pioneer DJ Trace. 'Early Frankie Bones, Joey Beltram, Frank De Wulf, Orbital, *Sueno Latino*, Fast Eddie, Tony Scott, and Doug Lazy being good examples. The hip-house, or hip-hop dubs, really started to gel with the Euro techno, and that was the catalyst that developed into UK hardcore.'

What became hardcore found its expression most prominently at rave events, and famously at Rage, the pivotal club night that took place at London's Heaven venue. Helmed by Fabio & Grooverider, who had already been DJs playing the house circuit for years, it became an experimental laboratory or Petri dish for new dance-music mutations via the medium of the two DJs' sets. To start with, Frankie Bones and Joey Beltram mixed with classic house sounds, though Fab & Groove gradually began to gravitate towards the UK breakbeat house records that were trickling out (see chapter 4).

In Dalston, Hackney—then one of London's roughest areas, in stark contrast to its gentrified image today—was the cavernous Four Aces club, which played host to Labyrinth, a hardcore hub with a legendary atmosphere. 'It was a club, not a rave as such, but for me at that age it was as close as I was going to get,' says Fracture. 'I'm telling you, man, Dalston was the Wild East back then. No rules. We'd have sorted out supplies before and just turn up with no money and pay £1 to get in. Didn't have money for booze and probably not water either. Just went there and raved hard. Memories of inside are hazy, but it was dark and a series of small rooms. The crowd was very mixed, but it was definitely rave-y. It had quite a strong piano hardcore vibe, but also played a lot of jungle. There would be rude boys in Versace sunglasses, and then some bloke with a ponytail and white gloves.'

## EARLY PIONEERS

As the 1990s began to unfold, the hardcore scene became a bit less euphoric and somewhat darker. *Mr Kirk's Nightmare* by 4hero on Reinforced was a prescient sign of this evolution.

Reinforced had started when four black guys—Marc Mac, Dego McFarlane,

Ian Bardouille, and Gus Lawrence—met studying electrical engineering at a college in north London and decided to band together. Marc and Ian had started a soundsystem called Solar Zone in 1986, and now they set up their own pirate radio station—Strong Island Radio, named after the classic '88 hip-hop track by JVC Force—thanks to Gus's propensity for building radio transmitters. The station obtained a cult following, and they soon started to produce their own music together.

Initially coming at things from the UK hip-hop, funk, and reggae angle, they were influenced by some of the rave DJs on the station and got more interested in house when they heard the bleep & bass sound emanating mostly from Yorkshire. 'Ital Rockers' *Ital's Anthem* was a big favourite with us at the time, because it had massive dub bass,' Marc Mac tells Matt Anniss in *Join The Future*. 'What they were doing up north was almost *dub-ifying* house.'

4hero (or 4 Hero) began to move with more of a house groove; early 1990 cut *Risin' Son* was a raw hip-house joint. With a house bassline, a rolling Johnny Pate break, and fat Detroit key stabs, the track is practically the blueprint for a sound that would shift with astonishing alacrity over the following few years. They recorded it on a borrowed DAT machine, then pressed up 820 copies and sold them out of the back of a car.

Their next EP may have been led by the mutant bass track *Combat Dance*, but it was track two—the first appearance of *Mr Kirk's Nightmare*—that caught the imagination of the breakbeat hardcore scene. It opens with a spoken-word sample taken from a drug awareness seven-inch from 1971 that dealt with the post-hippie generation gap, *Once You Understand* by a studio group named Think put together by producer/songwriters Lou Stallman and Bobby Susser, detailing the unfortunate exchange between a father and a policeman tasked with telling him his son has died of an overdose. 'Mr Kirk...you'd better come down to the station house, your son is dead,' the sample runs. This nihilistic warning shot freaked out a lot of heads when it was played on various dancefloors. Cutting to the core of the smiley-faced, rampant substance abuse at raves of the time, it was an eerie precognition of the drug-induced paranoia and darkside sounds that would filter into late-period hardcore.

Sampled and referenced by everyone from Richie Hawtin and Kid606 to Instra:mental, the track itself is propelled by layers of industrial-strength drums and a deadly, dark synth bassline, with needling atonal bleeps adding to the unease. The sense of tension and drama in the tune would go on to become a key ingredient in drum & bass—a way to create anticipation and excitement in the dance.

*Mr Kirk* was rinsed on newly legal dance radio station Kiss FM and sold more than twenty thousand units before it got banned from the airwaves. But not before DJ Rap had got caught up in an unfortunate incident involving the track, which led to her being virtually blacklisted from playing in London for a couple of years. Somebody had died at the Telepathy rave she was DJing at; unaware of this, she dropped *Mr Kirk's Nightmare* shortly afterwards. 'A faux pas is when you do something intentionally,' she says. 'It wasn't intentional. I was in another room, I didn't know someone had been stabbed outside of the rave or I wouldn't have played that record—no one would. It was a popular record at the time, it just so happened that someone had been murdered outside—I had no idea.'

Rap unjustly took the blame for the unfortunate coincidence, and a lot of hate came her way. 'I lost all my bookings for six months,' she explains. 'That's why I went up north. It was blown up into a big thing. I couldn't get booked in London, so I started playing the Eclipse [in Coventry] and all those things. I only came back down when jungle was just hitting.'

4 Hero signed a distribution deal for Reinforced, and they remained undaunted when the company went bust and left them with an eight-grand cutting bill to pay off. 'We decided to carry on, make up the eight grand, and continue,' Marc Mac told *Melody Maker* in 1996.

Chiefly putting out their own 4 Hero stuff and material by Marc and Dego under other aliases (Manix and Tek 9, respectively), the Reinforced crew were introduced to Goldie by his then-girlfriend, Kemistry. After starting to do artwork for the label and then some A&R, G soon blagged some studio time— going in with Marc in the daytime, and Dego at night—which resulted in the Rufige Cru release *Krisp Biscuit/Killer Muffin* and then the *Darkrider EP*, with its menacing title track sampling Darth Vader from *Star Wars*, while pivoting towards the dark side. The groundbreaking *Terminator* would soon follow.

Operating out of an innocuous suburban street in Dollis Hill, northwest London, 4 Hero themselves had released the album *In Rough Territory* in 1991, rounding up some of their twelves. *Callin For Reinforcements* was an early 1992 label comp, while their Enforcers picture discs would become collector's items. The futuristic *Journey From The Light* was another move towards proto-jungle, with assorted hardcore stabs, roughneck beats, and time-stretched oddities. In 1996, their one hundredth release, *Enforcers 9 & 10*, featured Goldie, Randall, Lemon D, and Leon Mar (aka Arcon 2), but by then 4 Hero were already piloting towards a parallel universe.

### REGGAE INFLUENCE

The breakbeat-laden sound was gaining traction up in Manchester, too. In 1990, A Guy Called Gerald, fresh from the UK acid house he'd help create with tunes such as *Voodoo Ray*, made *Specific Hate*, a cut grounded by a swung-out *Funky Drummer* loop. A reference to his former band 808 State (with whom he'd made *Pacific State*), it contained the same Elysian pad zephyrs and dreamy feel, adding acidic bleeps for something wholly original.

'The rave thing started to pick up at the beginning of the 90s,' remembers Gerald. 'Some of the gigs that I was doing, I was going in at a slower-tempo, acid-house kind of style, playing live. All I had to do really was pitch the tempo up. I remember one gig in particular, at Eclipse [in Coventry], where I'd been on tour and I was doing this live performance, and I was going after a DJ that was playing at 150bpm or something. I was like, *What am I going to do? I can't let this crowd down.* I had written a few things with b-lines and breakbeats in them, and I pushed those into the mix.'

In 1991, Simpson hit upon a super-minimalist, reggae-influenced sound with the immense *28 Gun Bad Boy*. Driven by a rolling dub bassline, skeletal bleeps and breaks, plus soundclash ragga samples, it had a cavernous sense of spaciousness and a concentration of rhythm that were unusual in the everything-but-the-kitchen-sink hardcore sound.

Simpson had grown up in Manchester, the son of Jamaican parents, and at the beginning of the 90s a Caribbean influence began to increasingly permeate his new tracks, along with the electronic sounds he had already been creating. 'I come from a Jamaican background, so that was thrown into the mix,' he says. 'When I heard more hardcore rave stuff, I thought that tempo, with that breakbeat, was where I wanted to go, but using a half tempo b-line, from a dub track or something. Then I was grabbing bits off old-school tapes of soundsystems. In the end, I wanted every single track to have a deeper b-line, so I was trying to find ways of doing that, with different analogue synths.'

Tunes such as '91's *Anything* (which would eventually be included on the later album *28 Gun Bad Boy*), with its stop/start breakbeat, ominous synths, and dub bass, again point to a jungle blueprint. Crucial to Simpson's new sound was sampling, which allowed him to combine all his musical influences into the unified whole that represented his cultural upbringing.

'It was at a time when the technology made sampling a lot cheaper,' says Simpson. 'Before then, with sampling, you'd need to have something like a Fairlight or a Synclavier. They were mad expensive machines. I was speeding up breakbeats from hip-hop tunes and using little bits and snippets from electro-funk tunes, sampling everything from vinyl in those days for making loops. I was putting everything that was in my mental discography on the tape, making sense of it that way.'

Sampling, Simpson thinks, is what enabled a fresh sound to be developed. Free from traditional musical rules, the new producers could run riot with ideas. Often, the most oddball ideas were the ones that worked. 'In the end, the best and purest sound came from a sampler,' he says. 'It was a really good time for experimenting, because now, there's rules. Back then, there were no rules really. Everything went, you know what I mean?'

Gerald was taken to Rage by Goldie, and he found people were going crazy for some of his tunes. He was amazed. 'Jungle was really new and fresh—we had our own microcosm with no-one else involved, and I think that was one of the scary things for these big labels,' he told *DJ Mag* years later. 'These microcosms appeared all over the country and people started to do their own raves. And people started thinking for themselves, and the culture was unique. There wasn't really anything happening on that level; punk was a similar thing back in the late 70s/early 80s, but the government started thinking they didn't want this going on, and that they'd have to start to tap phones and stuff.'

Renegade Soundwave's *The Phantom* was not created to be an early rave anthem—but it quickly became one. Like other records of the time that dodged the narrow beat template of four-to-the-floor, *The Phantom* arrived at the end of the decade amid the smiley-face festooned acid-house era, but like Humanoid's *Stakker Humanoid*, it stood out by virtue of its difference. Driven by an accelerated, shuffling drum groove, funk guitar samples, echoing vocals, and a relentless dub bassline, and possessed of a crepuscular atmosphere suited to the unhinged energy of a sweaty rave, *The Phantom* was another blueprint for doing things differently.

Renegade Soundwave comprised London trio Danny Briottet, Karl Bonnie, and Gary Asquith. The latter had been in the 4AD electro-punk band Rema-Rema, who had an industrial, post-punk attitude that they applied to experiments in sampling, dub, and dance music.

'Reggae was a huge part of growing up, I was going to soundsystems,' Broittet says. 'Me and my mate Baz were going to soundclashes and all kinds of things while we were still in school. Everything with the bass, that just became normal. From that, we mixed up beats from hip-hop, bass from reggae and the indie-punk attitude that we grew up with as well. We grew up in London and those were all the things we got exposed to, so they were channelled into that.

'Every pirate radio station you'd put on, you'd hear *The Phantom*, or in people's cars driving past. It was a massive buzz because, at the time, it was really real. It was that whole DIY thing. DJs you didn't even know were playing it. That was wicked.'

The first of many 'Renegades' in rave culture—from Omni Trio's *Renegade Snares*, to the Renegade Hardware label, to Ray Keith's Renegade project—Renegade Soundwave had an outlaw, anything-goes attitude in their fast and loose sampling and seamy lyrical content. Another of their earliest tracks, *Ozone Breakdown*, also contains the constituents of what became hardcore.

In Peterborough, Shades Of Rhythm, an acid-house outfit who would go on to have a succession of hits, made one of the earliest forays into dark hardcore with 1990's suitably scary-sounding *Exorcist*: nothing but a devilishly effective, pummelling break and a demonic, percolating acid line.

Meanwhile, in nearby Stevenage, Hertfordshire, Rob Playford was getting his soon to be influential label Moving Shadow up and running with his 1990 production as Charlie Say's (sic), *Bass N Buzz*. Related to the bleep & bass records coming from Sheffield and Leeds at the time—tunes by Unique 3, Nightmares On Wax, LFO, and Forgemasters, which relied on heavy sub-bass and metallic, often abstract synth riffs—*Bass N Buzz* foregrounded heavy low-end frequencies, yet added a bolshy forward drive of its own. With breakbeats sitting over its 4/4 rhythm, the track had a punchy industrial grind that related to the Belgian new beat and Euro techno that had grown in popularity in UK clubs and raves. While records such as this were not 'jungle' in a sense that is recognised now, they were beginning to become more focused on the possibilities of drum manipulation and minimalism.

Playford used to co-run the 2000AD and Ibiza raves in the late 80s, but when the police started clamping down on the illegal parties, he thought he'd better stop for a while. Having studied software engineering, he started producing music with a computer, a keyboard, and a sampler, then distributing his own records from the back of his van. Moving Shadow was born.

When Playford met Sean O'Keeffe and Simon Colebrooke—two Hertford DJs and ravers who shared a taste for hip-hop, Belgian rave, and Italian house—they initially asked him to help them make their own tunes from a stack of vinyl sample sources. 'We badgered him a bit, and he let us come in,' says Sean. 'We didn't know what the hell we were doing. He was able to interpret and channel what we wanted and make it happen. In the very early days we didn't have a clue. Over the months and then a couple of years, we learned the process that we would need and how to explain this, what that was called. We'd have these samples and he'd say, Oh you can't use that—because ABC—or That one's no good.'

In 1991, after their eponymous debut as 2 Bad Mice, they released the *Hold It Down* EP, which—as well as the layered breaks and funk samples of the title track—contained *Bombscare*, which was built around a sample from Belgian act Neon's *Don't Mess With This Beat*. The central descending organ riff, explosion snippets, and breakbeat detonations of the tune bridged the gap between existing club staples and the new sound that was now becoming fully established.

The EP also contained *Waremouse*, a stripped-bare pulse of offbeat skeletal drums and ghostly FX, which was another early sign of where things were heading. '*Waremouse* had a concept behind it—it was deliberately stripped back,' recalls Si. 'It was made on the back of hearing a DJ who used to do the circuit called Frankie Valentine. He was a much lesser-known DJ, but was halfway in between that Kid Batchelor, Trevor Fung, Richie Fingers crew, who were more on the house-y side, and then you had Fabio, Grooverider, and Frost on the other side. He had a tendency to play quite raw, stripped-back stuff—even if it was techno 4/4, it would have that real stripped-down, essentially drums and bass feel. On the back of hearing him playing in some warehouses, you'd come back and say, I can't remember any of those tunes, 'cause none of them necessarily had any standout hook, but it was an aesthetic—a vibe you took away from that, which was raw, stomping, reverb-y, dark, stripped down. So, when we went in to do *Waremouse*, it was with that vibe in mind. That's why it has the big reverb on it, to give the feel of the half-empty warehouse.'

2 Bad Mice's *Bombscare* propelled the *Hold It Down* EP into the UK Top 50, and the guys also helped Blame's *Music Takes You*—almost a sister track to *Bombscare*—into the charts by remixing it. Moving Shadow was off to a flying start. Soon, Rob got other people involved in the label, and his studio became like a revolving door. 'The whole thing was like a rolling ball of fire!' he told *Melody Maker* in the mid-90s.

As the 90s progressed, Moving Shadow became one of the pivotal labels in the scene, helping to bring the likes of Omni Trio, Blame, Foul Play, Dom & Roland, Aquasky, and EZ Rollers to the fore. 'We just reflect what's going on, really, and live it,' Rob told *Melody Maker* of Moving Shadow at its height. 'Whatever's happening in the scene, that's what we end up putting out. We like to be a little bit different—a tiny bit adventurous—but apart from that it's just reflecting what's going on around us.'

Hardcore was developing its own characteristics, from its percussive element to the faster tempo. Although the noise factor, carried over from Belgian techno, was an important feature of this fully developed hardcore sound, the music was increasingly becoming broader in scope. Lennie De Ice's dub-wise approach with *We Are I.E.* would be hugely influential, but concurrently in 1991 emerged bona fide anthems like House Crew's *Keep The Fire Burning*, which pitted a diva vocal against delirious sampled techno stabs and funked up drums. The product of the Production House label, which had started out as Phil Fearon's outlet for more conventional house records in 1987, House Crew was Floyd Dyce, one of the earliest pioneers of the sound.

Another tune that had an enormous influence was *Total Confusion* by A Homeboy, A Hippie & A Funki Dredd. Made by the late Caspar Pound (who'd later start rave/trance label Rising High), Marc Williams, and Tony Winter, the tune's abrasive, chain-sawing synth buzz cut through a maelstrom of breaks and raps, its serrated noise something that would become another primary colour in the hardcore palette.

'You had things like *Total Confusion*,' Sean O'Keeffe of 2 Bad Mice says. 'At some point, that transition happened, from people saying it's a hardcore tune—meaning like anything else that is hardcore—to it becoming the umbrella term for a genre. It was the kind of stuff that was getting faster, with breakbeats, and a fusion of these Belgian rave sounds.'

Those Belgian sounds, exemplified by tunes such as Front 242's new beat anthem *Headhunter* or Zsa Zsa Laboum's *Something Scary*, had a raw, dark electronic edge. The newer Belgian techno records—like T99's *Anasthasia*, with its terrifying hoover noise that would be endlessly sampled in jungle/drum & bass; or Frank De Wulf's productions on R&S Records—were frequently drawn on by UK DJs in need of something heavier and harder to satisfy the demands of their audience.

'I was really into techno back then, especially coming from the rave scene,' DJ Krust says. 'Me, DJ Die, and Suv used to go to all the free raves around the country when they were happening—we'd go with Rob and Ray from Smith & Mighty, so we'd be in fields all night, listening to techno, jungle tekno, then maybe you'd hear one early prototype jungle tune. I really liked the whole techno thing, I loved R&S Records and stuff like that, so, when I started to make music in a serious way, I was listening to a lot of that, and figuring out how they were doing those bass sounds and what synths they were using.'

### THE PRODIGY

By 1991, the hardcore sound had fully crystallised, and a wealth of labels and artists were springing up, inspired by the plethora of raves, club events, and records that were evolving the movement. And XL Recordings, already a significant player in the UK dance scene, was about to have a run of rave record successes that would blow the whole scene up and put it in the headlines, and the charts, like never before.

Originally founded by Tim Palmer and Nick Hawkes in 1989, XL grew out of City Beats, a dance subsidiary of Beggars Banquet that released everything from UK issues of rap group Ultramagnetic MCs' Kraftwerk-sampling *Travelling At The Speed Of Thought* to the 303-laden hip-house of Moody Boyz's *Acid Rappin*. A young raver named Richard Russell joined XL as A&R in 1991, and the label initially dedicated itself to American house, with a UK issue of Frankie Bones & Lenny Dee's *Looney Tunes* EP and tracks by Junior Vasquez's Ellis-D project. However, the label's second compilation, *The Second Chapter: Hardcore European Dance Music*, offered a taste of things to come, featuring seminal tunes such as T99's *Anasthasia* remixed by The Scientist (a project DJ Hype would later be involved with), the hurtling breaks and keyboard noise of Cubic 22's *Night In Motion*, and Dutch producer Orlando Voorn's monstrously tough *Where Is Your Evidence?* as Frequency. It also contained The Prodigy's

*Charly (Alleycat Mix)*, an early introduction to the rave quartet from Braintree, Essex, who would later become one of the biggest bands in the world. *The Second Chapter* captures that moment in flux between the previous dance decade and something new—an amalgamation of what had come before, arranged in thrilling and unexpected ways.

The Prodigy's debut EP for XL in early '91, *What Evil Lurks*, had all the hardcore hallmarks, yet also a rambunctious air that until then had only been hinted at by the genre's progenitors. Even from the beginning, producer Liam Howlett's sensory overload of film samples, rap snatches from artists like Ultramagnetic MCs (who he'd eventually collaborate with), synth bass, and ram-raid riffs had a sophistication—yet gave off an aura of lawlessness and excitement that he'd hone to a fine art. Along with the electro-tinged *What Evil Lurks* itself was the early classic *Everybody In The Place*, a clarion call to ravers to get their groove on.

But it was *Charly* that would really get the group noticed. With a snippet that, like *Mr Kirk's Nightmare* by 4hero, pivoted around a slightly queasy spoken-word sample, this time from a BBC TV safety film from the 1970s that advised children to 'always tell your mummy before you go off somewhere', *Charly* played on the idea of young ravers succumbing to the illicit lure of the rave and the manifold dangers that tabloid newspapers had warned of—albeit in a tongue-in-cheek, cartoonish way. With a mangled, cut-up sample of Charly the animated cat 'talking' from the same ad, and layers of bouncy castle riffs, the tune had appeal beyond the rave scene, and it became The Prodigy's first major hit, reaching no. 3 on the UK chart.

With Howlett in the producer's chair, and Maxim Reality, Leeroy Thornhill, and the late Keith Flint upfront as the dancers, The Prodigy were a living embodiment of the rave scene, performing live, appearing in their videos, and talking in their interviews as a unit—a group of friends brought together by the uniting power of hardcore. The Prodigy had a madcap sense of humour, as evidenced by *Charly* and videos for tunes like *Out Of Space*—but there was a manic, truthful energy to them too that both real ravers and radio listeners could relate to. This energy would be translated into classic tracks such as *Your Love*, a piano-chord-pounding highlight of their early material, and also *The Prodigy Experience*, one of the first bona fide breakbeat hardcore albums. The latter demonstrated not just Howlett's command of club production but also his musicality, which he learned from studying classical piano at an early age.

While XL had already dabbled with the new rave sound, releasing Moody Boyz's (Tony Thorpe) *Funky Zulu* in 1990, The Prodigy opened the floodgates for a fresh wave. Initially, the label signed several singles by SL2, a group who made explicit the links between dancehall reggae, breakbeat, and techno in hardcore—and who, like The Prodigy, had a musicality and accessibility that made them appealing to the pop market.

Comprising John Fernandez, Matt Nelson (later known as hardcore DJ Slipmatt), and MC Jay J, SL2 had released several EPs already, on their own Awesome Records label, when XL offered to reissue their single *DJs Take Control*. Like a free party distilled into a potent tincture, *DJs Take Control* is among the most cleverly constructed and effective hardcore tracks, rushing from heavenly Detroit synth stabs to tumbling drum breaks, snatches of a house classic, and a bleepy bassline—all summed up by the line 'How's everybody feeling?'

As residents of the Raindance mega-raves, which had been staged since 1989 across the UK, Fernandez and Slipmatt knew what it took to make a crowd move. When issued by XL, *DJs Take Control* reached no. 11 in the UK chart; and when they put rapper Jay J upfront, their message spread further still.

Another track, *Way In My Brain*, replayed the ten-ton-heavy, digital reggae bassline of Wayne Smith's *Under Mi Sleng Teng*, had Jay J sing the 'way in my brain' hook, and added a sprinkling of synth stabs over its polyrhythmic, funky beat—a tantalising hint of where things would be going in a couple of years. The follow-up single, *On A Ragga Tip*, was even more successful, again synthesising dancehall reggae and rave, with Jay J's chanted hook sitting over speedy drum breaks and a skanking keyboard riff. With bags of pop appeal, it reached no. 2 on the UK chart, and the band added two dancers to their crew, Kelly Overett and Jo Millett, touring around the country and Europe—though *On A Ragga Tip* was the last track they released.

Long before the notion of signing Adele or Radiohead, XL really made its name from this initial hardcore rush. Around the same time, label heads Nick Halkes (who'd later manage The Prodigy) and Richard Russell banded together as Kicks Like A Mule to release *The Bouncer* on the Rebel MC's Tribal Bass label. With its 'Your name's not down, you're not coming in' pastiche of the archetypal club bouncer, it captured the imagination of ravers and shot to no. 7 in the UK charts.

## NETWORK CONNECTIONS

In the Midlands, Network Records was another vital early rave outlet. It was started by Dave Barker and Neil Rushton in Birmingham, the latter having helped to popularise cutting-edge American electronic dance in the UK, compiling the 10 Records album *Techno! The New Dance Sound Of Detroit*, which featured classics by Juan Atkins, Derrick May, and MK, among others. While his label initially focused on issuing hot US tracks in the UK market, it then began to sign British acts with a similar mindset, such as Nexus 21, the Stafford duo of Mark Archer and Chris Peat.

When Archer and Peat were advised to release their new, more rave-focused material under a different name, they settled on Altern 8, after a misprint on their debut release. Their second single for Network, *Activ 8*, was a rush of pure energy, with unhinged samples of various rave gems, nods to electro, house, acid, and crowd noises, plus a diva vocal. Laden with hooks, it had pop appeal, too. 'Altern 8 was just a melting pot of all the sounds from the UK, the techno from America and Belgium, as well as the New York sound of Frankie Bones and Todd Terry,' Archer says.

Self-styled rabble-rousers, Altern 8 dressed in chemical-warfare bodysuits and dust masks emblazoned with their logo for live performances, bringing a sense of humour but also an all-important public image to the faceless world of dance music. One of the more surreal sights of the era was Altern 8's appearance on the BBC's pop-music show *Top Of The Pops*, waving around a pot of Vicks VapoRub (a medicinal rub used by ravers to intensify the ecstasy rush) and karate-chopping their keyboards: a weird crossroads at which two incompatible worlds briefly collided. Altern 8 would go on to make several classic hardcore tracks, such as the brilliant *Evapor 8*, and one excellent hardcore album, *Full On Mask Hysteria*, before the genre fragmented and evolved in another direction.

Altern 8 weren't the only hardcore hits in Network's arsenal. True Faith & Final Cut's 1991 track *Take Me Away* merged the heavenly pianos of the previous decade with a full female vocal plus throbbing bass and breaks, sounding like a Ralphi Rosario cut transplanted into an Eclipse rave. In an example of the cyclical nature of sampling culture in dance music, the tune was later lifted by The Prodigy for their latter-day hit *Warrior's Dance*, while another Network release, Rhythm Quest's *Closer To All Your Dreams*, was an early example of speeding up vocals to chipmunk speed, added to a heart-bursting, delirious melody and drum-break combination.

Later, in one of several examples of cross-fertilisation between the UK and US dance scenes, Kevin Saunderson, the Detroit house and techno producer famous for his Inner City project, made the intense hardcore of *Straight Outta Hell* as Tronikhouse, inspired by the rave he'd heard emanating from Britain at the time. A coup for Network, the track is cited by many jungle innovators as an inspiration; rather than a hardcore producer lifting segments of a Detroit record (of which there are endless examples), it marked a moment when the USA would return the favour. Another Motor City innovator, Juan Atkins (Model 500, Cybotron), would explore a similar idea, working with artists like 4hero and Dutch producer Orlando Voorn as Frequency.

Hardcore was exploding in popularity, and, after the success of The Prodigy, SL2, and Altern 8, record labels were realising there was considerable money to be made from this scene. A parade of crass novelty records began to appear, often lifting TV themes and dropping a hastily assembled dance beat over the top. Some, such as Urban Hype's *Trip To Trumpton*, came from artists who had already proven their worth in the rave scene. Sampling the 60s animated children's TV series about the titular village, *Trip* was a reasonably amusing piece of 'toytown techno'. Yet tracks like Smart E's *Sesame's Treet*, with a loop of the theme song to the American kids' show, were impossible to take seriously.

With the scene beginning to fragment into multiple subgenres and styles, and hardcore strafing the top of the pop chart, some were starting to view it with derision. A snobbishness towards this form of dance music—now viewed as low rent and unsophisticated compared to the perceived elan of US deep house or serious techno—was increasingly taking root. Hardcore, though, was far from dead. In reality, this new form of music was just beginning—and about to take its next giant step.

## MUSICAL EVOLUTION

Some in the embryonic rave scene were reluctant DIY entrepreneurs; others took to it like a duck to water. Music head Danny Donnelly from Suburban Base undoubtedly falls into the latter category. At thirteen, he was already buying and selling records—finding old funk or soul albums in charity shops like Oxfam for 50p and selling them to specialist central London record shops for £15. When he couldn't get a job in a dance music shop after he left school, he decided to set up his own.

In 1989, at the age of seventeen, he met with his bank manager, got a loan (which his dad had to guarantee because of his age) to buy the lease, and opened the Boogie Times record shop—named after an old boogie record—on Victoria Road in Romford, Essex. Danny stocked the shop with old funk records, breakbeat, hip-hop, and then a bit of rave when he started going out to a few events. 'It wasn't intended to be a rave store as such, but it became that, as that's what was popping off,' he says.

With the rave scene kicking off big time, Danny became more and more immersed in it; but unlike the flourishing West End record emporiums, as a brand new shop Boogie Times couldn't always obtain the big new tunes from their suburban base on the edge of London. As fledgling producers dropped by the store with new tunes on DAT tapes, Danny started pressing up white labels so that he had exclusives that the other shops couldn't get. 'It was all about getting the under-the-counter white label, and there was stuff that I just couldn't get my hands on,' he says.

Danny would give exclusive pressings to DJ pals like Hype, Rap, and Krome & Time, and ask them to say when they played them that the only place you could get this record was Boogie Times. 'Overnight we were popping, and Saturday afternoons in the shop became like a rave in itself,' he recalls fondly. 'People would come in with flyers; Hype might drop in and be behind the decks. Andy C ended up working there for a while, so did Zinc—he was the Saturday boy in my shop. Andy used to come in in his school uniform.'

The first official Suburban Base release, *The Rush* by Kromozone, was close to early Warp bleep techno, although a slew of 1991 hardcore future classics such as *Far Out* by Sonz Of A Loop Da Loop Era and *I Feel This Way* by M&M featuring Rachel Wallace soon followed. Danny himself (as QBass) jumped into the studio to make the raw hardcore rave anthem *Hardcore Will Never Die*—a phrase that went on to become part of dance music culture. What these records had in common was emotion and excitement in abundant amounts; they were calculated to cause ripples of bliss and animation in the enormous crowds that raves of the time would attract. The melodic sophistication and layering of records such as these indicated that they were not simply throwaways to be played once and discarded, but instead emblems of a future society that might be possible—

or reachable for a short time, at least. 'It was a time of experimentation,' says Danny. 'There weren't any rules as to what you could do. We knew what it was to experience a record at a rave, so what's going to appeal to people?'

Tracking the release schedule of Suburban Base is like watching the evolution of the scene. 'As the music developed, hardcore to me didn't really appeal to my sensibilities anymore—it became happy hardcore, and there was a clear split in breakbeat rave; it went happy hardcore, and more jungle,' says Danny. 'Obviously, with my musical influences, my preference was the stuff with rare-groove samples in it, with reggae samples or hip-hop samples, and I went more down the jungle path.'

With their graffiti-style sleeve artwork, merch, and instinctive marketing savvy, Suburban Base remained one of the go-to labels of the era. Danny was one of the first to see the necessity of going international, opening up an office in Los Angeles in 1992 and securing a vinyl distribution deal.

'We put on a party in Orlando, Florida—at my own expense—in '92,' he says. 'I brought it to the US really early. I was the guy behind the desk trying to make this happen, trying to get global and get it out there.' He later got distribution deals in Japan and South America, too—the first UK rave label to do so.

Suburban Base, which released Remarc's *R.I.P.*, was one of the original hardcore labels that understood jungle, and evolved with it, putting out classics by D'Cruze, DJ Hype, DJ Dextrous & Rude Boy Keith, and DJ Rap. Another of its undeniable classics was Marvellous Cain's *Dub Plate Style*. A ferocious, Amen-fired ragga-jungle track with cleared samples of toasters Asher D and Daddy Freddy, it broke down into one of those glorious ambient interludes with a diva exhorting 'joy', highlighting the classic junglist mix of rough with the smooth.

Krome & Time, a duo who had been inspired by reggae soundsystems in Hackney through the 80s, first emerged as a hardcore duo via Suburban Base and tunes like *The Slammer*, but quickly shifted over to jungle. The classic *Ganja Man*, a wild dose of Amen breakage and soundsystem snippets, was followed by *The License* on Tearin' Vinyl, pivoting around a sample from the Saxon dances they'd attended in previous years.

After more releases involving Johnny Jungle, Cutty Ranks, Boogie Times Tribe, and Remarc, Danny called time on the label in 1997. He went on to create the *Pure* and *Euphoria* compilation series, creating fifty gold- and platinum-selling albums—*Pure Garage*, mixed by DJ EZ, et cetera—and running Euphoria events in Ibiza for eight summers. When the bottom fell out of the compilation CD market in the mid-2000s, he set up a film production company in Hollywood that's now had a number of cinema releases: 'All from a kid that used to play on pirate radio in east London.' Then, in 2020, he rebooted Suburban Base again.

### NEXT LEVEL

Hardcore in 1991 and '92 was a repository of ideas where imagination, within the loose boundaries of the forming genre, could roam free. Tracks would often change direction from minute to minute, dropping in new samples, riffs, rhythms, or vocals with scant regard for music theory. Geniuses quickly emerged who managed to harness the sound's lunatic drive and shape it into danceable and highly creative blends.

Acen (real name: Syed Ahsen Razvi) was another Production House affiliated producer whose *Trip II The Moon* demonstrated hardcore's limitless potential. Bolting a cascading, atonal piano loop to stop/start breaks that shifted temporal zones and rhythms, Acen sped up the track's 'take me higher' diva vox, creating a helium-lunged android vibe to suit the sped-up hearts and brains on the dancefloor. Loaded with mind-lacerating synth riffs and eerie atmospheres, it was truly a galactic quest that became ever more adventurous with each ensuing remix. The *Kaleidoscopiklimax* version is full of hyper-happy piano riffs and countermelodies, while *Part 1* ups the drama to ludicrous levels by dropping in John Barry's bombastic strings from the soundtrack to the James Bond film *You Only Live Twice*.

One of the most memorable albums that emerged during this transitional period between sounds was Nicolette's *Now Is Early*. Putting the singer's unique and captivating voice upfront, this set of haunting breakbeat songs spawned minor hits like *Single-Minded People*, but today it deserves to be seen as something of a lost classic. Produced by Shut Up & Dance, the album offered a singular blend of UK soul, sample tricknology, and bleeps; it would also see Nicolette go on to work with Massive Attack and Plaid, among others.

Nookie (real name: Gavin Cheung) would play a key role in the transition between hardcore and jungle, and his deliriously uplifting and soulful tracks, like '92's *Give A Little Love*, ignited raves by mixing sophisticated melodies, sampled vocal hooks, and polyrhythmic beat chopping that was miles ahead of most of the competition. He'd later go on to work with Reinforced, engineer some of

Ray Keith's early material, and produce a whole album with American deep house progenitor Larry Heard.

A track that acted as a bridge between house and hardcore was Jonny L's *Hurt You So*. Featuring a chopped-up Think break, dub-wise bass, and lush synth, it moved between segments that sounded more like pumping acid house, proving an irresistible tonic on the dancefloor—and useful for DJs transitioning between beats. Jonny L was classically trained, but he spurned that world when he heard something far more exciting at early raves.

'For me, acid house was the start of a type of hardcore,' Jonny L says. 'Then I remember the rave sounds of 808 State and Orbital, going harder and darker as tracks like Human Resource's *Dominator* led to the more breakbeat hardcore sounds of *Anasthasia* and Altern 8. My roots are in classical, then around my teens there was a mental shift of letting go, forgetting the order of right or wrong notes, and making hardcore tracks from the mood I was in at night-time. The rave was everything, with endless high-energy sounds and bittersweet music I couldn't get enough of. Using my bedroom studio, with a sampler, mixing desk, synths, drum machine, Atari computer and microphone, I would translate this, going for something new, far out. It was the young, raw excitement of trying to reach what was just out of reach.'

Jonny L made *Hurt You So* in the midst of an on/off relationship with his girlfriend of the time, the vocal hook dedicated to their many break-ups and make-ups. Though the sped-up chipmunk vocals that were becoming popular in rave tracks were often sampled from disco divas, Jonny L sung the hook himself. 'I sang the lyrics—*Can't you see I love it baby when it hurts you so, all right*—into the sampler, pitched it up to sound like a female voice, then made the backing track a combination of uplifting soul, four-to-the-floor, acid, and dub bass.'

If Lennie De Ice's *We Are I.E.* had a prototype jungle feel, then others between 1991 and 1992 were beginning to pick up that Jamaican-influenced ethos and sense of dub space and sparseness, translating it into the modern sound of electronic dance music. Bodysnatch (Mark Simon Evans) made *Euphony*, a raw, stripped-down track with the offbeat snare hits of the chopped-up James Brown *Hot Pants* break and sample snippets calling out 'just for you, London' and 'fresh', plus interjections of lush synth adding to its smoked-out atmosphere.

The Labello Blanco imprint was a vital link in the transition to jungle. From its earliest releases, the label foregrounded ragga vocals and dubby bass. Macka

Brown's *Dubplate Style* had the high-pitched voices and emotional pianos, but its sub-bass and ragga chat marked it out as part of the new wave; Strictly Rockers (Danny Coffey, aka Endemic Void) made tunes like *Strictly Rockin*, which coasted on Jamaican samples and dub chord clangs.

Brixton's Genaside II (Chilly Phatz and Kao Bonez) were among the earliest outliers of the jungle sound. In 1990, their track *Death Of The Kamikaze* mixed electro and breakbeat components, but it was their masterpiece *Narra Mine* the following year that provided one of the first jungle touchstones. Starting with rugged overdriven drums and bleeps, it becomes a spine-tingling song, Sharon Williams's lush vocal sidewinding through emotive synth pads guaranteed to make any raver's hair stand on end.

*Narra Mine*, in its first section, is as anthemic as Massive Attack's *Unfinished Sympathy*. Breaking down in the middle to just throbbing sub-bass and hi-hats, the music is stripped right back; the punishing beats return, and the unhinged ragga chat of Killa Man Archer, speeding up into a consonant blur, ups the tension and excitement in the dance. This second section presages the ragga-jungle era in its combination of breaks and an overt Jamaican dancehall influence, which would dominate the music for years and remains a core characteristic.

Dance Conspiracy, a trio made up of producers Sponge, Professor Stretch, and DJ Pulse (who would later help to pioneer the ambient jungle sound), hit big with 1992's *Dub War*—another tune that sat midway between the euphoria of hardcore and the bass pressure of jungle. Mixing a mystical, ancient-Egyptian-sounding horn sample that Public Enemy also used with snippets of ragga chat and heavy digi-dub bass in its breakbeat recipe, plus mystic synths and a cooing diva, it was a further vital link in the chain.

One of the first jungle DJs, Ray Keith had started out playing house music like several of the early pioneers (Frost, Fabio & Grooverider, Nicky Blackmarket), but moved over to hardcore and jungle quickly as the sound crystallised. He recognised the moment when the genre was starting to morph into something new.

'It was a natural progression,' Keith says. 'If you go back to my history, I was one of the originals from the hardcore scene. If you listen to my tune *Sweet Sensation*, or you listen to the Orbital *Chime* remix, which is '91, '92, that's all pretty jungle. That was hardcore jungle as they called it, 'cause it had the 4/4 beat. Then it changed into what we knew then as full breaks. One of the first people responsible for that was A Guy Called Gerald, with *28 Gun Bad Boy*. And then *Just 4 U London* came out [in 1992], it was that kind of spacey techno, but breakbeat.'

Ray Keith grew up in Colchester, Essex, the son of Mauritian parents who played an eclectic mixture of sounds in the house, from the traditional sounds of the East African island of their birth to contemporary pop. 'There was everything from Boney M to Elvis, to The Beatles, to Bob Marley,' Keith says. 'That was from my mum and dad, and my family are from Mauritius, so that *sega* beat, which is like calypso, or a form of reggae or samba—it was quite cosmopolitan. I grew up listening to that, and a lot of Indian music—my mum used to watch a load of Indian films. There was always singing in the house.'

After getting into the 80s electropop of bands like OMD and Japan, and then hip-hop, rare groove and house music came calling. Keith earned a reputation as a DJ around the local club circuit, before the bright lights of the big city beckoned. 'I had already started to DJ around Essex, and I was at a party and Alex P was there with a guy called James, and they were like, You sound like Paul "Trouble" Anderson. I didn't know who that was, but at the time he was on [influential pirate station] Centreforce. I stayed in my bedroom for three years and learned how to mix, and thought, *This is me, this is what I'm going to be doing now.*'

The breakbeat hardcore sound was a natural fit for Keith, and he began to push it in his sets and early productions. 'From my hip-hop days I'd already looked at certain things and thought to myself, *This is where we need to be.* If you're listening to Public Enemy or all those breaks, it was a dream then to have something of our own. At those times it was 150, 155bpm. *We Are I.E.* is an example of hardcore jungle or jungle tekno, so those tunes broke through. None of it was a decision—it's just how something evolves organically and becomes purer, deeper and darker. You're looking to push it.'

## NEED FOR SPEED

Part of pushing the sound forward into new terrain was speeding up the tempo. As raves demanded more intense sounds, some DJs who originally came from the house scene recognised the power of velocity. Breakbeats sounded better speeded up, and certain jungle pioneers stood out through their use of the

+fader. Previous forms of dance music had moved around a stately 120–130bpm, but hardcore rapidly pushed this up into manic stratospheres, initially around the 140–150bpm mark.

Nicky Blackmarket, a pioneering DJ who played a part in the music's metamorphosis, remembers speeding up the beats when he first began working at the famous Soho vinyl emporium Black Market Records. 'When I went into the shop in 1990, people like myself were speeding up the decks,' he says. 'You had the regular house DJs going, What're you doing? Then there's all us pre-jungle DJs saying it sounds good. It was the birth before the birth.'

Nicky Blackmarket grew up listening to his mum's jazz collection, before discovering electro and heading off on his own musical journey. He could've become a professional cricketer at one point—he had scouts interested in signing him up from Middlesex and Surrey teams, but a motorbike accident put paid to that, so he decided to become a DJ instead, cutting his teeth on early house-music pirate station Friends FM.

'It was a big thing,' Nicky says of the experience of playing on the station. 'You had no internet back then, so everybody tuned in to the stations. The rave scene wasn't split off like it is now, into genres. There was complete full excitement. I was just in awe of the whole thing.'

For Nicky, the first rumblings of what would become jungle began at the same epicentre many claim as the start of the earthquake. 'You could say it was Lennie De Ice with *We Are I.E.* The breaks, the b-line. And then people making white labels…we were doing it for ourselves then, and that's probably when you could say it was a big explosion of our own thing.'

Another DJ there at the genesis of jungle was Randall. A hip-hop scratch DJ initially, Randall McNeil was turned on to acid house in 1987 at Notting Hill Carnival—an epiphany that spurred his interest in electronic beats. 'The way it brought all kinds of people together, all getting down to the sound, was inspiring,' he told bassdrive.com. Initially playing Delirium warehouse events, before getting his own radio show on Centreforce, Randall became known for his technical method, which he translated over to d&b.

'We all signed on to the craft of acid house, and I learnt the format,' he later told Drum & Bass Arena. 'It all became numbers, just counting bars, matching them perfectly and finding the drop. It's exactly the same style I took into drum & bass.'

His big break was at a ten-thousand-capacity Living Dream rave in Leyton: when Colin Faver didn't show up for his set, Randall was given free rein to drop beats for nearly three hours. 'When you're put in a situation like that, you end up playing better. You have to really think about it. That was my signing-on date as a DJ people wanted to hear play.'

Along with the likes of Ray Keith, Nicky Blackmarket, Jumpin Jack Frost, and Fabio & Grooverider, Randall was at the forefront as house shifted in structure and tempo into breakbeat hardcore and then jungle. With residencies at Rocket Club, AWOL, Orange, and more, he perfected numerous stylistic tricks and blends that have made him, for many, the best DJ in drum & bass.

Describing Randall as his mentor, Andy C told *DJ Mag* in 2017, 'He'd blow your brains out. The way he'd roll things out, and his selections were out of this world. I can still remember some of those blends now. The genius of his switches, and how he'd take things where you least expect. It's not about transitions, it's about creating actual moments between the records. That's the art of DJing, right there.'

'When I was at Laserdrome, watching Randall, I was like, *That's what I want to do*,' Friction says. 'He was creating new key changes or emotions just by mixing two tunes together, creating new music with two pre-existing records. That was what inspired me to mix.'

The evolution into jungle sped up intensely between 1992 and 1993, as producers sought to outdo each other, and certain philosophies of music-making became more widely adopted. Reinforced Records, 4hero's label, was way ahead of the curve in this regard. While tunes like *Feel Real Good* by Manix (a Marc Mac side project) were propelled by ebullient pianos and mad energy, the B-side track *Special Request*—a title also used by Smokey Joe and later nabbed by Paul Woolford for his jungle alias—had a more stripped-back vibe, with soundsystem samples and those offbeat breaks that were becoming a feature.

The raw and rugged beats of the transitional hardcore-into-jungle sound were just the beginning. A new style was waiting in the wings, and the club Rage, helmed by Fabio & Grooverider, was its proving ground.

# 04 Rage: Fabio & Grooverider Incubate The Sound

'Have we got good memories of Heaven? Fabio has, 'cause I always used to catch him round the back with birds and stuff,' quips Grooverider, prompting heaps of laughter between the two pioneers. 'Yeah, it's a seminal club for us— it's where it all started. You ask any DJ who was around at that time where the music was born, and they'll tell you—it was born at Rage.'

Fabio & Grooverider are brothers in arms. Old friends who met on a south London pirate station in the mid-80s, they frequently finish each other's sentences and are on an almost telepathic wavelength. Despite having quite different personalities, they have much in common: both have parents from the Windrush generation, who arrived in the UK from the Caribbean in the 1950s to help rebuild Britain after World War II; both grew up in south London in the 70s, sharing a similar second generation black British experience; both were music headz from an early age.

If anybody can be justly called godfathers of drum & bass, it is these two. They were the first DJs in the modern dance scene to cut their own dubplates—a practice borrowed from the reggae soundsystems that proliferated in British inner cities in the 60s and 70s. They were the first d&b DJs to do rewinds. They were pretty much the first to make back-to-back DJing a thing, paving the way for untold partnerships in the 90s and beyond. But perhaps above all, they were residents at Rage, the London club night that incubated the sound as it emerged from hardcore at the turn of the 90s.

An afternoon at Grooverider's house in south London gives an illuminating spotlight on their history and importance to the foundations of the scene. In the mid-80s, Fab & Groove began DJing at Mendoza's in Brixton, a semi-legal after-hours joint just off the Railton Road. They also both scored shows on the pirate station Phase One. Growing up in south London, reggae had been a big part of their childhood soundtrack (soul and funk for Fabio as well), and, as the 80s unfolded, they both got bang into hip-hop. 'We were kind of soul boys who were into hip-hop—early,' says Fabio. 'Groove had a soundsystem in '85, Global Rhythm—we was into breaks, really.'

Grooverider remembers the exact day he got into house music, because he was in the Mi Price record shop in Croydon, and DJ Jazzy M—who worked there—played him proto-house cut *Baby Wants To Ride* by Jamie Principle. 'I was like, What kind of music's that? Give me one of those, and he started pulling them all out.' The guys started playing house tracks at Mendoza's and on the radio, but the first time Groove heard anyone shout 'Aciiiiiiieed' in a club wasn't at Shoom or somewhere.

'One of the first times we played at Mendoza's, this thing used to start about two o'clock in the morning and finish about 8:30am, during the week,' says Groove.

'It was an after-hours,' adds Fabio.

'I'd known Fabio from the radio station, but I hadn't DJed with him, and the first time I DJed with him, he's played some tune and then got on the mic, and I thought, *What's he gonna say?* The next thing, Fabio's gone, *Aciiiiiieed!*' The two of them collapse into laughter at the tale.

'I was like, What you *doing?*' remembers Groove.

'I really can't remember that, y'know,' says Fabio, although he was evidently familiar with the parlance at the time. 'I'd never been to Spectrum or Shoom, the first time I heard it in a club was when I was playing Mendoza's. I'd never been to an acid club before, so when he did that …' Groove makes a face to his companion that suggests a mix of bemusement and *what the fuck are you playing at?*, and the two collapse into uproarious laughter again.

The guys heard about new nights like Shoom and Spectrum through the grapevine, and when house DJ Steve Jackson suggested they check out Spectrum on its third or fourth week, Fab & Groove had a bit of an epiphany. 'There was a huge queue when we got down there, and then we had to go through the whole black thing of not getting in,' remembers Fabio. 'The bouncer was like, It's a private party—what, for two thousand people? He was like, Stand to one side, guys, and we was watching everybody go in. Then we saw Steve Jackson, the guy who'd told us about it, and he said, What are you lot doing out here? All right, I'm gonna go and call someone—but then he didn't come back out. We were just about to go home—it must've been about half-one, we'd been waiting about an hour-and-a-half outside, and the security guy went, Look, just come in. Hurry up and get inside.'

Fab & Groove had been to Heaven a few times before, but this Monday night was something else. The dancefloor was packed, a heaving morass; the DJ was up in the heavens, if you like—on the first floor, towering over the crowd like at the Hacienda; lit by a bright light, punctuating the smoke.

'Everybody was facing forward towards him. That never used to happen—DJs made people dance, that's what they did, you didn't face the DJ and hero-worship him, he didn't have that mass control over you . . . you danced. You did your thing, and that was it. But here it was like a moth to a light, everyone was drawn to this guy who was up on high—it looked like a pulpit.

'[The smoke] cleared, and it was Paul Oakenfold. I just remember me and Groove standing there, as two of the only black guys in there, and we were in disbelief. We didn't say a word for about an hour. Oakenfold played stuff like Yello, and he was mixing it up with Chicago house and Balearic stuff, and he just had the crowd mesmerised—in a total state of hypnosis. Every now and again he'd play a big tune and everyone would just roar . . . it was the most incredible experience.

'I remember walking away from there, me and Groove, and Groove said, Have you got house tunes? and I said, Yeah, yeah, and he said, This is what I wanna do. And that's kind of how Fabio & Grooverider was born.'

Three years later, they were headlining the club themselves. 'We were radio DJs, quite big radio DJs—on pirate radio we had a nice little following in south London—but there was nothing aspirational about it,' Fabio continues. 'I loved playing funk down at the local bar to eighty people, but this was the next level—and I wanted to be a part of it. That was the moment that changed everything for me. We'd known about house music, but we didn't know about DJ culture.'

The guys immersed themselves in the scene and started buying more and more records and DJing wherever they could. There's a great photo taken by photographer Dave Swindells of Fab & Groove in an underground car park at an impromptu rave after The Trip at the Astoria in central London in '88. 'Someone put on some music and people started dancing all across the road,' Fabio says. 'Groove was going to his car, someone opened up their boot and started playing music, and they were just having it—properly jumping up on the lampposts. That picture is sick, man.'

'Red bandanas—that's the early days, man,' smirks Groove.

'And me with fucking little sideburns as well,' laughs Fabio.

Most of the people around them were on ecstasy, but Fab & Groove didn't partake. They loved the crowds and the energy, and they got their buzz by DJing to loved-up, expectant hordes. As much of the youth of the UK was swept up in the acid-house revolution—going to illegal raves, and then assorted licensed ones as the 90s unfolded—Fabio & Grooverider became fixtures on the rave circuit along with the likes of Slipmatt, Ratpack, Carl Cox, and so on. From 1988 onwards, the duo played virtually every rave going. 'We done Energy, Biology, Sunrise—every big rave that there was out there,' says Fabio. 'We had our following from the early rave days, and we kind-of translated that whole thing into Rage.'

After a couple of years on the rave circuit, the guys were asked to populate the Star Bar at the top of Heaven nightclub in central London for a night called Rage. They jumped at the chance. Colin Faver and Ibiza regular Trevor Fung were playing the downstairs main floor, but it quickly got so rammed in the Star Bar that promoter Kevin Millins made a switch.

In terms of music policy, the promoter gave F&G free rein, and the guys were playing quite a lot of 4/4 tracks at first—Belgian brutalism, acid house from Chicago, New York house like David Morales's Red Zone material—but were drawn more and more towards tunes featuring breakbeats. 'We were playing house records with a breakbeat in them, and picking up on the breakbeat more than anything else,' remembers Groove. 'At one point we were getting hip-hop tunes and speeding them up so they could fit into our sets. People started picking up on that and started to make the true form of jungle at the time.'

'There was what Frankie Bones was doing from New York,' adds Fabio. 'He was quite breakbeat-y, he was doing the Bonesbreaks stuff, and the Bonesbreaks stuff used to have a little bit of a different vibe when you played it. When you played Bonesbreaks stuff, people just got down in a different way—and we noticed that from early. So anytime we could incorporate that … Groove used to play *[Amerikkka's] Most Wanted* [by Ice Cube] and speed it up, 'cause it had that kick kind of thing going on.'

In a symbiotic relationship between producers and DJs, the producers who'd attend Rage started clocking the way that breakbeat-ridden tracks would get a better reception at the club, so they made more breaks-ridden tracks to feed the scene. From speeding up hardcore tracks and cutting up breakbeats, Fab & Groove were inadvertently helping to forge a new sound.

'Then *We Are I.E.* came out—Lennie De Ice,' says Fabio. 'That was the first track that I can remember with those proper speeded-up breaks—that tune is what started it really for me and Groove. When we played that in there [Rage], it changed the game. We saw a different vibe in the club. Then lots of jungle stuff—Living Dream, Ibiza Records, people started to make jungle tekno and we were playing it down there, but there weren't a lot of it about. Me and Groove used to still have to play house and mix it all up, we couldn't really play a jungle set 'cause there weren't enough tunes.

'We were still into our house music as well, we were just open to whatever was going on,' he continues. 'We used to play five different genres of music, we didn't really think, *Oh, we can't really play this techno tune, 'cause it ain't gonna fit.* We didn't give a shit. John Digweed was our warm-up DJ, Carl Cox came down and played, Kevin Saunderson played...'

Goldie became a Rage devotee after being taken to the club night by his then-girlfriend, Kemistry. A convert to the scene, his goal became to get Grooverider to play one of his tracks down at Rage.

One night, Goldie passed Groove his new dubplate—*Terminator*. Groove put it on—and it cleared the dancefloor. A lot of DJs would have seen the crowd reaction and never played the track again. 'You've got to take your time with these things. Persist. This is why we are who we are, 'cause we persist,' says Groove. '*Terminator* didn't sound like anything out there, but to me it sounded good. Some tunes take five plays before people get them, and that's why, many years later, we're still doing the same thing.'

'I remember Groove coming up to me in the Hippodrome, saying there's this guy making some music, and he's different to anyone else I've heard...and then I saw Goldie come running over, and he was just mad!' recalls Fabio. 'Groove was really supporting his stuff, and when Groove got *Terminator*—no one else had it, and they were all kind of screwing. So what Goldie used to do was make different mixes for everyone—a mix for Groove, a mix for me, a mix for Doc Scott. He used to have to look after the boys. So Groove's probably got lots of Dillinja's and Goldie's early stuff, some of which never came out.'

'Yeah, I've still got a garage full of 'em round the back!'

## JUNGLE CATALYST

For a couple of years in the early 90s, Rage was where it was at. Amid mutterings of disapproval from some of the house heads who were not down with the amount of breakbeat material that Fab & Groove were playing, the guys continued playing to sell-out crowds every week. Just as these proto-junglists thought they might have to get 'real jobs' when the rave thing died away, they scored this crucial residency that acted as the catalyst for producers to start developing the jungle/drum & bass sound.

'A lot of the original Rage crew stopped going there 'cause we started to play jungle and shit, and I remember [promoter] Kevin Millins going, You know what, a lot of the old guys—all Colin Faver's lot—who used to come here don't come anymore, 'cause you guys are mixing it up with techno . . . But he didn't really give a shit, 'cause it was rammed in there. He was like, Don't shoot the messenger, I'm just telling you. He knew something new was happening.'

The guys tended to do three or four tunes each, every fifteen minutes, in their back-to-back sets. A lot of tracks would be passed to Fab & Groove on DAT during the week, and the duo would then go to cut dubplates down at Music House on Holloway Road. Over those crucial years of playing together every week, the pair 'broke' lots of important records at Rage—*Lighter* by DJ SS, Zero B *Lock Up*, and so on. They went from playing mutant strains of house, techno, and hardcore to jungle/drum & bass over the course of the pivotal club night's lifespan. By 1993, with so many jungle tunes starting to come out, a movement—a new genre, a scene—was formed.

Rage on a Thursday became *the* place to go in London as the darker sound developed. 'Most Thursdays it was like the Mecca—we all went to Rage, it was like the birthplace,' Frost says. 'We all got the vibe; it was the start of a beautiful period of music.'

'You'd have people like Prince, Grace Jones, and Boy George mixing with a bunch of east London ravers, it was very cosmopolitan—and super-cool,' Bushwacka, a Rage devotee, said in the mini-doc made in advance of Return To Rage, the seminal night's revival, in 2019.

The night carried on until early 1994, when the promoter pulled the plug. 'Kevin had enough, man,' laments Groove.

'He'd been doing it a long time, and I remember it was in the winter—it was a really cold winter—and he was just finding it hard doing it every Thursday,' adds Fabio. 'It was a big thing, doing that every single week for about four years.'

By that time, though, nights like AWOL had become established in London, and the hyperkinetic breakbeat sound had gotten itself a new genre name: jungle.

# 05 Tales From The Dark Side (And Beyond): Jungle Crystallises

By 1993, the building blocks that the early hardcore and jungle pioneers had put in place—from Fabio & Grooverider as Rage residents to Reinforced Records as an outlet for futuristic breakbeats—was bearing fruit. 'Jungle' was becoming more commonly used to describe the music, though where the term actually originates from remains a hotly contested subject.

'In the early years you had reggae and hip-hop, and it was the concrete jungle, the ghettos and the projects,' MC Det says. 'They were called the concrete jungle, 'cause there's no trees and bushes. Flip that in the music, and people were talking about the concrete jungle. Then you had hardcore music, that had certain samples in there, like *hardcore junglist*. Hardcore disappeared, and the word junglist stayed.'

'The first time I heard someone describe it was Ibiza Records boss Paul Ibiza,' DJ Storm says. 'He'd brought Noise Factory's *Box Bass* into [Wood Green record shop] Music Power, and Chris, the guy running it, said, 'That's wicked, it's got some bass in it, what are you calling that? And Paul said, Jungle.

'Paul said that his friend had told him, If I was sitting in a jungle smoking a zoot, I'd want to hear this. It had this doubled-up bass, but it was the first time I'd heard this word.'

'Paul, any opportunity he gets, wants to tell people that he coined the word *jungle*,' says DJ Ron. 'But with the timeline, you know what? He did have a massive part to play in the early stages.'

The importance of Ibiza Records to the development of jungle cannot be overstated. Noise Factory's 1991 track on Ibiza Records *Jungle Techno* foregrounded the use of the word 'jungle', and its use would be repeated on 1992's *Jungle Dream* by Progression and the *Jungle Rock* EP by the Ibiza Crew that are both on the same label. Paul Chambers, aka Paul Ibiza, was also the first promoter to use the word for events—his Jungle Techno raves, which later became Jungle Splash—and so had more of a hand in the evolution of the term than most, although there are varied stories depending on who you talk to.

'The first time I heard it was on a Top Buzz tape pack that was recorded at the Eclipse in Coventry,' Sean O'Keeffe says. 'It was over our first record, *2 Bad Mice*, part of a one-hour set. Pat was saying over the top of it, *jungle tekno, jungle tekno*. You talk to different people and they say it came from this or that, but that was a pretty early appearance. It was used to refer to something that was more tribal and dubby. This would have been in '92.'

Though some consider jungle to be specifically the dancehall-reggae flavoured records that dominated the scene between '94 and '95—tunes with full ragga vocals, dub samples, soundclash FX, and digital sub-bass—in the early 90s, the appellation was already in use to describe a sound that was new and separate to the ecstatic feel of what had come before. The early records of Goldie, 4hero, Lennie De Ice, A Guy Called Gerald and more had opened up a musical landscape that was becoming populated with a minimalist, drum-heavy, and darker sound. With harsher noises replacing the elysian flutters of hardcore, and dance drugs more entrenched than ever in the rave experience, these records were reflecting the sense of delirium and paranoia that some ravers were feeling on the floor—an illicit thrill spiked with a touch of fear. This in-between jungle sound, sometimes christened darkcore or darkside, was characterised by tunes like Goldie's *Terminator* (as Metal Heads), DJ Crystl's *Warp Drive*, and Q Project's evergreen darkside anthem, *Champion Sound*. For music writer David Toop, the mix of dark and light in hardcore and jungle is part of its power, something he describes in his book *Ocean Of Sound* as, 'Heaven and hell, in some cases both, in opposition or in balance ... [playing] moods of euphoria off an undercurrent of disquiet, balancing oceanic dreams with the clattering, libidinous rush of body processes and urban movement.'

Rufige Kru, a Goldie production alias assisted by DJ Freebase and engineer Mark Rutherford, delivered perhaps the greatest darkside release of all. *Darkrider*, released in '92 on Reinforced, had gritty sampled rave stabs, dramatic strings, chopped drums, and an impossibly evil sludgy bass sound.

Suffolk crew Hyper On-Experience, the duo of Daniel Demierre and Alex Banks, may have gone to more ambient pastures in their later careers, but with *Lord Of The Null Lines* they made one of the key darkcore tracks. Built from a moody synth bassline, dramatic piano, eerie keys, and a sample that described substance abuse burnout—'There's a void where there should be ecstasy'—it was an unsettling classic, made more potent still in its more junglistic Foul Play remix.

Another key architect of the heavier sound was Leicester's DJ SS (Leroy Small). He began as a hip-hop and rare-groove DJ, under the name Scratchenstein, playing alongside a crew called the Formation DJs, before discovering house and then attending his first rave. Quickly tiring of the euphoric end of hardcore, DJ SS released a series of EPs through the label Formation, which he ran with DJ partner Eidris Hassam, that contained teeth-gritting heavy tracks like *Breakbeat Pressure*, loaded with end-of-the-world synth stabs and collapsing drum loops.

'We wanted the heavy beats and bass—it was getting too cheesy, that's why we started switching,' SS says. 'That's not what we came in for. When we came in, it was underground. The music was proper. That's why I called that EP *Breakbeat Pressure*: we were trying to make sure we added some influence of bass with the breaks, we were always trying to put the breaks in from the hip-hop influences.'

Formation put out tracks by Tango, and Megadrive's extraordinary *Demon*, full of twisted Belgian hoover-synth riffs and even a vocal sample from American horror writer Edgar Allan Poe's short story *The Black Cat*. At the time, with the new breed of DJs and producers leaving the piano-laden and helium-vocaled hardcore sound behind, SS was very conscious of a split and the start of something new. 'I had that hip-hop perspective,' he told the website UKF. 'I wanted the breaks, the basslines, not white gloves and big pianos.'

Bizzy B had a significant role to play at the start of jungle and for some years afterwards. As a producer, he was chopping up Amen breaks before most, attaching them to raw rhythmic missives driven by terrifying synths and looming pads. The deceptively titled *Slow Jam* has a shredded 'Mentasm' synth, while *The Twisted Mentazm* was pretty much the last word in unhinged rave abandon, miles away from the cheesy euphoria of the recent past. The distinctive synth sound, which was a constant feature of hardcore and jungle afterwards, derived from New York techno producer Joey Beltram and Mundo Muzique's tune as Second Phase, *Mentasm*: just one of several synth sounds, like the Reese bass tone, that would come to signify hardcore and jungle. Bizzy B, though, took it further than most, along with manic break edits that many only caught up to years later. 'I have always tried to create an original sound and never really looked at being influential, but ... just [have] my own way of making beats that I enjoy,' he later explained to drumandbass.com.

His Brain Records imprint, meanwhile, would release jungle classics by Cool Hand Flex, Equinox, and Red Alert & Mike Slammer. 'I decided to call my label Brain Records as I had always been into off-your-nut-style music, and the Brain logo also represents mind-boggling-style music,' he added.

## CHAMPION SOUND

Q Project was the solo moniker of Jason Greenhalgh, aka Quiff, a former b-boy from Oxford who would go on to become half of the long-running d&b outfit Total Science after hardcore caught his imagination. In '91, he released his debut single, *Freestyle Fanatic*, yet it was *Champion Sound* that caused the most ructions in the scene. Built on a skippy breakbeat loop, with eerie tribal tones and ragga vocals intoning the title, its head-down hypnotic atmosphere is shredded by the appearance of an evil synth riff sent from Hades, a seething cloud of doom spreading discord and excitement among cheek-chewing dancers. *Champion Sound* was part of an influential new wave that was washing away the good vibes of before in a tsunami of malevolent tech-noise—and most were along for the ride.

'I met a guy called Graham Mew [aka Invisible Man] who had a Cheetah sampler,' Greenhalgh told the *Time + Space* blog, 'and after a chance meeting at an Oxford free rave, I convinced him to let me come 'round and do a track. The fourth tune I ever came up with 'round his little bedroom setup was Q Project's *Champion Sound*, which went on to be a big early jungle tune, so we started a label called Legend with two other close friends to release it.'

In Essex around the same time, Andy C and Ant Miles were setting up Ram Records. They produced together under the name Origin Unknown, and one day they made something very different. Using vocal samples from a BBC documentary about near-death experiences and a moon-landing commentary ('31 seconds'), *Valley Of The Shadows* was totally fresh. With its dreamlike, ascending synth ripples, eerie mood, and rolling breaks, it was an outrider of this darkcore wave. The vocal sample, which tells of being in a 'long, dark tunnel', spoke to the rave experience: that lost-in-music sensation intensified by ecstasy. The bassline on the track, meanwhile, was made in a typical instance of sampling ingenuity. The sine-wave test tone, found on both Akai S900 and S950 samplers, was pitched down and doubled up at different frequencies—resulting in a bass sound that would become a key feature on many early jungle tracks.

Due to its unusual nature, *Valley Of The Shadows* became the B-side of RAM 004, and some record shops professed to prefer the more conventional A-side, *The Touch*. But it resonated with DJs and ravers. 'The tune comes out, and the week after that, it was like, I need another three thousand, I need another three thousand, I need another five thousand,' Andy told *DJ Mag* in 2014. 'Literally, the phone would ring, and me and Ant would laugh 'cause we'd say, I bet that's the distributor. It just snowballed. It wasn't like today, where hype builds on tunes before—it all happened after it was released.'

## DARKSIDE DEVELOPS

As Tom & Jerry, 4hero were making all manner of early jungle tracks, some of which tended towards the darkside flavour they'd played such a part in inventing with *Mr Kirk's Nightmare*. Their '93 cut *Sun On My Head* alternates Detroit techno chords with the most ferocious, seething filtered synth drones and a bassline that threatens to drag you under, its beats popping and snapping beneath.

Some would credit early pioneers Tango & Ratty with the term 'darkside', thanks to their tough 1992 track *Tales From The Darkside* and the roughneck jungle tekno of *Final Conflict*. These tunes, produced by Coventry duo Tango (the late Jamie Giltrap) and Ratty (David Smith), were hugely popular at the time, spawning remixes by the likes of Micky Finn, and they sound remarkably contemporary today, amid the revival of the breakbeat-laden techno sound of Special Request and others.

Concurrently, Reading's Basement Records was acquiring a reputation for its jungle tekno, dark breakbeat sound. Top Buzz's 1992 epic *Livin' In Darkness* has the sinister synths and rolling drums characteristic of this period, and it remains a classic, while Wax Doctor's *The Stalker* has unstoppable acidic bleeps more redolent of a squat-party rave soundtrack than what we know as hardcore, allied to a rolling breakbeat and 4/4 kick drums.

DJ Trace was a rave convert who had had a life-changing experience at Rage and became a regular at the club. Taking up DJing himself, he worked at a record counter inside the club run by Dave Wesson, before moving to Wesson's new shop, Zoom Records in Camden. Trace would go on to operate the counter in Choci's Chewns in Carnaby Street and Lucky Spin Records, while building his reputation as a DJ. He remembers one venue in particular that was a proving ground for the dark sound.

'The Lazerdrome in Peckham, in 1993 especially, was the right kind of hybrid of outdoor rave and indoor venue,' Trace says. 'It had in some ways a Fabric-type atmosphere, with the huge sound and dramatic main room. It was here that DJs like Randall, Grooverider, Andy C, and myself on a few nights debuted the Creative Wax, Basement Records dark vibes that were around. For me, this club was where it all started to shift away from UK hardcore and move more towards jungle/d&b.'

Among the most innovative producers to emerge during this period of transition were Foul Play. The Northampton trio of Steve Gurley, John Morrow, and the late Steve Bradshaw had each been inspired by hip-hop initially, before gravitating towards DJing and coalescing around the growing dance music scene.

'I remember having the Street Sounds *Electro* compilations on cassette and playing them on repeat,' says Morrow. 'I was still really young but was already enamoured by the whole DJ, MC, graffiti, breakdancing culture that the older kids were into. It was a couple of years later, the Christmas of '86, I got my first set of decks, and this coincided perfectly with the whole *Jack Your Body, House Sound Of Chicago* thing that was happening at the time. For the next couple of years, I was probably buying 50/50 house and hip-hop. It was that golden time, and I was just at the right age to soak it all up.

'I knew who Brad [Steve Bradshaw] was long before I met him,' Morrow continues. 'He was a bit of a local celebrity around Northampton, being in a hip-hop soundsystem called Krush Inc and promoting events.' Bradshaw was responsible for bringing acts like BDP and DJ Cash Money to the town. 'He came over while I was DJing at a local event during the summer of '91, told me he liked my set and wanted to be my manager, and that he was confident he could get me gigs. True to his word, a month later I was playing on the main stage at the Astoria for Fantasy FM.'

Back then, Morrow was playing the diverse mix of sounds that typified that era, though hardcore proved the most exciting genre for him. 'It was the hardcore breakbeat stuff that was really my bag,' he says. 'Shut Up & Dance, XL Records, Reinforced, Rhythm Section. It was the perfect mixture of the house and hip-hop elements transformed into something new—there weren't any rules or genre constraints, people were just making it up as they went along, and the ravers loved it. Looking back, it was such a fast moving and fertile time for UK dance music—it almost seemed like a new movement had emerged overnight.'

By then, Bradshaw and Morrow were putting on their own local events, called Oblivion, and regularly booking talented DJ and producer Steve Gurley, who would prove to be the missing part of the jigsaw. 'Steve also had a studio,' says Morrow. 'He invited us over and we started working on a bunch of tracks that ended up being *Foul Play Vol. 1*, which we released on our own label Oblivion Records.

'When we first started out, myself and Brad were totally reliant on Steve. Although he'd never released any music before, he knew his equipment really well, so we were able to get great results right off the bat. We were extremely lucky to have him in the group. What myself and Brad lacked in experience we made up for in ideas and enthusiasm. We were both DJs and knew exactly what we wanted, and we'd turn up at the studio with a bag full of records to sample and a hundred ideas, and Steve had the skill to make it work.'

When they began making music, Foul Play had to rely on a software sampler, but they soon had more boxes of tricks at their disposal. 'There was a steady stream of different gear in the studio,' Morrow says. 'Steve would borrow a piece of kit from someone, we'd use it on a few tracks, and he'd give it back, but there were a few staple items. All of the early stuff was made on [tracker program] OctaMED; it was late '93 before we got our hands on an Akai sampler. The Yamaha DX7 was used on most of our tracks, especially for basslines, and the Drawmer Noise Gate, which gave us that staccato transformer effect, was also used extensively.'

Foul Play's earliest tracks were banging from the off, with tunes like *Ricochet* dusted with hip-hop breaks, rap samples, deadly sub-acid basslines, and clever arrangements. Yet it was with 1993's *Finest Illusion* that Foul Play really made a mark. With its slipping, sliding Amen breaks, subs, and ghostly stabs, it had a level of sophistication seemingly miles ahead of many other producers of the time. Its frenetic synth stabs mix with a sped-up vocal pulled from a modern soul classic, demonstrating the extraordinary alchemy possible by mixing samples together just right.

'I don't think it's a coincidence that hardcore and jungle thrived as samplers first became affordable,' Morrow says. 'My first attempts at making music, while still at school, were with a guitar foot pedal that had four seconds of sample time, looped using a 606 drum machine, and then using a four-track to add layers. It was time-consuming and frustrating. Then, all of a sudden, you had affordable samplers on your computer, and your whole record collection became an instrument. The complexity and diversity of all the elements that made up jungle has to be down to this sudden availability of cheap samplers to experimental youths with big record collections.'

Another track released by Foul Play in 1993, together with DJ Yomi as 4 Horsemen Of The Apocalypse, was *Drowning In Her*, a definitive moment in the prototype jungle evolution. With its terrifying opening that sounded like the demonic whinnying of a spectral steed, its moody synth atmosphere, nods to 4hero's *Mr Kirk's Nightmare* (the 'How?' sample), eerie vocal snippets, and complex beats, this darkside track really sounded like the future—and was, Morrow says, the result of the fevered spirit of creativity of the time, with producers all trying to outdo each other with tunes that would be one step ahead.

'The speed with which the music evolved through '92 and '93 was incredible,' he says. 'The complexity of the drum arrangements, the change in tempo and use of more half-time elements, combined with a switch to a deeper, more bassline-driven sound. It became something almost unrecognisable from the hardcore sound that spawned it. I'm not sure that we ever made any conscious decision to follow these changes, we were just kind of swept up in the challenge of outdoing our peers. If someone made a great record, you felt like you had to come up with something better, push your equipment that bit further. It was a healthy competitiveness from a group of young producers that almost all had some sort of history in DJ or soundsystem culture.'

Signed to Rob Playford's Moving Shadow by eagle-eared A&R Sean O'Keeffe in 1993, Foul Play released *Vol III* through the label, the same year remixing Omni Trio's *Renegade Snares* into one of the archetypal early jungle classics. Brilliant in its original form—composed of a shiver-inducing piano motif and tumbling snare drums that slipped in and out of the soaring synths— in Foul Play's hands it became an intense rush of tuned breakbeats, a disorienting hall of mirrors of pinging rhythms and diva wails that used the original piano to ingenious effect. A true evergreen club track, a new VIP version emerged later, during the height of ragga jungle, while High Contrast made a new version in 2003. The first remix, though, is considered by many to define the essence of the early jungle sound.

'We'd already remixed *Feel Good* for Omni Trio,' remembers John Morrow, 'and he must have liked what we did, as he asked us to remix the follow-up, which was *Renegade Snares*. The name of the track inspired how we approached the remix, as I can clearly recall someone saying, It's called *Renegade Snares*, so let's make it live up to its name. That led to the distinctive, DJ-friendly intro with the spanned snare patterns. The musical elements were already perfection—there was no way we were tampering with those!

'I don't really remember it being any bigger than lots of other tracks around at the time. We were obviously aware it was getting played a lot and going down really well, but pre-internet, you only really saw what was happening in your own little bubble. Doing the VIP mix a couple of years later helped prolong its popularity into the more jungle-dominated era, and it's one of those tracks that has aged really well, I think. It's only as the years have gone on that I've become aware how special the track is to so many people.'

## RENEGADE SNARES

Omni Trio was another astute signing to Moving Shadow. The project of Hertford-based Yorkshireman Rob Haigh, the Omni Trio sound was a highly original blend of hard breakbeats and bass and mercurial ambience. His first release for the label, *Mystic Stepper*, is all spacious synth, backwards drum effects, and lush vocal samples, propelled by booming soundsystem bass, while *Be There* floats in dub space with warm jazzy chords and dramatic touches of sound design, as Amen breaks surge in the backdrop.

Though these were some of Haigh's first appearances on wax under the Omni Trio name, he had started making music far earlier. In the early 1980s, when he was based in London, Haigh was part of the post-punk bands Fote and Truth Club, before going solo and releasing ambient records under the name Sema. He worked at Virgin Records for a spell, then moved to Hertford at the end of the decade and opened the Parliament Music record shop, where he became excited by the electronic dance music he was hearing and stocking.

'Part of what we did there was to cater for the growing underground DJ scene,' Haigh says. 'I was buying in loads of white labels and imports of real underground house, techno, and hardcore, including the newly formed labels Warp and R&S, Nu Groove and Transmat. I realised that some of this stuff was coming from a similar aesthetic as Cabaret Voltaire, A Certain Ratio, 23 Skidoo, and so on. It was fresh, alternative, and really exciting. It reminded me, in some respects, of the period '79 to '81 of post-punk experimentalism.'

An experience in the shop would convince Haigh to start to make his own breakbeat music. 'One day in late '89, a customer came into my shop and played me a minimal rave tune that he had produced on a games computer. I was so impressed that I offered to put it out, even though I didn't have a label at that time. A couple of months later, I got hold of the same computer—an Amiga 500—and started experimenting with sequencing. At that time, my music output had slowed down quite a bit; I had a handful of unreleased piano pieces and a few of the sort of repetitive minimal tracks that I had released on the LAYLAH label. I tried mixing some of the repetitive themes with the sequenced drum tracks, and after a year or so of experimentation, Omni Trio was born.'

Haigh's approach was different because he came from these post-punk roots. Though the roughneck rhythmic arrangements of jungle drove his music, influences from his earlier endeavours were inevitably present in his material, with twinkling ambience and a sense of melodic song structure both contributing to this sense of difference.

'Without even trying to be experimental, this music was anyway,' Haigh says. 'Sampling, sequencing, cut-and-pasting, time-stretching, chopping up beats, and so on were all new uncharted methods of working. If you add to that a love for post-punk, krautrock, minimalism, and dub, then that experimental mindset was bound to influence whatever I did. But I've never been one to be experimental for the sake of it—it has to be in service of the tune. It's about looking for new and fresh ways of creating a sonic landscape, groove or atmosphere.'

Though jungle tracks at this point would occasionally incorporate ambient interludes and intros, these ethereal sounds were central to many of Omni Trio's productions—a feature rather than a textural garnish. Few others, bar LTJ Bukem and his pioneering 1993 piece *Music*, were using synths in such a way at this time, with Haigh's tunes anticipating the atmospheric drum & bass sound heard via Good Looking Records and at clubs like Speed a few years later.

'It was natural for me to continue to work in that way, because I'd been doing ambient and atmospheric stuff before Omni Trio. Sometimes I would create a whole instrumental track and then work on the beats separately; other times, I would build them simultaneously, especially if I had a specific bassline in mind.'

The original version of *Renegade Snares* was arguably his breakthrough in the scene, and it came from a similar root. 'At the time I had a version of the musical element, the pianos and pads, written as a kind of Philip Glass minimalist tune with no beats,' Haigh recalls. 'Then I started experimenting with beats over it, and it came together quite quickly. Originally, I did two mixes of the tune: the *Roasted Rollin Mix* and a slightly more rave, demo version, which confusingly got titled *Original Mix*. The *Roasted Rollin Mix* is the definitive one—we just put the demo mix on the EP as a bonus track. In the intro of the *Rollin* mix there is this unusual breakbeat loop, and on the end of every bar I put a lone Amen snare, before eventually letting loose into a cut-up Amen break.'

In one sense, the rapid-fire fusillades of breakbeat shrapnel that come at you on *Renegade Snares*, and its Foul Play remix, are the reason behind its name, though Haigh says there's another more important reason why the track got its title, to do with the outlaw nature of jungle/drum & bass and its separation from mainstream culture.

'The title works on another level. The whole movement of jungle/drum & bass was a kind of renegade movement. It was on the outside of the mainstream, totally independent, and, like punk, years before it, it created a minor revolution with its back firmly turned on the establishment. I've always been drawn to counterculture movements and underdogs, and I had grown up through punk and post-punk, with its DIY ethos, so keeping this thing underground was important to me. By the mid-90s, I was approached by two major labels (and I was told that a third had spoken to Moving Shadow). But I wasn't interested, because I know how the business works, and the pressures and compromises involved. Besides, I was under contract with Moving Shadow and perfectly happy.'

By 1993, with the darkside sound in full flow, and ambient elements filtering into the music, jungle had become its own style, though it was where it went next that would come to define the genre. Ragga jungle would bring the soundsystem roots and strong Jamaican influences on hardcore to the very forefront—and take it into the spotlight for real.

# Foundations Pt. 1:
# Dubplates, Record Shops,
# And Pirate Radio

### DUBS

Exalted among the many musical innovations that Jamaica has given the world is the dubplate. An acetate pressing of unreleased music, produced especially for DJs and soundsystems, the dubplate was the secret weapon with which top selectors could annihilate their rivals in a soundclash. Originally consisting of dub or vocal reggae tracks, having a selection of plates in your record bag was a form of one-upmanship that could give you an edge: after all, the DJ with the baddest tunes wins the battle.

Successful soundsystems in Jamaica, and then in the UK, could draw ever-larger crowds with the promise of exclusive, exceptional tracks; and the dubplate idea, like other facets of reggae, was carried over to jungle/drum & bass.

Fabio & Grooverider were the first DJs from the acid-house era to cut their own dubplates—closely followed by Micky Finn. Before the existence of CDJs, a dubplate allowed a DJ to play a just-finished track before its official release— sometimes months and months upfront. 'Groove would play something brand new, and everyone would talk about it,' explains Fabio. 'That would create a buzz on the track—that's how you'd do the hype.

'We had access to music that no one else did, so it was really important that we went out there and did our thing,' Fabio continues. 'No one had these tunes. Groove would go and play a set down Blue Note, and some of these tunes would come out eighteen months later. He had instant access to Photek, Dillinja…and no one else would have access to them. So we were in control. Goldie never used to give his tunes to more than two people. Groove used to get it first, then me and Randall and [Doc] Scotty—and that was it. So we controlled everything. You couldn't get these tunes, no matter how hard you tried.'

Just as floor-rumbling bass and reggae samples were highly prized in the jungle scene, so too was having tracks that no one else had. It was a way for DJs to compete and keep crowds coming back, especially during a pre-internet era when pirate radio, raves, and record shops were the only places you could hear new music prior to its release. While dubplate cutting began in earnest in the UK in the 1980s, it was the Music House cutting facility that popularised making jungle plates. In the early 90s, more and more DJs began to walk through its hallowed doors.

A place that rapidly acquired a social dimension, as DJs from all areas of the d&b scene met and got to know each other while they waited in line for their plates to be cut, Music House (and other cutting houses, such as JTS Studio) became an information network and hub in a similar way to pirate radio. 'It forced people to have to sit with [others] they may not normally socialise with,' J Majik told Drum & Bass Arena. 'Music House brought all the styles together and made you sit together. You didn't send a DAT to them by post or send a cab down there. If you wanted it, you waited, and it forced interactions, which were great because, after spending five or so hours with someone, you understand them on a different level.'

The dubplates a DJ would cut also affirmed their identity to the scene: the music they had access to would reveal a chain of musical and familial connections. 'That was really important, what dubplates you had in your bag showed where you came from,' says DJ Storm. 'People were like, Who are these girls with all these Reinforced dubplates? They go around with this guy with the crazy gold teeth. People would say at Music House, Does anyone know that guy with the gold teeth? *Yeah, we do.*

'The more you went down there, the more you became part of the community. Because that was the beauty of Music House as well, you'd meet people you'd never met before. It was exciting, I met so many DJs down there: Frosty, Kenny Ken, Shy FX, Roni Size. It was face to face there, and if someone turned up, you might be lucky that you were there at that time and they allowed you to cut [their tune]. We were there for hours, we loved it.'

Storm was never a dubplate elitist, though. 'I think you should play a good combination of vinyl and the latest plates,' she said in 1999. 'For me, DJing is about dealing with what you've got, and making it something spectacular.'

Dubplates are typically cut onto acetate, a usually ten-inch slab of metal that wears out far quicker than vinyl but has a warmth and depth of tone that makes them ideal for playing out. Another advantage of dubplates was as a litmus test, allowing DJs to check how the tunes sounded in a club environment, gauge the crowd reaction, and decide if the tunes needed any additional changes, or even if they were suitable for release. Dubplates were also a way for producers to create their own special remixes of their own most popular tracks. Called VIP mixes ('Variation In Production'), these versions would be the secret weapons of DJs, sometimes eventually making their way to official release.

Started by Chris Hanson of the UK reggae band Black Slate in the 80s, and originally based in his home in Finsbury Park, then on Holloway Road, Music House later moved to nearby Tottenham Hale. It featured renowned cutting engineer Leon Chue (who sadly died in December 2020) among its employees.

'When it first started, it was mostly reggae,' Chue says in the *Dubplate Classics* documentary programme on YouTube. 'You'd have soundsystems cutting. Chris [Hanson] started in his house. He was in Black Slate and could see the decline in touring, and wanted to do something else. He sold his car and bought a mono cutting machine, then started cutting dubs. Me and my brother and sister all worked with Chris, 'cause my dad [Paul Chue] was working with him before.

'Why I'm here is 'cause of jungle and 'cause of Kool FM. I didn't know anything about Grooverider, Micky Finn, Kenny Ken. I just knew about Brockie, MC Det, DJ Pressure X, Mampi Swift. When I came here to see my dad, the big tune at the time was [dancehall song] General Degree's *Papa Lover*, the Stretch remix, so my eyes were opened, like, *What's going on here?* And then my dad said, Brockie, you want one of these?'

Another aspect of the cutting process was the high quality of productions it brought about. While Music House was renowned for producing these dubs to a superior standard, and cutting them with the required bass weight and crispness—knowledge accrued through the reggae connection—it also encouraged producers to make sure their tunes were flawless, as they'd be standing in line with the great and good of the d&b scene, and they didn't want their material to sound lacklustre by comparison.

'It would keep you on your toes—you couldn't make a shit tune and go down there, 'cause everyone is going to hear it,' says Digital. 'You'd have to do your best to make the tune good. That would help you get a bit of a standard. Dubplate culture helped keep that standard up in people's sets. You'd think, *I'm cutting the best tunes here.* I'm from Ipswich, so that's how I got to meet a lot of people in London. I got to know what they're about and to know a lot of DJs and artists.'

In addition to Music House there was Jah Tubby's Studio, later shortened to JTS Studios. Based in Homerton, it had a similar journey from reggae to jungle, responsible for mastering reggae tracks for artists like Neville Brown and Frankie Paul, before later cutting records for hardcore and house acts like Phuture Assassins and Infamix (an early alias of B12). Another cutting house, Transition Studios in Forest Hill, would become a hub for the dubstep scene, itself a mutation/evolution of the bass sound that began with jungle.

Dubplates and vinyl persisted for the whole of the 90s and past the millennium. While DJs in other electronic music genres started switching to playing CDs on the new Pioneer CDJs that were sneaking into booths, drum & bass resisted for quite a while. America's top d&b DJ, Dieselboy, raised a few eyebrows when he played Movement in London in the early 2000s and played entirely digitally, but pretty soon—if gradually—most DJs made the switch.

Every early drum & bass DJ has their own story about when and why they switched to digital DJing. For Fabio, who used to get dubs thrown up to the DJ booth when playing Rage at Heaven, it was when he turned up to play at his night Swerve, and the DJ on before him was playing a new tune off CD that he'd just spent a load of cash cutting onto a plate. 'I started thinking, *Why am I doing this?*' says Fabio. 'Towards the end of buying plates, I remember once I was talking to my accountant and he said, Do you know how much money you're spending on dubs? It was something like eleven grand a year. One plate was £60 at one stage.'

Bowing to technological inevitability and switching to digital also allowed travelling DJs to carry many more tunes with them. Grooverider used to carry four heavy record boxes around to his gigs at one stage. 'I've always been into carrying thousands of tunes, it's always been my thing,' he says. 'Even when I was using vinyl, I'd carry more records than anybody else. So, for me, to slim it down and just put it in my laptop worked for me.'

Groove was an early adopter of Serato, the digital DJing system that allows you to play from a linked-in portable laptop computer. Fabio now uses USB drives after a decade or so on CDs, having got caught out once during a set when the CDJs were jumping, and he's never looked back. The guys certainly aren't vinyl purists anymore. 'I'm not one of those geezers putting records on thinking, *That's a great warm sound*—it's all about what's on it that counts,' says Groove. They believe they served their time playing off the physical format. 'We paid our debt to vinyl and dubplates, 'cause we were carrying 'em around for years—breaking our backs,' says Fabio.

'I've got two rooms full of shit out there,' says Groove, motioning towards his back garden. 'It's whatever you find is easiest to work with,' adds Fabio.

Beyond fetishisation, the use of dubplates was carried over into dubstep, and a select number of DJs still swear by their warm sound; new cutting houses have emerged to cater for the continuing use of dubs for DJs who play out on loud systems.

## RECORD SHOPS

Record shops, especially those with drum & bass links, were crucial for the development of the music in the 1990s. From Boogie Times in Romford on the outskirts of the capital to various Soho emporiums like Unity, record shops were a vital cog in the scene. Soon, most British cities had their own specialist section in a record shop, if not a shop entirely devoted to the sound.

Probably the most important was Black Market Records on D'Arblay Street in Soho. Nicky Blackmarket set up its jungle section in the basement with Ray Keith in 1992, to cater for the rave-y breakbeat hardcore stuff that was getting big, and Black Market soon became a hub for the emerging scene. The camaraderie both in front of and behind the counter was all part of the networking matrix—the kind of spirit that older DJs wax lyrical about these days—and most of the main playas would pass through at one time or another every month.

At times in the 90s, Black Market could resemble an auction house. Nicky or Ray or whoever would play a fresh white label over the shop's soundsystem, and record-buying DJs would bid for what was often purportedly the last copy in the shop. Lots of pirate radio DJs would come in hunting white labels, so they had the music a month ahead of the other jocks. Other DJs would call up the shop and demand that certain tunes were saved for them.

'It was a hierarchy,' says Miss Pink, who worked at Black Market (which was forced to change its name to BM Soho in the 2000s by the original owner— although everyone still referred to it as Black Market) from the late 90s onwards. 'You'd have the DJs and the producers who made the music, that would go to

Music House, and people like Nicky who would have four or five gigs a week and so were cutting dubplates and getting the tunes given directly to them to cut—or exclusive VIPs. There was that tier; directly off the press.

'The second tier was coming to us for white labels, which were test pressings from the distribution companies. We'd get ten or twenty, max, from distribution companies like Vinyl, SRD, and then New Urban. We'd release our first batch of fifteen or twenty white labels, and everyone was hungry to have them before anyone else had them. To the extent that it almost didn't matter what they were, just that they were new! 'Cos it had a white label.' A month later, the ordinary punter could get access via a label's full release, and if it was any good it would sell a lot of copies.

Record shops had their own culture—one that was decidedly male. Miss Pink was the first—and only—woman to work in the central London hub. 'It was a boys' club—absolutely,' Miss Pink says. 'I had to prove myself. Nicky recognised I knew my shit—I knew what was going on.'

Along with Music House, Black Market was like a living and breathing London HQ for the scene. 'Black Market was amazingly important. Nicky is an ambassador for the scene—Nicky Nine-Jobs, he's the hardest-working drum & bass DJ,' says Miss Pink, who preferred to play squat parties herself, infecting the monolithic acid techno soundtrack with some junglist business alongside other London free party devotees like Sexyrubbersoul, Offshore, and the High-Rise Drifters collective.

Immediately standing out thanks to her pink dreadlocks, Miss Pink would get a lot of stick in the shop, she says. 'Every week someone would come downstairs, and I'd be the only person behind the counter, and they'd say, Is Nicky here? No. Is Ray here? No. Is Ash here? No. Is Crazylegs here? No. Is Profile here? No. Do you want some records?'

The inherent sexism was frustrating for someone who really knew their tunes. 'However, I've met a lot of people since then who've come up to me and said, You sorted me out with so much stuff,' she says.

Vinyl shops started to drop off by the mid-2000s, although d&b's long association with wax and dubplates led to more longevity than most. By the end of the twenty-first century's second decade, a smattering of new outlets had popped up, like DNB Vinyl in Croydon, Disc World in Deptford, and the annual Clashmouth record fair in the capital.

## PIRATES

Pirate radio is one of the most important pieces of the jungle jigsaw. Without rebel radio, it's doubtful that this form of dance music would have exploded in the way that it did. 'It was probably the pinnacle for jungle coming through, because, to start with, the only place you could hear this music was on pirate radio,' says MC Det.

Though pirate radio itself began way back in 1964 with offshore pop stations such as Ronan O'Rahilly's Radio Caroline—transmitted from a boat in international waters and therefore not subject to broadcasting laws, and so evading the authorities, hence the pirate appellation—pirate radio really came into its own in the 1980s. With the success of genre-based pirates such as Invicta and Horizon, both of which played soul, DJs began to set up their own stations playing reggae, hip-hop and rare groove, in big cities rather than offshore. The first incarnation of Kiss FM was among the most successful of these, but when house music and rave culture hit in the late 80s, demand for the new music far outstripped supply. Pioneering pirates Centreforce, Sunrise, and Friends FM rushed in to fill the gap, playing continuous mixes of the kind of underground house and techno that was electrifying the illegal and legal raves of the period.

Launched in 1989, Centreforce was the first pirate station to put acid house on air seven days a week. It formed a symbiotic relationship with the mega-raves, promoting upcoming events in a way that would become a signature of hardcore and jungle pirate culture. Transmitted from Newham, east London, the station was an early proving ground for some of the biggest jungle DJs before the breakbeat sound was properly established. Kenny Ken and Randall were just two of the names that played on Centreforce. 'Before you went into that era, Centreforce bridged the gap from the acid house into the more urban rave hardcore, then into the early jungle,' says Sean of 2 Bad Mice.

Operating for just a year, the station was pivotal in playing the early rave mutations that would be the basis of the incipient hardcore and jungle sound, as the records changed from being four-to-the-floor to more sample-based and breakbeat-driven.

Another station based in east London, Sunrise FM, began even earlier, in 1988, with a varied musical diet consisting of rare groove, soul, and reggae, before house music began to dominate its playlists. Like Centreforce, it was a vital early source of dance music knowledge and a community hub, though it lasted a lot longer into the 90s. 'You had no internet back then, so everybody tuned in to the stations,' says Nicky Blackmarket, who got his start on the pirate station Friends FM. 'The rave scene wasn't split off like it is now, into genres. It was the rave scene, before it was even called the rave scene … there was complete full excitement.'

Parallel to the growth of the nascent hardcore and jungle scene was the explosion in pirate stations, which proliferated as the 90s got under way. Just as Radio Caroline and its ilk were born to provide the music that wasn't being played by mainstream radio, the dissident DJs of the enterprising new pirates broadcasted the underground dance sound of raves and clubs to an ever-increasing audience, who couldn't find their preferred style elsewhere on the dial. Stations such as Pulse, Rude, Fantasy, and perhaps most notably Kool FM built huge listenerships with their transmissions of renegade beats, and, with the practice illegal and constantly in jeopardy from the radio authorities, the stations acquired an aura of illicit cool. Often setting up in high-rise estates, many pirates broadcasted from the tower rooftops, giving the signal a greater range in a convenient instance of serendipity. 'Without the tower blocks, the stations would have got nowhere,' Rinse FM founder Geeneus notes in the documentary *Born & Bred*.

In addition to popularising the biggest new tracks and whetting listeners' appetites with tunes played long before their release, pirate radio made stars of many of its DJs. The likes of Brockie and DJ Ron at Kool FM, and MCs like Det, became big names in clubs and at raves thanks to their association with pirates.

'Back then, there was an excitement, like, *Can this really be true that we are just normal guys from the 'hood and now these people are coming to see us?*' says DJ Ron. 'I remember with everything going on, I was still taking the bus. I was sat at the top, and I could hear these people who were my age at the front, going, *Blah, blah, blah, DJ Ron.* They didn't know what I looked like, and I thought, *Woah, you know something, you might be well known!*'

As with Centreforce and other early outriders, the newer pirates would advertise upcoming events and encourage listeners to phone the station for shout-outs. In this way, pirates became an early forerunner of social media, providing community hubs that encouraged interaction and built fiercely loyal fans. Sometimes nicknamed 'the information centre', pirate radio provided a voice for a rebel scene ignored or shunned by the mainstream.

'In the early stages, it was like this huge community centre,' adds DJ Ron. 'Everybody turning up, having just left their mum's dinner table, and now they're playing and having a laugh.'

'Pirates were instrumental,' says DJ Trace. 'Back then, there were no smartphones or internet. The radio was the social network. This would come from shout outs coming through to the studio brick phone, the Motorola DynaTAC being the most stable at the time. You would have people saying things like, *Shout-out to so-and-so*, or *I'll be over in half an hour*, or *Meet me at this place*. It was also where you would find out where to go, with the adverts that were played in between each DJ changeover.'

'We'd go up on the rooftops and set up the rigs,' says MC Det, remembering the family feel in the pirate radio scene of the time. 'You'd go into the flats and all the other radio stations would be there, Defection, Centreforce, and Rush. They'd be setting up their rigs as well. I became part of that community, and that was all due to Brockie asking me to come up there. I joined a boys' club when I was nine years old—it was a multiracial boys club. I left there when I was probably twenty-two. I was used to having that club thing. Brockie used to be one of the workers in the youth centre in Hackney Downs. He was used to that group thing too. Being part of Kool FM just felt like joining another club.'

The pirates had a symbiotic relationship with dubplate culture, as these stations were another means of DJs testing out new tracks and gauging reaction to them. Sometimes the tracks were so fresh, they'd been made or cut that very day. Such immediacy is a regular feature of online platforms like SoundCloud today, but it was unthinkable on mainstream radio in the 90s.

'I'd use it as a testing ground for records that were made literally that morning or the day before,' DJ Ron says of his Kool FM sets. 'They were played there, and I got the responses. Obviously then there wasn't the benefit of the internet—all the responses were from people phoning in.'

The cultural activity of pirate stations, generated far from the commercial mainstream and largely by black and working-class people, did not please the powers that be. A moral hysteria was whipped up by the news media, and the Radio Communication Agency, part of the Department of Trade and Industry, endeavoured to take pirates off the air wherever possible, confiscating equipment and precious record collections in the process. The RCA's position was that pirate broadcasts interrupted the bandwidth used by emergency services, and—

in a very tenuous argument—that they spoiled the enjoyment of listeners to legal stations. Broadcasters, when discovered by RCA investigators using transmission-tracing technology, could face big fines or even two years in prison. TV news reports would detail with sensationalist glee the 'alarming lengths radio DJs would take to protect their stations', describing how tower blocks were becoming fortresses, and how police would be deployed in helicopters under the cover of night to perform daring raids on these illicit strongholds. Legend told of boobytraps, razor wire, concrete barricades; of the 'cat-and-mouse games' of bungling detectives and one-step-ahead radio engineers, setting up aerial equipment elsewhere to keep the beats flowing. Far from discouraging listeners, DJs, or radio owners, it made them part of a rebellious cabal, united against the authorities: renegades to a system that ignored, misunderstood, or was hostile towards them. Tunes sprung up pillorying the news reports, sampling and repurposing their words, speeding them up over rapid breakbeats and synth riffs, taking ownership of these fragmented misperceptions of their culture and twisting them to their own ends.

The most offensive suggestion by the police in their opposition to the pirate radio stations was that they must have some connection to organised crime: that the promotion of raves and club events was somehow shoring up the drugs trade. Utterly misunderstood was the dedication of DJs and station owners to the music; the time and money spent on a passion for jungle/drum & bass.

## GOING LEGAL

Pirate stations like Rude, Defection, and even Kool FM would frequently be shut down by the authorities. But they persisted. In the early 90s, Sarah from the Groove Connection DJ booking agency started agitating for legal stations like Kiss—which had been a pirate until 1989, and was after all supposed to specialise in black music and dance music, and jungle was the hot new street sound—and BBC Radio 1 to start a jungle show. Eventually, Kiss relented, and Fabio & Grooverider would present a Wednesday night show on rotation with Frost, Kenny Ken, DJ Rap, and LTJ Bukem, with Hype and Randall coming on board soon after. The popularity of the show was such that they soon added another Friday night slot, which Fab & Groove went on to helm.

Drum & bass evangelist Brian Belle-Fortune, aka DJ Zy:on, was instrumental in securing a jungle show on BBC Radio 1. After writing a long, passionate letter to station controller Matthew Bannister—audaciously titled 'Will Matthew Bannister really dare to be different?'—suggesting a jungle show on the national broadcast network, he was called into an interview with Radio 1's Andy Parfitt and effectively given the green light to develop *One In The Jungle*.

Brian started scheduling a range of DJs and MCs to represent the scene in the slot, and—after an hour's show the week before detailing the history of jungle/drum & bass—the first *One In The Jungle* show was broadcast on July 20, 1995, featuring Goldie and his chosen MC, GQ.

The BBC's in-house magazine, Ariel, trumpeted the arrival of *One In The Jungle* to the nation's airwaves. 'A passion for jungle music and a long shot to the top put unemployed graduate Brian Belle-Fortune on the road to the Radio 1 job of his dreams,' began an article entitled 'Brian's Big Break'—a good bit of PR for a station that had been criticised for not reaching enough minorities in reports from the time. BBC bigwigs Liz Forgan and Alan Yentob had said, 'Bridging the gap that now exists between many members of the African Caribbean & Asian audiences and the BBC is not going to be easy.'

As Brian details in his book *All Crews*, the show met some resistance from some semi-clueless Radio 1 execs in those early months. The powers-that-be insisted on pre-recorded shows, which made MC interaction with listeners via live shoutouts impossible. And sometimes the equipment at Broadcasting House wouldn't be up to it—pirate stations with their often cobbled-together setups invariably handled the technical side better than some of the Beeb's in-house professional radio engineers. And yet the shows were consistently firing: Rap and Moose, Kenny Ken and GQ, A Guy Called Gerald, Shy FX, Roni Size with Dynamite MC, and Brockie and MC Det were among those who contributed to this landmark first series.

Cruelly, Brian Belle-Fortune was sidelined by BBC management before the first series concluded, and Wilber Wilberforce, who is also black—and who produced Fabio & Grooverider's Kiss FM show—was drafted in to produce the second series. Many of the guest hosts in the second series were people Brian had selected. 'With the second series, they said they wanted someone in-house, so they recruited Wilberforce ... from outside,' says Brian. 'Go figure.'

A few years later, BBC Radio 1 sent out a press release crediting Wilberforce with the concept and title of *One In The Jungle*. 'I felt gutted, angry, hurt, and bemused,' says Brian about this historical revisionism. '*One In The Jungle* was my baby. From the outside, the BBC presents itself as the paragon of honesty, professionalism, and integrity. Inside, it's a hungry beast which devours people. I haven't heard Wilberforce setting the story straight, so I can only conclude that this was an inside job.'

With his fingers burned, Brian returned to work in the NHS as an ICU nurse—his passion for the music undimmed. 'I'm not bitter,' he says.

In early '98, Fabio & Grooverider were given the reins to *One In The Jungle* permanently, and they would continue this ambassadorial role for the next fourteen years. Friction took over in 2012, before passing the baton to Rene LaVice six years later. Meanwhile, in 2002, the BBC launched 1Xtra to exclusively cater for black music, and Bailey took the controls for the drum & bass show during the digital station's first decade, with DJ Flight also regularly on the 1Xtra airwaves.

The importance of national radio exposure can't be over-emphasised. While the 90s pirates filtered the music into bedrooms and onto car stereos, transmission levels only extended a few miles at best. Early internet 'pirates' such as InterFACE helped spread the sound worldwide, but in the 1990s there was nothing like the power of Radio 1 to reach the parts others couldn't reach.

'Growing up in the 90s, in a small, monocultural town in the northeast of England, underground music wasn't exactly readily available,' remembers Sam Binga, now an established 'third wave' drum & bass producer himself. 'There wasn't any pirate radio, and the internet wasn't such a thing back then. So, when Radio 1 decided that they needed to reconnect with the youth . . . *One In The Jungle* was a sort of lifeline, or a window into another world that I didn't really know existed.'

Another third-wave DJ/producer, punky junglist Rockwell, used to tape Fab & Groove's Radio 1 show every Friday night. 'I'd set my alarm every forty-five minutes to turn the tape over on my rubbish stereo,' he told *DJ Mag*. Radio was crucial in reaching under-eighteens who couldn't go to clubs, and youth in far-flung parts of the country—or later the world—who had no drum & bass clubs or events or festivals anywhere near them.

# 07 Goldie: The Alchemist

If there's one figure who's become *the* public face of jungle/drum & bass, it's Goldie. Alchemist, pioneer, instigator, agitator, irrepressible visionary—he merits a chapter to himself, so great has his influence been on the scene. He's like the living embodiment of the scene's soul—its spirit, if you like. He wasn't there at the beginning—he was living in America—but when he did touch down in London, his influence was seismic.

Goldie's music has reached levels of sonic experimentalism that nobody could've imagined at the turn of the 90s. For well over a quarter of a century, he's helmed Metalheadz, a groundbreaking record label and club night that has become a byword for quality, innovation, and staying true to the craft. And he's been an ambassador for the scene as a whole, spreading the drum & bass gospel worldwide. Repeatedly. Whether it be acting in James Bond films or on the BBC soap opera *EastEnders*, popping up on TV reality shows such as *Big Brother*, winning the hearts of Middle England with his waltzing on *Strictly*, or conducting orchestras on *Maestro*, he's reached the parts other DJ/producers could never reach. All the while, though, he's somehow stayed true to the underground, and—in interviews and by unsung practical deeds—has bigged up his crew, the drum & bass scene, and extended family. 'It's the same model,' he says. 'I realised very early on that it's about crews. The crew is the family. And family is what will save you.'

Born Clifford Price to a white Scottish mother and a black Jamaican father, Goldie spent most of his childhood in care and foster homes, where he experienced horrendous abuse—something he has been very open about in later years. It was art that first saved him from quite possibly descending the road into criminality and a lifetime spent in and out of institutions. Falling in with a breakdance crew, Goldie was an early adopter of graffiti—one of the foundation pillars of hip-hop—in his teens in the early/mid-1980s, and painted dozens of pieces around his estate in Wolverhampton. He had a real aptitude for art, and soon he was appearing on regional TV news stories and suchlike. Along with a young 3D from Massive Attack, he got picked out for a film called *Bombin'*—produced by Gus Coral, directed by Dick Fontaine—about the graffiti craze taken up by a swathe of British youth, and taken to New York to hang with the TATS graffiti crew from the Bronx. 'I just wanna change things, y'know?' Goldie says in *Bombin'*—a maxim that has held throughout his life.

A prolific graffiti artist for the whole of the second half of the 80s, with gallery shows and assorted commissions, Goldie returned to the Big Apple to visit the TATS Cru again in the late 80s, before moving to Miami in search of his biological father—and to get a bit of warmer weather. Surviving on his art and by making gold teeth, he was largely oblivious to the acid-house movement kicking off back home. By the time he returned at the start of the 90s—leaving the Midlands behind and moving straight down to London—the rave scene was in full swing.

Staying in Swiss Cottage, north London, with Gus Coral, who became like a father figure to him, Goldie started making his way in the capital, doing bits of design work. He met the Soul II Soul collective, connected with producer Nellee Hooper from Bristol, and started sitting in on sessions with Howie B, who was engineering for the group.

After being taken to the breakbeat hardcore club night Rage at Heaven by his new girlfriend, Kemi, who he'd met when she worked in the trendy Red Or Dead shop in Camden, he fell in love with the nascent jungle scene. Big time. Along with Kemi and her best friend Jayne Conneely, aka DJ Storm, they became a little crew themselves. Goldie was the duo's MC for a short while on some of their pirate-radio excursions, before he decided that he wanted to make a go of music-making himself. 'He always said, he would be the famous producer, we would be the DJs playing his tunes, he'd have a label and club,' Storm recalls, prophetically.

Falling in with the Reinforced Records gang, Goldie started making futuristic rave tracks that he hoped Grooverider would play down at Rage. 'I fell in with the right crew, 'cause that crew were looking at bastardised Detroit music from Europe, rave culture, and breakbeat,' he says.

Goldie describes his working relationship—his 'apprenticeship' and 'honorary degree'—with Mark and Dego from 4hero/Reinforced as like 'light and dark'. He recalls, 'I'd work with Dego in the morning, and Marc [Mac] in the evening. In terms of its DNA, that was the light and dark of my music. Marc was darker, Dego was lighter, so I'd have these tunes that were crossbred. That's how I made music—from then on.'

Most electronic music producers at the time used a combination of old analogue gear and new-fangled digital equipment and computers, and Goldie's early collaborations and experiments were no different. Rufige Kru (or Cru) also incorporated Mark Rutherford and Linford Jones into the equation. The first Rufige Kru EP on Reinforced—released towards the end of the summer of 1992—was an early example of the duality in Goldie's music. So, while the skippy darkcore anthem *Darkrider* was rinsed by Randall at AWOL, *Believe*— with its piano stabs and female vox—was more uplifting; *Menace* was a bleepy steppa that flitted from muted *Mentasm* stabs to a dreamy female vocal in the breakdown, while *Jim Skreech* remained on rave's hardcore continuum.

Goldie had quickly realised that producing electronic music could be like aural soundscaping—sonic art—and set about testing the limits of the equipment. 'Joyriding technology', as his b-boy maxim would have it. 'It's not about what the equipment does, it's what it doesn't fucking do. It was about being on the crucible of change. You've got to push the envelope.'

One night in the early 90s, Goldie was working late with Mark Rutherford on a tune inspired by an Arnold Schwarzenegger movie and its notion of time. They were working at John Truelove's studio setup in Arlington Street in Camden, and the other Rufige Kru mainstay, Linford, had gone to get the last Tube home. Goldie started messing with a piece of equipment called an Eventide Ultra (HF) Harmoniser 2000, which was originally designed for guitarists. 'I was obsessed with it,' he says. He managed to get it to time-stretch breakbeats so that they stayed in time but could be pitched up and down—a discovery that was crucial to the growth of jungle/drum & bass as the 1990s unfolded.

After finishing the arrangement of this new tune, *Terminator*, they started mixing it down while rushing on some MDMA. Rutherford temporarily lost the ability to see, so Goldie had to direct his use of the mouse on the Atari computer. They refined and EQed the track, Goldie standing on the mixing desk for some of it, until they passed out and woke up in the morning. They were astonished when they listened back to it afresh: 'It blew our minds.'

Goldie cut *Terminator* onto a dubplate for Grooverider to play at Rage, but the first time he dropped it, 'Everybody just walked off the dancefloor. I was devastated—I was gutted.' Grooverider persisted, though, and within a few weeks the futuristic breakbeat cut was the biggest tune in his sets. Goldie had arrived. Making his way in the scene, he started branding up Reinforced dubplates with the image of a robotic-looking skull wearing headphones—'it was like music will last longer than all of us'—on one side, and the Reinforced logo on the other. 'I used to call them *dubplates for the metal headz*—so it's actually my name, and he stole it from me,' Grooverider jokes.

'The head looked like Massive, my pit bull [terrier], when I used to squeeze his head together,' Goldie says. He adapted the Metalheadz logo from a designer named Darren Bartlett, buying it off him for £100.

Goldie actually used Metal Heads as the artist name for the landmark *Terminator* release on Synthetic in '92, before adapting it—and the logo—for his own imprint, launched with the help of Kemi and Storm. The first eight Metalheadz releases quickly set the standard: singles by Peshay, Alex Reece, and Wax Doctor; Doc Scott's amazing ambient jungle cut *Far Away*; Dillinja's *The Angels Fell*; J Majik's breakthrough track *Your Sound*; and then Photek's *Natural Born Killa* EP. The label was off to a flying start, feeding forward-thinking new music into the scene, but Goldie was also busy making his own new music—now with Rob Playford, the mastermind behind Moving Shadow, itself one of the scene's most important imprints.

The d&b scene at the time was still firmly underground, but Goldie had the vision to start shopping the resultant *Timeless* album around to major record labels. After a meeting to which Goldie took his pit bull, the album was snapped up by the keen A&R ears of Pete Tong for release on ffrr, the dance subsidiary of London Records. Released on July 31, 1995, it smashed into the Top 10 of the UK album charts.

Headed up by *Inner City Life*, the hit single that's almost like drum & bass's in-house theme tune—with its achingly soulful Diane Charlemagne vocal and atmospheric string samples—and with other future classics like the Pat Metheny-influenced *Sea Of Tears*, a gorgeously emotive *Kemistry*, and the heavenly *Angel*, *Timeless* catapulted Goldie into the mainstream. The album ably demonstrated the depth and meaning of the music, and its crossover success thrust drum & bass out of the underground and into the wider consciousness, paving the way for Roni Size/Reprazent to win the Mercury Prize a couple of years later.

The mid-90s was also when Goldie launched the Metalheadz Sunday sessions at the Blue Note on Hoxton Square in east London. This was well before the gentrification of the Shoreditch area that happened just before and after the millennium. Every Sunday night, without fail, the intimate, two-floor venue would shake to bad-ass basslines and steely platinum breaks. As it was the end of the weekend, DJs like Grooverider, Doc Scott, Randall, Kemistry & Storm, and Peshay would be there, and pretty soon a whole set of breakbeat fiends were joined by a smattering of celebs like some Spice Girls, Kate Moss, Robbie Williams, or David Bowie, mingling—with no VIP area—among the working-class Hackney junglists, b-boys and gals, hipsters and fashionistas, and futuristic drum & bass polyrhythms. 'It was like the Studio 54 of breakbeat,' Goldie remembers.

The community the Metalheadz club night built was like family for Goldie—people he was happy to see, Sunday after Sunday. 'You're just standing there smiling every week, thinking, *Wow, look what we've done, this is amazing*,' Storm told Red Bull Music Academy. 'It's becoming this awesome family that Goldie wanted.'

Goldie was effectively the scene's first rock-star figure, a naturally media-savvy individual who could spin a good yarn as well as represent on a big stage. He dated Björk, took *Timeless* out live for a few shows, hung out with Noel Gallagher—probably the biggest star in music in the mid-90s—and set to work on his second album, the follow-up to his platinum-selling debut.

### SATURNZ RETURN

'The record company thought I was gonna make *Timeless 2*, but I actually went the other way, which is what I always do as an artist,' Goldie says. 'I knew I'd be crucified for this album before I'd even made a note, because *Mother* was gonna happen. I can't as an artist make what I don't believe in—I just can't.'

When he was a kid, Goldie's overstretched single mother—a white Scottish woman named Maggie—was unable to cope with him and his younger brother, so Goldie was put into care at the age of three. He went through various foster families and children's homes, where he experienced horrendous physical, emotional, and sexual abuse. His talent for art—specifically graffiti—undoubtedly saved him, but he still had issues. Abandonment. Sexual trauma. Shame. As he became famous and started taking lots of drugs, however, this was all masked by his larger-than-life, braggadocious character and whirlwind demeanour.

'I was going to all these mad parties, but I was the loneliest guy in the world,' he says. 'I had to voice all this stuff about my mother, because I couldn't speak to her. This is an album, at the peak of my career with drum & bass music, and I choose to make an album which no one's gonna understand. It was like Greek tragedy: the story of a boy with trauma who just wanted his mother.'

By the mid-90s, Goldie was nearing thirty years old. In Western astrology, when you're twenty-nine and a half, Saturn returns to the degree in its orbit that it occupied at the time of your birth—and, as it does, a person reportedly crosses over a major threshold and enters the next stage of life. When you're in the period when your Saturn returns, you're supposed to leave youth behind and enter adulthood. Experience maturity.

This time of turmoil clearly had an effect on Goldie. In his autobiography, *Nine Lives*, he explains how his journey inwards for *Saturnz Return* was engineered by Rob Playford again to begin with, until they irrevocably fell out. Sound designer Mark Sayfritz and beat-fiend Optical then took on the lion's share of production after he split with Playford.

*Saturnz Return* features big names like David Bowie, Noel Gallagher, and KRS-One, but it begins with an hour-long instrumental opus that's emotional and deeply affecting. *Mother* is an extraordinary piece of sonic art. 'It was a serious piece of engineering—by any fucking standards, man, considering what was available at the time,' Goldie says.

The first few minutes are principally the sounds of gas and air. 'I had two mics set up with butane and a light and a lighter and a wet towel, 'cause the gas was choking everyone, and I was going between microphones,' Goldie recalls. 'This was before you could do certain things with new technology.' The Metalheadz man would scowl and hiss and use the gas canister to create the effect of a baby emerging into the world, before the lament 'I can feel my mother' comes in— soon accompanied by strings—just before the eight-minute mark. This is no quick-fix pop ditty.

The lament becomes more disjointed, 'and all of a sudden the track descends and pulls away from its mother—and I'm put into care,' Goldie narrates. 'And I'm in care, and then you hear the ticky-ticky-ticky-ticky [beats], and it's the whips, it's the abuse, it's the cock, it's the beatings, it's the people-manipulating, and it's the strap—it's *Angel Heart* Mickey Rourke, it's the black magic, it's all of this Pandora's Box.'

When the increasingly fierce breaks come in around the twenty-minute mark of *Mother*, it's symbolic of a child learning how to fend for himself. 'Optical's programming these breaks and we're getting these nasty snares, then it descends and tears away, and then [I cry], *NO ONE FEELS MY PAIN!* and it rips the whole fucking tune apart. The whole tune just goes *BAM!* I'm just an angry fucker about what's happened to all my shit,' Goldie explains.

After about thirty-seven minutes, the track starts descending. The 'I can feel my mother' refrain is reprised, and it drifts towards a denouement. There's a bell near the end that Goldie terms 'The Bell Of Resolution'.

'The idea of it coming out the back-end and coming into this infinity…it just says at the end that I forgive her,' Goldie says. 'I found this empathy in the record. I found this real…I'd punished myself for years, beat myself up. I'd done a lot of drugs, trying to numb myself from all the pain. It was a lot to deal with. It's not important to anyone else—it's important to me. It's important that I will always wear my art on my sleeve, unfortunately, but it was important to write something about me growing as a human being.'

It is profoundly affecting to sit in the same room as Goldie when he's alluding to the abuse he experienced as a child. It's not something he's done very often—mainly in therapy—but you get the feeling that fewer music critics might've criticised the purported 'self-indulgence' of *Mother* if they'd known the full extent of Goldie's backstory. This was an artist doing what true artists do—using life experiences to reflect something about themselves. Written to expunge his feelings of rejection, love, and understanding towards the woman who brought him into the world, *Mother* is ripe for reappraisal.

Goldie was determined that this should be a double album—and he got his way in the end. His tender, time-stretched ballad sung by David Bowie, *Truth*, follows *Mother* to complete the first part of the album, disc one—apart from a hidden track, *The Dream Within*, that follows three minutes of silence.

'Writing *Truth* for David was probably one of the greatest things that ever happened to me—who writes for David Bowie?' Goldie said in 2017. 'It was a piece of history for me.'

Disc two begins with the raw blitzkrieg rush of *Temper Temper*, featuring

Noel Gallagher playing Hendrix-y wig-out guitar over aggy junglist riddims, with Goldie himself exorcising angry demons with his vox. 'I said to Noel, I've got this idea, *Temper Temper*,' Goldie recalls. 'I'm always losing my nut, losing my temper, 'cause I was doing a lot of gear. I wanted to write this song, which was me venting 'cause I'd just done this sixty-minute piece that took me forever. And I just wanted to be a bit of an upstart and make this record. So he agreed to do it, and we did it—and it was mental.'

Goldie's hip-hop hero KRS-One features next—'coming thru for the UK crew'—on the punchy, ahead-of-its-time hardcore hip-hop missive *Digital*. The US rapper's commanding lyrical mastery amid the bleeps and sirens and fractured breaks is uncompromising and future-facing.

*I'll Be There For You* is a steely, Metalheadz-style slab of sonic sorcery that samples Malcolm McLaren's *Buffalo Girls* in another nod to b-boy culture, while *Believe* is a soulful jazzy cut that recalls cats like Working Week or the Brand New Heavies. *Dragonfly* is a flighty, flute-driven percussive feast that uses rich organic sounds within the polyrhythms to conjure up a widescreen natural panorama, before *Chico—Death Of A Rockstar* is all fiendishly frenetic Amen breaks and subterranean Reese basslines—another track that could've been made for his Metalheadz club night. The mood switches with *Letter Of Fate*—a ballad where the mournful voice overlain with a half-whispered mantra is actually Goldie's voice backwards, based on a suicide note he'd written years earlier that he found tucked away inside a book Afrika Bambaataa had given him.

Side two of the album concludes with *Fury—The Origin*, a bad-ass d&b interlude with trancey pads, strings, and skittery breaks. *Crystal Clear* is more soulful and jazzier, a melodious funk piece featuring Diane Charlemagne that wouldn't have been out of place on 4hero's masterpiece *Two Pages*. And, finally, there's *Demonz*, a clanking, abstract slice of breakbeat junk.

Not long after starting to record *Mother*, Goldie was invited to New York to produce Madonna's new record. He turned it down. He also wouldn't let his record company hear anything of his second album until a celebrated unveiling of its lead track in 1997—a scene lightly satirised in John Niven's wicked novel about music industry excess, *Kill Your Friends*, a decade later. In the book (and subsequent film), Goldie is clearly the drum & bass superstar, 'MC Rage', who ushers assorted record company employees into a room to hear the first reveal of *Mother*—something Niven himself actually experienced as a marketing executive for London Records at the time. Goldie read *Kill Your Friends* on a plane a decade later, laughing out loud frequently. 'It was brilliant,' he says. 'As much as you have your internal belief, there's an A&R man who's got a fucking coke deal to go to and he's gotta fucking sell units.'

On its release, *Saturnz Return* received a mixed reception. It reached no. 17 in the UK album charts, but some lazy music critics couldn't get past the length of *Mother*. Even Pete Tong, his A&R man, thought it was too long. 'The stupid thing about that album is if sixty minutes had been hacked out of it and *Mother* had been, say, twenty minutes long, there's a very good album hidden in there,' Tong says in Goldie's book, *Nine Lives*. 'But there was no telling him at the time, especially since it involved his mother!'

Was Goldie wounded by the mixed critical reaction to *Saturnz Return* at the time? 'Wounded by critics? I was probably more wounded by cock, and people beating you with a fucking strap and burning your fucking fingers,' he says pointedly. 'Putting you on a dog lead and carrying you round a fucking front room in your underpants, and you're doing the circle like a dog while they're at church. Leave it out. Critics? Fucking have 'em for breakfast. Not in the slightest.'

The record company made a lavish video, with Goldie and Noel at the centre of it, for *Temper Temper*, but not one for *Digital* with KRS-One, so that single didn't crack America as it might've done. The album sold a respectable hundred-thousand units in the UK, more in America, and both singles cracked the UK Top 20. 'I hadn't taken on board that by recording *Mother* I'd carried out an autopsy on myself, but I forgot to sew myself back together,' Goldie says. 'I knew I was gonna get crucified. It's tragic opera, a story of a son and a mother, and a lot of pain.

'As an artist it served its purpose,' he continues. 'I was with her when she died, and then I went to the chapel of rest and did what she told me to do—play her *Mother*. So I sat in a small room, played *Mother* to her, and sat there and thanked her for bringing me to this planet. And it felt like every elastic band from my [umbilical] cord went back to her. And then it kind of freed me, really.'

### MASTER OF REINVENTION

Goldie started recording a third album for London Records, but it wasn't really happening at the time, and soon after the millennium he parted ways with his manager, Trenton—and also with Pete Tong. He moved to Hertfordshire to try to escape the temptations of London and cocaine, and busied himself with his newfound acting career in James Bond and Guy Ritchie films (*Snatch*) and with a part as a local gangster in *EastEnders*. But drum & bass music was his anchor. It still is.

'Like so many artists who don't stay within the parameters of what they are first known for, Goldie gets really unfair criticism for working in so many different areas,' David Bowie once said about him. Bowie was somebody who knew about reinvention. 'He'll have the last laugh, though, as he's bloody good in most of them.'

In the years following *Saturnz Return*, Goldie created the fearsome *Malice In Wonderland* album with Heist under the Rufige Kru name, released various DJ mixes, and pretty much carried on as normal—touring, gigging, partying, and so on. A turning point for him came when he got into Bikram yoga around 2010. 'I got into it after a really horrendous water-skiing accident, doing one reality TV show too many,' he says, referring to his appearance on *The Games*. 'It's totally saved my life. Still now—it clears the water.'

The self-taught, self-educated artist worked with the Heritage Orchestra to realise *Timeless* at the Royal Festival Hall on the twentieth anniversary of its release ('total vindication,' he said of this milestone concert), and then moved to Thailand. 'It's a part of the world where I can go and nobody knows me,' he says. 'Thailand for me was about reinvention, being totally chilled, and very clear water—literally, and physically speaking. The Thin White Duke [David Bowie] would always say to me, *Reinvention is the best thing you could ever possibly do.*'

Goldie briefly returned to the UK in early 2016 to pick up an MBE for his contribution to British music. Accepting the award from Prince Charles at Buckingham Palace, he said, 'Art and music is so important for young people—the arts need to be supported, and I think there are so many Clifford Prices out there like me.'

Goldie also attended the BRIT Awards in early 2016, where glowing tributes were paid to the recently deceased Bowie. 'That's probably the last thing he would've wanted,' said Goldie, whose work with Bowie was overlooked by the music industry mainstream on the night. Nobody asked Goldie about Bowie, even though 'a drum & bass kid from the Midlands wrote a track for him'.

During his time prepping for the *Timeless* concert on the South Bank, ideas for Goldie's next artist album started germinating. He started writing stuff down in notebooks, 'and it all started coming. Get up at five in the morning, walk along the beach. Sunrise. On the other side of the island, sunset. Boat trips. Beaches. Yoga.'

Once he'd written everything over two years—the words, the sounds, the ideas, the concepts—he recorded it all with pal James Davidson from Ulterior Motive in a couple of months at his Treehouse studio in Thailand. *The Journey Man* was born—a very mature album dripping with honeysuckle soul, but unmistakably drum & bass nevertheless. 'I'm happier than I've ever been now,' he says. 'The music tells you that a little bit, doesn't it?'

The crossover success—on its own terms—of *The Journey Man* raised up the profile of drum & bass in the mainstream once more. And Goldie remains the de facto spiritual heart and soul of the scene. His story threads right through the history of the music, from its early days to the present. He's journeyed a long way from his darkside hardcore roots, but even from his Thailand base, he's still rooted in drum & bass.

# 08 Ragga Trip: The Ragga Jungle Sound

'At the end of the day, it's all dancehall,' Smiley from Shut Up & Dance once said. 'Dancehall is the start.'

Around 1993, jungle crystallised into a unique musical shape. Driving this was a group of mostly black British DJs and producers who drew heavily on their Caribbean heritage and parents' record collections, in addition to the hip-hop breaks and house synths they'd been exposed to in recent years. What emerged was a sound influenced by inner-city UK life but that also embraced the musical culture of their families' generations.

Reggae was very much in the UK's musical mix already, and in terms of hardcore it had cropped up in everything from the Prodigy's *Out Of Space*, in the form of a Max Romeo vocal sample, to A Guy Called Gerald's scene-starting *28 Gun Bad Boy*, to the synthetic dub skank and strolling bass of Babylon Timewarp's genre outrider, *Durban Poison*. But reggae became a primary source of inspiration, distinguishing jungle from hardcore in a number of ways.

First and foremost, jungle stripped back the attention-deficit sample mania and electronic euphoria of its earlier musical cousin, becoming a spacious zone where the drums and bass ruled—as they do in dub reggae. The vibe was no longer crazed but a form of energetic beat meditation. There was room for the breakbeats to become a key feature, giving them free rein to slip and slide all over the place with polyrhythmic abandon—the only limit being the producer's imagination (and studio skills). The bass was pushed right up in the mix and rolled like classic dub, albeit with sine-wave sub and 808 boom rather than bass guitar.

Secondly, the samples that *did* feature in the music were often drawn from dancehall. This modern, digital style of reggae had developed through the 80s into the harder, rawer ragga sound, popularised by toasters like Capleton,

BEN MURPHY & CARL LOBEN

Ninjaman, and Shabba Ranks, and producers like Steely & Clevie. As the latest iteration of Jamaica's most famous musical export, it was more widely appreciated by a new generation, who related to its rapping and modern production. Identifying the first tunes that can be categorised specifically as jungle is a hotly contested subject, but from the roots of Lennie De Ice's *We Are I.E.*, A Guy Called Gerald's early works, and Bodysnatch's *Euphony* came more categorically junglist tracks like Potential Bad Boy's *Jungle Fever* ('93) and *Brok Wild* ('94), Noise Factory's *Breakage 5* ('93), and Renegade's *Terrorist* (made in 1993 by Ray Keith with engineer Nookie but released a year later).

Thirdly, the sound accelerated in tempo. Whereas hardcore had generally hovered around 140bpm, jungle upped the ante towards 150–160, and it became faster with ensuing years, effectively doubling the tempo of reggae so the bass could play half-time, while the beats shredded at hyper-speed on top.

Dancehall had developed a big following in the UK, with London soundsystems like Saxon—respected even in its musical birthplace of Jamaica— bringing MCs such as Papa Levi and Lady Di to the forefront through the 80s. In time, American reggae historian David Katz has suggested, Saxon's 'aggressive approach at the microphone and use of special effects began influencing acid house and jungle productions'.

It was inevitable, with these influences in place and the strong heritage of Caribbean music in the UK, that the black British youth who had experienced hardcore and house would seek to fuse it with the sounds of their culture and make a unique style. It could be said that jungle was the first entirely new electronic dance genre to be created in Britain, and its rise to fame was rapid, fuelled by ragga chat, soundsystem effects, and rib-rattling sub-bass. Made up of elements that had almost entirely been innovated by black musicians in Jamaica, America, and Britain—among them hip-hop, funk, soul, house, techno, and reggae—this music had a distinctively black British identity. Jungle was a sound that could only have come from the UK, and specifically multicultural London.

Some of the earliest pioneers of what became jungle started out in soundsystems. The Ragga Twins, aka Flinty Badman and Deman Rocker, were involved from the beginning, and they had a role in shaping the genre. Flinty was in a small soundsystem, Sir Cruise, with friends while he was still a teenager, before he and his older brother joined up with Unity Soundsystem, both of them chatting on the mic, inspired by Jamaican artists and local sounds alike.

'In 1984, Deman joined Unity sound, which had been running for two years,' Flinty says. 'They broke off from Fatman Sound. A guy called Ricks built Unity sound, then he invited Deman to join. I joined Unity in '85, until '90. We wasn't getting in the studio enough to make songs, but we wanted to make records too, you know what I mean? Like [UK dancehall MCs] Tippa Irie, Tenor Fly, we were good mates with them. We were thinking, *How come we're not making a record?* 'cause we were going to all these dances and mashing them up. Tearing down the place. We decided to leap off the soundsystem thing, but we didn't have nothing planned, really. We went and got jobs.'

While working in a pawnbrokers, Deman Rocker met Smiley from Shut Up & Dance, which set in motion a chain of events that would see them anointed as some of the first jungle MCs. 'He had made a song called *Lamborghini*, which had sampled Deman's voice off one of the Unity recordings,' Flinty remembers. '*Deman sends request to all the acid people.* Deman had the lyrics about acid, 'cause in the reggae days we'd hear the news and would write lyrics about what was happening. He sampled a bit of that, and came to see Deman, and said he wanted to put out this song, but it had this sample, could he get permission? Deman said, Yeah cool, but what could you do to get us into recording? He didn't know what the tune was—that it was a hardcore acid tune—'cos Smiley hadn't played it to him. Smiley was like, Come down, and he said he was going to bring his brother with him. He was like, Cool, I know both of you.

'We arranged a date to go down there, and lo and behold, we got to Shut Up & Dance, and I was like, *Rah, these two guys had a sound called Heatwave!* We had our soundsystem in our uncle's basement, and every weekend, we'd have a blues. We invited them down there a couple of times, so when I saw them, I was like, Ras, you're Heatwave, Smiley and PJ right? And PJ used to go to primary school with us. The connection was already there.'

In the studio, they worked on new material with Shut Up & Dance, some of which became early instances of hardcore and ragga cross-pollinating. 'They said what they wanted to do—do a dancefloor one and a vocal thing on the other side, a hip-hop reggae thing, which would highlight our vocal skills, and the instrumental thing would be for the rave. We ended up doing *Spliffhead*— they said they just needed a sample for this song, so we were just doing a few things and picked out *Ragga Twins deh 'bout*. Before that, they said it would be best if we went as a group, not as a single artist. We had to make up the name, and Ragga Twins was the best thing we could come up with. There was already Double Trouble out there and some other ones, and we didn't know of no twins at the time. Although we're not twins, twins is two people, so Ragga Twins stuck. We done them two singles, *Spliffhead* and *Ragga Trip, Illegal Gunshot* and *Hooligan 69*. They just blew up—it was amazing to us, we didn't know what was gonna happen, 'cause we was still going to reggae dances. We wasn't really into the rave thing yet.'

But the rave side of things soon captured their attention, when they saw how powerful and popular it was in the flesh. 'We started doing shows up and down the country,' Flinty says. 'We ended up doing one at Essex County Showground, and we was headlining with The Prodigy. It was like an open air outside thing. It was a nice hot day and we'd just done the show with loads of people, twenty-five thousand or something. We were buzzing off the vibes, and thought, *Let's just stay here.* Now we've done our show, we'll stick around for a bit backstage, have a smoke and a drink and then chip off. It captivated us from that day—we thought, *This is absolutely amazing.* The vibes were electric all the way through, it wasn't just our PA going off and that's it, the whole thing was going off. The Prodigy came on and the vibe was mad. We ended up going to Plymouth one night, done the show and stuck around in the party, and then the next DJ came on. We were standing there looking at the guy going, I know who that DJ is. We went back up and it was Jumpin Jack Frost. We were like, Nigel, what are you doing here? We were like, if he's into this, if this is what he's doing, then this is the place for us. He was a hardcore reggae man.'

Ragga Twins were among the very first to chat lyrics over hardcore beats, and they went on to record a whole album with Shut Up & Dance, the excellent *Reggae Owes Us Money.* Though their connection with Shut Up & Dance came to an amicable end, they continued to MC at raves, and soon noticed a very different vibe in the music that had a resemblance to the genre they'd started out in.

'We stayed in it, and it started to change. More reggae people were coming into it, more black people were coming to the raves, and then the producers started using more reggae samples, and eventually it started turning over into jungle with loads of reggae basslines or whatever.'

Though American rap had been a huge influence on hardcore, there were scant examples of MCs rhyming over the latter. But as the ragga element came to the fore, toasting over the beats became a more natural component. With the strong connection to Jamaica in the UK, it felt more honest somehow than people copying the American rhyme style.

'No one was really MCing at the raves [initially],' Flinty says. 'They were just hosting and bigging up the people, not chatting lyrics. Then we ended up on pirate station Kool FM, run by Eastman, another guy who had a sound back in the 90s called Eastman Sound that we used to chat on. He said, Come on my radio station. They never really had MCs on there chatting lyrics before, so we started doing that. They started getting more listeners. We were jumping on anyone's set, then they started to get more guys coming in and wanting to MC. The whole DJ/MC thing started blowing up. MC Navigator was with us, then Det came a bit after that, you had Shabba D, all these guys started chatting lyrics over jungle, which turned into a whole scene.'

The freestyling of ragga or rap lyrics and hooks over jungle breaks—made famous by MCs like the aforementioned Navigator and Det, and others like Skibadee and the late Stevie Hyper D—started to become a thing. Flinty remembers a particular moment when he recognised how well it worked.

'It was one night at an event called Roast, and Grooverider was playing,' he says. 'Deman just decided to go up there and pick up the mic. He was chatting and the place lifted off, I was like, *Ras!* I was in the crowd and he just went and done it. The next week, I went to Roast again, it was every Sunday, but Deman never came. Rider was playing again. I thought, *I'm gonna jump up there this time.* Same thing happened—it went mad. So we thought, *Yeah, this thing can work. We can do this.* There wasn't a booking for MCs then, we would just go to raves and chat. Then the first person to book us as MCs was Jungle Fever. We done a set with Andy C, a half hour of him playing tunes and us chatting lyrics.

'It's the same vibe as reggae, but obviously in reggae they'll play the vocal track then split it onto the version, and we'd chat. This was purely instrumental. We thought, *This is where we should take our thing.* Still make records, but in dances it would just be freestyling.'

## DANCEHALL CONNECTION

While some were creating their own rhymes to fill the dubby spaces jungle had opened up, many were using a sampler to make the dancehall connection. Behind the wave of bona fide ragga jungle were artists both seasoned in the hardcore scene and brand new, and one of the most important was Mikail Tafari.

Previously known as Michael West, before he changed his name in line with his Rastafarian faith, Tottenham-based Tafari had success in the pop charts as Rebel MC in the late 80s with hits like the reggae-influenced *Street Tuff* with Double Trouble, which featured lyrics like 'Is he a Yankee? / No I'm a Londoner.' While that material was slick and mainstream accessible, his 1991 follow-up album, *Black Meaning Good*, hinted at the rich mix of jungle, with roughneck hip-hop breaks, a dub-wise atmosphere, a sample potpourri from sources as unexpected as Enya, and guest ragga MCs like UK legend Tenor Fly—and this was just lead single *Tribal Base*. The following year, Tafari produced the Amen-breaking, sample-stabbing beat for ragga rappers Demon Boyz's *Jungle Dett*, before fully immersing himself in jungle, releasing a series of dizzyingly tough and danceable records under a host of pseudonyms, including, most famously, Congo Natty.

Under the name Conquering Lion, he made speedy, rolling tracks of clipped breaks, deep dub bass, and a plethora of samples grabbed from recent and not so recent reggae and dancehall hits, lacing them with mystical synths. 'Reggae wasn't really focused on the sub-bass feeling, but in jungle we enhanced that frequency,' Tafari told the *Guardian*.

*Inah Sound* was telling in its dancehall rat-a-tat drums, which mimic the boom tap, boom tap of ragga yet send them over hyper-speed rhythms. *Dubplate Special* was even better, with its soundsystem bleeps and blips, and little samples that drew from rare groove, soul, and house classics, nodding to the diverse musical roots of this new hybrid.

Arguably Conquering Lion's finest moment was *Code Red*, which along with samples from Reggie Steppa's classic *Drum Pan Sound* has a full vocal chat from Jamaican MC Supercat, dub echoes, and rolling bass, drawing an explicit link to soundsystem heritage and giving it a futuristic respray. With toasted vocals attached and the drum breaks landing on the offbeat like dancehall, it appealed to revellers who enjoyed both rave and ragga. More and more people started to make their own takes on this reggae-driven breakbeat sound.

'I started to get records sent to me, and Rebel MC [Congo Natty] was starting to make records,' says DJ Ron. 'By him making some seminal tunes, and me being the first person to have them, that raised the game again. It's like everything—people hear something, they want to make those kinds of records, because they see people having success. Slowly, more people were making what you would credit as jungle tracks—with ragga samples, breakbeats, deep basslines, acid sounds, things like that.'

DJ Ron, who would make his name as a DJ on pirate station Kool FM alongside other jungle innovators like Brockie, remembers the club Roast at Turnmills in Clerkenwell, east London, as being a seminal spot in jungle's evolution.

'My friend was telling me, There's this event, I can get you to play there. Fabio was already playing there, Tamsin; it wasn't your archetypal jungle rave, 'cause you had Matthew B playing, Richie Fingers, Trevor Fung. Even those names, it's quite a cross-section of DJs. That was the early Roast. I got in there, and it was completely packed. I'm there in the party and I don't really know anyone, but then I clocked my friend Bart, and just by the power of the gods, a DJ didn't turn up as another was finishing. At that time, everyone was playing hour-and-a-half sets. Until this moment, I was the epitome of a bedroom DJ. All I'd ever played to was people in a bedroom. I'd done the odd gig, but this place was completely packed, mobbed, and this guy goes, This guy's got his records. I got up and started playing and it was going off, but then my mate Bart is coming back to me, saying, Play more of the breaks, so I'm getting out of my comfort zone, playing more of those. People were going nuts in there, yelling *Rewind!*, smashing the place up. Then the next DJ didn't turn up, so I played for three hours, and then they made me resident. But it was a mixture of all of us that helped us push it to a really well-known residency at that time.'

As the jungle scene and sound began to grow, the sub-heavy synth bass that had featured in classic dancehall tracks, from Anthony Red Rose's *Tempa* to Wayne Smith's *Under Mi Sleng Teng*, became a natural companion to breakbeats. They could run half-time while the beats chattered along at double the speed. You could dance to jungle as you would dance to reggae, and dance styles that were big in the ragga scene, like the bogle, crossed over to the new scene. Ragga fans went to jungle events too, and though hardcore raves had themselves been ethnically mixed, these dances attracted a bigger black audience than before.

'When we started the ragga jungle stuff,' says Bryan Gee, 'a lot of my friends and family could relate to it, 'cause it had lyrics from reggae tracks.'

'It just got rawer and rawer, then we started adding the reggae element to it,' says DJ SS. 'It was about a vibe. That was a key element. It was something people knew, and their mothers played to them—they reminisced on the soul, reggae, and funk. That's what it's all about, something people could connect to.'

'A big thing among the black community in the blues parties was reggae, revival, and soul,' says MC Det. 'It was mad because the rave scene and the new jungle had all these sounds sampled in. There was a lot of rare groove, old-school reggae tunes and upfront reggae tunes, popular tunes of the time, and they were being played in the blues and stuff. If you listen to something like Leviticus's *Burial*, that was the crossover—it was based mainly around what was going on in the blues. You found a rare groove tune that everybody liked, then you put a breakbeat under it.'

Eastman of Kool FM co-founded the Jungle Fever event in 1993, but though its name chimed with the music that was played there, he says it was named for a different reason. 'Jungle Fever came from the Spike Lee film,' Eastman said in an interview with *Vice* magazine. 'The film's about mixed relationships, about black and white, which I thought was fitting, as rave culture was doing more for race relations in the UK at the time than anything else.'

Commandeering huge warehouse spaces, pitching up not just in London but elsewhere in the UK, from Milton Keynes to Coventry, Jungle Fever became one of the pioneering events to push the sound. 'There were other parties at the time, other people doing things, but they played a bit of this and a bit of that,' Eastman said. 'Jungle Fever was always a main-room event, one of the first to use jungle in the title and to play it from start to finish, all night.'

In jungle, the musical ideas tested out in hardcore's most adventurous tracks—like beat choppage, time stretching, sound manipulation—could be mixed with found-sound shrapnel of everything from barking pit bulls to police sirens, soul divas to horn licks, and chest-caving low-end bass. The samples peppering the tunes sounded like the emanations of passing cars pumping out pirate radio, from soul to reggae to hip-hop, to jungle itself: the inner-city 'concrete jungle' experience captured in aural snapshots.

The jungle sound germinated from record labels like Paul 'Ibiza' Chambers's Ibiza Records, home to pioneering tracks from Noise Factory and Potential Bad Boy, as well as Jimmy Low's Labello Blanco, which initially introduced reggae aspects to hardcore, before putting out jungle anthems by Dr S Gachet, Smokey Joe, and Rogue Unit.

Kenny Ken, one of the original champions of the jungle sound, followed a familiar route through hardcore—the Centreforce pirate station, and events like Labyrinth and Crazy Larrys—in his early DJ career. His earliest musical obsession was reggae, and he followed the Unity Soundsystem in his youth, later applying the style to frenetic breakbeats in his sets.

'My style is very reggae influenced, I love bass,' he has said. Though best known as a DJ, his 1994 collaboration with MC D.R.S., *Everyman*, remains one of the greatest vocal tracks in the genre, mixing roots lyrics and chatting with rapid rolling Amens.

DJ Brockie was also key to innovating jungle from the very start. One of the first DJs on Kool FM, he pushed the more minimal, ragga-influenced jungle style as soon as it came into being, with MC Det adding a lyrical flavour to his sets and helping to set in motion the more vocal side of the scene (see chapter 11). Also the boss of the Undiluted label, his productions alongside Ed Solo have found their way onto True Playaz and Sonic Art.

Jungle evolved rapidly, and one of its greatest virtuosos was Remarc (real name: Marc Forrester). From Brockley in southeast London, he was introduced to reggae by his Jamaican dad. 'My dad had a small soundsystem when he first came to the UK,' he says. 'So from as far back as I can remember, music, mainly reggae, has been a part of my life. When I was young in south London, it was all about soundsystem culture. It was definitely all about Saxon Soundsystem for me, but south like everywhere else had nuff big sounds, including Coxson and Shaka.'

Later introduced to hip-hop and rare groove at blues parties, then hip-house by his younger brother Ray, Remarc started DJing at local shindigs, before getting into the nascent hardcore sound and securing a regular slot on pirate station Weekend Rush. He learned the basics of production from his friend Lewi Cifer, and the duo made the rock-solid and unsettling *Ricky*, a classic track that bridged the gap between the darkside sound and the new jungle with its screams of 'Ricky!' sampled from early 90s movie *Boyz In The Hood*; its rapid-fire, layered breaks; and its dub bassline. Starting out with just an Akai S950, a six-channel mic mixer, and normal stereo speakers, he would help to define the jungle style, fusing a love of soundsystem music and breakbeats.

'I just followed on from what the likes of Shut Up & Dance, Rebel MC, Paul Ibiza, among others, had been doing for years previous,' he says. 'We used to mix reggae records with hardcore on the radio, so naturally when I learnt to produce,

I incorporated my musical tastes all into one, of course heavily influenced from my love of soundsystem/clash culture.'

In 1994, Remarc started to release the kinds of tracks he would become famous for. *Sound Murderer*, backed with *Drum N' Bass Wise*, would bring about a monumental shift in the genre.

With *Sound Murderer* lacing a rare-groove soul track with speaker-busting sub and sampled soundsystem chat, what made it stand out most was its delirious rush of Amen breakage, splintering the drums into micro-snare shards, transposing them into different keys and creating futuristic drum glissandos. The effect was an exhilarating rolling sensation, like perpetual motion, and it would have a considerable influence on jungle/drum & bass as a whole. While some had already been experimenting with chopping up breakbeats, Remarc took it further than anyone, yet he still made it danceable and accessible. With *Sound Murderer*, he seemed to suggest, he was assassinating musical rivals with the strength of his beats—a new form of the soundclash that was such a feature of reggae soundsystems.

'I didn't intend on pushing anything further than anyone else, I was simply having fun and learning at the same time, making what I liked, basically,' Remarc says. 'If you listen to my releases from back then, you can hear the experimentation going further and further with every track as I was learning and going deeper.'

Back then, though, cutting up breaks in such a way was a truly time-consuming and meticulous procedure. 'Every edit, stretch, mad twist-up in them tunes were done via sampler and MIDI parts. I would usually go over the track several times, adding edits in here and there for days. I still hear chopped up Amen tunes, but I can pretty much hear when a software plug-in is being used to do it.'

In '95, Remarc put out perhaps his greatest track via Suburban Base, *R.I.P.*, a minimalist slab of Amen rollage with impossibly slick drum cut-ups, samples of 'junglist', and the central 'RIP, rest in peace' ragga vocal, throwing down the gauntlet for others to attempt to follow in his footsteps. More outlandish was *Thunderclap*: a seething Reese bass powered by a metallic percussion blur that's dizzying in its complexity, it would prove the template for extreme subgenres focused on drum manipulation, like breakcore and drill 'n' bass.

James Stephens, a producer who made some of the earliest proto-jungle tracks as Noise Factory, took on the alias Family Of Intelligence to produce ragga-laced classics like *Champion Of Champions*, full of dancehall vocal samples and snippets of gruff gangsta lyrics, while the associated Kemet label, run by Mark X, became a vital outlet for the sound. Kemet Crew, a collective of producers who released on the Tottenham-based label, put out an album via major label RCA, *Champion Jungle Sound*.

Stretch, who today runs the excellent AKO Beatz label—a reliable source of new jungle beats—made one of the greatest ragga jungle tracks as New Blood. *Worries In The Dance* had shivers-down-the-spine air-raid sirens, massive woodblock percussion hits, and scattershot samples of dancehall tunes, soul divas, and roots gems amid its chopped Think break, and is one of the best thrill rides in the entire genre.

The Moving Shadow label, another there at the beginning of hardcore, remained on point, releasing Dead Dred's *Dred Bass* in '94. With its time-stretched sample of Dr Alimantado's *Gimmie Mi Gun*, asking 'What the time you have, the dread?', gunshots, and warping synth bass sound—quick to become a jungle signature—the track was an instant signifier of the genre.

Ray Keith's track as Renegade, *Terrorist*, made with engineer Nookie, was another key Moving Shadow single. With its ominous reggae piano intro (inspired by synth-pop band Japan's *Nightporter* and replayed) and a combination of evil Reese bass with a second dub-wise bassline, not to mention its doubled-up break, it too would become an instant classic.

'I was annoyed with all these samples, and I was like, Right, this is my interpretation of what electronic dub should be,' Ray Keith says. 'Originally, I used to listen to a tune by Smith & Mighty, *Anyone*, and the bassline in the middle of it, not the Reese but the other bass, was influenced by that.

'I made that tune in four hours. I wanted a dubplate for the weekend, but whenever I did something, I wanted it to be different. I would make myself uncomfortable and push it, otherwise there's no point. Why am I going to regurgitate something that's been done already? I needed to push the sound. I remember I gave it to three or four DJs, we were all playing Orange that weekend, and I must have heard it about ten times in the dance. Everyone started with it or finished with it, and it just smashed it.'

## MCS
Guest MCs were becoming more prominent at jungle club nights and events, and especially on pirate radio, while ragga toasters continued to be a key feature

in the music. Increasingly, these vocals would be more than just samples. The UK reggae label Fashion, started by the south London record shop Dub Vendor in 1980, opened up a new label in 1994 to meet the demand for the new sound. Jungle Fashion teamed established Jamaican and British vocalists with producers to create official hybrids, and sometimes had vocalists cut entirely new jungle tunes. Cutty Ranks, Poison Chang, and Tenor Fly were some of the acts to bridge the gap between the genres, while DJ Rap, Kenny Ken, and Marvellous Cain provided the beats. DJ SS's version of Cutty Ranks's *Limb By Limb* became a hardy perennial of the scene. Greensleeves, another long-running UK reggae label, also latched on to the new craze, releasing *Bad Boy Lick A New Shot* by Ninja Man, Bounty Killer, Beenie Man & Ninja Ford in 1994.

'The thing about jungle is we were really taken by surprise by it,' said Chris Lane, one of the founders of Fashion Records, in the liner notes for Soul Jazz compilation *Rumble In The Jungle*. 'We'd always assumed that we'd be making reggae records ... and then we found that these young black kids didn't want to play their parents' music. Suddenly reggae records weren't selling in the same way, and everyone was going on about jungle. I was listening to this stuff, all speeded-up with synthesised basslines added, and loads of samples. In the early 90s, any time I turned on a jungle station, within two minutes I would hear a sample of one of our tunes, be it Cutty Ranks or General Levy or someone random. And I was getting into it.'

The classics came thick and fast between the two golden years of this ragga-jungle sound. *Burial* by Leviticus was pretty much the perfect jungle track: opening on swirling digital ambient chords, it slams in on rolling breaks, a funk sample you could hum along to, and the classic MC chat of 'Big, bad and heavy / Any sound test and tonight dem ah go bury.' With a little diva snippet in there too, re-sung by Yolanda, *Burial* has hook after hook, and is another example of the magpie nature of the genre. Made by scene pioneer Jumpin Jack Frost, it was one of a cohort of tracks that would become famous beyond the scene.

'When the reggae style of jungle came out, a lot of people who grew up in the area where I did were like, *Yeaaahhhh*,' says Frost. 'When before they were like, What the fuck is all this about? I got really embraced by my community then—Frost, our hero, Brixton ... before, people didn't give a fuck.'

Sometimes, the jungle sound had more surprising elements in its sampladelic mishmash. As Sounds Of The Future, DJ SS was behind one of the biggest anthems of the time, *The Lighter*, which lifted a classical piano theme from 70s film drama *Love Story*, matching it with obese bass splurges and fleet drum breaks for an instantly recognisable and rewindable classic.

'I never sampled *Love Story*—we replayed it,' SS says. 'My mate who I was working with, he's a bass player, and he was in the studio just jamming. I said, What's that? Play that again, to this tempo. It was just a vibe. It was about hooks, things that people could remember. The whole thing was underground, so you had to try to get people to listen to that music. Something they'd know—then you drop the beats and bass.'

Sampling everything from famous classical composers to pop divas, DJ SS would look anywhere for inspiration, and on his roughneck classic tune *Black*, he played a fragment of an eerie synth riff that came from an even more surprising source. 'That was a Christmas song, if you listen to the whole riff,' he says, 'but I took out the rest of it 'cause it was too cheesy!'

In 1994, at west London's Notting Hill Carnival, the famous celebration of Afro-Caribbean and black British culture in the UK, jungle began to make its presence felt. Soundsystems around the event had up till then pumped out primarily reggae, dancehall, hip-hop, and soul sounds, but jungle, with its proximity to Jamaican rhythms, became another piece of the puzzle, electrifying a younger crowd and adding lightning-quick breakbeats to the dub bass that usually abounded there. Sounds like Rampage and 4Play added the evolving style to their main ingredients of funk, hip-hop, and ragga. Jungle totally bossed the carnival that year.

In clubs, jungle soon had a host of legendary dances. AWOL—started at Paradise Club in Islington in 1992 by Kenny Ken, Micky Finn, Dr S Gachet, Trevor Fung, and Swane—became a vital proving ground for jungle. By 1994, it was packed with junglists, often decked out in designer gear like Armani and Versace and MA2 bomber jackets, in slick counterpoint to the baggy casual gear of the hardcore era. Rather than pills or speed, clubbers would more likely be found puffing on a spliff or sipping champagne, and the dancing was focused-intensity rather than saucer-eyed abandon. In later years, AWOL would commandeer massive clubs like SW1 in Victoria and Elephant & Castle's famous Ministry Of Sound.

Roast was another key event in jungle's evolution, starting in '91 and originally taking place on Sundays at Turnmills, between midday and 8pm (hence the 'Sunday roast' name). Grooverider, Top Buzz, Ron, and Micky Finn were regular DJs there, and were some of the first to crystallise the jungle sound.

'Roast was definitely the birthplace of jungle,' says DJ Tamsin, another resident. 'That low ceiling at Turnmills . . . the dark, sweaty vibes. The banging on the walls when a TUNE dropped. Shouting, *RELOAD, RELOAD!* I've never experienced that kind of excitement about music before. It was raw. Special.'

When it moved to Linford Studios, the dancehall element became more evident in the music. As Brian Belle-Fortune points out in his classic jungle/ d&b history *All Crews*, the club's predominantly black crowd 'could relate to the music embroidered with reggae sounds and dancehall-style MCs'.

### THE COMMITTEE

As the jungle events got bigger, MCs became more of a focus in the scene, with DJ and producers more in the background. By 1994, the scene had become too successful to ignore, and the media suddenly wanted a piece of it.

One of these MCs was the London-born Paul Levy. He started chatting on the mic while still at school, and he came second in an MC competition in 1986, which spurred him on to take up the art seriously—taking a lot of influence from Jamaican dancehall soundsystems and artists.

'I came from an era when it was like DJ and MC running the place, like Yellowman and Beenie Man and Eek-A-Mouse,' he says. 'I was definitely inspired by these kinds of people, and also English soundsystems like Saxon and MCs like Papa Levi, Smiley Culture, Tippa Irie, Macka B—basically putting all these influences together and developing my own character.'

He started out running with local soundsystems in northwest London like Java [Nuclear Power], Vigilante, and TipperTone. 'I came with my own style, a hiccup style, which gave me my own signature, so basically I incorporated a lot of influences and put in a bit of my own flava—and that's how I became General Levy,' he says.

In the early 90s, the General released the *Double Trouble* album with Jamaican dancehall artist Capleton, following it up with *The Wickeder General* on Fashion Records, and having quite a lot of dancehall success. Fledgling jungle producer M-Beat then approached him to do a track, as he'd already been sampling Levy's vox in his own tracks anyway. 'It was a new venture for me, and a new vibe for these guys,' says the General. 'We put it together and made a song—*Incredible.*'

The success of *Incredible* was, well, incredible. Along with Shy FX's *Original Nuttah*, it became huge on the scene—smashing it at 1994's Notting Hill Carnival and busting into the Top 10 of the UK's national charts—and when the General started playing huge shows, the media came calling.

Jungle's appearance in the pop charts meant that print magazines suddenly wanted a piece of the action, but many in the scene were distrustful. It was easier for a latecomer journalist to access a latecomer singer or ragga MC, but that meant they would not truly get to the heart of the matter. Interviewed straight after an event in east London, General Levy was quoted in style mag *The Face* as saying, 'I run jungle at the moment. I came along and bigged up jungle. I took it national.'

In the close-knit London jungle community, which prided itself on the fact that no individual was bigger than the scene, there was outcry. Levy's reported boast did not go down well. An ad hoc grouping was quickly formed by leading DJ/producers to address the fact that the focus of the scene was shifting to spotlighting the MCs, and this new Jungle Committee's DJs decided to stop playing *Incredible* in their sets. What's more, its members were forbidden from performing on the same bill as General Levy—in some instances, cancelling residencies or regular slots they'd held down for years. Levy was blacklisted, and it adversely affected his career for a long time.

Purportedly instigated by Congo Natty, the committee was primarily concerned about the media attention falling predominantly on MCs and singers, in a similar way to how the focus in rock, pop, and hip-hop tends to be on the front people. Some of its initial attendees had been in the scene for years, and they were justifiably concerned about latecomers stealing their thunder.

The Jungle Committee's efforts effectively forced Levy into a public apology. In the September 1994 issue of *The Face*, after saying how he understood how much work people in the hardcore/jungle community had put into the scene, Levy wrote, 'I am part of a scene that is working to promote black music in this country. Anyone who wants to do the same I support and will big up. It is the DJs who supported jungle (Randall, Micky Finn, Ray Keith), the shops (Blackmarket, Unity), the radio stations and the public who run jungle. It is music by the people of the world. No one individual runs any type of music. I am one voice trying to further the cause of black music in this country.'

There was undoubted strength in the committee, although some in the scene refused to get involved, or thought it was aiming at the wrong targets. 'What a pile of shite,' said Dego McFarlane from 4hero in Martin James's book *State Of Bass*, first published in the late 90s. 'We had no involvement in it. Fucking kids. Boys all talking shit.'

'There was a committee, and I was not very welcome in it because I refused to not play that record,' says DJ Rap. 'It was a great record, and I was going to play it as often as I could. The committee said we couldn't play it, so I decided to play it every single set at the beginning. So I was invited to one meeting, and that was it. I wasn't allowed to be part of the committee—boo hoo.

'Was it a necessary thing at the time? I thought it was a load of rubbish,' Rap continues. 'The thing I loved about the rave scene is that we were free, with no sheriffs. Now was not the time to start policing anyone.'

It took years for General Levy to be accepted back into the core fold after the *Incredible* saga. Many moons later, he's still bemused by the whole affair. 'The *Face* interview was a misinterpretation, really,' he says. 'I basically said to the guy, Jungle is a UK thing, it was born in the UK, we created this. It was a statement that was made to say to the people, the public, that this was our music. Other countries have got hip-hop or reggae, and now we've finally got our own thing that was organically born in England. You know what I mean? But the way it was interpreted in the magazine was that I was saying I made it, I created it, me-me-me,' he continues. 'It was a misinterpretation, taken out of context.'

General makes the point that he was interviewed immediately after coming offstage at a two-thousand-capacity gig with M-Beat at Walthamstow Assembly Halls in east London. 'It was a really exciting moment for me as an artist, it was definitely overwhelming. I was hype, you know what I mean? And I'm twenty-two years old, so of course I'm gonna be...y'know, and I'm saying, Bwoy, this is great music, we made this music, we should be proud of it. I think the way he took it [the journalist] was turned around.'

Levy thinks that he was made a scapegoat for the underlying feeling of some long-serving DJs and producers that the media might focus too much on MCs, and that the DJs and producers would be relegated to merely providing the backing for ragamuffin mic-men, rather than largely making cinematic, instrumental, sample-based music.

'It was like a sacrifice. It was like, *We want to keep this thing instrumental.* I didn't really understand that at the time, 'cause I was a reggae man coming from reggae music, so I didn't really understand this thing about not wanting any vocals on a track, wanting to keep it instrumental—I didn't understand that concept at all. So I maybe stepped on some people's toes unintentionally and unknowingly, but they then used that statement and twisted it and turned it around to give us a bad name. Assassinate our characters.'

Levy didn't hear about the committee until many years later, and even now he's still a bit bewildered about it. 'Am I sorry the whole affair happened? Well, yeah, it was just ridiculous. Have I spoken to any of the main people since? Well, I don't know who these people are, 'cause nobody ever approached me face to face to say, Hey, I've got a problem with you. It's always been shadows.'

He's been forgiven by the scene now and had a career rebirth, but at the time it caused him a lot of angst and depression. He also got dropped by London Records as a result of the furore. 'They got scared: *Oh god, how are we gonna market him, everybody hates him!* So I lost a lot of money, a lot of my career I've lost through being blacklisted. Most people won't know how much I lost—only I know, and my family. Even with *Incredible*, I was never paid the full money for the tune. Crazy.'

A lot of water has passed under a lot of bridges since this 1994 furore. What the committee did do is further grow a tight scene away from some commercial temptations—it became not so much a way of life as necessarily a business for some. In hindsight, the *Incredible* saga forms a crucial time in the development of the scene—when the more MC-led 'jungle' split off from what started to be called 'drum & bass', which was more concerned with producers painting musical soundscapes.

## LYRICAL EDGE

Along with *Incredible*, the other massive jungle hit was Shy FX & UK Apachi's *Original Nuttah*. With its eerie horn intro, UK Apachi's motormouth rhymes, and rolling Amen breaks, it made jungle an instantly recognisable sound to ears outside the scene—and made the UK Top 40.

Production wiz Shy FX (Andre Williams) grew up in Tottenham, surrounded by music: his grandfather ran the Third World record shop and was best known as early UK soundsystem pioneer Count Shelly. At home,

BEN MURPHY & CARL LOBEN

blues parties would make the walls of his home reverberate. Working for a soundsystem himself from an early age, he couldn't help but be intrigued by the hardcore breakbeat sounds he'd hear around his estate, and, after making his first dancehall production, he was compelled to make his own version of the embryonic jungle style, sampling a beat from another twelve-inch and a Capleton a cappella to create the tune *Jungle Love*, released by Permission To Dance in '93. Then, after UK rapper Skinnyman helped him get a job as a tape op at Sound Of The Underground Records (SOUR), he persuaded the label to put out his next record.

'They agreed to put out *Gangsta*, and it went nuts for them,' he told *Trench* magazine in 2019. When the label suggested doing a collaboration with one of their MC mates, UK Apachi, Shy FX thought he'd give it a try, unaware of the massive tune they were about to create.

'Apachi came into the studio, did his job in two takes, went home, and it was done. It felt like it was writing itself,' he continued. 'Everything on the tune sounded like a hook. There wasn't a part that felt like a verse—it was nuts!'

Blowing up on pirate radio, it was one of the biggest tunes at Notting Hill Carnival in 1994, too, and it set Shy FX on the path to becoming a key producer in the many movements of jungle/drum & bass, from jump-up/hardstep tunes like *Wolf* and *The Message* to later more soulful missives like *Shake Ur Body* with T Power.

Jungle wasn't just party music. Some artists sought to reflect the harsh realities of what they saw happening on the streets in their tunes. Shy FX's *Gangsta* (aka *Gangsta Kid*), the tune that was remade into *Original Nuttah*, featured ragga MC Gunsmoke and related a London gangland execution in its intro.

'*Gangsta* came about because we were hearing a lot of tunes that were sampling films and all the rest of it,' Shy FX says in the 1994 documentary *Jungle Fever*. 'We thought we should do something more original than that, get some London talk so everybody can relate to it. Incidences like that do happen, that's why you put it in there in the first place.'

A sense of rebelliousness and an urge for a new generation to define itself also drove the roughneck lyrical and musical edge of jungle. Just as hip-hop (or punk) had shocked older generations, jungle became a route by which youth could stand apart from their elders and say, 'This is our thing.' Though the reggae and soul samples threaded through the music indicated black British musical heritage, it was about presenting it in a new way that felt relevant to a youthful movement.

'Rebellion, true rebellion,' the late Peter Harris, founder of Kickin Records, says in the same documentary. 'Jungle is about making music that adults hate and kids love. It's like the old rock'n'roll story. If it's loud, they hate it. I think jungle is popular because the youths can let off on it. It's an escape from their society.'

Jungle's hard-edged sound and uncompromising lyrical content became a negative focus for some who sought to discredit the music. Just as pirate radio had been portrayed as a cover for drug dealing by the police and news media, jungle was painted as the preserve of 'undesirables' by some of the mainstream and music press. As with American hip-hop, the finger was pointed at the supposed negative influence jungle was having. The troubling subtext is that it sought to denigrate a multicultural scene, most of whose pioneers were black.

For a number of reasons, ragga jungle had receded into the background by the end of '95. Some found the vibe of the music too moody; some DJs and producers in the scene disliked the vocalist-led direction, and wanted jungle to be a mostly instrumental form, as it had originally been. The media, having courted MCs like General Levy, sought to distance itself from the jungle sound, instead wanting a more 'musical' form to promote. Running parallel to the ragga-jungle sound, the drifty elements of ambient and techno were being combined into the breakbeat recipe at clubs like Speed and on LTJ Bukem's Good Looking Records label. A schism opened up between what was perceived as jungle—the ragga variant—and what people increasingly described as drum & bass. Some thought there was a racial component to this rebranding, as if by banishing the Jamaican and black British parts of the music, it could become more palatable to a white crowd.

'There was this thing in the dance media at the time, very early on—they were saying this jungle music is dangerous in a way; the people that go to these dances are crackheads,' A Guy Called Gerald says. 'Straight off the cuff, it was given this bad name. Was there a racial component? I wouldn't call it straight-up racist, but it was definitely a separatist kind of thing, like, *Don't go to these dances with these people*. It had this dark undertone to it. It was segmented off. When the marketing thing of drum & bass kicked off, that was pushed more. When labels got involved, it had to be a more watered-down kind of thing, a process of making remixes of tunes.'

Meanwhile, jungle itself was morphing, drawing more from American rap. The breakbeats were a US import originally, of course, yet the sound started to incorporate samples from Stateside MCs, like the raw atmospheres of New York's Wu-Tang Clan and the wiggly keyboard lines and sun-baked synth bass of West Coast gangsta rap by the likes of Dr Dre.

From Lemon D's funked up *Urban Style Music* for Metalheadz, to Ganja Kru's *Tiger Style*, to Capone aka Dillinja's ferocious *Soldier* on Carl Collins's great Hardleaders label, a new path was being mapped out for the underground. There was even cross-pollination between the two scenes, as Goldie was tasked with remixing Houston rap legend Scarface and guest MC Ice Cube's *Hand Of The Dead Body*. Goldie and Rob Playford turned the track into a plaintive gangsta paean, with rough drums tumbling over a gorgeous keyboard figure and pads, the MCs' raw street reportage sitting perfectly on top.

DJ Zinc's 1996 release *Super Sharp Shooter* was an instant dancefloor classic, with its rap vocal snips, spelled out title (courtesy of crafty sampling of LL Cool J), cut-up synth squiggles from The J.B.'s, Amen breaks, and warping bass. Hype's track *Playaz Anthem* took the gangsta-rap vibe and followed it through to its logical conclusion, looping a section from a Brian de Palma movie and dropping it over soul-diva vocals and rugged bass and beats.

The rap-tilted variant of jungle would become hardstep (sometimes called jump-up), a direct subgenre that made the drums more straight-ahead, removed the unnecessary melodic aspects, and pushed punishing synth basslines upfront for a guaranteed dancefloor recipe. Tunes such as Urban Takeover's *Bad Ass*— made by Micky Finn and Aphrodite and spliced together from film dialogue, rugged beats, and noisy b-lines—would rule in this rowdy new club style.

The ragga and dancehall side of jungle never *really* faded, of course. In fact, it has remained an underpinning component of the entirety of the genre. Whenever the music became too techy, too melodic, too abstract, there were always producers, DJs, and ravers keen to keep the fire burning. The Amen break became a constant feature, even in the most clinical productions. MCs were now a key part of pirate radio and at raves and clubs. The sub-bass of dancehall soundsystems would permeate every side of the sound, while ragga lyrics, dub effects, and reggae vocals would periodically return. And while these elements were woven into the very fabric of the genre, there were always artists who continued to promote the ragga jungle sound, such as Congo Natty or Kenny Ken.

To some, the term 'jungle' would come to embody that golden mid-90s era, which is celebrated today by huge artists like Chase & Status (witness their *Return II Jungle* album and live tours). The sampling, invention, and heaviness of it stands in stark contrast to the cleanliness of much d&b production now. The essence of jungle persists because its champions have largely kept it away from the mainstream, and its fans are some of the most passionate of any genre. Soon, the style would bifurcate into punky tech-noise and blissful ambient undercurrents—but it would resist any attempts at dilution.

# 09 Inner-City Life: Jungle's Regional Expansion

'We did the first drum & bass raves in Leeds—a partner and I put on the first drum & bass raves in Sheffield, I'm confident of that,' remembers DJ, producer, and label boss L Double. 'We did the first jungle rave in Huddersfield. There was jungle tekno being played. At the Sheffield thing, we brought up about seven or eight DJs, Micky Finn, DJ Ron, Roni Size—he turned up in his Mk2 Fiesta. That was right at the beginning. I felt like we needed to be spreading this. I'd done a lot of travelling to London and recognised it was a London thing, as far as the vibe of the music scene, but I wanted to bring some of that energy back up here to the North.'

Though hardcore and jungle may have been born in London and the surrounding counties, it didn't take long for the scene to propagate in other spots around the UK. The North and the Midlands took to acid house and rave culture along with the rest of the country, and once the initial burst had died down, it left several enclaves where producers and DJs could formulate their own takes on the breakbeat sound.

Yorkshire has a rich history in terms of its contributions to electronic music, from the synth-pop of Sheffield's Human League to the bleep techno of Leeds groups LFO and (early) Nightmares On Wax. It's lesser known for its hardcore and jungle, though L Double (real name: Lee Johnson) has been on a mission to represent for the county and his city of Huddersfield from the beginning.

When he was growing up, L Double would hear reggae playing in the house courtesy of his dad, and crooners like Frank Sinatra and Shirley Bassey from his mum. But soon something would come along that would really inspire him. 'Hip-hop was the first thing that was *ours*—our first real new music that wasn't passed down by someone else's generation,' he says.

Falling in love with the American sound, he joined a hip-hop crew, and then another US import, house music, came into the picture. 'I can remember being on the outskirts of it all, when we were all into every other permutation of music except for rave at that stage, and rave was coming across like a tsunami,' he says. 'Friends were dropping like flies, one minute they were like, Yeah, man, we're hard hip-hop, R&B, reggae, then next week it's like, *Man down*, as he was seen at a rave! One less of the crew. Going to these things originally as outsiders, wandering around the flat tops and the polka dots, we were going, Woah, this is an amazing vibe in here. It was opening your eyes and ears, hearing and looking at what the collectives were doing as one. It started from there. We'd been into Chicago house, which predates it all. Labels like Trax, DJ International, going way back, I've got all that era of music, the whole nine. I'd go to Jumbo or Crash Records in Leeds and spend my six pounds on an import.'

L Double would join bleep techno group Unique 3, whose 1989 anthem *The Theme* managed to bridge the gap between rap, house, and heavy, soundsystem bass pressure in a way that prefigured the mixtures of hardcore and jungle. As Unique 3 began to tour festivals and raves to perform PAs of their hit tracks, L Double started to notice new sounds and styles coming into the mix.

'Around '91, we were doing shows, and passing the mic to whoever's in there, introducing Grooverider, Fabio, Micky Finn, Frost. We were doing performances in between what they were playing. We would go on and say, Did you hear that thing that Frost played? We were hearing madness, from early Moving Shadow and early Reinforced, like Manix's *Feel Good*. I watched Seal come on stage for his first PA with Adamski, his first time, at Shelley's!'

When Unique 3 broke up, L Double, inspired by the rising breakbeat sound, struck out on his own. After several hardcore releases, he started to make roughneck jungle, launching the Flex Records imprint in 1994 with the fierce Amen brock-outs of *Little Rollers Volume One*.

'When Flex really kicked off, it was because I didn't have anything left to give to a major label-type situation. I'd heard everything I'd needed to hear with the Unique 3 stuff. I just thought, *This drum & bass thing is me*,' he says. 'Breaks were my thing. It felt like a bit of liberation, the fact that I could do it, and then it started selling and I was making my money back—result! It was like, Oh, this is actually fun.'

As L Double's reputation grew, with solo ragga jungle releases, and high-profile singles like his Metalheadz EP under the name Asylum, *Da Base 2 Dark/*

*Steppin' Hard*, he was also putting on club events around Yorkshire, viewing a significant gap in the market.

'We started the whole events thing, moving on to work with major players in the town [Leeds house club] Back To Basics, and we did events in Sheffield at the Arches,' L Double says. 'We carved it out, there was nothing going on here, and that's being polite! I think that's one of the reasons why we get a little nod. A partner and I hired the old swimming baths in Bradford for one event. It was crazy in there. You couldn't get venues, so this place is empty. *You want to try it?* Too right, imagine that?'

L Double gained a reputation for his raw, roughneck approach to jungle, and a style that came to be briefly known as hardstep. Characterised by thumping, sub-heavy synth bass, irresistible straight-ahead breakbeats, and a peppering of samples from American gangsta rap, hardstep, like ambient jungle and techstep, was an essential ingredient in the mid-to-late-90s dancefloor recipe. L Double's tune with Shy FX, *The Shit*—along with tracks on labels like True Playaz, Dope Dragon, and Urban Takeover—epitomised the sound, while his tunes on Flex Records at the time can be considered classics of the era.

Starting a regular radio show on Yorkshire's Galaxy 105 station, he set out to bring drum & bass to a wider audience in the North. 'I was trying to connect down south to up here. I started doing interviews with Reinforced, A-Sides, Bukem, Smokey Joe, Red One, Andy C. It was my duty in a way. Like, *Let's get this music out to the masses, 'cause this is what we do*. It felt like no one knew what was going on then. It went well—I had the most listened to specialist show on Kiss and Galaxy 105. I was competing with all the house guys, the whole nine.'

From there, he was recruited by former Kiss FM man Wilber Wilberforce for the BBC's new national 'urban' station, 1Xtra, and became one of the channel's earliest champions of d&b. 'I demanded the first national drum & bass chart in the UK—that was part of my prerequisite for going on to the new digital station,' L Double says. 'Mainly because I'd done the rest at Kiss/Galaxy. That didn't interest me anymore. I wanted something that could make our music more official. When I turn on these big radio stations, there's a chart, so why was there no drum & bass chart? We had to devise a system to do it.'

Jungle evangelists like L Double were pivotal figures in spreading the gospel in the North. He used to sell records to independent record shops out of the back of his van, and it was after a visit to the Eastern Bloc shop in Manchester that he helped kick off the production careers of two important figures in the city's scene. Suggesting a collaboration, L Double asked Marcus Kaye, aka Marcus Intalex, what his goal was.

'I said, To get a tune into Grooverider's box,' Marcus told Joe Madden in 2011. 'And two weeks after making the tune, L Double gave it to Grooverider, who played it on Kiss and said, This is the best shit I've heard in perhaps years! So I was like, I must be doing summit right!'

Mark McKinley, aka Mark XTC, had also started off doing distribution rounds as a teenager, before landing a job at Spin Inn record shop in Manchester city centre in 1989-90. A budding DJ, he rode the transition from hip-house and hardcore into early jungle via tracks like Lennie De Ice's *We Are I.E.*, 2 Bad Mice's *2 Bad Mice*, and lots of Ibiza Records stuff. Spin Inn was the only shop selling jungle at the time, and he'd get a lot of the white labels before the shops in London. Soon, he was charting them for *Mixmag Update*.

Manchester resident A Guy Called Gerald had been instrumental in kicking off jungle via releases like *28 Gun Bad Boy*, but it was only when Goldie took him to Rage in London that he connected his music to the jungle scene. Manchester's acid-house history has been well documented, but jungle was a consistent undercurrent in its music culture since the early 90s.

'Back in the early 90s, jungle was not accepted in mainstream clubs—especially in Manchester, which had earned the nickname Gunchester,' Mark XTC says. 'We had a fantastic amount of talent around—MC Trigga, DJ Sappo, Future Cut, Da Intalex (myself and Marcus Kaye), ST Files, RaggaBeats, Platoon, Tonn Piper—and we all used to play quite a lot of different venues, with many different races. There was a club called the PSV (Darkhouse), which was predominantly black people, I would say 80/20, but it wasn't about that. Because the jungle thing was new for everyone, you had many different people from various backgrounds coming out raving to this new sound.'

Mark had known Marcus from DJing together at Angels in Burnley, where the latter was a resident in 1990–91, and Marcus used to buy so many records off Mark in Spin Inn that he soon offered him a job there. When the boss of rival shop Eastern Bloc, John Berry, came in and poached Mark to manage the place—effectively taking his jungle clientele with him, as well as the R&B and hip-hop buyers—Marcus moved to Eastern Bloc with him. As Da Intalex, the pair got a slot on regional radio station Kiss 102, which changed its name to Galaxy 102 in 1993.

Da Intalex's first release on L Double's Flex imprint, *What Ya Gonna Do*, mixed a classic soulful vocal sample with booming sub-bass, a sparse jungle dub atmosphere, and rolling polyrhythmic breakbeats, before a blissful elysian interlude of glimmering ambience. It helped put them on the map nationally, and they set up Intalex Productions to funnel tracks by themselves and local talent such as ST Files, aka Lee Davenport, into the scene. After a few years, Da Intalex parted ways when Mark wanted to pursue a teaching career, and Marcus—who also ran the Guidance night in the city—along with ST Files secured releases on 31 Records, Hospital, and Metalheadz around 2000. Mark XTC would later himself have tunes signed by Dillinja and Ray Keith, and he is still DJing, producing, and teaching the next generation to this day. 'This is one of the best feelings you can get, as it shows the love for the music is not dying in any shape or form,' he says.

The classic junglist juxtaposition of rough with smooth was especially potent in Marcus Intalex's hands, with tunes like *Love & Happiness* sampling a classic house vocal and lacing it with hard-stepping beats and warm Donald Byrd jazz-funk chords, resulting in a liquid drum & bass classic. Beyond his productions, he would also help to bring through many of today's biggest Manchester artists (Skeptical, Chimpo, DRS) in the genre via his Soul:r label, and he was especially keen on the experimental edges of the genre, typified by acts like Instra:mental and dBridge, or dubstep/techno producers like Martyn. (He also made some excellent techno music in the 2010s as Trevino.)

It took Marcus a long time to make his mark beyond Manchester—he certainly earned his stripes—and as his reputation soared in drum & bass's second decade, he didn't hold back with some of his passionate, straight-talking opinions. 'I can get frustrated with the sound of drum & bass, but the best way to make a difference is to get your own music out there and let that do the talking,' he said in 2011. 'Be positive, be proactive. There's too much negativity in the scene in general. Get out there and do something, instead of fucking whingeing. I've learned that.'

## NORTH-EAST AND THE MIDLANDS

Newcastle is often brushed over when considering the various places drum & bass has taken root across the UK, but the northeastern city also gave rise to its own tight-knit scene. Phobia (aka James Smith), one-third of Chroma, summarised the influence of Newcastle playas best when talking to Dave Jenkins in 2020. 'Hidden Agenda weren't far away, Original Sin and Sub Zero were just starting up, and Taxman not long after. Craggz & Parallel Forces. Jubei was up here for a few years. Sato. Tyrone. This city has been home to a lot of talent in the genre.'

Smith ran the Turbulence night for sixteen years, and when it stopped it left a hole in the city's scene. Various young DJs and d&b enthusiasts started their own nights—Motion Sickness, Dilate, Lively Up, and so on—and they continue to support each other when they bring big names into town or promote special events. 'We give each other sets, tell each other dates we have stuff planned, and try not to clash too much,' says Nicky Taser. 'It's nice—everyone's friendly and supportive.'

Other parts of the country had their d&b champions too. Coventry, the city that had given birth to The Specials and the multi-ethnic 2-Tone movement, became a hotbed for drum & bass talent. Catalysed by local clubs such as the Eclipse, which hosted events by rave promoters Amnesia House, in the early 90s it cultivated a group of artists who went on to become some of the most important acts in the genre.

Coventry's most famous export is Doc Scott (real name Scott McIlroy), the renowned DJ, 31 Records boss, and Metalheadz affiliate. He got his first pair of decks at fourteen, drawing inspiration from Fabio & Grooverider. 'I owe them a great deal,' he told *Melody Maker*. 'From the beginning, it fascinated me how one person, the DJ, can control the emotions and actions of so many people.'

Initially making his name as a DJ at events like Amnesia House among others, Scott put out a series of early hardcore and proto-jungle releases with suitably medical sounding names, such as *Surgery*, *Nite Nurse*, and—of course—*NHS*. Later, as jungle became properly established, he joined the hallowed ranks of the Reinforced label with titanium-coated monster tracks like *VIP Drumz*—a darkcore classic—and became a regular feature of seminal clubs like Speed and Metalheadz Sunday Sessions at the Blue Note.

Skanna was another important artist to emerge from the Coventry dance scene. John Graham would later go on to make trance and progressive house as part of Tilt and as Quivver, but he started out making hardcore and jungle, with the seminal *Heaven* EP one of the first to flirt with the ambient style. Other Coventry producers of note include Neil Trix, who ran the city's Bangin Tunes record shop and label, and was also part of FBD Project; and the highly prolific trio Essence Of Aura, who put out music through Moving Shadow among other labels.

Thirty-six miles north of Coventry, in the city of Derby, Simon 'Bassline' Smith had been a soul DJ who, in 1987, went off to DJ in Tenerife for three years. Returning with acid house in full swing, he quickly slotted into being a jobbing DJ on the hardcore rave scene at the turn of the 90s. 'You could see on the dancefloor the dance moves changing into more of a shuffle with the breaks, or a simple head-nod,' he says. 'Me and the other DJs around at the time were experimenting with speeding up records from 33rpm to 45.'

Simon had grown up on reggae and hip-hop, so he was naturally drawn to proto-jungle tracks with sped-up breaks and deadly sub-bass—from where he earned his 'bassline' nickname back then. 'Tracks like A Guy Called Gerald *Anything*, Bodysnatch *Euphony (Just For You London)*, Tic Tac Toe *Ephermol*, Tronikhouse *Straight Outta Hell*, Lennie De Ice *We Are I.E.* were big for me at the time,' Simon says. 'If you listen to the releases from then, you can hear the transition. At that time the music was still dominated by the kick-drum, and the difference between music with a 4/4 kick-drum and a break is massive. With the kick-drum, it's headed towards a house direction. When the kick-drum was taken out and the focus was on the breaks and the sub-bass, that was exciting.'

Smith set up his own label, Absolute2, and put out early releases by Doc Scott and Nookie. Not much was going on in Derby, though, so Simon spent much of his time in Birmingham or London—the latter, especially, in record shops. 'Frequenting all the major underground record shops, like Bluebird Records, Music Power; City Sound, where Ray Keith worked before Black Market opened; Red Records, other shops around Brixton and Soho,' he recalls. 'Having played mostly outside of my hometown in the early 90s, most people thought I was London-based. I spent a lot of time in London on a weekly basis, so it felt like I was part of what was going on around that time there anyway.'

Another key lynchpin between cities, linked by record shops and raves, Bassline Smith would play huge events nationwide alongside rave DJs such as

'Evil' Eddie Richards, Fabio & Grooverider, Carl Cox, Colin Dale, and Jumpin Jack Frost. 'In the Midlands, we had raves like the Rag Market in Birmingham, Perception, the Amnesia parties, Time, the Eclipse in Coventry, the Bass Place in Birmingham,' he says. 'These nights were the pinnacle at the time. Ravers flocked en masse. It was awesome. At that time—'90 or '91—it was off the back of peace, love, and unity, flower power in the Summer of Love. Nobody looked at colour or creed. Having said that, it's fair to say that the majority were probably white, and the majority of the DJs were black. But no one was looking at what colour the next man was with any judgement. More importantly, the raves were classless. It was people from all classes—the poorest looking to escape their everyday life, and the richest looking to find themselves away from the pressure of parents, universities, schools or high-powered jobs. Even football hooligans found peace and love at raves.

'What I also found inspiring was that it was a new beginning,' Simon continues. 'In terms of the people that were coming into the raves, they were very excited, and we as artists and DJs were excited about what we were seeing in front of us. The horns and the whistles made the atmosphere in the dances feel so unreal. Those times of playing music to a crowd that was so into it, living and breathing the music and the culture that came with it was so inspiring. At the weekend, ravers went out; they didn't look left to see what that person was wearing, they didn't look right to see what car that person had. They were all in a rave, raving to one music that made them all feel free and happy. That was what was exciting then, that still excites me now.'

In about 1998, Simon met Andy Wright and Ben Wiggett from the Drumsound production outfit at the riotous local Derby drum & bass night Technique. Teaming up, they became one of the most successful groups in UK drum & bass; touring the world, releasing on Good Looking, V, Prototype, Urban Takeover, Formation, Trouble On Vinyl, and Breakbeat Kaos, and garnering more and more Radio 1 airplay. After they linked with the Utah Saints from Leeds, old friends of Simon's from the rave days, for an update of their Annie Lennox-sampling hit *What Can You Do For Me*, their status as Annie Mac favourites was cemented even further.

Elsewhere in the Midlands, DJ SS helped put Leicester on the drum & bass map. A pioneer of the darkside hardcore sound and later ragga jungle, he started out as part of the Formation hip-hop DJ crew before discovering dance music.

'We went to a rave in '89, I think it was, saw Fabio & Grooverider, and that was it—changed,' he says.

In Leicester, he became known for putting on and playing at a series of parties, the most famous of which was Total Kaos. 'We started doing the Total Kaos thing on Tuesday nights,' he says. 'We had Carl Cox down, Sasha. I think the first big thing we did was Nemesis 90. We rented out a skating rink, it was a daytime party, twelve till twelve. I remember going to Grooverider, Do you want to play this party? and he said, I can't do it mate, I'm playing somewhere else, and I said, Groove, it's a daytime thing, and he said, Ah, wicked! From then, me and him connected. We had Carl Cox, Sasha, Groove, Fabio, Micky Finn, all at this one party in Leicester.

'It was brilliant, really good, and it unified people. I remember doing that event, seeing one of my old-school hip-hop mates, and him saying, What're you doing, you sell-out? And then I saw him in the queue later and he said, Can I get in? You're calling me a sell-out and now you want to get in? It changed people's mindset, because no one had seen nothing like that before.'

DJ SS would go on to release massive EPs like *Breakbeat Pressure (Part 2)*, which explored the darkside sound, releasing many classics of the style through his Formation label; as noted previously, he also recorded some of the biggest ragga-jungle tracks ever with *Black* and *The Lighter*, made under the name Sound Of The Future.

### STORM FROM THE EAST

In the east of England, the county town of Suffolk, Ipswich, became a surprising outpost for jungle/drum & bass. The town's Essential Selection record shop, run by Rob Solomon, was an early rave hub, selling tickets to events and rave tape-packs in the early 90s. After playing in a local reggae soundsystem, Solomon put out some hardcore of his own under the name Origination, and would collaborate with another Ipswich resident, Photek, on his earliest material. One of the earliest women pioneers in jungle, Jo, hailed from Ipswich, and released the eerie eight-bit video-game-referencing classic *R-Type* in 1993.

The local scene also gave rise to the excellent Certificate 18 label run by Paul Arnold. Initially putting out Photek's first twelves under a host of names, it soon became a trusted label for uncovering new talent like Ipswich artists Klute, Digital, and Motive One.

'Working in Essential Selection, I was introduced to Rupert Parkes [Photek],' says Paul Arnold. 'He brought in a few demos that were super-fresh, like nothing I'd heard. They deserved to be released. Rob Solomon, owner of Essential, linked me with the Prince's Trust, where I was able to get a grant to press the first few records.'

Klute (Tom Withers) had previously been a member of punk band The Stupids, a favourite of John Peel, but adapted naturally to jungle, releasing the eerie FX and drum shrapnel shredding of *F.P.O.P.* via the label. Digital (Steve Carr), one of the most prolific artists in the genre, got his start there too, hooking up with Danny C as Authorised Riddim and dropping the Amen breakage and soothing ambient synths of *Split Personality* on Certificate 18.

Growing up listening to reggae like Gregory Isaacs and Dennis Brown and setting up his own soundsystem to DJ at parties, Digital got hooked on hip-hop via his brother and tunes like NWA's *Straight Outta Compton* and Mantronix's *King Of The Beats* (both of which contained the Amen break). When he saw how dancers went mad to rave tracks, he wanted to get involved with the sound himself.

'I'd been playing reggae already, and as soon as I heard lots of music that related to me, I just thought that was the next step for me to take,' he says. 'I was DJing all the time since I was a little boy. But the big step was going to a few different parties where I took my own soundsystem as well, and I got to play with Danny C's records. The vibe was electric compared to what I was used to.'

Around that time, Digital remembers a bubbling scene around East Anglia and Essex. 'There was a lot happening around Ipswich actually, Colchester, Clacton at a place called Tutus. You had Carl Cox there, Matthew B, different guys. There were a lot of the Ipswich guys there coming out of the reggae scene. As a reggae DJ who played a bit of hip-hop as well, there was a certain vibe in a reggae dance—nice, a bit of brandy, a bit of weed and that—but then I went to this place where everyone was going mental. The vibe was different, let's just say that. It was more vibing than the reggae dance.'

After his initial collaboration with Danny C, Digital struck out on his own, with his debut, *Touch Me*, an intricate slice of Amen choppage, metallic bass tones, and lush synth sweeps made in collaboration with Photek; his more ambient-influenced works emerged under the Natural Mystic moniker. Quickly,

Digital gained a reputation for his skilful edits and crisp productions, especially evident on early classic *Space Funk*, released under the name S.O.S. 'Because I used to go around with Photek, Source Direct, Certificate 18 crew, all those lot, they were into their edits, so I learned a lot from them. *Space Funk* is full of loads of edits—four different sets of edits in one track.'

Digital reckons that the limitations of sample time would force him and other producers to be more creative. 'A Roland W30 was the first thing I had, with fourteen seconds of sample time. Then I had an Atari ST. The technology changes the sound of music in any genre. To make an effective track I didn't really need lots of sample time, I just needed to get freaky on the piano scroll, you know what I mean? If you haven't got a million seconds' sample time, you're not doing anything else, are ya? You've got a string and you've looped that, you've got your pad and can play it low or high for a different effect, you've got one-shot stabs. You're gonna run out of time pretty fast. So you have to spend time on the drums.'

Building up a sizeable discography over the ensuing years on Metalheadz, Creative Wax, 31, and his own Function label, Digital came to be known for his distinctive use of breaks, never settling for simplistic rollouts. 'It was trying to have an individual sound. There was not a lot in my tracks, but I chose breaks and samples carefully. I think I've got better and better at it. I can do whatever I want now. At the time, I used to work with a guy called Mark—he used to help me do breaks as well. There were parts of it I thought I was good at, like the bass. So I made sure I had my own style. It does take a long time. If you're going to copy someone, you can pretty much do that straight away. But if you're going to do your own thing, you've got to nail it.'

Another vital force to arise from Ipswich was the late Spirit (Duncan Busto). A buyer at the town's Redeye Records shop, his catalogue of releases is immaculate, with tunes like 1996's *Mendacity* micro-shredding the Apache beat over gorgeous ambient washes worthy of Bukem himself, while his regular collaborations with Digital would always push the musical boundaries. When the scene became dominated by the kick-snare-powered techstep sound, the duo endeavoured to do something more interesting with the template.

'At the time, I thought it was too simple—why was everyone doing the same thing?' Digital says. 'I never really understood that, coming from the early 90s, when everyone did their own thing. But everyone was like, I need to use a two-step break 'cause everyone else is doing it. I did think it was quite boring, but myself and Spirit said, We're going to do a two-step break, but we're going to select the breaks. So we selected a decent break for *Phantom Force*, not just a boring boof-chak.'

As a relatively small town away from metropolises like London or Manchester, Ipswich punched way above its weight. 'Ipswich has always had a strong music scene,' reckons Paul Arnold. 'It's an hour away from the M25, and many early raves, forged with the growth of independent dance record shops, brought together creative minds, giving access and exposure to early electronic music, influencing and introducing bedroom producers to the possibilities of their own UK rave, jungle, hardcore soundscapes.'

Without a city to be centred around, DJs and producers like Rob Playford, Source Direct, Wax Doctor, DJ Pulse, J Majik, Justice, and Blame whirled around the home counties—driving into London for record shopping and raves, collaborating locally, checking out new beats in cars. Bukem started building his Good Looking empire in Watford, twenty miles north of London.

Now, with all these micro-pockets across the UK, a bubbling London scene, and an increased media spotlight on jungle/drum & bass, it would not be long before ears would start to prick up across the Atlantic, and around the world.

# 10 Touch Down On Planet V: Bryan Gee, Jumpin Jack Frost, And V Recordings

Brixton in the 70s and early 80s was a tough place to grow up if you were a young black youth—there was poverty, unemployment, and persistent harassment by the police, for starters. A stop-and-search policy, Operation Swamp, was introduced in 1981, and riots ensued after nearly a thousand black men were stopped by police during a five-day period in April for 'acting suspiciously'—sparked by a misunderstanding between the community and the police after a young black man was stabbed. Brixton *burned*. As *Ghost Town* by The Specials shot to no. 1 in the charts, other inner-city areas like Handsworth in Birmingham, Moss Side in Manchester, Toxteth in Liverpool, and Chapeltown in Leeds had riots too.

The subsequent Scarman Report into the Brixton Riot found unquestionable evidence of the disproportionate and indiscriminate use of 'stop and search' powers by the police against black people. Most of Lord Scarman's recommendations in his report weren't implemented by Margaret Thatcher's Conservative government, however, and there were more riots in Brixton in 1985 after a mother of six was shot by police during a raid. 'There was a lot of injustices with the police, racism was rife—it was hard,' says Jumpin Jack Frost, aka Nigel Thompson, who grew up in the area. 'We had to go out there and make our way in life.'

At the age of eight, a young Nigel was encouraged to play records—calypso and reggae tunes—at family gatherings by an older cousin, Denise. At ten, the TV show *Roots* was a big influence. 'None of us knew anything about slavery up until that point, although we'd been exposed to racism,' he writes in his book *Big Bad & Heavy*. 'However, we were shocked by *Roots*. I just couldn't believe what I was seeing. I asked Mum if all this slavery shit was for real. *Oh yeah, this is what happened. Black people were taken from Africa in slave ships and forced to work, blah blah blah.* I was so *angry*.'

Frost started getting into trouble at school, but he was also inspired by the Jamaican soundsystem culture around Shepherd's Youth Centre in Brixton, and in his early teens he would skank with pals at dances headed by Jah Shaka, Frontline International, and other reggae systems. He soon became a box boy for Frontline International, and he then started chatting on the mic himself for a short while as MC Boga. He got into doing some petty crime, like 'popping' chains and shoplifting blank cassette tapes up in the West End to sell to soundsystem guys so that he had money to go to dances.

Frost got caught up in the Brixton riots as a youth, and at seventeen he was fitted up for a crime he didn't commit—accused of stealing from a woman's handbag on a Tube station. He was sent to a youth detention centre that was more like an army boot camp. 'I admit that I was a bad boy, but it was weird to be banged up inside an institution like this when you hadn't actually done anything wrong,' he says in his book. 'I'd been framed. Maybe it was karma? I don't know.' Four months later, he was out. 'Did it put a halt to my bad behaviour? Did it fuck.'

Frost's misdemeanours became less frequent, though, when he started going to Jazzie B's Soul II Soul parties at the Africa Centre in Covent Garden. He was gifted three thousand records—funk, soul, rare groove, jazz—and started learning to DJ with pals who had decks, before kicking off the Hit & Run Squad to play at house parties and local community centres.

One Sunday night, he stopped by the Normandy pub on Brixton Road, where a dreadlocked guy was playing funk and rare groove. They started chatting about their mutual love of funk. 'I used to see him around the way, and he was one of those guys that you didn't really want to get involved with—ha ha ha,' smirks the dread, who became known as Bryan Gee.

Bryan had grown up in the Cheltenham/Gloucester area in a tight Jamaican community. Reggae soundsystem culture was a big part of the local scene, and he got involved with his local system, becoming the selector for Challenger. After moving to Brixton, he found himself on the wrong side of the law and briefly ended up in prison, but as soon as he got out, he launched his own soundsystem, Kleer FM, and started DJing on pirate radio and at parties and events around south London.

At their meeting on that fateful night, Bryan persuaded Frost to do a demo tape for the pirate he was playing on at the time—Quest FM in Balham. He recorded one, but Bryan said it wasn't good enough.

'Then I came up to your house, and you walked me through how to do the demo,' says Frost, as the two reminisce together in 2017.

'Serious?' asked Bryan.

'Yeah, and from there it was all right. At first it was all over the place.'

The pair soon switched to shows on Passion FM in Brixton, and after going to a rave at Clink Street near London Bridge they became evangelists for this new music style—acid house. 'It blew my mind,' says Frost. 'Colin Faver and Eddie Richards were playing down there—they were a massive part of my growth. Once you went down there, you was hooked.'

In 1988, they started playing an illegal rave in Lambeth called Car Wash—so called because it was actually in a car wash—alongside another couple of black DJs from the rival pirate station Phase 1 named Grooverider & Fabio, who had also embraced house music and received stick for it from some of their contemporaries. 'We loved the fact that this music saw no colour,' says Bryan. 'For the first time, racial barriers came down. Black, white, European, hip-hop, indie, rare groove…all these genres blurred into one movement and one culture.'

Frost was originally named DJ Underworld ('What was I thinking?') before switching to his current moniker when Passion FM was applying for a legal license, and all the DJs on the station changed their names. 'We all had silly names, it was meant to be a joke, but my show took off,' says Frost. 'I got a call from a guy called Tony Colston-Hayter saying, I want you to come and play Sunrise, man. There was no way I was changing my name back.'

Frost and Bryan started going around to record label offices, blagging upfront promos to play in their sets. 'We just wanted to play the music first,' says Bryan. 'I had a show on Passion called the Promo Show on a Thursday night, so that was part of my mission every week. We built up a relationship with all the club promotions guys, they all knew us, and one thing led to another.'

Bryan got a job with Outer Rhythm, the dance offshoot of Rhythm King, which released important records such as Moby's *Go*, LFO's *LFO*, and Leftfield's *Not Forgotten*, and part of Bryan's job was to take the latest promos to club DJs such as Fabio & Grooverider at Rage. Frost, meanwhile, became a resident at Hell at the Fridge in Brixton—south London's answer to Rage. But in 1992, in a wave of cuts, Outer Rhythm was discontinued, and Bryan was made redundant.

Taking with him a sack of the demo tapes the label had been sent, Bryan continued listening to a load of them in an A&R capacity. 'There was these guys from Bath that we signed called Absolute II, and they were saying, We've got this boy from Bristol, his name's Roni, he's making some really cool stuff, have a listen to it. I called Roni up, told him I'd got his demo from Absolute II, and me and Frost went down to see them.

'They were doing jungle and early breakbeat stuff, but I could hear that soul and that funk in it—something different from what the London guys were doing,' Bryan continues. 'They had a different vibe, and the way they were rolling their breaks and everything just sounded different.'

'I think DJ Krust was actually our main focus at first, 'cause he'd been involved with Fresh Four and all that,' thinks Frost.

'It was both of 'em,' says Bryan, 'so we went down to meet them. They brought their friends Die and Suv along, and we just clicked straight away. It just felt good, it felt right. We said to them, We wanna release some of your music, and they were down for it. I heard something in these guys and followed it up—and I'm really glad I did.'

'We thought, *We're gonna start a label with these guys*,' says Frost. 'It was a very slow process at first, 'cause we were all kind of learning at the same time. Bryan knew the mechanics of how to run a label, but not like now. We all grew together.'

'V were the first people to really recognise our talents,' says Die. 'Bryan and Frost were there breaking the tunes, they believed in us.'

V Recordings—with its iconic sun logo—was born, and this Bristol/London axis of love remained strong from thereon in. Early releases from '93 onwards included records by Roni Size and DJ Krust, as well as material by Trinity, an alias of a young producer whiz-kid named Karl Francis, who engineered the original of Frost's crucial, monster-jungle tune *Burial* under the name Leviticus, and was also known as Dillinja. (The *Lovers Rock Mix* of *Burial* on the flip—with Frost's sister singing on it—was engineered by Optical, who would go on to become a vital force in drum & bass, both solo and with Ed Rush.) Dillinja's mate Lemon D, and then Bristol boys Die and Suv, made up the totality of V's first twenty-five releases. These were the foundation artists that V built their label on, before Ed Rush & Optical, Ray Keith, and Adam F started popping up on one-offs.

One of V's first releases—Roni Size's *It's A Jazz Thing* from 1994, which sampled Lonnie Liston Smith's strung-out *Shadows* from 1974's epic, smooth soul-jazz fusion album *Expansions*—caught the ear of a young DJ named Gilles Peterson. This jazz fiend had made his name on pirate radio before getting a show on Kiss, and he had surfed the acid-jazz wave—initially with the Acid Jazz label he'd started with Eddie Piller in 1987, and then with Talkin' Loud, which had Norman Jay as its A&R for the first few years. Owned by major label PolyGram, Talkin' Loud broke acts like Young Disciples, Galliano, Omar, and Incognito, while Gilles carried on DJing on the radio and in the clubs.

With his keen ear and love of jazz in all its forms, Gilles played *It's A Jazz Thing* and other jazzy jungle at his Monday nighter at London's Bar Rumba, That's How It Is, which he co-hosted with a geeky, bespectacled kid named James Lavelle, who had started up his own label called Mo'Wax. London was bustling with energy; music heads were hustling at Speed or Metalheadz or 101 other happening club nights, and everything was cross-pollinating in a time that the media dubbed 'Cool Britannia'—the 90s version of the Swinging Sixties. Meanwhile, down in Bristol, the Full Cycle crew were getting organised. Roni, Krust, Suv, and Die banded together with local mic-man Dynamite MC and singer Onallee to become Reprazent.

In the new spirit of the age, V Recordings wasn't precious about exclusivity. The Bristol crew were so prolific anyway that it made sense for them to have their own imprint—Full Cycle—and to sign Reprazent to a major-label subsidiary to further their ambitions. The deal with Talkin' Loud was brokered by Simon Goffe—Reprazent's new manager, and someone who Frost and Bryan had known since the rave days when they ran a record shop at the back of a shop on London's Oxford Street. Goffe had had his own club promotions company, Secret Promotions, with a young assistant called Nick Halkes—who went on to co-found XL Recordings and sign The Prodigy—and was a soul DJ too, with a big interest in jazz. He knew Gilles Peterson from when they were on pirate radio together and would book him as a DJ for his club nights. They now run Brownswood Recordings together.

### CLASSIC MATERIAL

In the run-up to Reprazent's *New Forms* album coming out on Talkin' Loud, Goffe suggested that V take on a PR person—the first time they had ever done so. 'Roni was about to release his Reprazent album, and Simon wanted the *V Classic* album to get the right exposure,' says Laurence Verfaillie, who'd recently set up her own agency, Electric PR, after a long spell at Creation Records with Alan McGee. Laurence had started doing PR for more electronic acts, and after a Damascene conversion to drum & bass one night at Metalheadz, she started working with some d&b artists. 'So reluctantly, Bryan and Frost agreed to get me on board,' she says. 'V was my big break. At the time I started hanging out with these guys they were not very keen on publicity, so everyone was very happy that Goldie was such a good spokesperson for the scene.'

'I kept saying to Alan McGee that jungle was the new punk rock,' Laurence continues. 'People were not ready to compromise to get any exposure in the mainstream—it was basically, *This is what we do, you take it or fuck it.* I loved that, even though it made it very hard to work with these guys at first.'

*V Classic* rounded up some of the finest tracks on the label so far, including Roni's *It's Jazzy* and Krust's *Maintain*, as well as hot exclusive dubplates like Dillinja's brutally deep pounder *Unexplored Terrain* and Goldie's stellar remix of Roni's *The Calling*. As well as coming as a series of five twelve-inches, *V Classic* was expertly mixed by label chief Bryan Gee on one of the first commercially available drum & bass CDs.

Laurence secured a fair amount of press for the *V Classic* comp, including a big feature on Frost in *Muzik* magazine. Immediately following this, Frost told her that people in the queue at Music House—waiting to get dubplates cut— were all asking him, 'Hey Frost, how did you get that big piece in *Muzik* mag?' Soon Andy C, Hype, and other big guns were knocking on her door.

Both Frost and Bryan had had brushes with the law in their youth. An establishment that denied black people opportunities, and a police force riddled with systemic and institutional racism in the 80s, meant the odds were stacked against them from the start. It's no exaggeration to suggest that both turned their lives around thanks to the power of music. 'Bryan was a real calming influence on me,' says Frost, undeniably more the firebrand of the two. 'It's not just a lazy cliché—music really did help save people from a life of crime and punishment.'

Jungle's roots in inner city pressure chimed absolutely with the experience of the V pair as young men in Brixton. The reggae and the rage; the unity and community. In the Bristol bunch they found kindred spirits who infused their tracks with a slightly different Bristol *je ne sais quoi*; soul power in motion, a brand new funk.

## MERCURY RISING

Movement at Bar Rumba was incredibly important to V. In 1997 in the capital—outside of the weekend raves—the steely Metalheadz sound was repped by Goldie at the Blue Note, while the more soulful, oceanic Creative Source/Good Looking strata was floating at Speed at the Mars Bar, and then Swerve. With Bryan installed as resident DJ alongside some of the Emotif/Botchit crew like Tonic and BLIM, V had its soulfunkjazztricknology sound represented—just down the road from Piccadilly Circus. Black people often used to be excluded from West End clubs; now here was a night where hooray-henry Sloanes bopped next to Hackney b-boy and b-girl junglists, black and white together side by side—jigging to the riddims from the off. You'd often find Lady Miss Kier from Deee-Lite—a d&b convert—sitting at one of the tables at the back. It was fitting that when Reprazent won the Mercury Prize, on August 28—a Thursday—the crew headed to Movement to celebrate in style.

Buoyed by their Mercury success, Reprazent headed out on a major two-month tour of the USA, with Bryan and Frost as their support DJs. 'We had these two massive tour buses loaded with TVs and mirrors and everything—rock-star business,' recalls Frost. 'We travelled round America from city to city on these buses, and it was like living the life of a rock star—crazy.'

'Every night was party night,' says Bryan in Frost's book. 'You would do a show, then go back to the coach with some groupies. Then, after an hour or two, you'd be off to the next town. Then it was wash, change, have some food, do a soundcheck, show-time and party. Every day! It was proper rock'n'roll, man.'

Reprazent's success nicely teed up the *Planet V* album a year later. The album's rammed launch party at Mass in Brixton on March 6, 1999, had Frost, Bryan, Peshay, Ray Keith, Ed Rush & Optical, Adam F, Dillinja, Lemon D, Andy C, and DJ Marky all playing the London Room, while Roni Size, Krust, DJ Die & Suv, and Bill Riley took control in the Bristol Room. V was at the heart of the scene—and smashing it.

Frost had monthly residencies at Twilo in New York and the Viper Rooms in LA, as well as one in Toronto, disappearing off for a week at the end of every month for this superfly North American jaunt. Back in London, he'd party with fellow Man Utd fan Goldie and occasionally go to matches, although by then he'd also started taking so much cocaine that he could scarcely remember anything after a while; he neglected his label duties, and he was pretty much absent when Marky had his chart success with *LK* in 2002. Bryan and label manager Shirley Hutchinson ran the operation, achieving a Top 20 hit in the national charts from a small flat in Elephant & Castle.

Frost now says that he was masking depression and anxiety with his drug-taking—which soon escalated into crack use—but he carried on regardless until he checked himself into rehab. 'Being in rehab gave me space to think about things for the first time in years,' he says. Amid the daily schedule of group therapy sessions, one-to-one counselling, and the gym, he underwent counselling for depression. 'If only young men, black men especially, would just face up to depression and get it treated,' he writes in *Big Bad & Heavy*. 'Don't battle these things out alone.'

Having been out of the game for over a year, he was reunited with his family, and with Bryan, who smoothed his transition back into the scene. 'These dark times made us both stronger,' says Bryan. 'We were both much wiser, and I was really proud of him for turning his life around.'

The success of V in bringing through first the Bristol crew and then the Brazilian bunch (as detailed in chapter 19) laid firm foundations for the label to become one of the most important in the scene over the next two decades. Today, it still remains a mark of quality with pretty much every single release.

# 11 Foundations Pt. 2: DJs & MCs

## KEMISTRY & STORM

Beyond the ingenuity and innovation of the pirate radio broadcasters, bedroom producers and studio whiz-kids who drove the evolution of jungle/d&b, there was another kind of originator who would push the limits of their chosen art: the DJ. Arguably the greatest DJs in electronic music, whose technical skill surpasses those in any genre, have arisen from this movement—and some have chosen to focus mostly on selecting and blending tracks, rather than making them. Kemistry & Storm were one of the greatest DJ duos in this regard: a team whose style has come to influence countless d&b players since.

The late Valerie Olukemi Adeola Olusanya (Kemistry) and Jayne Conneely (Storm) helped shape the sound of drum & bass with their pioneering sets at LTJ Bukem's Speed night and Metalheadz's Sunday Sessions at the Blue Note, while their edition of the long-running and prestigious *DJ Kicks* mix series, recently reissued by !K7, remains one of the best and most high-profile d&b compilations.

With divergent tastes, Kemistry & Storm blended styles together into a coherent, seamless whole, while their expert ears helped shape the output of the Metalheadz label, which they co-founded with Goldie in 1994. They were an inseparable unit until the tragic death of Kemistry in a road accident in 1999. Today, Storm remains a prominent DJ on the club circuit.

The two DJs first became friends after bonding through music. Storm had grown up competing in Irish dancing competitions, playing accordion, and had been part of a marching band, but Kemi showed her that there was a whole world of other sounds to discover.

'When I met Kemi and her group of people, they were in a nine-piece band,' Storm says. 'There were lots of influences and I think from there, my mind was opened to lots of different things. That was an exciting time for me 'cause I met people who sat down and talked about music, and it was like, *Wow, this is interesting.* Their band was called Swamp Women. The lead singer was a bit Joy Division, and my partner who played guitar and saxophone, he was into Bowie and Eno. Then they had an African bass player, who brought lots of different things. I learnt about Black Uhuru. We all knew Bob Marley, but to learn about those different things, then I had something new to listen to. So Kemi and I were like little sponges. I take things in really quickly.'

After first meeting Kemi at fashion college in Northampton, Storm connected with her crew of friends, and soon they were heading to clubs in London. Electronic music came to the fore, and Kemi's more esoteric taste drove their appreciation for weird dance sounds.

'We were kind of down the same lines, but she found more obscure things,' Storm says. 'She lived in Sheffield for a few years, and she discovered Cabaret Voltaire, and worked at FON Records, so she had a bit of experience working at a label. I'd really not discovered the underground dance scene at all, but Kemi had obviously had a few forays with it, and there was obviously stuff going on in Sheffield that was really interesting. She came back and said, I've been to one of these raves. You look at all the little points in our lives and it was leading to this.'

After studying at the College Of Radiography in Oxford, Storm shared a flat with Kemi in London. The latter was working in fashion boutique Red Or Dead in Camden, and was part of a crew of ravers who went to house clubs. With their interest piqued by listening to Randall DJing on pirate station Centreforce, it was one club that would set them on the path to becoming DJs themselves.

'The guys who'd decide where we'd all go out, this Red Or Dead crew, they'd heard about these two DJs at this club, Heaven. It was called Rage. We just tagged along for the ride. On the first night you had to get membership, with the old laminated-card thing. We literally got to hear about an hour of Grooverider, but it changed our lives. We'd been going to Silver City in Wood Green, a few little illegal raves, but really Heaven was on a proper big scale, with a big rig. They'd really thought about it. It had lights and strobes, and an amazing system. It was a life changer, we were like, *Wow, we've heard this guy Grooverider, now we want to hear the other one, Fabio,* 'cause everyone was saying that they played differently.'

Between 1990 and '91, the duo began buying rave tunes and started thinking about getting some turntables and a mixer. Then Goldie came into Kemi's life, and they struck up a relationship. That was to prove another catalyst for Kemistry & Storm. 'Things changed for us—it accelerated our progress. He was such a force and there were no boundaries for him. To meet someone like him at that stage in our career made us a bit fearless.'

The trio became Mach 3, and they started DJing on pirate station Touchdown FM, with Goldie as their MC. 'It was hard work, 'cause it was six till nine on a Sunday morning,' Storm says. 'You had to take your own decks—you could use their mixer, but the decks were dodgy, and it was in this little squat. You had to get through this hole . . . it was pretty exciting. You knew you were doing something a bit anti-establishment, and we quite liked that.'

Moving to rival station Defection FM, Kemistry & Storm started to refine their style, learning how to stand out from the crowd. 'I don't know where we would have been without our radio show. It gave us discipline, to put a set together every week, trying to be different, not play the same tunes. You could back then, because the amount of promos you were getting was ridiculous. There's a lot of music about now, don't get me wrong, but coming through the door were however many pieces of vinyl—it was incredible. I kept a book of it right from the beginning, and you can see how many releases there were in a month, it was ridiculous. If you didn't do that, you could use your B-sides. That was really becoming a DJ, and using what you'd got.'

With Goldie making his debut on wax with Icelandic crew Ajax Project's 1992 darkside EP *Mach III*, Kemistry & Storm started getting known, too. 'He had his first EP, so people were getting to know us—'cause we're not from London, the three of us. We had to make our own little family out of what we were doing. Goldie was great for pushing us forward—he used to give all our tapes to Fabio and Groove, and the next thing, you were on [DJ booking agency] Groove Connection, which was the biggest agency going at that time.

'Music Power down in Wood Green, we became friends with the manager of that shop, he was really good at sorting us out. We were very polite and very well mannered, and I think people were happy to give us stuff 'cause they knew we would try to play it. Paul Ibiza was amazing, that was a really hot label [Ibiza Records], and he would give us two of everything, he was the only person who would give us one each.'

Over time, the two DJs began to recognise that each of them could focus on a musically distinct style, merging them or swapping them as appropriate. 'Me and Kemi wouldn't play each other's tunes. We knew each other's style. I still think you can hear me doing that now, thinking, *Maybe Storm wouldn't have played that, but Kemistry & Storm would have played that.* People were saying we did this rough with the smooth thing, and we were like, *OK,* so that became our tagline.'

In the early 90s, there were few women DJs in the male-dominated dance scene, let alone in jungle/d&b. Kemistry & Storm were inspired by the example of scene pioneer DJ Rap, and they also found strength in each other.

'I don't think Kemi and I felt any boundaries. We had Rap out there and thought, *Wow, if she can do it, that must be really hard on her own. There are two of us, so it will be easier.* And I have to say it was, because we had each other. We could talk when things weren't going right, then we'd make a plan and try and stick to it. We didn't think about us being women, like, *We're going on a mission right now.* Reinforced didn't treat us that way, and they were the first organisation we encountered. We didn't think about it until we turned up at some gig and someone said, Oh, you're women!

'When we sent our promo tapes out, you could look at a flyer or pick up a fanzine and there was the promoter's number, and you phoned them. And you said, *Can I send you a tape? I've got these DJs I'm looking after, they're called Kemistry & Storm*—we never said we were women. We worked very hard and realised early that this was the way—you gotta be really good to get out there and make a difference. It seemed that our tapes were different, and obviously attractive to certain promoters. We'd thought about that, and because we were a bit older and had careers, we had a bit more experience in how to do business.'

In 1994, two momentous things happened for Kemistry & Storm. First, they became residents at legendary London club night Speed, influencing the development of new strains of the genre that would variously be called ambient jungle or, the term that stuck, drum & bass (see chapter 13); and then, with Goldie, they started Metalheadz, helping to steer the flawless label's direction and sound, and signing classic after classic in that golden era for the music.

'What Goldie wanted to do was have a label and show respect to the people that had turned him onto drum & bass, like Doc Scott, Peshay, Alex Reece, and Wax Doctor. J Majik was his wunderkind. Metalheadz didn't really sell well until

J Majik's *Your Sound* and Dillinja's *The Angels Fell* came along. I think the beauty of those is that everyone could play them. There were three stonking tracks from Dillinja, who was so hot right then; you had this perfect execution of the Amen break with J Majik, with some beautiful sounds in. You can still play it today and the crowd will go crazy.

'There were a lot of classics that came out of Metalheadz. People would tell me Metalheadz is dark, but then I'd say, well, you had Alex Reece's *Pulp Fiction*. That wasn't a dark tune—look at the stuff Photek did on that label. Actually, the beauty of a Metalheadz track is drama—all the really good releases have it. They make you think, they make you sit up. It brought that out in the artists, because Goldie gave them such freedom. We became this family really quickly, and when the gigs started coming in, we really shared it round, everybody had a little piece.'

From the label sprang the club night Metalheadz Sunday Sessions, possibly the most hallowed of all d&b events. Also starting in 1994, at Blue Note in Hoxton, it became an incredibly popular night, frequented by celebrities as well as the d&b faithful. With DJs like Goldie, Doc Scott, and Kemistry & Storm at the helm, it was an experimental canvas where DJs could try out the most futuristic new plates on an open-minded crowd; soon, there would be events on a Saturday too, at the Leisure Lounge.

'The Metalheadz DJs at Blue Note did really well. How many organisations could have run a Saturday and a Sunday? You'd go to Leisure Lounge, which was packed; you'd go to Blue Note, and that was packed. For us, it happened quite quickly. It was a phenomenon, and it blew up.'

Cementing their position at the heart of the London scene, Kemi and Storm did a lot of work behind the scenes at Metalheadz as well as being out there DJing every weekend. Between '97 and '98, Storm clocked up seventy thousand miles in her Golf GTI, driving the pair across the UK for gigs. 'A lot of the time you have to make things happen in the drum & bass scene,' Kemi told *DJ Mag* at the time. 'Create things. There's always room for hands-on nurturing.'

The duo transcended different crews, and they largely stayed out of the scene's internal politics. 'It's really funny when you hear it all,' said Storm in the same *DJ Mag* feature in the late 90s. 'We try to stay out of it in London. We just listen to it and laugh at it, really. But if there's some politics that reflects on you or what you believe in, then you've got to say your piece. You can do that in the drum & bass scene, because we're hopefully all trying to push it in one direction—forwards.'

The duo were honoured when Germany's Studio !K7 asked them to put together the latest of its *DJ Kicks* series in 1998, following on from the likes of Carl Craig and Kruder & Dorfmeister. Representing the full spectrum of the scene with tracks from Dillinja, John B, Dom & Roland, Digital & Spirit, DJ Die, Lemon D, and Goldie, the release not only pushed drum & bass deep into Europe and raised their profile significantly beyond the scene, but also inspired another legion of young women to take up DJing. Heading towards 2000, the pair appeared unstoppable.

On April 25, 1999, in the early hours of the morning, Storm was driving herself and Kemi back from a gig—as she did most weekends. Freakishly, the van in front of them dislodged the steel body of a cat's eye in the middle of the road, sending it spinning through their windscreen. It hit Kemi in the passenger's seat, killing her instantly. It is one of the only times an incident of this nature has ever been recorded, and the only time it has resulted in a fatality.

The core of the drum & bass scene came out to show respect at Kemi's funeral and wake, and memorial gigs are frequently held on anniversaries to remember her. Such a lovely soul, she was a shining light at the heart of the London drum & bass family, never forgotten.

Storm, devastated, took some time out before eventually going back to DJing, and she has remained a stalwart of the scene ever since.

### FLIGHT

Another female pioneer in the orbit of Kemistry & Storm is DJ Flight. First breaking through when the duo handed her mixtape to Goldie and asked if they could bring her into the Metalheadz crew, Flight has since become one of the great DJs of the jungle/drum & bass underground, championing the most cutting-edge beats via her BBC 1Xtra and Rinse FM radio shows and *The Next Chapter* podcasts. She's held residencies at Metalheadz Sunday Sessions and at the home of the liquid drum & bass sound, Swerve, while her Play:Musik label has released a host of key singles from upcoming d&b talent, as well as her own collaborative productions with Breakage under the name Alias. A passion for this music—and for the forward-thinking sounds within it—drives all that she does.

Flight listened to Kiss FM as a teenager, before her friends and their older siblings brought pirate-radio tapes into school. Her interest was piqued by hardcore and the incipient jungle sound. Around the age of fifteen, she started going to some underage club nights, and she became obsessed with the subterranean beats transmitted by the pirates.

'I listened to Pulse FM, Don FM,' she says. 'When I got a bit older, I would listen to Heart FM—I think they were called Face before that. I could never pick up Kool because I grew up in southwest London, and I never had an aerial that was good enough. Then I started listening to Flex—that was the first pirate I played on. On Eruption, I'd listen to Zinc and MC Rage.'

What initially appealed to Flight was the sheer variety in the genre: the way it managed to draw from so many sounds she already knew, while presenting them in a brand new way. 'It was just this weird mishmash of loads of other music that I really liked and I was growing up listening to,' she says. 'Reggae, soul samples. You could hear bits of 80s New Romantic pop sometimes—obviously a lot of that music was dance-y anyway. Hip-hop as well, in the breaks. It was a real melting pot of everything coming together.'

Flight's first real rave opened her eyes and ears to the potential of the music. 'I went to the last-ever Elevation at Crystal Palace Sports Centre—I'd just finished my GCSEs. That was when it properly cemented it for me—just seeing the mixture of people, those were the first places I felt completely at ease and comfortable, because they were such a mix.'

Some of Flight's friends had decks, and they would put on jungle/d&b events, but seeing Kemistry & Storm play was a huge inspiration—and convinced her she could try DJing herself. 'It was at SW1 Club, Innovation, part of a London club tour they were doing,' she says. 'They went on after Rap; everyone was having a great time, and I saw these other women standing at the back of the DJ booth, and just assumed they were Rap's mates. Then they came on, and I'd never seen a picture of them. I'd noticed their names on flyers but never knew what they looked like. They absolutely smacked it, they were just so different—they had different tunes to everybody else that night, Stevie Hyper D was MCing for them, and I was just blown away by the sound, and the look of them as well. I found it completely fascinating and interesting that there were two women, one was white, one was black. Kemi had locks, she was light-skinned and mixed race like me, it just made a real impact. When I saw her, I thought, *Maybe I can try this as well.*'

Flight sought to distinguish herself from the start by reaching for less obvious tracks, and she had a steady stream of exclusive dubs from friends like Digital, Total Science, and Dylan. 'Storm said, when I first started giving them mixtapes, they liked the fact I would make use of B-sides on records. I wouldn't always go for the obvious A-side—I was properly making use of the vinyl I had. I guess sometimes I have made the point of steering clear of certain tunes that everybody is playing, unless it's something I love to death that I must play, then I will.

'Seeing Kemistry & Storm, and Fabio, was a massive influence,' she adds. 'Seeing them stick to their guns and play music that they fully loved, that was always my inspiration. I've tried to carry that throughout.'

While Flight has since become a club staple, known for her sets not just with Metalheadz and at Swerve but also at clubs around the world, it's radio that has proven the most important component in her rise. From her pirate days to shows on legal stations, radio has enabled Flight to hone her skills, push innovative artists, and build that sense of community upon which drum & bass thrives.

'I'd only been mixing a few months when I started doing overnight slots on Flex FM,' she says. 'It did wonders, practicing mixing. I didn't have my own decks for ages, I was going to my friend Brian's to practise, until Storm gave me Kemi's decks after she passed away. Practising, working out what tunes go well together, being able to showcase a sound that maybe other people weren't playing so much on the radio, getting to know people ... it was just like a community, really. It helps you build up a profile as well. If people like what you're playing, they'll definitely tune in each time you're on.'

Flight's listening tastes are wide, and she sometimes plays house and other genres in her sets. Focusing on the deeper end of d&b for the most part, her aim is to create a musical balance when she DJs, and not just smash it out for the sake of it. 'I try to incorporate light and dark. But there's still a feel of soul throughout it. There's got to be some kind of feeling. I can't just play tear out—it has to have some kind of colour to it.'

Though supported by most in the scene, Flight has also faced discrimination, principally for being a woman in a male-dominated industry, indicating the extent to which sexism—and also racism—are endemic in our society, and even present in some pockets of the d&b scene.

'You pick it up with actions,' Flight says. 'While you're playing, the sound engineer or someone will come up and lean over while you're in the mix and touch the mixer, do something. I can deal with that myself, thank you—or, if you want me to turn it down a bit, just ask me to do it, you don't need to come and put your hands on the mixer during my set. The amounts I've been paid, regularity of being booked at places, being invited back, being a black woman as well. I've obviously experienced racism when I've played abroad, but not necessarily from the people that have booked me or that have been at the party, more from the place in general. It's definitely there, but I wouldn't like to say that it's hindered me in any way. When I started, I never used to pick up on anything like that; when you're younger and having fun and stuff, there's less responsibility, you don't really notice the things that are wrong with society until you get a bit older and you start noticing things.'

Despite these experiences, Flight has stuck with drum & bass, and it remains her greatest musical love. 'Sometimes I wonder why I'm still into it. You hear tunes and it is actually really weird music when you think about it. But it captured my heart and soul years ago, and I just stayed with it.'

## ANDY C

Through his older sister, Andrew Clarke started listening to pirate stations like Sunrise and Centreforce when he was barely into his teens. She snuck him into a rave near his hometown of Hornchurch, in Essex, and that was it: 'From that moment, that's all I wanted to do.' He soon met a DJ called Red One (aka Scott Bourne, now his manager) through work experience from school, and went to one of the parties Scott was putting on in Bishopsgate, where he witnessed a DJ called Just Jones from Syndicate FM drive the crowd crazy. Inspired, he got himself a pair of cheap decks—Citronic belt-drives—and started practising like crazy in any spare moment he got. He started making mixtapes for his mates, and became 'DJ Andy C' for his first gig at a club called the Prison in Stoke Newington, where Bourne was promoting a night.

Andy was soon getting other slots, while simultaneously messing around at home on a Commodore computer that he did a bit of programming on as well as playing games. Linking with local pal Ant Miles, together they made a shuffly hardcore hip-house tune, *Turn On*, under the name Desired State. Throughout '91 and '92, they released hardcore tunes on labels like Karma, Dance Wax, Strategy, and Out Of Romford Records, but they kept getting knocked for payment, so, one day, Andy's sister suggested he start his own label. Ram Records was launched in 1992—named thus because Andy's star sign is Aries—just as he finished his GCSEs. The first release was the *Sour Mash* EP by Andy C.

Both Andy and Ant got jobs with a distributor, delivering records to the independent shops in London, and Andy ended up working in the Boogie Times record shop in Romford that was also the HQ of Suburban Base Records—home to many a hardcore hit. 'I was in Boogie Times so much that they was like, You know what? You might as well come and help us behind the counter,' he recalls fondly.

One day, Andy and Ant made a tune that was slightly different to their usual output. They recorded it in four hours and called it *Valley Of The Shadows* (and themselves Origin Unknown), although the guys at Boogie Times preferred their other new track *The Touch*, so they put it on the B-side of RAM 004. Catching the darkcore zeitgeist, *Valley Of The Shadows* took off in the raves, and distributors had to keep phoning up Andy for thousands more copies.

Ant didn't want to do any Origin Unknown gigs, so Andy did a string of rave PAs at places like Laserdrome and Roller Express, in between DJing, running Ram, and his vinyl-delivery job. He believes that the fact he was on the delivery runs and meeting everybody face-to-face helped him a lot with his integration into the jungle/drum & bass scene. 'I was selling records to the shops, giving records out to the DJs, going to Black Market and cutting Ray Keith and Nicky Blackmarket a dubplate of the remix, or being at Music House and cutting dubs,' he says.

One night he'd be riding with Randall or hanging with him down at AWOL ('it was church'), the next he'd be flying to Japan as Moving Shadow's new resident DJ after impressing label boss Rob Playford at one of their Voodoo Magic nights in Leicester Square. He was only just eighteen.

Andy grabbed his mentor, Randall, for a collaboration on Ram in 1994—jungle double-header *Feel It/Sound Control*. While the former was decent roughneck jungle, it was again the B-side, with its riot of Amens, spooky synth, and time-stretched beats—that endured. By now a stalwart scene DJ, forever cutting dubs down at Music House, Andy picked up his first official accolade in 1999—for 'Best DJ'—at the *Knowledge* Drum & Bass Awards. His signature 'double-drop' DJ technique, which involved layering two tracks over each other so that they have their 'drop' at the same time—often executed with three decks—earned him the scene nickname The Executioner.

He knuckled down and made a couple of Origin Unknown albums with Ant in the late 90s, and also a Ram Trilogy album with the addition of another Essex boy, Shimon. With Shimon he scored a chart hit with the triple-time swagger of *Body Rock*, which sold thirty-eight thousand pieces of vinyl in the UK in chart-registered shops alone, reaching no. 28 in the UK charts. 'If you listen to that record, I don't think you'd have thought it was a guaranteed daytime radio chart record,' he smirks. 'It just really caught people's imaginations.'

But for most of the noughties, Andy chiefly concentrated on DJing. His *Nightlife* mix series, begun in 2003, became an almost biannual snapshot of big tunes in the scene, while he scooped several mantelpieces worth of punter-voted trophies at various d&b awards and the 'Top 100 DJs' poll, where he was regularly the highest-placing d&b DJ. Finding that he'd always be booked to play tents rather than the main stage at festivals, despite being a huge act, Andy created his audio-visual concept show, ALIVE, in 2012. 'My main thing with drum & bass has been, *Give us a chance, put us in front of a big crowd and we'll entertain people*, 'cause it's that kind of music,' he said in his *DJ Mag* cover story in 2014. A massive learning curve, ALIVE involved Andy also triggering visuals via a computer language called Boolean programmed into his equipment, as well as mixing tracks. The show involved touring with a whole crew for festival and large venue shows, and put the drum & bass DJ four-square in front of main stage audiences.

Ram would put out early releases by Sub Focus, Chase & Status, and the solo DJ Fresh—after Bad Company—in the noughties, and later also helped launch Wilkinson, Rene LaVice, and the Calyx & Teebee behemoth, becoming a huge brand by also promoting bigger and better events. Andy would often headline these Ram shows, and he also started doing standalone All Night Long gigs—at huge venues like Brixton Academy and Alexandra Palace in London—which culminated in a sell-out DJ gig at the 12,500-capacity Wembley Arena in November 2018. In 2019, he was the first DJ to be invited back as a quarterly resident at London's boutique electronic music hotspot XOYO, following his successful thirteen-week run in 2017. Again pulling in a cross-section of d&b scene DJs to support him, the series sold out in less than three hours.

'It's still like a hobby to me, in a way,' Andy says, looking back. 'It's one of them things like when I was at home when I was fifteen, mixing in my bedroom, dreaming of being able to do it in front of a crowd, learning how to manufacture a record, finding out the company that prints records, finding out how you put a

record label on a record, thinking it's some smoke and mirrors magical process…
everything is like that, so we set goals. It's like a mad hobby that's turned into
a profession, and we're now really fortunate to be in a position where we can
dream ideas and set goals to try to realise them. That's the fun part of it.'

## HYPE

DJ Hype (Kevin Ford)—who's half-Iranian, via the biological father he never
knew—grew up in a quite different east London to the one we know today.
'We were living in what I call original Hackney, when it was raw, violent, and
crazy, not the gentrified Hackney of today,' he later told *DJ Mag*. Falling in
love first with reggae and then with hip-hop, he set up the one-deck Sticksman
Hi Fi soundsystem with Smiley (of Shut Up & Dance) and MC Daddy Earl,
which later would be known as Heatwave—building their own speakers for the
sound, which Hype still has in his basecamp today. 'By fifteen years old, we had
developed into a soundsystem that played not only reggae and dub but soul, rare
groove, and hip-hop, plus Daddy Earl would reggae MC, Smiley and PJ would
rap, and I would cut and scratch my way through all these different music styles
all night. We even had our own little drum machine. It all sounds like nothing
now, but back then it was quite a new thing to do it all at the same time and do
it all well. I would ride around on a BMX looking for empty-looking houses to
break into and hold our illegal parties.'

Ford got seriously good at scratch DJing—doing well in competitions such
as the DMCs, and ultimately winning the London Mixing Championships
in 1989. He'd simultaneously got into production as a youth via the Islington
Music Workshop and the National Association for the Rehabilitation of Young
Offenders. He made a track, won a competition, got featured on regional TV
news, and started a music engineering course. When the rave scene kicked off, he
would hear other DJs playing on pirates while working in a local warehouse. He
thought most of them were shit, but they seemed to be getting loads of club gigs.

Originally called Doctor K, he became DJ Hype at his first pirate station,
WIBS. He spun tunes at the Fantasy FM pirate, and, one day, was passed some
tapes to listen to in an A&R capacity by Peter Harris from the nascent Kickin'
Records. He only really liked one set of tunes, by a half-Greek synthesiser whiz-
kid from Essex named Phill, who had been nicknamed The Scientist, and he
ended up co-producing a couple of tracks with him.

*The Exorcist* took influence from 1974 funk jam *The X-Sorcist* by The Devils. With its bleepy keys, hardcore hip-hop beats (nicked and sped-up from a KC & The Sunshine Band cut), and 'Send 'em to the cemetery' Malcolm X sample, it took off on the rave scene in 1990 and cracked the UK Top 50. Buzzin' follow-up *The Bee* also cracked the UK Top 50 as The Scientist embarked on a series of solo rave PAs, conveniently forgetting to mention Hype's involvement in the productions in accompanying interviews—and royalty payments.

Hype was stung, but his DJ career had taken off. By 1992, he was playing raves like Dreamscape and doing the Rocket in Kensington on a Saturday to two thousand people, before it all suddenly stopped when the DJ agency he was on fell apart. Undeterred, he went back to producing on his cobbled-together setup and started releasing tracks on Suburban Base like the frenetic jungle cut *The Trooper*, the hyperkinetic *Shot In The Dark*, and punchy madcap killer *Weird Energy*. Soon he'd landed a show on Kiss, too, where he could put his fine selections and motormouth caustic wit to good use.

Hype's anonymous Ganja Records imprint fed more goodness into the scene—as collected together on label compilation *Still Smokin'*—and by early '96 he'd decided to semi-formalise the working relationship he had with new pal DJ Pascal, who released on Suburban Base as Johnny Jungle, and also this new kid who'd bring him tunes to check out, who went by the name of DJ Zinc. Ganja Kru, initially a solo moniker for Hype, became a trio—a kind of supergroup of three on-fire DJ/producers, and pretty soon one of Zinc's tracks, *Super Sharp Shooter*, had blown up on Ganja, via a beefed-up remix that Hype had suggested he do.

The Ganja Kru formed their own True Playaz label, running all aspects of their operation themselves. 'You eat, sleep, shit it,' Hype told *Melody Maker* in 1997. 'You wake up to it, go to bed to it. This is it.' The gang became one of the last established artists to sign to a major in the mid-90s gold rush, opting for a deal with Parousia, whose parent company was BMG. They quickly reissued *Super Sharp Shooter* on a showcase EP, and it reportedly helped sway the minds of US hip-hop heads like Ice-T and KRS-One towards jungle/drum & bass when they heard it. 'People probably associate us with hip-hop because of the success of *Super Sharp Shooter*, but that's just a part of what we do,' Hype said at the time.

True Playaz started a regular night at the End in the late 90s, transferring over to Fabric just after 2000. Having nights at arguably London's two best clubs helped cement their position at the heart of the scene. Sporadically putting out releases on the True Playaz label and the rebooted Ganja as the 2000s progressed, Hype began his association with DJ Hazard after releasing some of his tracks on Playaz and Ganja, and he helped bring him through into the scene. So much so, in fact, that by the later 2010s, he was regularly touring back-to-back with the Birmingham man, who won the 'Best DJ' gong at the 2017 Drum & Bass Awards, displacing Andy C, who had held it for an eternity.

Hype had recorded the landmark *FabricLive 03* in 2002 to help set the blueprint for the club's impeccable in-house mix series, as well as doing comps for Ministry and Warners, and he was still at the top of his game, running Playaz nights at Fabric—along with trusty cohort Pascal—right up until the COVID-19 lockdowns began.

### ZINC

'At raves there was a much bigger mix of people—black and white, rich and poor. That was a big part of the attraction for me,' says Zinc, aka Ben Pettit, who grew up in multicultural Forest Gate, where the pubs tended to be all-white.

After starting to play out with DJ Swift on the Impact FM pirate station, he was juggling a day job and learning how to produce. He made a few tracks and people said they liked them, but DJs would never play them in their sets. When he played Hype some of his tunes, he appreciated his brutal honesty. 'He was ultracritical, but that clicked with me,' Zinc said in 2004. 'I needed someone to bounce from a bit, and Hype was perfect.'

Zinc had made a few tracks with Swift, but the original of *Super Sharp Shooter* was the first track he made on his own—produced in Swift's spare room on minimal equipment while he was still working his office job during the week and behind the counter at Boogie Times in Romford, Essex, on a Saturday. They released the original on Ganja in 1995, but it was the revamped version the following year—complete with a chopped-up sample of LL Cool J spelling out 'The S, the U, the P, the E, the R', taken from 1989's *It Gets No Rougher*—that truly smashed it. 'To say this record changed my life is an understatement,' Zinc told *DJ Mag* in 2004. 'It was actually similar to a lot of other tunes around at that time. I was just lucky that mine was more popular than most, and even now I have no idea why.'

The LL Cool J spell-out was a genius way to start *SSS*, immediately marking it out in a rave set. Hype had made Zinc pay more attention to his basslines—he got this one from a sample CD on the front of *Future Music* magazine—and when it hit, after some faux gunshots and Sensurround panning before the drop, it was more meandering and potent than the original when paired with some nifty Amen work. Ravers would flail and pogo around the dance, as the track became one of the biggest—and most memorable—in the drum & bass oeuvre.

The success of *Super Sharp Shooter* and signing to BMG offshoot Parousia allowed Zinc to leave his day job to become a full-time DJ/producer, and he's never looked back. *Six Million Ways*, as Dope Skillz, quickly followed, half-inching a vocal snippet from Method Man & Redman's *How High*, and he raided the same hip-hop track for the 'When I raise my trigger finger' sample that kicks off *Ready Or Not*, a hastily constructed Fugees bootleg from their hit of that year that was initially meant just as a dubplate secret weapon. After smashing it at raves like Jungle Fever in late '96, *Fugees Or Not* found its way onto bootlegged white labels, which sold like hot cakes, perhaps because there were comparatively few vocal tracks in drum & bass sets at the time.

Zinc carried on releasing tracks with Hype and Pascal, while the success of his cross-genre breakbeat garage instrumental *138 Trek*—so named because of its 138bpm tempo, making it considerably slower than d&b, some of its shuffling beats actually taken from a Barry White track from 1973—led to him setting up his own Bingo Beats label and releasing material by himself, as Jammin, and others. Zinc actually sampled himself for *174 Trek* on True Playaz in 2001, and that same year released a magnificent slab of liquid spy-mania funk, *Casino Royale*, which would have been used in a Bond film if there was any justice.

Exploring different tempos led Zinc to his debut artist album, *Faster*. 'It was like I'd been sitting alone in one big room in a huge dark house, and suddenly all the lights came on,' he said in the cover feature for *DJ Mag* in early 2004, 'and it hit me that there was a load of other rooms I could go and explore.'

*Faster* gradually upped the tempo as it progressed into drum & bass. It was initially going to be released on Polydor after Zinc became the latest to sign to a major, but he ended up taking it back from them, dissatisfied. 'I signed to them as I thought it would be the best way to reach the maximum number of ears,' he continued. 'I really expected them to have good, clever ideas and powerful distribution, and it turned out to be the opposite, so I told them they're shit and I've taken the LP back. It stalled the release for a few months, but I've learned valuable lessons from it.'

Zinc went on to work and split releases with the likes of Ray Keith, Marky, Makoto, and Shy FX, while around 2007 he moved away from drum & bass to concentrate on house music. Setting out his stall with the *Crack House* EP and aligning himself with assorted 'fidget house' acts like Jack Beats and Redlight (aka Clipz), he worked with others such as US heavyweight A-Trak, and Ms Dynamite, with whom he had a hit on 2010's *Wile Out*. But he always kept a link with his first love, drum & bass, and towards the end of the decade he made a triumphant return to the scene with an acclaimed set at the Metalheadz night at Printworks in London.

## DJ RAP

Charissa Saverio moved around a lot when she was a child. Born in Singapore to an Italian father and an Irish-Malaysian mother, she moved with her family to Southampton in her early teens, and at sixteen she left school behind and moved to London. 'I had a sheltered life, there was no music—the only thing was piano,' she says, adding that she was grateful that she did have lessons at the time.

Charissa found herself living in east London in the late 80s. 'A lot of times I was squatting with other girls, models and stuff like that, doing whatever we could to make money,' she says. 'Sometimes that meant doing a bit of glamour modelling, things that we didn't wanna do, but it was just hard to survive when you're on your own and crashing in apartments and stuff. We'd do whatever we could. I call these years the Dysfunctional Years, breaking away from everything—a lot of drugs, the squatting...'

She was in her late teens when the rave scene started kicking off. 'Coming from the background that I did, the freedom and the love that I felt when I would go out was night and day to what I'd been experiencing,' Rap recalls. 'I didn't really have a great childhood, so for me it was like, you walk into a field and there's fifty thousand people there and they all wanna give you a hug. You're home. It was the acceptance, the lack of sexism, the lack of racism—it was unconditional love. My party crowd became like my extended family. At the time it felt like the only family I really had. It felt like I belonged. I felt like I was home.'

She had her 'lightbulb moment' in terms of wanting to be a DJ herself at a London party called Ibiza Rave, when Dem 2 dropped Shut Up & Dance's Suzanne Vega-sampling breakbeat tune *£10 To Get In*—and it went off.

Recognising the power in a DJ's hands, she says, 'It was amazing what he was able to do to us, and look at what he was getting back—it was like the biggest giant hug. Artists are fucked up, they're fucking dysfunctional people who need a lot of attention and love, and probably the reason that you become an artist is that you're trying to recapture something that you never had. So for me, watching what he got in return, as well as what he was giving, was equally exciting.'

The very next day, she tried making her own mixtape with one deck and a tape recorder; a friend taught her some basics, and soon she'd made a couple of Balearic tunes with her pal Jeff B under the name Ambience, and started DJing on pirate radio stations Rave FM and then Fantasy FM. 'That's really where I started to learn how to mix—on air,' she says.

After her initial break, she started getting lots of DJ gigs, including a residency at the big Telepathy raves. As pretty much the only female DJ on that circuit initially, she had to be doubly good. 'Once people saw what I could do on the decks, every single promoter booked me—I was everywhere,' she says. 'How did male DJs take to me? As a female, we have to put up with guys hitting on us, we have to put up with men trying it on, we have to put up with all that shit—that's normal, unfortunately. But I feel that I never really experienced true sexism until I got to America. For me, the guys in the UK have always been very protective, very sweet. Quite flirty, of course—in that everyone will try it on when they can—but really supportive.

'Jumpin Jack Frost took me under his wing, Fabio was supportive—definitely,' Rap continues. 'Much later, Roni Size, when he was around. There's a lot of DJs that were really cool: Kenny Ken, Cool Hand Flex—most of them were just great. I got teased by a bunch of 'em, I got a lot of stick, but I think that was just banter—although sometimes it got a bit much. The two guys I'm still closest to today are Fabio and Frost.'

Rap started making hardcore records for Suburban Base with Aston Harvey, later of The Freestylers, but when she started going to AWOL a lot, she parted amicably from him because she wanted to go more into the darker jungle sound. By then, she'd set up her own label, Proper Talent, and learned to produce on her own. Floaty rough jungle cut *Spiritual Aura* was her big breakthrough solo tune, while her liquid double A-side of *Intelligent Woman* b/w the female-positive *Switch* (featuring MC Outlaw Candy), plus her explosive remix of Top Cat's

*Ruffest Gun Ark*, lit up the floors. 'Although I certainly never got it easy, the moment I produced big records, the sexism—or perceived sexism—went away for me,' she says.

She was sometimes excluded when it came to receiving dubplates, though. 'Most of my dubplates were from Clayton [from Renegade Hardware], Hype, Roni ... it was always the same people that gave me dubplates. But the reality is that most of my dubs were my own stuff. I was never one of those who was constantly given the new stuff. That's where the sexism comes in—although I don't think that's the right word. Let's call it elitism. Because I was doing so well, it was definitely a thing of not sharing some music with me on purpose—I know full well that happened sometimes. Not so much now, thank god.'

'At Music House, the boys would share a lot more music with each other than the girls would get,' she continues. 'I was there—that happened. But I didn't really give a fuck—I've always been the kind of DJ who played more for the crowd anyway. I wasn't there to educate them. I made do with what I had, and I still slayed everybody. It didn't matter that I didn't have the most upfront music.'

When the major labels came calling, Rap signed with Sony and made the 1998 album *Learning Curve*. With Rap attempting to reposition herself as an electronic pop star by singing on most of the tracks herself as well as producing, the long-player was more big beat and trip-hop than drum & bass. 'I wanted to do something different that combined all the styles,' she says. 'There wasn't really any d&b on there, it was just d&b-influenced. Sony wanted something that had that commercial edge, but they didn't want something that was cheesy or commercial.'

Sassy lead cut *Bad Girl* was a Top 40 hit, as was the follow-up, *Good To Be Alive*. But while there were more strong tracks on *Learning Curve*—*F**k With Your Head* was like *Mezzanine*-era Massive Attack—that stood up next to anything by Björk at the time (and she wrote, sang, and produced most of it herself), it didn't cut through quite as much as it might've done in the UK.

In 2001, Rap moved to America to tour the album, and she ended up doing big pop shows with people like Julio Iglesias and Christine Aguilera, and festivals such as Coachella. 'People don't realise that in America, not only was I flying the d&b flag but also killing it with tech-house and the pop stuff,' she says. 'It was a bigger place to explore more, whereas in the UK people love you and then you do well and then they hate you. You're meant to stay in your lane, and I didn't want to do that.'

Not only was Rap doing her big pop shows, she was also playing DJ sets right across the USA as drum & bass sought to establish itself in America. 'For a little while, I was probably one of the highest-earning DJs in the world,' she says. 'It wasn't easy, 'cause this music was fairly new. It wasn't the easiest music to get through to a completely different country and culture. A lot of gigs were great, and a lot were like, *What am I doing here?* It was huge gigs all the time. I had huge agents—I didn't really play small gigs. I played every major gig you can imagine in the world, up until 2011, and when the gigs started getting smaller, I kind of quit. I don't enjoy doing tiny little gigs, I enjoy big crowds.'

Like Goldie and Adam F, Rap got into acting for a while. She appeared in several independent films and theatre productions before the pull of music brought her back. She set up an online production school for learning Ableton and other production skills, while also getting up to speed with new techniques herself. She then relaunched her own label as Propa Talent, and nestled back into the international scene as one of its prime movers and ambassadors.

### MCS

From early on in the music, a renegade mic-spitter was a crucial part of the show. While white MCs at early raves tended to come over more like East End barrow boys selling a pound of veg, the predominantly black MCs who hosted jungle dances borrowed techniques from reggae soundsystems—dancehall chat, toasting—or US hip-hop. MCs like hardy perennials the Ragga Twins, for instance, came straight from the Unity system, via Shut Up & Dance.

Literally the master of ceremonies, the MC was there from the start to vibe up the dance, to nice up the area. MCs brought personality to the pirates, and a certain coded rave slang to clued-up clubbers. And at jungle shows, the MC was the bridge between the dancefloor and the decks, giving ravers something humanistic to cling to amid the futuristic polyriddims and big bad bass.

MCs seldom recorded in the studio in jungle's early days but, outside of the dances, the way some of their rhymes and catchphrases became known was through tape packs. Key phrases and exclamations would be learned and repeated by young ravers—often too young to get into the shows—across the country, as tapes were passed around or sold via underground networks.

One MC who did commit his vox to wax in the early days was London's Stevie Hyper D. He made his vocal debut on bleepy hardcore track *Teknoragga* with Liverpool electronicists Apollo 440, but it was really in the rave environment that he came alive. Stevie pioneered double-time rhyming, his super-fast flows matched the bpm of the music. He developed regular 'sung catchphrases' like 'I'm just a junglist soldier/ Fighting to keep the jungle ali-i-i-i-ve' and 'Junglists are you re-e-e-eady? Oh Lord a-mercy mercy', while accompanying the likes of Nicky Blackmarket, Kenny Ken, or Clarkee at jungle events.

'He had everything—the lyrics, the flows, the hooks,' says IC3. 'He would turn jungle and drum & bass tracks into full-on tunes. Certain tunes you would hear and say, I remember this track where Stevie Hyper D would have the set lyrics, which had a massive impact.'

Other MCs like Rhyme-Time, Navigator, Five-O, Fearless, Bassman, Moose, GQ and Skibadee came through in jungle's early years, their ability to chat bits of reggae as well as tap into post-hardcore freneticism proving crucial to the development of the jungle sound. One of the most significant MCs to arise from the jungle scene, MC Det, has a typical tale to tell. Born and raised in Hackney, he grew up surrounded by music. His dad was in two bands, and Det was captivated by the 80s scene, going to see legendary rap groups Public Enemy and Eric B & Rakim at their first London show and attending some of Soul II Soul's club events. With his brothers, Det had a soundsystem, which they'd set up at blues parties in Hackney and play a mix of reggae, rare groove, and soul. When he got on the mic at these events, he'd gravitate to the funkier sounds and had more of a rap-style flow. 'All my friends were much better than me at chatting reggae,' he says. 'Later on in the morning at the blues, when the other guys were chatting over reggae, I would rap over some of the rare groove beats.'

Det lived across the street from DJ Brockie, and he looked up to him—though he wasn't keen on the rave music Brockie was into at the time. 'He's an older guy than me, so he's one of the elders,' Det says. 'I was in awe of what he was doing as a grown man, not just in music, he always had nice cars and stuff like that. I used to see him in the early hours of the morning with his eyes bloodshot red and with dark glasses on sometimes. He was part of that hardcore, acid-y kind of time. We didn't like the music, we used to call it devil music—we weren't feeling it!'

One day, Brockie asked Det if he wanted to come up to Kool FM to check out what he was playing. Over the next two weeks, Det visited a few more times. After helping Brockie set up the rooftop aerial rigs, Det felt invested in the station and began to get involved himself, chatting on the mic. 'Kool FM used to be a reggae, R&B radio station and would only play rave music on Friday and Saturday,' he recalls. 'Then it extended with the rave scene, and we'd kick off with jungle on Thursday. The rave music would finish on Sunday night. It was exciting.'

When Det began to MC on Kool FM, he'd focus on maintaining the vibe and adding flavour to Brockie's set, rather than flowing continuously over the music. This meant coming up with catchphrases and memorable couplets, instead of whole chunks of freestyle lyrics. Most of all, he realised he couldn't just rely on the rhyme styles he'd used in the past over slower genres like soul and reggae. 'When I went onto the music, it was so fast,' he says. 'There were so many sounds that you don't get in hip-hop. I listened to the breaks that Brockie would play, and I just knew that the raps I had pre-written in my head already, they wouldn't fit with the pattern of this music. The scene wasn't about rapping or chatting, I thought. I think it was about creating really great hooks that people could use when they played. So I changed *Big shout* to *Maximum boost*. People used to say *Maximum boost* and didn't know where it came from— that was me. That became quite popular.'

Various forerunners to Det inspired him to forge his own path. In particular, he mentions Mad P as an early influence. 'I remember when Mad P came to London. He would work with Top Buzz and used to do a lot of raves in the country and the Midlands, and there was an event where they came and played at Roller Express. Everyone said they were coming down there to perform, and, man, the building was more packed than I've ever seen it in my life. Instead of three thousand people, there were five thousand. I remember standing outside the event and they opened the back doors, it was so hot in there. People were spilling out, trying to get in. Mad P was on the mic, and I wanted to see what he looked like. Back then, there were no mobile phone pictures. I was standing up at the back, on my tiptoes, watching him chat his iconic lyrics.'

Like other MCs of the time, Det sought to distinguish himself as a British rapper, chatting in a London accent and throwing in cultural references unique to the UK. In this way, jungle MCs set themselves apart from Jamaican or

American vocalists, and they carved out their own distinctively British niche—something that Rodney P from UK hip-hop act London Posse was also instrumental in pioneering. 'You could speak like yourself now,' says Det. 'I think my best hooks that made me come through more were because I was saying British things, I'd throw a little cockney in there. People used to love that. You'd say something in Jamaican and then flip it, the same thing but cockney. It made people want to get involved. It felt more like ours when we did it that way. The Ragga Twins and Navigator chatted reggae, but English reggae, like Tippa Irie. We started to rap more like the British stuff.'

Det points out that jungle production itself developed in tandem with MCs. When hardcore became more stripped back and dub-wise, giving rappers more space, it began to evolve into jungle. 'What people started to notice was, that little eight-bar loop that's in a track, that was usually the baddest part of the track,' he says. 'So you've got guys out there hearing that who think, *I like that bit of the tune, I'm just gonna loop that, and that's gonna be the main frame.* When an MC would speak over a track, like Mad P and those guys, over hardcore, it was always over that eight-bar break, so that motivated producers to catch that loop and to build on it.'

As Kool FM and jungle grew in popularity, Det began to make appearances at numerous events. But many venues weren't set up for a vocalist to appear over the soundsystem. 'They had to change the technology to fit that sound,' he says. 'Ninety percent of the clubs I went into with Brockie back in the day never had a facility set up for an MC, or they didn't have a mic in the building. I spoke through headphones for a lot of years; there was a lot of clubs where I couldn't MC at all because they had no connection. If they wanted someone to MC back then, they'd get in a PA system. Over the years, every club around the world has changed their soundsystem, and we made that happen.'

In 1996, Det was the first jungle MC to cut his own album. Featuring production from Shy FX, L Double, T Power and Elementz Of Noize among others, it's a vivid snapshot of the jungle scene at its height, with the masterful ragga roll-out *We Nah Ease Up* among its highlights. But Det admits that at the time, there was some reticence among the junglist scene about committing their material to an album or—especially—signing a record deal.

'I didn't know what kind of album I wanted to put out,' he says. 'We had this new music off the back of hardcore. You want to sell records, but you want to sell this music as well—you don't know how to do it, because none of the tunes had full vocals in. On that album we tried every angle: a tune with just one word in, a tune with sixteen bars in it, a tune with just a loop in it. Every way. Just in case, whatever style came through, we had covered it.

'Nobody would take a deal,'cause we were afraid as Londoners that some guy from up north is gonna come and get all the praise for this music,' he continues. 'We've seen it time after time. The producers were very afraid, so they wouldn't take any deal. It was kind of like an unspoken agreement—don't take a deal or they'll take our scene away from us. And then, one day, Goldie took a deal! Everyone's jaw dropped. Oh my god! Everyone started rushing deals now. You got a pat on the back for saying no, but after that people were going deal crazy. I even got a deal with SOUR Records, it was just that time.'

**INSTRUMENTAL**

Not all MCs were rooted in reggae and rave. For instance, Cleveland Watkiss, born in Hackney to Jamaican parents and around hosting in the Speed/ Metalheadz era, started out with Courtney Pine's Jazz Warriors in the late 80s. MCs like Bukem's long-term compatriot Conrad, and Dynamite MC, who came through with Full Cycle/Reprazent, developed a more languid style. After the General Levy furore of '94, however, there was arguably a subconscious shift towards a more instrumental form of the music.

'The producers and the DJs kind of hijacked the scene,' reckons Det, before going on to talk about how MCs were not as respected—or well paid—as their DJ counterparts. 'The promoters would know that the DJs felt this way, so they'd get MCs to work for next to nothing. It was kind of a fight for MCs, and today it's the same fight. Trying to get ourselves heard, trying to get the support from the DJs—it's still not really happening.'

'It wasn't about people taking the mic and chatting all over your tune…MCs had to take the back seat,' Goldie told Red Bull Music Academy about the early days of his Metalheadz club night. 'Rage never used MCs—it was just about the music. This music has its own body and soul—it doesn't need an MC to fucking tell us what it is.'

'It wasn't like we all hated MCs,' Photek also told RBMA in 2013. 'It was just that there had to be one place where there were no MCs. I mean, everyone was listening so closely to the music. We didn't need hyping up or [someone] to tell us what was going on [at the Metalheadz night at Blue Note]. It was the sanctuary for producers to hear their music played by the best DJs.'

Still, most DJs would play out with an MC—whether their own favoured mic-smith or the resident in-house guy. And it was usually a male MC, although ball-of-energy MC Chickaboo paved the way for other women such as Lady MC, Dyer MC, and Lady ST by the late 90s, alongside a second wave of male MCs like DRS, Darrison, Wrec, Visionobi, and Kemo breaking through.

'Instead of taking our own MCs into the studio, top producers would prefer to go and sample rap or ragga, or go and get MCs from other genres,' another 'second wave' MC, Eksman, told *DJ Mag* in 2013, while giving props to Zinc, who got him on the raucous *Drive My Car* in 2004.

Roni Size has been instrumental in his work with vocalists. Aside from Dynamite and Onallee in Reprazent, and Leonie Laws in Breakbeat Era, he brought through New Zealand-born MC Tali just after the millennium. Falling in love with d&b around 1996, Tali had approached Roni at a Reprazent after-show in Melbourne. After a short conversation, she did a rhyme in his ear, and Roni immediately gave her the mic. 'I MCed over Die's set, then hung out and partied with them for twenty-four hours, and talked about where I wanted to go with music,' she said in 2004.

Roni gave Tali his contact details, and she duly moved to England. Then—after hooking up with Reprazent again at their Hammersmith Palais after-show—she MCed with Krust and Die at Fabric, and subsequently moved to Bristol. After a year or so with the crew ('These guys are like my brothers, I've been very fortunate that they've taken me under their wing and I've become like a sister to them'), Roni suggested she make an album of her own. He put the full weight of Full Cycle behind her—production and promotion-wise—to try to blow up the resulting *Lyric On My Lip*, hoping to aid her evolution into a solo artist to rival Lady Sovereign or Ms Dynamite. The title track did scrape into the UK Top 40, but ultimately it didn't quite happen for Tali in terms of crossover success.

Since then, MC tracks, especially with the MC credited in the title, have remained relatively rare, despite the success of Stamina adding his extra flava to Marky & XRS's *LK* at the start of the century. SP:MC featured prominently on *Dreadnaught* by Icicle on Shogun Audio in 2011, and Dub Phizix & Skeptical foregrounded Strategy on the half-time *Marka* around the same time, but most young UK rappers started making their way in garage or grime instead—where they were generally afforded more prominence. It took a few MCs banding together as SASASAS to make waves in the jump-up scene—Skibadee and Shabba D from old-school jungle joined by Stormin' from grime collective Nasty Crew and hotshot newcomer Harry Shotta. This MC 'supergroup', partnered with veteran DJ/producer Phantasy and Macky Gee, only came together for a one-off show in 2014, but the initial reactions were so strong that they became a huge draw internationally as the decade unfolded. Tragically, Stormin' passed away from skin cancer in 2018, at the age of thirty-four.

Latterly, the Ladies Of Rage collective has sprung up to promote female MCs in drum & bass, and there are other women active in the UK, like Melody MC, Dotty, Starz, and MC Y-Zer, and plenty more internationally.

# 12 Jazz Notes: Roni Size, DJ Die, Krust, Suv, And The Bristol Scene

Bass is deeply embedded in Bristol's musical culture. In addition to the famed 'Bristol sound', the city has produced many of jungle's most significant artists, from Roni Size, DJ Die, and Krust, to Suv, Substance, Decoder, Redlight/Clipz, and TC. A love of low-end rumble is a shockwave running through the creations of many Bristol producers today, from Pinch and Joker to Shanti Celeste and Batu.

Located in a pocket of southwest England that borders Somerset and Gloucestershire, Bristol has its own special atmosphere. It's urban, yet the countryside is right on its doorstep. The city's musical history is deeply intertwined with its cultural narrative and demography. It has a diverse population, with a large black community of mostly Caribbean descent, in addition to a significant Asian populace. In this small but vibrant conurbation, close proximity is a fact of life, and a constant cultural exchange is taking place.

'There's a real cross-section of people here, and we're all crammed in together,' says Bristol DJ and producer Krust. 'The city isn't that big, so you've got to imagine all these cultures packed in this tight area rubbing shoulders every day, listening to each other's music and language, eating each other's food. Blacks mixing with whites, Indians mixing with whites, Chinese mixing with blacks, all in a tight environment.'

Reggae has long permeated Bristol's music scene, with many soundsystems starting up around the St Pauls and Easton areas of the city through the 1960s, and operated through the 1970s by names like Jah Lokko and Excalibur to cater to the Caribbean community. By the 1980s, this reggae sound, heard booming from speaker stacks across town, would come to cross-pollinate with other new musical forms, and it would change shape as a result. An early example is the Bristol post-punk band The Pop Group's 1979 debut single, *She Is Beyond*

*Good And Evil*: produced by Dennis Bovell, aka reggae producer extraordinaire Blackbeard, who worked with everyone from Linton Kwesi Johnson to Janet Kay, its ricocheting shimmers of echoed percussion and cavernous sense of space were heavily influenced by dub. *She Is Beyond Good And Evil* was a tantalising indication of how the music could combine with other styles, and this hybrid creation was something Pop Group singer Mark Stewart would cultivate in his influential solo material, recorded with the dub/hip-hop band Tackhead.

A vitally important crew influenced by the city's bass culture was the multiracial Wild Bunch. Their soundsystem would play in clubs and warehouses, and at the St Pauls Carnival in the city, mixing hip-hop, reggae, disco, and electro-funk together in a way that was totally fresh. 'Wild Bunch were instrumental to the scene here,' Roni Size says. 'They went away to America and Japan, came back, and were playing music that no one else had. They were the first crew to make a name for themselves outside of Bristol.'

'Back then, there were people at school just passing around tapes of the Wild Bunch,' adds DJ Die. 'Those were gold dust recordings—they were your rites of passage—it was like currency back in those days.'

'If you listen to what was going on then, it's what today is called multi-genre,' says DJ Krust. 'It was crazy: you'd go to a lot of Wild Bunch parties, and you wouldn't know what was coming next. It could be a house tune, a ragga tune, a lover's rock tune; it could be Sade, Pet Shop Boys, Tears For Fears…that built in us a sense of what good music is, what moves the crowd.'

Comprised of DJ Milo, Claude Williams (Willy Wee), Nellee Hooper, Grant Marshall (Daddy G), Robert Del Naja (3D), Andrew Vowles (Mushroom), and Adrian Thaws (Tricky), The Wild Bunch blended their influences and mixed them together in a way that would prove hugely influential. They released several records of their own through the 4th & Broadway label, but quickly split in the late 80s, with Marshall, Del Naja, Thaws, and Vowles starting a new group, Massive Attack, and Hooper becoming a successful record producer.

The Wild Bunch weren't the only hip-hop-skewed crew making power moves in the city, however. According to DJ Die, hip-hop thrived in 1980s Bristol. 'There were loads of other crews in the city, all throwing down, doing house parties and things in warehouses,' he says. 'There were a lot of illegal parties going on in St Pauls and around there. People were just swapping around the music, and the films, the books, *Subway Art*—these were all blowing us away, at thirteen, fourteen, trying to breakdance. There are so many of us from this same era that all have the same influences.'

Like Massive Attack and The Wild Bunch, Smith & Mighty were a Bristol act heavily influenced by dub, making their own hybrid tracks. Rob Smith and Ray Mighty brought a soundsystem sensibility to their hip-hop and soul songs, foregrounding the kind of chest-caving sub-basslines they'd heard issuing from speakers around their city. 'They are godfathers, man,' says DJ Die. 'They were a big influence on us.'

Smith & Mighty's *Walk On*—a cover of the Dionne Warwick classic *Walk On By*—has the sparse drum machines and heavy bass of digital reggae, electro bleeps, but also the raw breakbeats and scratching of hip-hop, minting what latterly came to be known as the Bristol sound. For the duo, it was a natural combination of the things they were into.

'At the time, Bristol was being left alone by the rest of the world, so we were left to try out things, and mix it up,' says Rob Smith. 'Whereas I think other areas were doing more purist sounds, we were taking bits and pieces from everything and mixing it up to see what came out. We were really into reggae when the hip-hop thing started to happen; we were a bit reluctant to let go of it, so we were still doing reggae but with breakbeats.'

At the end of the 80s, in Bristol as in the rest of the UK, house music and raves were in full flow. Smith & Mighty weren't immune to their allure, and they began creating more electronic material, from the prototype dubstep of *Brain Scan* to moody 4/4 like *The Dark, Dark House*. Inspired by the musical free-for-all of the Bristol scene, their early discography is a time capsule of this proto-rave era.

'The scenes in Bristol crossed over quite a lot,' Smith says. 'There were punks and rastas and soul boys and everything else, and there was one main club where everyone went, the infamous Dug Out club. Everybody met there and exchanged ideas and talked about forming different types of bands. The soil was very rich, with that attitude to mix things up.'

Free parties in the countryside inspired Smith & Mighty to make breakbeat hardcore tracks of their own, among them the bass-heavy, Amen-driven *Killa*, packed with sampled reggae chat and rap snippets. On their rave excursions, they'd take along some friends who would go on to forge a Bristol sound of their own.

'We were going to a lot of the orbital raves at the time, just in the countryside, out in a field or whatever,' Smith says. 'We used to travel with DJ Krust and DJ Die, before anybody was anybody really. We had this big seven-seater Citroen, which we all piled into. I remember the music at the time, you'd get all these DJs playing Detroit house stuff, and then the acid thing was going on. DJ Die said to me one time, Have you noticed that some beats are flat, and some are kind of jungle beats? That's the first time I heard that term. Then there were Frankie Bones and people like that playing stuff with breaks in, and things like *We Are I.E.* It was really interesting to hear it breaking up and splitting off. Obviously, the breaks got faster, and people started pitching it up. I always feel there's this parallel between technology and genre. When a new piece of kit came out, people were trying out that bit of kit. When sampling started happening, people realised you could play a breakbeat on lower C and then play it on an upper C, and it's like, *Oh, wow, check that out.*'

### SIZE MATTERS

Roni Size grew up listening to a lot of reggae and dancehall, which he heard through his brothers and at local soundsystems in the 80s. 'As well as funk, the stuff that really captured my imagination was digital reggae from Jamaica,' Size says. 'My brother used to have a soundsystem, Lasertronic; there was a sound called Raiders 32. We always used to clash each other back in the day, it was a pretty interesting time.'

While DJing on Bristol's pirate stations, Size was starting to make his own digital reggae tracks, and he was increasingly influenced by hip-hop too. Production became an obsession for him, and at an initiative called the Basement Project at a Sefton Park youth club, he dedicated himself to learning how to make beats on a computer and understand the provided hardware equipment inside out. Later, he became a music teacher for the Basement Project, showing other budding beatmakers how to operate drum machines and software. 'As soon as I knew you could make music on a computer, that was my mission,' he says.

The Basement Project had a considerable amount of equipment, and Size had access to 'a Roland 707, Notator, a sequencer, a nice studio master desk, and some Tascam reel-to-reels'. Even then, he was obsessed with studio gear, researching the machines that were behind his favourite dancehall reggae records. 'I wanted stuff like what they were using in Jamaica: the DMX drum machine, the LinnDrum, and Pultec EQs. I wanted to get that extra shine.'

Hardware samplers, though, would send him on a whole new path, as he discovered the infinite possibilities of a large record collection and a limitless imagination. 'I was making UK hip-hop anyway, but it wasn't until I had a Roland S-330 sampler that I realised I could start using breaks from my brother's record collection,' he says. 'I was just sampling, making nondescript music. I was learning how the equipment needed to be manipulated. When I started to hear some of the early jungle techno, where people started throwing in breakbeats, sub-basses here and there, I thought, *Wow*. I recognised some of the breaks, like the Amen. I thought, *I have those—let's see what I can chain together myself.* Back then, I was just putting in bits of reggae, bits of soul, bits of R&B, breaks, and stringing it all together, seeing what stuck, really.'

DJ Die (real name: Dan Kausman) moved to Bristol when he was twelve and quickly got into music. 'I went to the cinema once, to see *Beat Street*,' he says, 'and that was it. Traded in the Doc Martens for Puma States. After that it was hip-hop, hip-hop, hip-hop, then acid house.'

He remembers his earliest electronic music epiphany vividly: going to the Thekla venue and a club night called Def Con, he was bemused by the weird new sounds being played. 'It was the popping club in town on a Friday,' Die says. 'They'd play a lot of rare groove in there, James Brown, a bit of hip-hop; rare groove, in those days, that was the vibe. One night, I was in a corner, soaking it up. The rare groove stopped, and this kick drum came in, and I was like, *What's this?* And then the acid came creepin' in. I thought, *What the fuck is this?* It was a total, mind-blown moment. It was *Acid Tracks* by Phuture. I realised, *OK, there's something else going on now.* It was a big revolution. Then the whole acid thing hit, it was '88, '89, the Summer of Love. Suddenly people would turn up in clubs wearing white gloves. It was a new sort of spirit. They'd obviously got their hands on Es, and it was just an explosion, everyone trying to throw parties. Adamski would be coming through town, or Guru Josh was playing live. I was always trying to get in. I used to help carry this soundsystem into this club called the Locket Hill, just to get in. That was it, just getting in where you could.'

Die was DJing as much as possible, and going to the free parties scattered around the countryside. He began to play at raves like Circus Warp—a series of events thrown by travellers around the southwest of England—and soon linked up with Jody Wisternoff (later of Way Out West) to form the group Sub Love.

Their debut 1992 EP, *Twisted Techno*, was a varied collection of suitably bass-heavy beats and breaks, drawing from ragga samples, Belgian horror synth riffs, and snippets from well-known pop hits.

After becoming a regular DJ fixture at raves around the country, Die was travelling all over to dance, too, heading to events thrown by Spiral Tribe and Universe. At one party, he ran into an old friend who was another dedicated raver. 'I linked up with Krust, who I'd met in the late 80s at some of the house parties and squat parties that they used to throw as the Fresh 4,' he says. 'I bumped into him again at a free festival on Chipping Sodbury Common. We linked up across the dancefloor. I said, What are you doing here? And he was like, We're both here for the same thing. We had that moment.'

With Smith & Mighty, they'd head off on rave missions, rolling as a unit. 'We knew them, and they were into their raving from a bit before, the M25 parties and stuff like that. We had a taste of it and were like, *Yeah, we want more*.

'We'd go to wherever the rave was,' Die continues. 'You'd call the Batphone and find out the address. We were part of that whole convoy: we'd go off on this magical mystery tour to find a free rave. I was a budding DJ who tagged along and would wait for their turn to play. You'd put your name on the list, almost. You'd get there and then some other DJ would come waltzing in, pushing their way through, but you had to stand your ground. You'd be waiting behind the decks with your headphones and records, like, *I'm playing next.*'

It was when Roni Size met Die and Krust that the scene was set for a new chapter in Bristol music. 'I met Roni on the street, and he gave me a tape,' Die says. 'It was cool, some early ragga jungle. I bumped into him at a Universe party, and he was raving. We hung out for a while and listened to a Bukem set, then got in the studio shortly after that.'

Their first sessions resulted in Roni Size's exceptional *Made To Fit* EP. With stripped-back nods to hardcore in its synth sounds, the minimalist grooves and creative drum edits of tracks like *Det-Strumental* had all the hallmarks of what would become jungle. *Refresher*, meanwhile, had waterfalls of soul piano and soundsystem chat amid its avalanche of micro-spliced breaks.

### UPPER KRUST

DJ Krust (Kirk Thompson) grew up surrounded by a similar blend of musical influences. As part of the group Fresh 4, with his brother J Thompson (later known as Flynn), Paul Southey (Suv), and Judge, he was another who helped to instigate the Bristol sound most often associated with Massive Attack. Their cover version of Rose Royce's soul paean *Wishing On A Star* had the lush vox of Lizz E tied to a rolling *Funky Drummer* break and samples of classic rare groove, all doused in capacious reverb: summery weed-haze bliss. Fresh 4 quickly succumbed to the predominant rave sound, and their follow-up single was a rap-laced house track, *Release Yourself.*

'Back then, when the Fresh 4 thing was going on, we were listening to rave,' Krust says. 'Fresh 4 were DJs, essentially, so we were doing these crazy warehouse parties where you'd play hip-hop, breaks, rock; you'd do scratch sessions, rap sessions, you'd play house music, techno tunes, then have a vocalist come in and sing on a house tune. The whole thing was experimentation.'

Krust was increasingly enraptured by the breakbeat rave sound he was hearing at events, and after hooking up with Smith & Mighty, Die, and Roni Size, he began to make his own beats in the new style. 'I really liked the whole techno thing,' he says. 'When I started to make music in a serious way, I was listening to a lot of techno and figuring out how they were doing those bass sounds and what synths they were using. I was sampling a lot of those techno tunes, and then eventually I moved onto using Moogs, ARPs, and Novations, and learned how to programme the basses myself. The Roland S-760 sampler was a big thing as well—we'd spend days just making bass sounds and recording them onto DAT, and then sample them back into the 760, and use the filters.'

Krust's first track was *Resister*, backed with Roni Size & DJ Die's *Music Box* on their label Full Circle (which later became Full Cycle). With its dreamy shoegaze rock samples and rapid drum breaks, and subsequent drop into booming 808 bass, it was an impressive calling card. *Music Box*, meanwhile, created an entirely new style. Laced with warm, jazz-funk Fender Rhodes keyboard samples that seemed to circulate in the stratosphere, it had more in common with the dusty crate-dug hip-hop of the time, but with added speedy beats and swelling bass.

'At the time, Roni was using Notator and the Roland 550 sampler,' says Die, 'which is something we stuck with as it developed, and just a few effects units. But Roni had some tricks with the 550. There's this forwards/backwards effect—you hear it on the *bling!* sound on *Music Box*. That was a function that the 550 had that the Akai samplers didn't have, and also there were loop points. To save on time, you could loop the little hi-hat part.'

This was heady sampladelia that could work on a dancefloor, very different to the way that hardcore producers had used snippets of old records in the years previous. 'We'd go digging in the crates, all over,' Size later told *DJ Mag*. 'It just happened to be a lot of 70s jazz or funk, or just rock records. You'd hear great loops and you'd use them. For me it's all about coming at it from a b-boy mentality.'

'Your record collection was your pride and joy,' he adds, 'so whatever you had in your collection was what you were going to sample. That was my history.'

'We were definitely hip-hop minded kids, digging in the crates looking for those special sounds with flavour,' says Die. 'We were borrowing, but we were being creative with it as well. Sampling two-second bits and making textures, and you'd never know. We made *Music Box* in '93, the first record on Full Cycle. It was just forming. Shut Up & Dance and Ibiza Records were a massive influence. They paved the way, those labels and artists stood out. There was early Doc Scott stuff, DJ Crystl stuff, LTJ Bukem, the whole Birmingham thing. Those magical two years, it all changed after that, but it seemed that that was the golden pocket right there. In '93, jungle was really kicking in: more roll-out in arrangement, more drum-and-bass bits, less drops.'

These tracks were swiftly adopted by DJs and club/rave crowds, with *Music Box* in particular having a seismic impact whenever it was dropped. Soon, as previously detailed, London DJ Bryan Gee approached Roni Size to secure some releases for a new label he was starting with Jumpin Jack Frost.

'Bryan was working at Rhythm King, and he was an A&R,' Roni says. 'He knew two of my friends who I was giving music to at the time. They let me use their studio, and when Rhythm King folded, Bryan took the tapes with him, and on my tapes was the phone number. He contacted me, came to Bristol, and we forged a working relationship from there on.'

'He loved what we were doing and could hear the potential,' adds Die. 'Along with Frost, they gave it the stamp of approval. They were certified, they had respect already in London, and they brought us in.'

After a couple of singles came the big breakthrough: Roni Size and DJ Die's 1994 split EP *The Size Of Things To Come*. On it was one of the perennial jungle classics, Roni Size's *It's A Jazz Thing*, which took the ideas first suggested by *Music Box* to dizzy new stratospheres. *Jazz Thing* was Size's early masterpiece, its flanged drums seeming to ping back and forth between the speakers and a great deluge of percussion, before a spine-tingling double bass riff and glissandos of Rhodes keys, taken from Lonnie Liston Smith's *Shadows*, enter the picture. It was jazzy drum & bass but minus the noodling and guff.

Krust released the follow-up on V, *Jazz Note*, drawing from the deeper end of Detroit techno (despite its title), daubing viridian synth tones over crisp breaks, soaring pads, and 808 hits, minting a distinctive style of his own.

Now Bristol had a new sound—jungle—and Krust, Die, and Roni Size set up Full Cycle proper as an outlet for their material. 'Full Cycle was the label that allowed us to not have to second guess what we were doing,' says Size. 'It was like, *Actually, do you know what, this is what we're doing, this is what we like and this is what we're putting out.*'

'My background is hip-hop, so I grew up with *Wild Style* and the premise of being a b-boy,' adds Krust. 'That premise was, *Don't bite.* You need to be original, you need to be fresh, so when we started Full Cycle, everyone understood that ethos. We all came from the hip-hop era, we all had fat laces, we all were graffiti writers, breakdancers, rappers, DJs; we tried everything. There was no bigger crime in our crew than copying each other, or using the same sounds too many times. It was always about pushing the boundaries and going to the next level. You go into the studio and Die would be making a beat. You're like, *Fucking hell, what's that?* Or you go into Roni's studio and he's making a beat, the same thing. We were constantly pushing each other forward, trying to outdo each other— there was that healthy competition.'

Meanwhile, more and more jungle beats began to issue from the city. Flynn & Flora—Krust's brother J and Flora Fiakkas—started their own label Independent Dealers, and began to release distinctive and underrated jungle tracks with a somnolent musicality. *Dream Of You* was a gorgeous roll-out of splintered Amens and susurrating pad swirl, with a vocal sample of *Anyone Who Had A Heart*, continuing Bristol's strange infatuation with Burt Bacharach songs (see also: Smith & Mighty), while the tougher *Flowers* has more pummelling beats and psychedelic jazz samples. Their follow-up for Full Cycle, *String For String*, was possibly even better, with its endlessly unfolding drum rolls and 4/4 kick.

Not to be outdone, another former member of Fresh 4, Suv, would make an essential entry on V Recordings with DJ Die. *Out Of Sight* mined a similar minimalist funk vibe to the rest of his crew: all intricately stitched rhythms and twilit jazz chords.

Bristol club night Ruffneck Ting, run by Substance and DJ Dazee, became a vital pitstop for visiting junglists, with Grooverider, Bukem, and Fabio regular guests at the event, which took place at various venues around the city. It became a label, too, releasing the classic female-vocal-led ragga jungle cut *Rude Girl* by Substance, a track loaded with warping sub synth and time-stretched Amens. More Rockers, a project from Rob Smith and Peter D Rose, took the Smith & Mighty sound into overt junglist territory, with splintered breaks, raw synth bass, and diva vocals—especially potent in the form of *You're Gonna (Make Me)* and its incredible remix from Roni Size and Krust.

### CONSTITUTING REPRAZENT

The jungle sound was in full flow in Bristol in 1994. Ragga chat, dancehall bass, and R&B samples merged with jazz-funk and rare groove snippets on dancefloors. This combination made sense to Bristol crowds, who had grown up with a similarly diverse soundtrack around the city.

'There were a lot more black people in the raves [by then],' says Die. 'You'd go to the raves and it would be going off: flame throwers, champagne, batty riders. It was like stepping into a movie. Those elements were definitely appealing for people—the reggae, the soul, it was like a rave on steroids. But then jazz brings something in, like, *Let's put some jazz ingredients in and that will spice it up*. People would love it.'

Roni Size brought his dancehall side back to the fore, with ragga jungle releases under the names Firefox and Mask, full of warping synth bass and springy, time-stretched drums. He also started a side label dedicated to this more club-centric sound, Dope Dragon. 'We were making so much music at the time that we just wanted to put it out,' he says. 'Some of the styles were different. Firefox was my reggae style, and Mask was more geared towards me being a young kid, into hip-hop, comic books.'

Concurrently, he formed a new collective with Krust and Die: Roni Size Reprazent. A kind of super-group but without the prog-rock guitar solos and monster egos, Reprazent were courted by Gilles Peterson and Norman Jay's Talkin' Loud label, which released their astonishing debut EP, *Reasons For Sharing*, in 1996. With the spelunking sub frequencies and forceful funk of *Share The Fall*—all scuttling drums and the lush jazz vocalisations of Onallee—the shimmering ambient keys and live-sounding percussion of *Down*, the abstract kettle-drum hits and atmospherics of *Sounds Fresh*, and *Trust Me*'s rolling double bass and weeded-out vibe, Reprazent's sound was bold and new.

'Reprazent was born after putting all the music out on these independent labels,' says Size. 'We were approached by Talkin' Loud, a label we always looked up to 'cause of Galliano and stuff, and Gilles Peterson running it. Rather than sampling all the breaks and the records that we had, it allowed us to start contacting all the musicians that we knew in Bristol. We could go and start recording our own sounds. That's what we did. It was like having a wish list fulfilled. The idea of recording your own stuff was great.'

With Suv, singer Onallee, MC Dynamite, lightning-quick drummer Clive Deamer, double-bass dude Si John, and others, Reprazent continued to use the same composition techniques but sampled live playing to piece together new drum tracks and musical elements. They were made to perform live, and they became a massive draw on the festival circuit.

Reprazent's debut album, *New Forms*, was released at the height of drum & bass's popularity. Simultaneously experimental and sophisticated, while maintaining that raw dancefloor minimalism, it had a broader appeal to a market outside the drum & bass crowd. The title track is an ice-cool transmission of double-bass funk, shivery sound design, and the dream-come-true lyricism of US rapper Bahamadia; there's the clipped futurism of *Digital* and the bright soul flavour of *Watching Windows*, going up against tougher tracks like the rib-rattling bass splurge and Dynamite MC rhymes of *Railing*.

*New Forms* offered a bird's eye view of jungle's myriad strains and interpretations. It peaked at no. 8 on the UK album charts and was entered and then shortlisted for the Mercury Prize for best album that same year. The label didn't think it had a hope in hell, but Reprazent gathered together their crew, with Roni calling up Frost and Bryan Gee from V—who put out their first records—to come along to the awards show anyway. 'Prior to that night, I'd never heard of the Mercury Prize,' says Bryan. 'I'm underground, I didn't have a clue what it was—I just knew that it was a big thing, and I was told to wear a suit. We went to the Grosvenor House Hotel and I was like, *Oh my god, this is really a major deal.*'

Reprazent were up against Radiohead's *OK Computer*, The Prodigy's *The Fat Of The Land*, and The Chemical Brothers' *Dig Your Own Hole*—as well as the Spice Girls' debut—and at 16/1 were rank outsiders to win. A few of the Talkin' Loud crew put money on Reprazent to win, but they weren't too confident, given the competition and the fact that the label hadn't spent much, comparatively, on album promo.

Announcing the winner, the chairman of the judging panel, Simon Frith—music critic and Professor of English Studies at Strathclyde University—said, 'We have been arguing for quite a long time. We do think that Radiohead's album is a classic, but in the end we all agreed it was to be Roni Size's *New Forms*.' The Reprazent table was stunned, and then they went ballistic as Frith explained the lengthy process it had taken to reach a majority decision. 'It was the record we were most happy to tell buyers, This is the one to go out and buy,' Frith concluded.

The Reprazent gang took to the stage, and Roni said, 'A lot of people have supported us, and I thank them. People said we were crazy, but we believed what we were doing. We all have been working hard for this, this is not just about me.' He later revealed that the £25,000 prize money was going to be donated to the Sefton Park community music project where he first got the chance to learn his trade.

'To win it was one of the craziest nights ever,' says Frost. 'It was on TV and I was there with a big cigar and all that, and straight afterwards we all went down to Bar Rumba for a massive party at Movement. It felt like a win for the whole scene. Probably one of the highlights of my life.'

Signing to a major label was perhaps always going to be double-edged for junglists. The Talkin' Loud deal had given Reprazent more financial muscle, but being part of a major label wasn't without its difficulties. Press officer Paulette Constable reports that there was no budget from the label to promote the album until the Mercury win. 'Talkin' Loud was in no way supported by Polygram,' she says. 'Every day was a fucking battle.' She describes the press department as 'toxic' and 'a vipers' nest', with the head of press refusing to sign off her expenses to take journalists out to get them onside for the Reprazent campaign.

When the Mercury win was announced on the night, Constable was pulled off the table by the Polygram bigwigs and taken to a corner to be told that the label management wouldn't be giving any interviews to the assembled industry press corps. 'They were so sure that it was going to lose that there was no stock of the album in the warehouse,' she recalls. 'Mercury is a music-industry plaudit, and normally the head of the record label blahs about how much they believed in the artists and how much they have given in terms of promotion and distribution.'

Even after the victory, some critics were sniffing that the judges were just trying to be 'trendy', rather than shining a light on the most futuristic music out there. Nevertheless, the Mercury win gave the whole genre a massive boost at a key moment. 'It was a great thing for us, and for the drum & bass scene,' Size says. 'It felt special—it was a good time. It opened up people's eyes, and when they saw the band, they saw that it wasn't just kids in bedrooms—there was a drummer, bass player, actually playing this stuff live.'

## OTHER BRISTOL SOUNDS

While the Full Cycle crew dominated the headlines, they didn't have a lock on speedy Bristol breakbeats. Elsewhere in the city, darker rumblings were afoot. Mark Caro, originally from Birmingham, was releasing titanium-reinforced tracks under the name Tech Itch. He'd first surfaced under the name Plasmic Life, releasing eerie Amen choppage on Bizzy B's Brain label, but he settled on Tech Itch for his main moniker, setting up his own label, Technical Itch, too. He was poached by Moving Shadow after Omni Trio personally recommended him to the label, going on to make gems like *The Dreamer*, with its granite break crunches and warping, buzzing bass.

At the same time, another Bristol-based artist and associate of the Ruffneck Ting collective, Decoder (Darren Beale), was creating next-level beats across town, and Tech Itch released his blistering debut *8 Tap*: a ragga-jungle-influenced, early hardstep/jump-up delight with bowel-loosening subs. The pair would become a crucial force in the incipient tech-step sound that was already making its presence felt in London via the No U-Turn label.

During this late-90s period, DJ Krust would make his own definitive statement of futuristic technoid d&b, the masterpiece album *Coded Language*, while Die would make titanium bangers like *Clear Skyz*—all atmospheric pressure, filmic sound design, and wobbly bass. Reprazent, meanwhile, did a ton of shows following the Mercury success, having been rapidly catapulted onto big stages alongside the likes of Oasis and The Prodigy. 'We find ourselves appearing at jazz festivals, rock festivals, dance festivals—in all sorts of areas,' said Roni at the time, on taking d&b to new audiences. 'People don't know where to put us, which is great. We love that.'

Between touring, Roni and Die busied themselves with a new project involving another Bristol singer—self-described 'sassy gobshite' and ex-traveller

Leonie Laws, fresh from the southwest's 'free party' scene. 'I was a member of the audience in the techno days—when girly singing was the devil's work,' she says, 'so I didn't see my contribution for a while.'

Signing to XL, Breakbeat Era slipped out their eponymous debut single in '98 and cracked the UK Top 40. Saucy follow-up *Ultra Obscene* was rinsed by Grooverider, Andy C, and Ed Rush as a dubplate over the summer of '99, before the track and the album of the same name again punctured charts in late summer, backed up by a series of live shows. But by this time, Roni was also working on the second Reprazent album. 'How do I juggle everything? By being organised,' he said. 'We're more organised than we've ever been.'

Some of the sketches for new tracks were worked up on the tour bus or during soundchecks for the live shows they played following the release of *New Forms*, and they adopted an understandably harder edge. 'We made *New Forms* without ever being on a stage as a unit,' Roni said. 'When we got in the studio to make *In The Mode*, we had over two hundred shows under our belts, and a better idea about what was needed to create an impact on stage. This record was made with a view from the stage.'

Tougher tracks with super-optimised dynamism included collaborations with US hip-hop mic-men Rahzel from The Roots and Method Man from Wu-Tang Clan, as well as vocalist Zack de la Rocha from rock/rap rebels Rage Against The Machine. What was immediately noticeable, however, was how commanding and self-assured Reprazent's own mic-man, Dynamite MC, sounded amid these hip-hop heavyweights.

'Do you know how hard it is to get someone's vocals sounding right with the music?' said Roni. 'Fucking hard, but I learned. Working with Method Man, Zack, and Rahzel, you have to do them justice, bring out the best in them. Dynamite and Onallee too. You can hear every word, which is good.'

Lead single *Dirty Beats*, featuring Dynamite, preceded the album's release in October 2000; Reprazent performed it live on *Top Of The Pops* ('no miming'). Onallee still featured on two-and-a-half tracks, but the album definitely felt more hip-hop-influenced and militant. 'There's a lot of jazz on *In The Mode* too, you just can't hear it as clearly,' Roni told *DJ Mag* at the time. 'Drum & bass always changes, it goes through a dark era, it goes through a light era. It's always done that—you can't be light all the time.'

By the time *In The Mode* dropped, the guys' home nation was in the grip of

UK garage fever, and Reprazent were having to field bullshit questions from the media about whether drum & bass was now dead. 'England kind of had enough of what we were doing, which is disappointing,' Krust told *DJ Mag* in 2000. 'They never really gave it a chance to grow. It was blown up in the first five minutes and, all of a sudden, it was rubbish—and that's bollocks. Any music takes a long time to develop, and then once you develop it you've gotta execute it and follow it through. And when you follow it through, you've gotta back it up. That's what we're doing now—backing up what we started.'

Asked in the same *DJ Mag* cover feature whether d&b was the UK's answer to hip-hop, Dynamite had this to say: 'In the sense of a culture, a movement, a generation coming up through the rave scene and the whole chase of being in the car park, following the lead car, finding the field and then setting up the rig and then dancing . . . yeah, in the way that hip-hop had the breakdancing, the graffiti, the turntables and everything. But drum & bass needs to be identified in its own right. It's universal, 'cause people are making this music all over the world now.'

'There are similarities,' added Krust, ''cos that's our ghetto music, and that's their ghetto music: borne from frustration at an establishment not wanting to support a homegrown talent, so fuck 'em, we do it ourselves. That's the attitude: *Fuck you, we'll do it ourselves.* That's what drum & bass is about. We're hip-hop people anyway, and if you blatantly need to hear a rap to say [something is] hip-hop, then that's what you need. But there's a lot more going on in our music than just that—and phat beats, phat basslines are what hip-hop's about as well.

'This is our answer, but it's our own individual thing,' Krust continued. 'It's what we needed as ghetto British people with hardly any identity. Before, we were just copying everyone else, mutating all these other musics—acid and house and hip-hop and this, that, and the other. When jungle and trip-hop came out, that was truly British music from the ground up. We took a piece of everything and made it our own. With trip-hop, you could feel the tension. Drum & bass is about feeling something.'

**FUTURE SOUNDS**

Though this period marks the zenith of what we think of as Bristol's music scene, the city has continued to produce d&b talent ever since. TC (Tom Caswell) began to make a name with his neck-snapping, jump-up beats in the early 2000s, while another Full Cycle affiliate, Clipz (Hugh Pescod), started out creating simple and raw jump-up club tracks like *Slippery Slopes* before broadening his remit under a new name, Redlight, to make fidget house, breakbeat, and dubstep.

Beyond the city's diverse population and the strong Caribbean/black British influence on its music, Bristol has thrived, Krust reckons, precisely because it's not London or Manchester. Away from the spotlight, it's been able to develop its own styles. Bristol's artists make trends; they don't follow them, a philosophy evident on Krust's excellent experimental d&b record from 2020, *The Edge Of Everything*.

'We're far away from the big bad city, so the industry doesn't necessarily come here,' he says. 'But on the other side of that, we do get left alone, so we're allowed to experiment and come up with new formulas. It's a weird juxtaposition: Bristol is quite laid back, so on the face of it, Londoners would call us *country*, and you wouldn't think there would be this progressive attitude. But underneath that sort of façade of people being stoners is this work ethic that is really pioneering.'

The acts that Bristol has produced have been a huge source of inspiration, Krust says, spurring artists on to make their own innovative material, and that's a tradition that continues. 'I come from the tradition of Smith & Mighty, Wild Bunch, Portishead, Tricky, Massive Attack,' he says. 'I'm in that lineage of trying to be creative, trying to represent my culture. What those guys created was a blueprint. When I found jungle and I started to create that, I felt it was my duty to be as pioneering as those guys. When we did Full Cycle, there was a ferocious appetite for making music and a ferocious appetite for pioneering. You can see it in the city now—it's back. There's energy here, where people are being super creative, you've got people like Joker, and the other young guys out here doing their thing. Some of the stuff I'm hearing, it's like, *Fucking hell mate*.'

Bristol's spark of innovation is indeed undimmed, as new crews like Rotations—a large collective of DJs and producers—and Invicta Audio continue to rep drum & bass in the city, alongside a myriad of other artists influenced by the form in some way or another.

# 13 New Horizons: The Dawn Of Ambient Jungle

There was a flipside to the rugged beats, raw samples, and pummelling sub-bass happening in early 90s UK dance music. Amid the wild abandon of acid house, hardcore, and jungle, there was chill-out culture. DJs like Mixmaster Morris and groups such as Global Communication and The Orb played and made mellow ambient records, infused with all the synths of the past masters but with an ear cocked to modern dance beats. Chill-out rooms proliferated in clubs and at raves, offering a calming counterpoint to the frenzies elsewhere, and records like Aphex Twin's *Selected Ambient Works Vol. 1* and the Warp *Artificial Intelligence* compilations offered armchair raving to soothe dancers into a post-ecstasy calm. Blissful beatific textures proliferated through the work of Sueno Latino, B12, and Carl Craig—and jungle was not immune to the musical worlds conjured by digital synths either.

While swirling tones had already become a regular feature of jungle as early as 1993—mainly in the intros or breakdowns of tracks, before an avalanche of breakbeats and bass—some pioneering artists dared to imagine ambient atmospheres as a key feature.

LTJ Bukem (real name: Danny Williamson), a classically trained DJ and producer from Watford, was introduced to the jazz fusion of Chick Corea and Lonnie Liston-Smith by his schoolteacher, Nigel Crouch, at a young age. He started going clubbing and had his own soundsystem—Sunrise, not to be confused with the big rave brand—for a while, and despite working as a chef was still going out nearly every night.

When he started making some inroads into the rave scene, he had the idea to foreground lush textures in his productions. One of his earliest tunes, 1991's *Logical Progression*, followed the early hardcore template to some extent, with its 4/4 kick-drum, breakbeat, and pianos, yet it also had an oceanic, dreamy quality.

The follow-up made the ambient aspect explicit: 1992's *Demon's Theme*, which was rinsed by both Fabio and Grooverider at Rage and rapidly became a rave/club classic, placed soaring digital chords in the middle of the action, providing a dramatic juxtaposition to the intense rolling drums of the Amen break that hammered away below. As if to explicitly state a link with the ambient past and future, *Demon's Theme* featured, among its samples, the bird call also used on 808 State's *Pacific State* and a synth lift from Rhythmatic's bleep-house missive *Frequency*, as well as a small snippet of pan pipes from Germany's arch cosmic rockers Tangerine Dream, arguably one of the first bands to pioneer the ambient/new-age sound.

Bukem's ingenious idea worked not because it lulled the listener into a blissful stupor, but because it existed between two states, at once dreamlike and rhythmically rugged; dancefloor-ready yet stimulating to the mind. The follow-up was even more gorgeous—1993's *Music* centred around a hypnotic techno loop and soaring strings, plus orgasmic moans from a Raze house classic. Combined with offbeat rolling Amen breaks, it felt like a camera panning over a verdant landscape, before a low melodic bass note added a sublime additional musicality.

'You had a record collection, you loved a piece of music from it, took a snippet, and off you went,' Bukem told *XLR8R* in 2019. 'Whether it was a must-have beat, new synth sound, catchy music, or a vocal sample—I guess this was often my starting point to creating something.'

Bukem was acknowledging his influences with his sample choices, though the ambient elements that would increasingly populate his tracks also emanated from further back in time. Heavily inspired by jazz and soul in his formative years, he also had in his mix the cosmic tones and searching melodies of 70s greats like Roy Ayers and Pharoah Sanders. At eight minutes, forty-nine seconds long, *Music* wasn't afraid to stretch out either, just as these exploratory jazz epics had done. Larry Heard's *Washing Machine* had been a big game changer for Bukem. 'Cosmic soul, man, that was my link between Lonnie Liston-Smith and the electronic age,' he told *DJ Mag*. 'That blew my head off. Took me somewhere I'd never been before and I didn't want to come back.'

'Personally I'm a big soul head, and people often look at me weirdly when I tell them this,' Bukem later told *FACT*, 'but what I see is that there's a parallel from soul to jazz to reggae to 80s soul to hip-hop, early house to hip-house to the early acid to techno to drum & bass. In that way they're all connected.'

**BELOW LEFT** FABIO & GROOVERIDER AT AN IMPROMPTU CAR-PARK RAVE AFTER THE TRIP, CENTRAL LONDON, 1988. PHOTO BY DAVE SWINDELLS. **TOP RIGHT** BABY JUMPIN JACK FROST WITH HIS MUM, INGRID, IN SOUTH LONDON. **BELOW RIGHT** BABY FABIO WITH HIS MUM, JENNY, ALSO IN SOUTH LONDON.

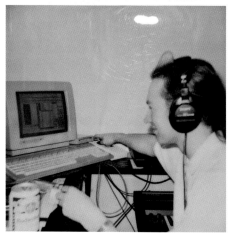

OPPOSITE PAGE, TOP BOOGIE TIMES
RECORDS. BELOW LEFT DJ HYPE IN
BOOGIE TIMES. BELOW RIGHT SEAN
O'KEEFFE OF 2 BAD MICE, DEEP BLUE.
THIS PAGE FOUL PLAY.

THIS PAGE KEMISTRY & STORM. PHOTO BY TRISTAN O'NEILL. **OPPOSITE PAGE, TOP LEFT** DJ RAP. **TOP RIGHT** BRYAN GEE AND JUMPIN JACK FROST. **BELOW** A GUY CALLED GERALD IN THE STUDIO, HAMMERSMITH, 1994. PHOTO BY LADY MISS KIER.

OPPOSITE PAGE METALHEADZ AT BLUE NOTE, LONDON, 1995. PHOTO BY DANIEL NEWMAN. **THIS PAGE, ABOVE** ANDY C. **LEFT** MC DET.

OPPOSITE PAGE, TOP CLUB FLYERS.
BELOW GOLDIE, LTJ BUKEM, AND
ROB PLAYFORD LARKING ABOUT AT
CREAMFIELDS, 1996. PHOTO BY DANIEL
NEWMAN. THIS PAGE MOVEMENT AT
BAR RUMBA, 1997. PHOTO BY DANIEL
NEWMAN.

**THIS PAGE** SANCTUARY, BIRMINGHAM, 1997. PHOTO BY DANIEL NEWMAN.
**OPPOSITE PAGE, TOP** LTJ BUKEM ON THE COVER OF *DJ MAG*, MARCH 2000.
**BELOW** RONI SIZE. PHOTO BY SARAH GINN.

OPPOSITE PAGE, TOP MARCUS INTALEX IN THE MIX. PHOTO BY JAMIE SIMONDS. BELOW LEFT TONY COLMAN AND CHRIS GOSS OUTSIDE THE RED DOOR OF THE FIRST HOSPITAL RECORDS HQ. BELOW RIGHT DJ MARKY WITH A FABRIC AWARD. PHOTO BY OLIVER J. BROWN. THIS PAGE CALIBRE. PHOTO BY SARAH GINN.

www.giprint.co.uk

The solid centre
for your
stadium operati

ston Smith

gip

bolt
growwithbolt.com

TOP LEMON D AT VALVE SOUNDSYSTEM, BRIXTON ACADEMY. PHOTO BY SARAH GINN. **ABOVE** DBRIDGE. PHOTO BY KHALI ACKFORD. **RIGHT** SHERELLE. PHOTO BY ALEX LAMBERT.

**RIGHT** GOLDIE. PHOTO BY CHELONE WOLF. **BELOW** FABIO & GROOVERIDER. PHOTO BY CHELONE WOLF.

Bukem began to attract attention for his different take on jungle—though, to start with, his style was simply considered part of the rich blend of influences the genre could exhibit, and he could be found on many a club or rave flyer amid acts more known for playing hard beats. Still, his open-ended approach made his Good Looking Records label a home for other like-minded producers who were also interested in exploring the combination of musicality with tough drums and bass. D.O.P.E. (Ben James and Ray Stanley), who ran Rugged Vinyl, linked up with Bukem to deliver the early ambient-jungle epic *Travelling (Slow Train To Philly Mix)*, interlacing a submerged soul sample, subtly shifting synth notes, vocal snippets, and beats that slip and slide in an impossibly fluid fashion.

Around the same time in Hertford, Omni Trio (Rob Haigh) was beginning to combine the ambient music he'd already been making as Sema as early as 1984 with the hardcore and jungle beats he'd heard and been excited by while working in the town's Parliament record shop. With tunes like '93's *Mystic Stepper* and *Renegade Snares* (see chapter 5), he was another formative influence on ambient jungle. And in Coventry, Skanna (John Graham) was another artist experimenting with ambient elements as early as 1993. His *Heaven* EP followed two roughneck jungle cuts with *This Way*, a track full of soul soothing, sampler-stretched pads and warm bass booms.

In Luton, Justice and Blame began fusing influences from other dance genres with jungle beats, spurred on by hearing LTJ Bukem, and producing early ambient-tinged gems like *Anthemia*. 'Drum & bass was all in a minor key then, with *Mentasm* stabs, and it was all quite dark, being pitched that way,' says Justice. 'Myself and Blame at that point weren't really feeling a lot of stuff that was coming out. We started listening to other stuff—to progressive house, to US garage, and went to places like Garage City. Hearing the sounds they were listening to, it was like, *Wow, these sounds are more in that major scale*. And then we heard LTJ Bukem's *Music*; he'd done *Logical Progression* already, which was quite early. I remember hearing that and thinking, *This is so different to what's going on now*. It was the sound we'd been searching for—something different to break that monotony.'

By 1994, with jungle fully established as its own discrete genre and the ragga-infused Amen break variant becoming recognisable even to the mainstream pop world, the ambient vibe was in full flow too. Records by Sounds Of Life (later to become one half of Source Direct), Blame & Justice, Peshay, Spring Heel Jack, and many more all provided a mellow contrasting sound with the dominant jungle club/soundsystem style. Artists more associated with the heavier incarnation, like Photek (as Aquarius, *Dolphin Tune*) and Doc Scott (*Far Away*) tapped into the ambient mode, and 4hero's galactic drum & bass masterpiece album *Parallel Universe* featured tunes like the chilled and jazzy vocal gem *Universal Love*. Wax Doctor, who had made his name making raw hardcore and proto jungle on Basement Records, delivered the sublime, style-defining *Kid Caprice* for Metalheadz, taking the break from Kurtis Blow's *Do The Do* (one of the earliest of many tunes to do so since) and merging it with a cascading ambient melody and languid funk flute to mesmeric effect. There was a collective realisation that jungle had many more musical applications, and that its fast tempo opened up exciting avenues when combined with influences from elsewhere.

This jazzier, more ambient style of jungle soon had a club to call its own. Just off Tottenham Court Road, near the old Astoria venue in central London, the Mars Bar hosted Speed from late 1994; LTJ Bukem could be found holding court there alongside resident DJs like Kemistry & Storm and Fabio.

'Things started happening,' says Storm. 'We were in Reading one day, at Vinyl, and this guy came up to us called DJ Lee and said, I love what you're playing, and you know I've been talking to Bukem and I want to start this club, I want a main dancefloor for what you're doing. [That] was Speed. The first night, Nicky Blackmarket and Bukem played. We met Photek there, which was really amazing, and then we said, We need to get as many producers as possible down here, because their stuff isn't being played out there at the moment and this is a club where we're highlighting it. It was the first place I met Marcus Intalex—his stuff was being played.

'I said to Lee, How much is this club? and he said three hundred quid,' Storm continues. 'So I thought if we could get 150 producers paying £2 each, we could cover the costs. That was all we were looking to do in the beginning, and when it got going, Fabio was brought in. Then you had a set from Fabio and Bukem, and it was Doc Scott, DJ Lee, and Kemistry & Storm as the warm-up. Because it was so hedonistic, that club, people started coming really early, because they wanted to experience the whole night. It was exciting. It established, if you want to give it a name, drum & bass. You were still playing stuff from Ram Records and True Playaz in there, if you could make it work.'

One of the regulars at Speed was J Majik, the producer responsible for a host of classics, from *Your Sound* to *Arabian Nights* for Metalheadz. First breaking through at the age of fourteen in 1993 with the storming *Six Million Ways To Die* under the name Dextrous—the tune that led Goldie to sign him to the label—J Majik was inspired by the fresh sounds he heard at the club. 'I thought, *How long can you keep making music with a ragga vocal in?*' he told *Melody Maker* at the time. 'Now production has improved, it's become more mature.'

Like Rage, Speed was one of the seminal jungle club nights, and its signature combination of roughneck breaks and the more atmospheric side of the genre attracted a growing crowd of devotees. Bukem's Good Looking label (and its Looking Good offshoot) was concurrently putting out a steady stream of soon-to-be classics. The Wild West saloon bar brilliance of PFM's *The Western* was followed by *One & Only*, a soul-soothing ambient hyper-ballad, combining crisp breakbeats with a yearning lovelorn vocal, aquatic chords, and a lush 808 bassline that made it equally powerful on the dancefloor. 'One of the most monstrous basslines I've ever witnessed was PFM's *One & Only*, dropped by Bukem at the End,' Dead Man's Chest told Red Bull Music Academy in an article about ambient jungle. 'Utter devastation, and from one of the most blissed-out ballads in d&b history.'

Aquarius's *Drift To The Centre* showed Photek's mastery of the mellower mode, while Seba & Lotek's *So Long* managed to make the swift velocity and damaging power of the Amen break a calming energy flow rather than a maelstrom. Bukem's own masterpiece, *Horizons*, with its inspirational Maya Angelou sample ('The horizon leans forward, offering you space to place new steps of change') and dramatic chord stabs, began to get him noticed outside the jungle scene, too. He headlined at the Big Chill, taking ambient jungle to a fresh set of left-field electronicists, and he started doing his Logical Progression nights at Ministry Of Sound and other prestigious venues in the UK and beyond.

Around the same time, soulful tracks began to emanate from across the scene. Adam F's *Circles* pivoted around a haunting electric piano sample from jazz-funk boss Bob James, though with its mystic atmosphere, double bass, and extraordinarily lush arrangement—breaking off on a musical tangent with a new bassline towards its conclusion, only to re-form around that heavenly riff at the end—it was so much more than just a sample-based piece. Meanwhile, DJ Pulse, who had originally broken through as part of the hardcore outfit Dance Conspiracy, started his Creative Wax imprint as an outlet for some of the best ambient and jazz-tinged jungle. In between, he released the soulful, synth-drenched likes of *Let You In* and *Voyager* on Moving Shadow—tracks with the warm feel of deep-house pioneer Larry Heard, but translated into the breakbeat realm.

DJ Tamsin, a resident at Roast, tapped into the ambient style with the sublime *Innocence*, mixing booming subs with gorgeous synth melodies. 'I'm a pretty chill person,' she says. 'I loved the freedom of the jazzier atmospheric jungle. I wish I'd had the opportunity to make more. It was always an inspiring experience.'

The wider music industry eventually recognised this new strand of jungle—and its marketability. Bukem's remix of *Feenin'* by the massive American R&B group Jodeci was released via major label MCA, and the media, especially the dance press, latched onto the sound. In the past, there had been a snobbishness towards hardcore and jungle in the magazines and weekly music papers, where they were sometimes viewed as less worthy of coverage than the more 'sophisticated' likes of house and techno, and either too cheesy or too raw to be given column inches. Now, with the advent of Good Looking Records, LTJ Bukem, and Speed, journalists started to write more approvingly about the genre. Goldie's *Timeless*, released the same year, also contained more ambient-leaning material, like *Angel* and *Sea Of Tears*, so music scribes had something they felt was worthy of writing about, while Bukem, accompanied by the smooth tones of MC Conrad, did an *Essential Mix* for Radio 1 in 1995—an indication that drum & bass could be canonised like other dance genres.

A big problem at this time, though, was rebranding. To differentiate the mellower sound, some began to describe the music as drum & bass rather than jungle. Some promoters used the term to compartmentalise DJs they saw as playing material that was less hard than jungle—and less lyrically focused than the ragga style that predominated.

'Speed was a really interesting club, more musical than Metalheadz was,' says DJ Storm. 'All of a sudden, when you were being booked by a big rave, you were seeing this: jungle in room 1, and in room 2, drum & bass. We were being moved into that room, and I was like, hang on a minute, I'm a junglist. Why are you doing this? I think we all got a bit annoyed about this, saying, Why shouldn't our stuff be on the main floor? The promoter would say, You lot have got a slightly different sound, it's drum & bass, not jungle. I never saw jungle as about a lyric—for me, it was about the bassline.'

The producers and DJs making or playing the more ambient style simply saw it as an extension of jungle—another branch of the tree, rather than a replacement for what already had strong roots. These artists played the same clubs and raves, mixed ragga stuff alongside mellower material, and were deeply embedded in the scene. 'In drum & bass, I don't consciously play across the spectrum,' Doc Scott, who made and played everything from mechanical techstep to mellower ambient jungle, told *Melody Maker*. 'Anything goes, I'm just into good beats at the end of the day. Whether a track has a jazz-tinged edge or an ambient feel or is some industrial techno kind of thing, it doesn't matter. I don't enjoy DJing on just one level.'

Nevertheless, the ambient producers and sound were placed in their own category, and for a while their style became the epitome of cool. Out of this arose the unfortunate terms 'intelligent jungle' and 'intelligent drum & bass'—a troubling genre descriptor that, while it aimed to describe the musicality and depth of the new sound, ended up insulting the entire community. By talking about 'intelligence', the implication was that all other iterations of jungle were somehow stupid or unsophisticated. Considering that most jungle was made or played by black and working-class artists, there was more than a hint of racism and class snobbery embedded in the idea. By rebranding the sound, the name seemed to imply, it could suddenly become acceptable to the ears of white middle-class hipsters.

'It looked like styles were being played off against each other during the mid-90s boom, when drum & bass became really trendy with various magazines,' DJ Flight told Red Bull Music. 'People began differentiating between jungle and drum & bass. Jungle was seen as rough with too much trouble kicking off, and a bit cheesy; d&b was *mature*, for a more refined listener. There was probably a fair bit of underlying racism, too.'

In another sense, the notion of 'intelligent' jungle or drum & bass was a needless complication. 'The name is so condescending to every other form of drum & bass,' T Power says. 'You're talking about a niche scene that is restricting for a lot of people to get into anyway, primarily 'cause of the tempo, and the groove is complicated. It's why house is so popular, even though it's the lowest common denominator.'

Whatever the implications of the genre name, or what people chose to call it, this ambient jungle sound produced many classic records, and it would prove a gateway drug for listeners getting into the sound for the first time. In 1995, 4hero, having already delivered the jazz-tinged classic *Parallel Universe*, produced a self-titled album for R&S ambient offshoot label Apollo under the name Jacob's Optical Stairway. It nodded to their love of Detroit techno, adding deep jazz elements, astral synths, and soul vocals, creating a classic of the era that remains puzzlingly underrated today.

LTJ Bukem's era-defining mix compilation *Logical Progression*, released in 1996, was a snapshot of the greatest tracks to emanate from this micro-scene. It contains tracks like Chameleon's *Links*, made by Tom Middleton and Mark Pritchard (who were behind the ambient/chill-out classic album *76:14* as Global Communication), many of Bukem's best tracks, cuts by Wax Doctor and Moving Shadow's JMJ & Flytronix, and a tune apiece by DJ Trace and DJ Crystl, on hiatus from their usual roughneck material.

The *Logical Progression* series and its companion set, *Earth*—with their lush, sophisticated design on both vinyl and CD—helped set up Good Looking as the scene leader in this particular lane. 'All my money goes straight back into Good Looking, 'cause that's my dream,' Bukem told *DJ Mag* in 2000. 'My dream isn't to drive a Ferrari, do crack, have two mansions and seventeen birds a night. Those things don't turn me on ... I've turned down the money, I've turned down the drugs. People have offered us millions for Good Looking. They've offered us money that makes most record deals look like pocket money. What would happen? OK, so I'm sitting there with ten million pounds. Phew. Blinding. But what have I got? I've got nothing. My label's gone to someone who's given me ten million pounds. I'm a music man at heart, and my whole music and everything I've built have gone somewhere else and I can't control it. I'm like, You couldn't do a worse thing to me than buy my label off me, for any amount of money. ...I've got fifteen staff and twenty artists. I work fifteen hours, seven days a week, for the last ten years, and I don't see it stopping for the next ten.'

Bukem's work ethic was well documented in a late-90s documentary shown as part of the BBC's *Modern Times* series, although his wideboy manager Tony Fordham, who featured heavily, was the character most viewers ended up talking about, due to his amusing antics in business meetings in Japan and on the road with Bukem and his MC, Conrad. 'Bukem's fee can be as much as a thousand pounds for two hours at the turntables with his MC,' runs a quaint voiceover early in the film.

It wasn't until early 2000 that Bukem released his debut artist album, having preferred to tour the world several times and build up Good Looking for the duration of the 90s. *Journey Inwards* allowed him to explore jazz, breakbeat soul, flute-licked funk jams, and trip-hop, as well as drum & bass. 'I'm passionately into drum & bass, but I'm a music man,' he said in a *DJ Mag* cover feature to celebrate the album's launch. 'I like other styles of music, and I buy them and play them and DJ them and want to make them.'

Meanwhile, T Power (Marc Royal), who had started out releasing hardcore with the Sandman on Soapbar Records, was making extraordinary LPs of sprawling ambient jungle. *Self Evident Truth Of An Intuitive Mind* and the epic *Waveform* aimed more for mystic atmospheres than bass heft, yet did compelling new things with the jungle format, adding jazz, techno electronics, and multi-layered cinematic elements to the mixture.

Having been first inspired by hip-hop, T Power got into production in the mid-80s, using a basic ZX Spectrum computer and a hacked Cheetah drum machine to make beats. Rave, with its breakbeats, was immediately appealing, but soon he was drawn to sounds outside of that scene. 'I loved Black Dog intensely, *Spanners* is still one of my favourite electronica albums, and I used to listen to Autechre and stuff like that,' T Power says. 'The rave thing was very open at the beginning, and then, as we began to find this path through, we started to develop a collective vision of where the music might go. That's when the rules and the structure really started to feel restrictive to me, and I started to look outside the scene for interesting stuff, and obviously Warp was right at the forefront of that.'

Tunes like *Lipsing Jam Ring* show this distinct touch of Warp, glimmering with chrome textures and Autechre-like steel snares, while dark surges of synth strings merge with chattering jungle breaks and exultant diva breaths. *Self Evident Truth Of An Intuitive Mind* goes further still, borne of an experimental impulse and influences beyond the core jungle precepts. 'I was being influenced by people outside the scene like Mixmaster Morris, and Rising High at that point, which was going in various directions,' T Power says. 'Something was changing. It was just a culmination of events that got me to that point where I was suddenly gifted the opportunity to put down what was in my head. I finally had enough equipment where I could do that, and enough understanding of how to manipulate breaks. That whole album spewed out of my head in, like, four days. There's no way I could recreate that kind of workflow now. It was just years and years of everything being backed up. That's just how it came out, and it was all these seemingly disparate influences that came together. And it kind of worked.'

Though he was an early contributor to hardcore and jungle, T Power's music never quite fit in. Identifiably similar, yet drawing on more techno elements, it was unusual at the time, and for this reason has aged especially well. 'I was always considered an outsider. I didn't care about fitting in with anyone and I was very outspoken, probably too outspoken, and left myself open to criticism.'

Some of his tunes resonated more than others, though. *Mutant Jazz*, his track with MK Ultra, was a languid, sax-y jazz lilt lounging in a beatific dream. Contrastingly, the single *Police State* was a fourteen-minute, unsettlingly cosmic affair with robotic snare prangs, *Blade Runner* synth swirls, and bright keyboard melodies, dissolving into pure ambience, only to re-emerge as a raw, energetic roller towards its close. This kind of longform track was highly irregular— something that only artists like Goldie did.

'Goldie did it with his album, and Photek, but they were guys who were embraced by the cognoscenti,' T Power says. 'I never was, but *Police State* went down really well. That was one of my more successful releases. There's no question if I hadn't done that, somebody else would have. Other people did, but they were people who weren't embraced by the scene.

'*Police State* would have been one of the first releases where I got a very small ProTools rig, so now the idea of having to sample and record stuff, the idea of there being a limit to that, had gone out of the window. I had as much sample space as my hard drive could handle, whereas we were limited to sample times in Rolands and Akais and E-mus. That changed it. Making *Self Evident Truth* was a massive technical undertaking, 'cause it was on Cubase on the Atari ST, so it was just on a floppy drive. All you could really save was the MIDI data. Getting into hard-disk recording, that changes everything. As with any technology, all of these things that are technically challenging become very easy, you start focusing on other things. You can get more anal about the actual sound of what you're doing. The mix sounds get better, for example. I had a Korg Prophecy, Korg Trinity, a JV-1080, a Supernova, there was a bunch of outboard [hardware equipment], and we had guitar pedal routings for things and fed sound through them.'

Around the same time, Jonny L, who had been on hiatus from rave culture for a few years after his hardcore hit *Hurt U So*, returned with the lush Rhodes keys and vocals of the *2 Of Us* EP on XL Records, inspired by the sound he was hearing emanating from the scene of the time. 'I like the freedom to mix hard with soft sounds, as with rave/hardcore, d&b seems to work especially well doing this,' he says. 'I was excited to be on Richard Russell's XL Recordings, finding my way forward within the d&b sound. I remember some classic LTJ Bukem nights at Ministry Of Sound, string harmonies over rough breakbeats, faster tempos, flowing basslines on an extremely loud soundsystem. The feelgood vibe was attracting more ladies to what was usually a more male-driven sound.'

The Moving Shadow label produced a definitive snapshot of ambient jungle that was another useful primer for the uninitiated, just as *Logical Progression* had been. *Storm From The East*, though devised as a guide to the best producers from the east of England—mostly around Suffolk—had lush ambient tracks from Photek, PFM, EZ Rollers, and JMJ & Richie.

Wax Doctor's *Heat* single for R&S—a label usually more tilted to techno and house—was another late highlight in ambient jungle's brief bloom, and found him shredding the Apache break and lacing it with warm Detroit chords and subtle trumpet licks. Meanwhile, his frequent collaborator Alex Reece was a producer who tended towards the ambient or deep house-influenced sound. After initially making hardcore, his soulful tracks for Metalheadz—*Fresh Jive*, the lush *Basic Principles*, and *I Want You*—were indications of his mastery of both beat and musicality. The music the pair made together, as Unit 1 and Jazz Juice for DJ Pulse's Creative Wax label, was way ahead of the curve.

In 1995, Reece made a seismic contribution to d&b history by creating the divisive tune *Pulp Fiction*: a classic that, with its minimalist kick-snare, two-step beat, would eventually influence the sound of drum & bass as a whole, replacing the breakbeat polyrhythms of the past with a uniform computer-generated, boom-chak clank. Still, most of the music he made was more synth driven and dreamy, and, as a result, Reece became a poster boy for the ambient jungle sound. Picking up remix work from trip-hop label Mo' Wax (he reworked both DJ Krush and Attica Blues), he was one of the first d&b artists to be snapped up by a major label, signing to Island Records subsidiary 4th & Broadway for the 1996 album *So Far*. Though it had pleasant and breezy pop tracks like *Feel The Sunshine*, with its Björk/Emiliana Torrini-esque vocal, it lacked the warmth and transcendent feel of his earlier material.

As ambient jungle abounded, its popularity became widespread, and compilations like React's respectable *Artcore* series moved to capitalise, collecting together the best tracks of the subgenre for the casual listeners who didn't buy twelve-inches. And the term 'intelligent', though often derided, was still used occasionally by the most respected artists in the scene: Reinforced released a *Jungle Book: Intelligent Minds Of Jungle* compilation in '95, the same year that DJ Rap called her artist album with Voyager *Intelligence*.

The notion of an intelligent jungle sound would soon come to signify something else, in the form of the hyper-edited, technical drumfunk of artists like Nucleus, Paradox, Seba, Equinox, and Fracture & Neptune. 'The ambient style was more experimental,' says T Power. 'We wouldn't have had choppage as a subgenre without it, and there were lots of interesting people to come through 'cause of that.'

## IT'S JAZZY

While 1996 was arguably the height of the ambient style's popularity, change was already in the air. Those who liked the musicality of ambient jungle began to err more towards jazz as a source of inspiration, sampling it and employing live musicians. Project 23, a collective led by Cleveland Watkiss—who had appeared on Goldie's *Timeless*—treated drum & bass as more of an organic live band experience, creating the LP *23* for eclectic independent label Dorado. And as noted elsewhere, Roni Size, who had already explored multiple styles of jungle, put together the band Reprazent with a similar urge to merge the live and digital worlds.

Fabio's label Creative Source, which initially featured many early ambient jungle classics, like Carlito's *Heaven*, became far more jazz- and soul-focused in its approach to drum & bass. This particular form would soon come to be known instead as liquid funk, while in reaction to the popularity and breeziness of the ambient style, some producers decided to go the opposite way, pushing a harder, darker, industrial techno influence. Soon, jazziness and techstep were opposing forces, battling it out to become the dominant end-of-the-century sound.

# 14 Milestones & Mavericks: Pushing The Sound Forward

## AFRO-FUTURISM AND THE JUNGLE ALBUM

By the mid-90s, the creative possibilities of jungle/drum & bass were being fully realised, with some of its greatest producers pushing the music to astral heights. And some had begun to view the album as the next logical progression for d&b.

The first truly groundbreaking full-length was 4hero's second album, *Parallel Universe*, released in 1994—a musical, diverse creation that remained true to the tenets of the genre. Its opening track matches spacious jazz-influenced Detroit chords with warm live saxophone and a soul vocal espousing the importance of *Universal Love* sung by Carol Crosby, while on the title track, the beats sway and side-wind to a mystic synth line as a warm sub thrums underneath. This was drum & bass with an Afro-futurist feel, Marc Mac and Dego the cosmonauts beaming the genre's concrete jungle setting into an alternate dimension less governed by hard beats and more by atmosphere and space. On tracks like *Terraforming*, the sample suggests 'we could go and terra-form Mars'—an intimation that they might wipe the slate clean and create an elysian vision of drum & bass far in the stratosphere. *Talk Around Town*, meanwhile, interrupts its heavier bass barrage with a drop into sinister acid bleeps, like a wormhole opening into a frightening forbidden zone of the deep cosmos. Reviewing the album at the time, Simon Reynolds said, 'At its best, *Parallel Universe* is black science fiction in full effect, Sun Ra's *Disco 3000* meets William Gibson.'

Afro-futurism describes science-fiction concepts and ideas as imagined by people of the African diaspora. It's a term developed by the writer Greg Tate, formalised by Mark Dery in 1993, and since popularised by fellow cultural theorists like Kodwo Eshun. In the hands of black musicians (and novelists such as Samuel R Delany or Octavia Butler, or filmmakers like Ryan Coogler, the director of the Marvel Studios blockbuster *Black Panther*), Afro-futurism becomes a method of imagining alternative futures and transcendent states, and of presenting something utopian (or dystopian) that connects with the black experience and history in a new way.

Galactic visions have long been a feature of African-American and more recently black British music. In the States, astral travellers populate the philosophies of cosmic jazz artist Sun Ra and the songs of George Clinton's bands Funkadelic and Parliament, with their *Mothership Connection* and UFO landing imagery. It's there in the Detroit techno of Cybotron and Model 500; in the imaginings of Carl Craig, Jeff Mills, and Drexciya; or in the echo-deck hallucinations of Lee 'Scratch' Perry. In its futuristic manipulation of rhythms, bass frequencies, and sounds, and its hyperkinetic absorption of different forms of music of black origin, remade in a cybernetic structure, Afro-futurism pervades the world of jungle/drum & bass too.

In an interview that accompanies his book *More Brilliant Than The Sun: Adventures In Sonic Fiction*, Kodwo Eshun talks about how science fiction manifests itself on 4hero's classic record. 'I follow breakbeat science,' he says. 'I follow it to the conclusion of tracks of people like 4hero, specifically *Parallel Universe*, where I turn the emphasis and focus on the science in breakbeat. And the thing I notice about breakbeat science, about the way science is used in music in general, is that science is always used as a science of intensified sensation. . . . In this way, science then refers to a science of sensory engineering, so *Parallel Universe* announces this, when it has titles like *Sunspots* or *Wrinkles In Time*, these are the points where the laws of gravity and the laws of time and space collapse, and they're simultaneously saying rhythm is about to collapse when you enter these zones. So you've got someone like Goldie who does *Timeless*, and *Timeless* is obviously referring to simply the infinite loop of the breakbeat, which Goldie's trying to tap into.'

Just as 4hero conjured new worlds beyond the stars in their own image, and would continue to do so on their cosmic, self-titled techno/jungle fusion record as Jacob's Optical Stairway (and Marc Mac side-project Nu Era), and on their subsequent double-album opus *Two Pages*, A Guy Called Gerald explored this Afro-futurist idea with another one of the genre's classic albums, *Black Secret Technology*. A celestial voyage of molten synth pads and lush soul vocals, album track *So Many Dreams* finds its breaks coated in titanium, time-stretched into metallic twists and sensual, sinuous turns. *Finley's Rainbow*, featuring Finley Quaye, repositions the singer's reggae style amid dreamy drifts of electronic and multi-layered melody: it's a futuristic new conception of what black British music could be, driven by cutting-edge technology but rooted in established modes of expression.

Though Gerald Simpson is still most famous for acid-house hits such as *Voodoo Ray*, he was there making breakbeats during the hardcore period, and his pioneering *28 Gun Bad Boy* is considered by many to be one of the very first jungle records. *Black Secret Technology* represented the next step, as Gerald realised he could combine the sounds he'd grown up with—and sounds from further back in history—and synthesise them into something new that continued the vibrant continuum of black musical culture.

'Back then, jazz was a big influence,' he says. 'Drummers-wise, Lenny White, Steve Gadd, those jazz fusion drummers. I discovered them through jazz-funk—I listened to a lot of Herbie Hancock and Weather Report too. I found that with fusion, jazz-rock, it was really fluid. As someone who was a dancer and a listener at that time, an experimenter, it opened me up to the possibilities of the ways you could go.

'What I was finding was, music from all these different places, from America, from Jamaican cousins, different styles of music, you could jigsaw them together,' Simpson continues. 'You could just take a segment of that and it would create this whole new vibe. It felt to me like something was talking to me through this music, still does. So I got deeper and deeper into it and started to look at the earliest stuff—earlier than reggae and ska from Jamaica, like mento and then the cumina, the nyabinghi, all these different tribal things.'

For Gerald, there was a thread running through all of it, a rhythmic connection that, despite the new music's computerised creation, bore a similarity to ancestral African sounds. 'I was like, That is the genetic that was flowing through this music. *Black Secret Technology* was a way of saying, This is old ancestors talking to me through this technology. I was watching some TV programme, and there was this woman saying that there are these codes that are given out to people through different ways, through meditation—whatever—and this is called black secret technology. I thought, *That's the title!* It totally fits.'

Both *Parallel Universe* and *Black Secret Technology* provided possible blueprints of what the future, and drum & bass itself, could offer. It's no coincidence that Goldie's *Timeless* had connections to both: 4hero had already collaborated with Goldie multiple times and released his music through Reinforced, and Marc Mac and Dego worked on the *Timeless* album tracks *Still Life* and *Angel*. Meanwhile, Goldie linked with Gerald on his *Black Secret Technology* track *Energy*. It's possible to see threads of the Afro-futurism idea permeating the cybernetic soul of *Timeless*, with its assimilation of dub, R&B, and jazz-funk amid a storm of platinum breaks and hyper-modernity.

### BREAKBEAT SCIENCE: PUSHING RHYTHM TO ITS LIMITS

Far from the urban sprawls of Manchester and London, an unlikely source was about to produce one of the greatest producers in the history of the genre. In the Suffolk county town of Ipswich, a micro-rave scene had developed in the early 90s and had got the attention of young producer Rupert Parkes, later known as Photek. He'd grown up not far from London, in St Albans, Hertfordshire, where he'd first come across pirate radio stations and been intrigued by the weird sounds he was hearing, at once alien and somehow reassuringly familiar.

'Fantasy FM, Friends FM—some of these stations from back at that time,' Parkes says. 'There were so many great stations then, I think if you jumped on the FM dial you could pick up twelve amazing underground stations at any time. I was listening to hip-hop, soul, funk, reggae, then I started to hear stuff on the radio that had little bits and pieces of the music that I was already familiar with. At first, I was like, *This is weird techno*, then it all started to click to me, and it became relevant through the fact that there were these midtempo rave tunes with breakbeats in them.'

Hip-hop was the gateway drug for Parkes, and soon he was going to his first rave, electrified by this strange, break-driven music. 'The first rave I went to was Telepathy on Marshgate Lane [east London], in a warehouse,' he says. 'I was a complete newbie to the scene. I think it might have been Jumpin Jack Frost playing when I walked in, and I had my first moment of experiencing that. It was a black warehouse with no lights and one green laser. It's like, you stumble out of one of the other exits of this warehouse, and it's all rubble and pieces of concrete, and there's a complete wasteland outside—a total hazard, you know? That defined it for me. First of all, I had all this stuff in my imagination from listening to pirate radio. Then my first actual experience was Telepathy, and I think the next place I went was Labyrinth in Dalston Lane. I'm grateful that they were my first two rave experiences.

'Labyrinth was a madhouse! I thought, *This is literally a lunatic asylum*, when I went in there for the first time. As a teenager, walking into a completely unfamiliar environment—my only cultural foundation was hip-hop at this moment—I walk in with a particular outlook of the world, and it's lunatics dancing. Crazy, UV lights with people's teeth and eyeballs glowing in the dark. There were stairways that led up to a dark corner and you'd try and look like you knew what you were doing, and you'd walk up these stairways and it would be a dead end. I was completely out of my comfort zone in there, and then there's sweat dripping from the roof, condensation dripping, it's like, *Who spat at me, who threw their drink at me?* Everyone's together there, but it's intimidating the first time you walk in. By the time I went there the second time, it was like home for me. It had a huge effect on the music I made ever since, honestly.'

When he moved to Ipswich, Parkes was determined to start making his own version of jungle, but he had no idea how. After studying music magazines, he scraped together some cash and went to an equipment shop in the nearby city of Norwich, where he was shown just the gear he needed to start creating tracks.

'It was the nearest big shop that had professional gear. The guy showed me a Roland W30 Workstation. I think I had my eye on an Akai S-1000 sampler or something. I said, I think I need this, and the guy said, You probably do, but what are you doing for sequencing? I was like, What do you mean, doesn't that thing sequence things too? He said, This machine does it all, and from the sound of what you want to do, this could be it. So that salesman sold me the right bit of gear. It had a keyboard to tap with your fingers, it had a sequencer in it to record what you were doing, it had a disk drive in it so you could save all your work and it had a sampler in it with some preset synth sounds. It was pretty limited, but it had all the different elements that I needed. That's how I got started—I locked myself up in a room for six months, and all I did was figure out what I could do with a pair of headphones and this keyboard. It was another year before I met anyone else who made music. When I did, it rolled from there and there was this whole culture I didn't know about, of studios and music making, white labels and manufacturing records and this kind of thing.'

Meeting like-minded ravers magnetised by Ipswich's Essential Selection record shop, Parkes's earliest excursion on wax was a collaboration. 'Rob

Solomon, the founder of the shop, had a studio in his back garden with his brothers,' he says. 'He'd do a soundsystem with them, reggae and soul, they were just starting to release their own vinyl singles, so they understood a bit about how to make records, how to master, how to get them manufactured, how to distribute them. I learned a lot from them. Rob took an interest in rave music at that time, and he started Rude Boy Records and the alias Origination, which I was part of, but it was his creation. He had a big hit with the tune *Shine On*. I teamed up with him on a lot of stuff and I learned about how to make records and music from it.'

Parkes's first solo release under the name Studio Pressure, 1993's *Jump*, appeared on the Ipswich-based Certificate 18 imprint (which would itself become a significant player in drum & bass). With its sampled synth chords, layered breaks, and metallic bass clanks, the track had a distinct style that stood out from the crowd. Over subsequent releases, he would hone his sound into a hybrid of Detroit techno melody and mysticism, micro-spliced drums, and science-fiction atmospheres. On his own Photek label, Parkes emitted epics like *The Physical*, loaded with crushing sub-bass and beats that sound like a rhythmic transmission from deep space, all flanged textures and rhythms plus warping synths. *Fusion* matches breathy female vocals with dusty processed synth chords and endlessly unfolding, lush jazz breaks, and *Resolution* has a snaking synth sequence that sounds closer to something that would have come out on Warp Records at the time, allied to stop/start, hazy breaks. They all had an abstract dreamlike quality, yet also the roughneck edge and bass weight required for club play. This was something new.

'I wanted to make the coolest music I could think of—blow any other tune I liked out of the water with a new take on it,' Parkes says. 'I was really looking to push and do incredible music that I wanted to hear. It was within the boundary and format of that type of music. I had all these frameworks of things that I thought were good, or maybe combinations of things that hadn't been done yet that I wanted to hear. There were a handful of people doing these killer edits with beats. Really one of the biggest influences for me were Shut Up & Dance, because they had this hip-hop reggae element but were killing it in raves. The way they would chop and edit beats—when I realised what they were doing, a whole world of possibilities entered my mind.'

Detroit techno was a key influence on Photek, though like most producers making jungle at the time, he didn't have access to a raft of analogue synths. Instead, Parkes reached for the sampler. 'Because I didn't come from a synthesizer or music-studio background, I wasn't that guy who knew about Juno-106s or how to patch synths,' he says. 'I would just look for samples that contained the textures of those instruments. It was over the years that I realised if I go and buy the right synth, like a Roland D50, that sound is in there. I didn't need to go and forage for it. It's an instrument that you can go and buy, like a guitar. I didn't know that then. I just thought, *If I get this saw string and EQ it the right way, and put a reverb on it, then it's going to sound like that sound on a Carl Craig record*.

'There was a much easier way: just buy that keyboard and you'll be able to replicate that very easily. But none of that occurred to me, because I had no formal intro to making electronic music. Everything I did was totally improvised. I'd quite often find just a little flute sound, off some world music record. I'd trim it and put some attack and release on it, put it through a reverb, then I would get a flute-y synth sound. That was probably a preset on some other synth Carl Craig was using. He was a synth guy, he knew how to make that sound, and I improvised that out of collaging together a few samples. In pursuing that sound, I created a different one by mistake.'

Parkes's next step was far from accidental, though. The *Seven Samurai* EP drew on his love of films (already evident in the sampled dialogue from movies that littered his earlier work)—in particular, martial-arts flicks or the classics of Japanese director Akira Kurosawa—to create something highly atmospheric and rhythmically captivating. With the splashing drama of gong hits, East Asian percussion, and breaks that sound more like samurai katana swords clashing in a ferocious, balletic battle, he constructed something that resembled an elaborate movie action sequence rather than something you'd hear in a rave.

'Obviously, the title of *Seven Samurai* says a lot,' Parkes says. 'I started with the typical kung-fu flicks, and then it moved onto cinema classics like Kurosawa. As much as street culture, as much as raves, I was putting film score and film sound into music. I wasn't the first person who had sampled a movie, that's for sure. There were people like Depth Charge, who was incorporating Sergio Leone samples in his stuff, and I thought that was amazing, 'cause it tied that whole field together. A *Bounty Killer* sample in there, and suddenly it makes even more sense. I think I got that concept of tying a musical thematic with a little cinema bite that could be the glue that pulled that idea together. That concept had already been established, and at the time you had Wu-Tang Clan, *36 Chambers*, all this other hip-hop stuff that was incorporating this martial arts flavour into it. You put all that together with where drum & bass was going at that time.'

Photek took his martial-arts-inflected style to Goldie's Metalheadz label with the *Natural Born Killa* EP (an Oliver Stone/Tarantino film reference), matching sword-clashing breaks on *Consciousness* with the unexpected and sublime trip-hop of *Into The 90s*. There was a brief diversion onto Kirk Degiorgio's techno label Op Art with the spacious ambient d&b of *T'Raenon*, but more was to come from his cinematic, stealth-ninja persona, and that manifested when Parkes signed to major label Virgin's dance imprint Science. The single *Ni-Ten-Ichi-Ryu* (Japanese for 'two-sword technique') and its flipside, *Fifth Column*, refined the razor-sharp swordplay of his previous work, with sampled slams, clanks, and metal percussion, creating something that sounded like an elaborate and frenetic rhythmic ceremony. At once highly futuristic and ancient, like the Japanese culture Parkes had come to revere as a martial arts student himself, *Fifth Column* saw him pushing his production to its limit, sampling real-world objects like a film Foley artist to help conjure his cinematic atmospheres. He went to great lengths to mimic the sound of a shuriken throwing star whistling through the air to connect with its target.

'At that time, there was no internet, no email even,' he says. 'There were sample CDs, which were few and far between, with sound effects in. This was your access to sounds. So you had to be creative—you couldn't download a sample pack, or get someone to drop you a zip file with a shit ton of sound effects in it. So, for that shuriken sound, I got a throwing star, experimented a bit with a microphone to figure out how to capture [the sound], and what I realised was that throwing the star and just putting a mic in the room wasn't going to get it at all, 'cause they don't make very much sound. For movies where they fake the sound and exaggerate it, you have in your mind what that should sound like. So I first of all balanced it on my fingernails, and then flicked it in the air like you'd flip a coin, so that it had a bit of *pling* to it. Then you had the *shing!* coin-toss sound. I got a bicycle brake cable, and I whipped that round a few times to make a whipping sound. I did probably a hundred swipes and then had to edit them together to make it sound like it was something flying through the air. Then I got the actual throwing star and threw it into a piece of wood. That probably took a day and a half to put together, just to get that sound effect that lasted a second, a second and a half. But it was epic, it was worth the time.'

His beat manipulation and expert grasp of mood would inform his debut album as Photek, *Modus Operandi*, a record full of dark, tense jazz inflected beats. *The Hidden Camera* perfectly illustrates this, looking not to the soporific chill-out jazz flavours that some producers had begun to specialise in by this point, but instead to the psychedelic, dark vibes conjured by 1970s Miles Davis or Billy Cobham.

Another artist who would feature on the Metalheadz imprint and take drum & bass into new dimensions was Dillinja. Karl Francis, a south Londoner who had been raised on hip-hop and reggae music, had a deep connection to the latter, going to soundsystem dances in his early teenage years and growing fascinated with the technology behind their speaker arrays. Learning the intricacies of construction from an amp engineer for Jah Shaka, he endeavoured to build his own system aged sixteen, and before long he was making his own tunes too in his bedroom, influenced by time spent at the Digidub studio in Camberwell.

'Everything stems down to soundsystem culture. That's the root of it,' he told UKF. 'I did grow up with a lot of soundsystems around me in Brixton. Especially King Tubby's. I had friends with the same passion as me at school, so we bounced off each other. I've been obsessed with [soundsystems] from a young age.'

Stirring together ingredients from his musical influences, Dillinja over time crafted a unique style, merging the punishing sub-bass of his soundsystem knowledge with sped-up breakbeats from his hip-hop side. His first tunes, like 1992's *Tear Off Your Chest*, a collaboration with Batmix, had a straight-ahead b-boy block-party energy, mixed with that signature low-end. But by 1994, Dillinja was making sounds that were way ahead of the curve. *Deadly Deep Subs* on his own label, Deadly Vinyl, has ricocheting Think break snippets and spelunking dub frequencies, with eerie sample residues from Kevin Saunderson's early Chicago house track as Reese, *Just Want Another Chance*, adding a heady psychedelic synth component to its damaging rhythmic assault. *Sovereign Melody* from the same year demonstrated a gift for sample sorcery, splicing funk guitar runs and vocal drifts with ingeniously and laboriously cut-up drum breaks, again putting the Think beats through the wringer, before embarking on minimalist, dub-heavy sections where the throbbing bass takes centre stage. 'I got a little vibe from hip-hop and also jazz fusion,' he told *Atmosphere* magazine in 1994. 'It depends what sort of feel I get from what [tune] I started.'

Dillinja's genius was not only about futuristic, hyper-shredded beats and chest-caving bass; it was the highly prolific producer's ability to move between melodic sounds and heads-down, roughneck jungle. As Trinity, he made the hard-as-nails tunes *Chapter 19* and *20* on V Recordings—Amen rampages with dub bleeps and psychedelic touches of synth and bird song, plus bass you could feel as well as hear. *Gangsta* saw him delve deep into the reggae archive, with a moody dancehall synth figure and ragga lyrics put through the time-stretch mangle. Though associated with heavier tracks, Dillinja could also turn his hand to the atmospheric ambient sound: 1994's *Deep Love*, a collaboration with Mystery, chimed perfectly with the jazzy Bukem style.

Perhaps his most high-profile release of the time was his EP on Metalheadz, *The Angels Fell*. The title track, with its *Blade Runner* soundtrack samples, drew from a deep well of sci-fi inspiration. Starting off atmospheric, with drifting, re-pitched ambient textures and the wax and wane of electroid bass, its breaks seem to shatter, reflect, and reform, before dropping into a spinning portal of drums that slip in and out of FX chains, translating the sound-desk manipulations of dub into the breakbeat domain. The beats are time-stretched, filtered, delayed, and layered into avant-garde rhythmic passages that could work a dancefloor and still sound futuristic now. *Ja Know Ya Big* on the flip brutalises an Amen with tape-echo effects of the kind that few have even tried since, adding a lethal guitar lick before it drops into a barrage of bass so heavy it's like being hit with a boulder.

While his breakthrough material is among some of the best jungle ever made, Dillinja would go on to refine his style further, mastering first the kick-snare techstep sound and then jump-up, while remixing everyone from Björk to Faith No More and Jeru Tha Damaja, demonstrating both his wide appeal and also his extremely high hit rate. Tunes like *Threshold* (as Cybotron) show his adaptability to the techstep style.

'What you can do is look at the elements that are relative to the time and then, over a series of releases, make that sound your own,' he told *Knowledge* magazine. 'Steer it in your own original direction and put your own stamp on things, something that I've always tried to do throughout my career.'

Later, he'd collaborate with Lemon D and co-found the Valve label, and the two would employ Dillinja's soundsystem knowledge to build their own Valve system, which became famed for its power and potency. 'We used the same type of boxes King Tubby's [system] were using in the 80s, and put modern speakers in them,' Dillinja said. 'We built some high-end boxes as well. We changed them for professional ones in the end, because we needed to split the tops, mids, and bottoms more, but everything else was old-school built. So many people [were] saying how they'd never felt bass like it before. People *felt* drum & bass how it's meant to be felt. Not heard ... felt.'

Lemon D (real name: Kevin King) made a significant mark on junglist history with many 90s innovations. Adapting his artist name from French newspaper *Le Monde*, he was making hardcore back in '92 on the Planet Earth label, with EPs such as *DJ On Wax* considered classics today and changing hands for eyewatering sums on Discogs. By '95, he'd refined his production into a needlepoint-precise jungle method, with tunes like *Feel It* inhabiting that interzone between atmospheric bliss and Amen-shredded ferocity. His Metalheadz EP *Urban Flava* brought the hazy vibe of American jazz fusion and West Coast G-funk into the genre, with *Urban Style Music* a nimble-footed studio manipulation of cymbals, snares, flutes, and warm Rhodes chords. Deftly tripping from section to section while remaining cohesive, this was an audio journey that still made sense on the dancefloor, while its flipside, *This Is LA*, imagined Compton's Most Wanted at Speed, dropping wailing gangsta-rap synths over punishing breakbeat pressure. With its lush jazz sample and ingenious breakbeat sorcery, *I Can't Stop*, released that same year on V Recordings and recently revived by DJ Sherelle, cemented Lemon D's funk credentials. Going on to cut tracks for Prototype, R&S and Trouble On Vinyl, and co-found Valve Recordings with Dillinja, Lemon D is one of the greatest—and yet somewhat unsung—producers to make his mark in d&b.

In a genre where studio knowhow and scalpel-sharp editing skills are highly prized, Equinox (Marlon Sterling) is a cut above most. Releasing records since 1993, the producer has gained a reputation for his beat-chopping, taking the rhythmic contortion of jungle as far as it can possibly go. Starting out working with mentor and hardcore/jungle pioneer Bizzy B, and inspired by everything from Detroit techno and the Black Dog to Shut Up & Dance, he quickly mastered the art of break edits, releasing bona fide beat pressure at the height of the ragga-jungle explosion in '94.

'My uncles used to be DJs back in the 80s, playing soul, funk, electro, hip-hop, and house, so I was influenced by music from a young age,' he says. 'I was always buying records, and started mixing around '88, '89, so from acid house to Detroit techno, I followed the music through the rave scene. I was young, but I was listening to pirate radio until I was old enough to go raving, obviously with a fake ID. It was the *Bones Breaks* series that inspired me to start making music—I used to muck around with a little Casio SK5 keyboard, sampling loops and running them through my Amiga using a program called Future Sound. That was when I had an Amiga 500. I wanted to express myself through the music, whether it was angry, dark, whatever. Hearing people like Black Dog, A Guy Called Gerald, Carl Craig and the Detroit techno guys, 4hero and Bizzy B, all these guys inspired me, all the different sounds in the late 80s and early 90s. I didn't have much equipment, but I tried to do what I could then.'

Using a few bits of borrowed gear, he received one particular piece of advice at the time that resonated and helped set him on the path to forging his own sound. 'I was young and I didn't really know what I was doing, I had no one showing me, so I was mucking around,' he says. 'It was only when I met Bizzy B in '92 . . . obviously I was a big fan of his music, and he heard the demo tape of what I was trying to do, and then he showed me the light and gave me [software tracker] OctaMED. That was my main tool then. But before that, I was borrowing a Roland D5 synth and a Boss Dr Rhythm drum machine from a friend, and Future Sound. That's what I used to make the demos I sent to Bizzy, and from there I started using OctaMED, in '92. It was a four-track, with eight-bit quality sampling. I wanted to change my computer—I knew that everyone was using Ataris, but with the Atari I needed to buy a sampler, and I was a kid and I didn't have the money then. But Bizzy said, Nah, keep the Amiga. I used OctaMED and I was changed forever. Big love to Bizzy B and the Brain crew, because he's my foundation—the sound I've got all comes from the Brain camp originally.'

Where many of his peers began to make metallic techstep and moody kick-snare beats as the 90s came to a close, Equinox doubled down on the breaks-driven original sound. Tunes like 2002's *Coastal Vision* mix blissful ambient pads with cascading, funked out drums; the spacious *From Above* has the lush quality of prime Good Looking Records, with a harder-edged ear for beats. *Love Thy Brother*, meanwhile, with its classic roots-reggae sample, mixes crisp, multi-layered hits with techy loops, giving jungle a futurist sheen, and the titanium tough Amen roll-out *Acid Rain* for Inperspective Records proved there were yet more new ways to manipulate that most famous of breakbeats.

'There's something about Amen,' Equinox says. 'Energy! You can use it on a militant tip, or a mellow tip as well. No matter what style of music it is, when that beat kicks in, the energy goes off, everyone goes nuts. That break makes people come alive.'

Meanwhile, tracks such as *Breakestra Ting* found him uncovering hitherto unused rhythmic samples and meticulously slicing them into shards of sinuous mechanical groove. With several others, like Seba and Paradox, he was tagged with a new subgenre, drumfunk, which described artists inspired by classic jungle and dedicated to the (then) vanishing art of the drum edit.

'I love edits,' he says. 'I don't stick to simple breaks—no matter what break I use, it has to be chopped. It's more drumfunk than other stuff for sure, but I chop up my beats a bit more. I like quite scatty and long patterns. I love processing breaks.'

Equally central to Equinox's sound is a dedication to the dub, roots reggae, and soundsystem culture that had such a formative part to play in the creation of jungle/drum & bass. 'I'm heavily influenced from dub—the term drum & bass for me comes from the roots-style soundsystems from the 70s; Jah Shaka, Fatman Hifi, and Lloyd Coxsone, just to name a few. Those soundsystems were a massive inspiration to me growing up. It definitely appealed to me when the music stripped back to the actual drums and bass with effects and delays. Bass you feel in your chest, that's the foundation for me.'

Together with DJ, producer, and label owner Chris Inperspective, Equinox started the Technicality club night at Herbal in London's Shoreditch area in 1999—an event that sought to keep the original jungle ethos going at a time when the kick-snare drum & bass sound and techstep dominated the scene. 'We were friends and decided to do the night together,' Equinox says. 'It was his idea, [but] it was our decision to roll and do this, pushing the beats we wanted to hear out, as we weren't hearing what we wanted. Inspired by what Bukem did, he went off and did his little atmospheric thing with Fabio, doing the Speed night. If you want to hear a certain sound and you're not hearing it, you go off and do your own thing.'

A similar ethos was behind Equinox's Scientific Wax label, which acted as an outlet for old-school material at a time when few others were releasing it. 'That's what I did with Sci Wax—bring back the elements I wanted to hear. We've been doing this sound for ages now. We've stuck to our guns and do what we like. We struggled for a while, but we've never left it and we still do it, always have done and always will. People are sick of Amens? I don't care. I do it personally for myself and the crew on the label—we do it from the heart. We're evolving, but we're still doing our thing.'

Equinox's approach was without compromise, which is something he maintains to this day.

Drum & bass's broad-church nature is evidenced by the success of John B, who at first glance looks more at home in an electro-goth-industrial scene. The term 'maverick' is an apt description of this prolific producer, whose career began in 1996 via a series of releases on DJ SS's Formation label.

Tapping into both the steely vibes of techstep and the floaty feel of ambient jungle, his track *Secrets* featured on Grooverider's seminal *Prototype Years* compilation. But his 2001 track *Up All Night* on Metalheadz—an anthemic dancefloor smash that moves from a blissful acidic intro and vocal samples into a terrifyingly tough stomp of rave stabs and seething Reese bass—would make him a huge name in the scene. Rather than repeat this trick, he instead began to draw from sounds from beyond the genre, with tunes influenced by synth-pop, electro, and trance motifs. Launching the Nu Electro label, he put out tracks like the 80s-influenced *American Girls* and the excellent New Order-referencing *Blue Eyeshadow*, with its enormous synths and euphoric emotion, and has since remained in a category of one with his synth-driven, neon-lit productions that feel like a hyper-speed musical update of a John Hughes film.

St Albans duo Source Direct also deserve a mention when it comes to producers operating at the vanguard of the scene. Tapping into a similar source of samurai-swordplay breakbeats as that uncovered by Photek, *Snake Style* on their own label has a spooky, late-night cinematic feel in its eerie samples, while the drums tumble and chase in balletic movements. *The Crane*, all Amen tricknology and minimalist FX, intensified the martial arts vibe. After releases for Good Looking and other labels, they signed to Virgin's Science imprint and released the cult classic *Exorcise The Demons* album, and had their tune *Call & Response* featured in the Hollywood Wesley Snipes movie *Blade*.

## BE TRUE: MAINTAINING THE JUNGLE SOUND

At a time when the polyrhythmic manipulations of jungle had been more or less swept aside by the clanking kick-snare beats of techstep, there were a few true believers who helped maintain the sound via their club nights and record labels. Technicality at Herbal—run by DJ, producer, and label boss Chris Inperspective alongside the aforementioned Equinox—became a place where lovers of rolling beats and bass could reliably hear not just classic tracks but also new tunes made in the jungle style. Few other clubs were playing breakbeat-driven jungle then, so the original Technicality crew of Bailey, Equinox, Wilsh, Golden Child, Killa B & Blackeye, and Fracture & Neptune attracted a loyal following.

'We were like, *With you all going that way, we're going over here,*' says Chris Inperspective. 'Anyone who wants to come over here can come with us.' The event grew out of his Inperspective label, which he started in 1997 as a reaction to the dominance of kick-snare drum patterns. Putting out drum-shredding cuts by Equinox, ASC, and Breakage, Inperspective kept the fire burning for fans of beat edits and sub-heavy bass during fallow years for the original jungle sound.

'All the stuff I was listening to was all chopped up—there were no simple beats,' Chris says. 'And then, in '95, *Pulp Fiction* came out. I started Inperspective 'cause I was pissed off with *Pulp Fiction*, and I started Technicality 'cause I was pissed off that I couldn't get Inperspective releases played. I thought, *We'll start our own club.*'

A huge influence on attendees like Double O and Mantra, who went on to found the Rupture club night, Technicality was an inspiration, too, to artists who continued to make rolling beats when few others were doing so—tunes like Breakage's 2007 classic *Clarendon*, for example.

In the years since Technicality's heyday at Herbal, Inperspective has continued to be a vital presence in the dance underground, bridging the gap between generations of producers and contributing to the vibrant resurgence of popularity that jungle has enjoyed in recent years. Chris Inperspective, together with Chris Dexta of Diffrent and Rob Vndnnwnhysn of One Seventy, also launched Clashmouth, a drum & bass vinyl market event that brings together various independent labels in a way that has galvanised the underground dance scene.

'Originally I started going to record fairs, and I had a pitch,' he says. 'We had all these techno labels around us, going, *Great, there's loads of techno fans here, are there no drum & bass fans? Why don't we fill a room with jungle fans, it would be way better!* So I thought of a drum & bass-only vinyl label market. We did the first Clashmouth at [London bar] Café 1001 for about thirteen labels, the second one we had twenty-two. Now we've moved to House Of Vans, we have about forty-two labels. What's mad is that every event we do, the list of people that don't get in gets longer and longer. We're in a position where we might have to move again, the manufacturing industry in the UK absolutely loves us right now. We're encouraging all these labels to sell vinyl.'

In their own ways, each of these scene mavericks has maintained the rebel ethos at the heart of the jungle genre. Refusing to conform, challenging the mainstream, daring to push further than others, they epitomise the renegade flair of drum & bass. Each of these breakbeat scientists has pushed the boundaries, and, in the process, they have inspired many others to think differently, too.

# 15 DJs Take Control:
## The Mainstream, The Media, And Reckoning With Sexism

In the 1990s, the inner sanctum of drum & bass—an extension of the core that had made up the ad hoc Jungle Committee—ensured that the heart of the scene remained close-knit and protected against mass commercialisation. Not in an organised way but in attitude. Bastardisations of drum & bass weren't going to get through the net, because the DJs wouldn't play the tracks out—simple as that. As the 1991 Raindance old-school hardcore anthem by SL2 would have it, the DJs had taken control. 'We aren't going to get any Kylie Minogue drum & bass—we've got it locked off,' said V Recordings chief Bryan Gee at a Planet V event in Brixton in the late 90s.

'We tried to protect the genre from going outside and becoming washing-up commercials in Germany,' says Goldie.

There had been a real danger of a watered-down version of drum & bass being co-opted by the mainstream in other ways, however. These tracks wouldn't generally come from within the scene itself, but from opportunistic interlopers from outside.

Drum & bass producers started off chiefly remixing other drum & bass artists, but then a few got hired to remix house tracks too. Roni Size brilliantly overhauling *It's Alright, I Feel It!* by Nu Yorican Soul, aka house-music stalwarts Masters At Work (Kenny Dope and 'Little' Louie Vega), was a masterpiece that did wonders for the fledgling scene Stateside. Just as 'Fatboy Slim remix', or before it 'Andy Weatherall remix', had become a lazy record-industry buzzword for the ultimate in cool, so 'drum & bass remix' in 1996–97 became semi-ubiquitous—almost a cliché—as mediocre indie bands or wannabe-hip TV shows or adverts sought to extend their cool cachet.

Some of the junglists newly signed by majors were easy to turn to for A&R men. Goldie remixing Björk, Alex Reece taking on techno troubadours

Underworld, or Dillinja remixing Everything But The Girl—or indeed anybody at all—wasn't about to dilute the sound irredeemably. This was DJ/producers taking on remixes on their own terms, and their revamps only served to spread the drum & bass gospel further into other scenes. In this period, most d&b producers concentrated on their own original material, or remixing others from within the dance scene.

### 'COFFEE TABLE' DRUM & BASS

Everything But The Girl were an indie duo who shot to prominence in 1984 when their debut album, *Eden*, became a word-of-mouth hit among students and assorted alternative music fans. Just over a decade later, when Roni Size and his Reprazent crew were preparing *New Forms*, they sampled the album's opening salvo—the jazzy horns that begin lead single *Each & Every One*.

After a string of albums on which they switched up various styles, the group's Tracey Thorn and Ben Watt—along with a host of other rock and pop musicians—fell in love with the dance-music scene. EBTG gave house-music pioneer Todd Terry their track *Missing* to remix in 1995, and it soon became a worldwide Top 10 hit. John Coxon from art-core drum & bass act Spring Heel Jack had worked on the previous year's *Amplified Heart*, the mainly acoustic album that *Missing* first appeared on. He also worked on 1996's *Walking Wounded*, the band's highest-charting album to date, which saw them explore electronic styles more than ever before. With its gently coiled kicks and snares, sweeping cinematic strings, and muted off-kilter breakbeats, the title track was twisted into a 'coffee table' drum & bass UK Top 10 hit that nestled into the same ballpark as Bristol acts Massive Attack and Portishead. Indeed, Tracey Thorn had guested on Massive Attack's enduring *Protection* a few years previously. And Rob Haigh turned in a divine Omni Trio version that was more for clubs such as Speed, helmed by Bukem and Fabio, yet still kept the melancholia of his masterpiece *Renegade Snares*.

Almost at the diametric opposite end of the spectrum to *Incredible*, the M-Beat and General Levy ragga-jungle missive that had hit no. 8 a couple of years previously, *Walking Wounded* followed Goldie's peerless *Inner City Life* into the UK singles chart—peaking at no. 6 in April 1996—and further cemented d&b's rep without selling out to crass commercialism. With Coxon himself hailing from the scene—albeit the more experimental side—and Thorn and Watt respected for their craft, musicianship, and evident enthusiasm for fresh sounds, this was merely seen as a new flava rather than some mainstream sell-out. As if to underline his authenticity, Ben Watt became a DJ himself, at the age of thirty-five—urged to do so by producer/collaborator Howie B, who'd worked with Goldie in the early 90s—and was soon running his own London club night, Lazy Dog, and an acclaimed dance label, Buzzin' Fly.

Similarly, Liverpool-born electronic act Apollo 440—based around brothers Trevor and Howard Gray, and post-punk multi-instrumentalist Noko—had featured MC Stevie Hyper-D in some of their early 90s live shows. When they followed up their 1994 tech-trance album *Millennium Fever* with the more conceptual *Electro Glide In Blue*, then released *Ain't Talkin' 'Bout Dub* as a single in early '97, they were also kind of given a pass. The track kicks in with a searing, sped-up guitar riff sampled from hoary heavy-metallers Van Halen's 1978 single *Ain't Talkin' 'Bout Love*.

### TELEVISION: DRUG OF THE NATION

It was in the realm of theme tunes and TV advertisements that commercialisation was more problematic. There was nothing stopping an advertising agency commissioning or pulling from the music library metaphorical shelf a slice of 'drum & bass' made by a jobbing music producer who fancied having a stab at some d&b using an Amen preset. In a potentially cack-handed attempt to enhance their street cred, it could then be blared to millions—and there was nothing a bunch of London-based DJs could do about it.

As the undeniable sound *du jour* by '97–98, drum & bass popped up in everything from Sky One sound beds to ads for deodorant or home-improvement store B&Q. But again, the drum & bass scene was lucky to have fans of the music in the right place at the right time. As documented in Brian Belle-Fortune's excellent late-90s snapshot of the scene, *All Crews*, a couple of producers named Kyan and Ray, aka Survivors, made it their business to make drum & bass for TV ads. Regulars at AWOL at Paradise in Islington back in the day, their ambition had been to make a tune that Grooverider would play out—just like Goldie at around the same time. They did get the seal of approval from Groove, and other DJs like Randall, Kenny Ken, and Bailey, and through hustling via various music and media-related day jobs they 'were commissioned to make music for Kiss 100 FM, Lucozade, trails for Box TV, and the backing track for an Eric Cantona documentary', according to *All Crews*.

Most impressively of all, they scored the music for a new ad campaign for Red Stripe, a Jamaican lager popular at the Notting Hill Carnival and elsewhere. Using footage shot in Jamaica by the eminent black film director Spike Lee, it featured a DJ pumping out drum & bass and ended on the tagline 'Jamaica. Good and proper.' The advert's director, Paul Leeves, said at the time, 'I set out to make a film with a harder edge than the usual hammock and palm tree offerings we have become used to with Caribbean products. Red Stripe is a strong brand that now has a tough film to go with it.'

After missing out on signing Goldie, the wags in the EMI A&R department were evidently tickled when presented with a white label of the theme tune to kitsch 70s British sitcom *Are You Being Served?*—reworked in a drum & bass style. Created by the same writers as other 'classic' BBC sitcoms like *Dad's Army*, *Are You Being Served?* was set on the sales floor of a retro department store. The theme tune, written by in-house light-entertainment composer Ronnie Hazlehurst, features old-fashioned cash registers ringing and a lift attendant giving a breezy rundown of the goods for sale on each floor ('First floor telephones, gents readymade suits, shirts, socks, ties, hats, underwear and shoes, going down ...'). Reworking it into a drum & bass pastiche won't have taken the producers—who named themselves Grace Brothers, after the ageing owners of the department store on the fictional TV show—very long. No wonder its architects have keep their identities a secret on Discogs to this day.

Mailed out to regional radio DJs for a cheap laugh, the novelty track actually reached no. 51 in the UK singles chart in April 1996, and it could've had a detrimental effect on d&b in a similar way to how various kids TV themes infected rave (*Sesame's Treat*, *Trip To Trumpton*, et cetera). But it was brushed off by most as harmless, a bit of a laugh—and it may even have got a few bored, stay-at-home parents familiarised with a sanitised, Middle England-friendly version of this jungle thing that their kids were out raving to.

### THE THIN WHITE DUKE

David Bowie was the most iconic, if not important, musician of the last fifty years. His ability to experiment, trend-spot, paint lyrical images, and create new personas—chameleon-like—usually kept him one step ahead of the curve.

After dalliances with mod, music hall, and folk styles in the 60s, he created the androgynous Ziggy Stardust character and effectively kicked off the glam-rock movement. He moved to America after killing off Ziggy, recording *Young Americans* in Philadelphia with soul, funk, and disco musicians (his 'plastic soul' period), and formulating his Thin White Duke persona, before moving to Germany and—inspired by Kraftwerk and kraut-rockers like Neu! and Can—experimenting with electronic music with Brian Eno for the so-called Berlin Trilogy of albums, *Low*, *"Heroes"*, and *Lodger*.

The UK's early 80s New Romantic movement was heavily inspired by Bowie, who handpicked outrageously dressed Blitz club regulars for his *Ashes To Ashes* video, which catapulted him back into the mainstream. Then he teamed up with Chic funkateer Nile Rodgers for *Let's Dance*, before temporarily abandoning his solo career for the Tin Machine band project that predated Britpop.

Back with Nile Rodgers in '93 for the album *Black Tie White Noise*, which contains bits of soul, jazz, and hip-hop, in 1995 he was reunited with Eno for the quasi-industrial album *1. Outside*, during the making of which Bowie was apparently listening to a lot of drum & bass. According to collaborator Reeves Gabrels, someone from Bowie's office was recording Fabio & Grooverider's BBC Radio 1 show every week and sending it to him on DAT or cassette.

Bowie and his band went on tour with industrial act Nine Inch Nails to promote *1. Outside*, then did the festival circuit in the summer of '96. After their headline slots, they'd invariably go along to the dance tent to check out the sounds. 'I was an Underworld fan and David was a Prodigy fan, so we were having those arguments—like, *Who's better, The Beatles or the Stones?*' recalls Reeves Gabrels. 'We'd seen both of those bands live, and things just kind of naturally seep in when you're in that community.'

In the spring of '96, Bowie had recorded *Telling Lies*, featuring a typically obtuse vocal narrative over polyrhythmic percussion that was clearly influenced by drum & bass. It would later receive remixes by scene stalwarts A Guy Called Gerald and Adam F when readied for release as the first single from Bowie's next album, *Earthling*, which was started and completed very quickly in the autumn of '96. (It was also the first ever downloadable single by a major artist, but downloads didn't count towards the charts at the time.)

Reeves Gabrels started sketching out ideas using the Vision software for Mac, which predated Logic. 'We put the song ideas on computer and started building them from there—they had a legitimate electronic start,' he says. 'David's thing, and he would say this himself, is that he would function like an art director: *I know what I want the magazine to look like, but then I pick different people whose work I like and try to put them in slightly uncomfortable positions and situations to create.* It was a melting-pot thing.'

Reeves has a memory of him and Bowie buying the first *Breakbeat Science* compilation on Volume—featuring 4hero, Omni Trio, Roni & Krust, Trace & Nico, Boymerang, and so on—from the Other Music record store in Manhattan, and then using some of the studio time to listen to it or the tapes of Fab & Groove's radio show loud on a big system, rather than recording themselves. 'Instead of using the studio time we were paying for, we'd be using it as a place to listen to the albums we'd just bought on really good speakers!' Gabrels laughs.

Nevertheless, *Earthling* was recorded in less than a month in New York in a burst of creativity—Bowie's twentieth album, but the first he had recorded digitally. 'The whole process was invigorating and exciting,' remembers Reeves. Guitars were sampled and dissected, transposed out of their natural octaves. Rather than sampling other records, the single *Little Wonder* was predicated on a loop of Zack Alford's drumming that they chopped up to resemble an Amen break. The whole ethos of the album was to break purism rules, experiment, act the magpie—as Bowie had always done in his music career.

'In my head, it was like, *What if we take some drum & bass-style loops in place of the electronic part, and have the rock band come crashing in at different points?* There's a song on *Earthling* called *Battle For Britain (The Letter)*'—a loose-limbed, rocktronic breakbeat song that descends into discordant avant-garde jazz—'which is kind of an example of that,' says Reeves.

*The Last Thing You Should Do* pivots on cinematic Detroit chords and rhythmic breaks, while *Dead Man Walking* is more of a Prodigy-esque blitzkrieg. Other album tracks such as *I'm Afraid Of Americans* (the only one recorded with Eno), *Seven Years In Tibet*, and *Law (Earthlings On Fire)*, meanwhile, owe more to the industrial noise of Nine Inch Nails or Nitzer Ebb, but there was no doubting that the most important pop artist in the modern era had 'gone dance' in a way that was completely individual and devoid of pastiche.

Crucially, though, Bowie's intention was *not* to make a drum & bass album. 'If at any point the songs sounded too legitimately drum & bass then we had gone too far—that was wrong, because we were not that,' says Reeves. 'We liked drum & bass as a flavour, like we liked industrial. We worried about becoming too much of a drum & bass thing; we would change it up so we'd have the flavour of it but wouldn't become it.'

According to Reeves, Bowie was respectful and in awe of this new underground sound that had sprung up in the UK, and he didn't want to eclipse actual drum & bass people: 'David was aware that he was David, and if he really made a drum & bass record then he was fucking over all these people that have put their blood, sweat, and tears into actually being that thing—and are legitimately that thing.'

Nevertheless, because of the presence of breakbeats in a few of the songs, some critics were quick to categorise the album without really understanding it. 'It would bother me when people would dismiss *Earthling* as Bowie's drum & bass record,' says Reeves. 'It was lazy journalism.'

Bowie had turned fifty by the time the *Earthling* album came out in early '97. It reached no. 6 in the UK charts, while *Little Wonder* peaked at no. 14. Bowie had correctly identified that drum & bass production was the new cutting-edge, and—while peers like Rod Stewart and Elton John trod water—he was still pushing the envelope and experimenting. While doing so, he inadvertently helped a d&b aesthetic reach the parts that other artists couldn't reach.

Bowie didn't hire a fully formed junglist to work with him on *Earthling*; he did, however, do a track with Goldie, for the Metalheadz man's follow-up to *Timeless*, which Bowie loved. Rather than do a d&b track together, Goldie asked Bowie to sing a ballad that he'd written: *Truth*.

'I wrote the words one night after coming off a four-day bender,' Goldie says. 'I woke up and there's a record mailer next to the bed. At first, I thought it was a Dear John from the bird from the night before! My writing is really weird—it's like capitals, it's really ornate. I could be really hammered and my writing's the same. I picked up the mailer, and saw the lyrics and I thought, *Wow. When did I write that?* I can't remember writing it.' He wrote the words out on paper and faxed them to Bowie, who loved the song. 'About a month later, he got to the studio. He said he really wanted to go to Blue Note, so I started taking him there,' Goldie says.

After a slow start, Metalheadz on a Sunday had become the hottest ticket in town. 'It was the Studio 54 of breakbeat,' says Goldie. 'I'm sorry, it was.' The assorted celebs who did turn up were left alone as everyone was pretty much on a level in the dank, sweaty surrounds. 'I remember David Bowie's people were like, Oh, we can't let David go into the crowd, and we were like, Nobody's bothered about David Bowie,' said Storm. 'People will most probably say, Yeah, I was dancing next to Bowie last night, but now if Dillinja walked in, they would be like, Oh my God, it's Dillinja! Or, Oh my God, it's Photek! We had our own stars.'

After performing songs from *Earthling* on two of America's biggest TV shows—*The Tonight Show* and *Saturday Night Live*—Bowie started rehearsing at the Factory Studios in Dublin for his upcoming tour. During downtime, they were listening to Photek, Squarepusher, and Roni Size, who they went to see do a show in Dublin. 'We were hearing jazz in drum & bass as well, and Herbie Hancock,' says Reeves Gabrels. 'There was harmonic sophistication in Roni Size's stuff—it was exciting.' A local promoter named Brian Spollen took Bowie to various club nights, where no one would really bother Bowie apart from coming up to say hi.

During rehearsals, Bowie's band started trying to perform the Adam F and A Guy Called Gerald remixes of *Telling Lies* live. 'We were thinking of them as encores, which we could do alongside *Pallas Athena* and *V-2 Schneider* or whatever,' says Reeves. An idea started to form about doing 'secret' dance sets. One day in Dublin in May '97, Bowie asked Spollen to organise a gig at the Factory rehearsal rooms. 'I want it to be the kids that go to your clubs,' Bowie reportedly told Spollen, who added, 'You could only buy a ticket the night before at our club in The Kitchen, and then you had to ring on Saturday to get the venue details.'

'Before the band launched into the festival set which they'd been rehearsing this past month, there was the small matter of Bowie's current musical fixation for the new model dance genre known as drum 'n' bass,' the *Irish Times* reported. 'The first hour of the set was an extended experiment in psychotic loops and block-busting bass, and only the hardcore clubbers could endure the stomach-pummelling bass frequencies which throbbed from the speakers.'

The illegal party nearly got out of hand, but Bowie loved it. His band next played three shows at London's Hanover Grand in June, doing the dance stuff as encores. '[We] then decided that if we had a day off before a festival show, if they had a dance tent, we might be able to slide in there,' recalls Reeves.

At the Phoenix Festival in Stratford-upon-Avon in July '97, there was just a handmade chalkboard outside the dance tent advertising the acts for Saturday.

An unfamiliar name was on the line-up, slated for a late-afternoon slot: Tao Jones Index. Orbital were headlining later on, and Bowie was there at the side of the stage to greet Goldie after he came off from playing a mid-afternoon drum & bass set.

Tao Jones Index began in darkness, with no spotlight on any of the players. More of an experience—a 'happening', in the late-60s rave sense—than a gig, all the instruments were running directly into the soundsystem, so there wasn't any blast of the band coming off the stage. 'It was just like someone would do if they were a DJ, or if it was just keyboards and sequencers,' says Reeves. 'I'd seen Lo-Fidelity Allstars and really liked them, and they did something similar—they played, but the sound didn't come off the stage, it was going to the front of house.'

Bowie, in darkness, mainly played sax or improvised key lines from *V-2 Schneider* or *Dead Man Walking*. They did a d&b cover of *O Superman* by Laurie Anderson, with bass player Gail Ann Dorsey on vocals, and finished the hour-long set in tripped-out psychedelia.

The next night, Bowie headlined the main stage to tens of thousands, playing pretty much a greatest-hits set. Only a few hundred festivalgoers had witnessed the secret Tao Jones Index show the day before. 'I don't think we did more than three others that way,' remembers Reeves. 'Once we did the Phoenix one, the cat was out of the bag and everyone pretty much knew who and what it was, and then it became a drag, because we felt we were hurting the scene.'

Without co-opting it, Bowie had helped shine a light on drum & bass and further legitimised it to mainstream sceptics. 'We influenced him a lot—the energy of drum & bass really influenced him,' says Goldie. This wasn't like mainstream artists temporarily 'going disco' in the late 70s in the wake of *Saturday Night Fever*—Bowie absolutely meant it.

## REPRESENTATION

There were a few women DJs around London in the scene's early years, but apart from Kemi & Storm and Rap, most of them struggled to get many gigs outside of their local region. Asked if she'd experienced chauvinism in the scene by *Phoenix* magazine in 2020, Storm said, 'Yes, I have, some subtle and some very blatant. My advice is to stand up for yourself where needed, and in some situations don't sweat the small stuff. At the end of the day, if you have something to bring to this scene, you are determined and you have skills, then they will shine through no matter what sex you are.'

Drum & bass wasn't unique in being male-dominated—most music scenes were, and still are. Despite the individual efforts by many of the scene's stalwarts, like Fabio, Frost, Roni Size, and Goldie, to promote women DJs, the overarching culture was exclusionary and sometimes intimidating. Nevertheless, this didn't stop a raft of women getting involved in the 1990s, not just behind the scenes in 'supportive' roles but as DJ/producers too.

Xtreme, aka Suzanne Harris, co-produced breakbeat hardcore for Lucky Spin with DJ Harmony (Lee Bogush) before moving more towards a jungle sound. The Amen choppage of 1994's DJ tool *Boo* for Section 5 was a highlight—Randall picked it up for his Renegade Selector mix the same year—while *Wicked & Bad* on Deep Jungle, with its full raggamuffin vocal, did indeed live up to its name. Xtreme helmed the Lucky Spin show on Don FM for a time back in the mid-90s.

Fallout (Alisa Maher) produced a number of tracks with the late Midlands junglist Tango (Jamie Giltrap), as well as solo remixes for Moving Shadow and Creative Wax. Fallout also played some of the biggest raves in the Midlands at places like the Eclipse in Coventry and at Shelley's in Stoke-on-Trent.

Emma C. Grange made several tracks as Eternal Bass, some with pal Roach and some solo, and had others produced by Wishdokta, an early alias of Grant Nelson, who went on to be a UK garage pioneer. Emma DJed at big raves like AWOL and Roller Express before getting a job with royalties-collection body the Performing Rights Society (PRS).

Jo Millett, originally from Ipswich, was a dancer with SL2 before getting into production herself. Her bleepy *R-Type* track on Awesome Records in '93 is her most enduring track, receiving several represses and having the accolade of being the first proper release on Shogun Audio—now one of the scene's biggest brands—in 2004, with a new remix by label boss Friction (Ed Keeley) and pal Frenzic. And so the list goes on. As well as the aforementioned Tamsin, who was a resident at Roast, and Flora from Bristol pairing Flynn & Flora, who released three albums and 15 singles together, there was Wildchild, who also played big raves like Telepathy and Jungle Fever while holding down a Kool FM residency for many years. Helen Taylor had a couple of releases as Pure Science before releasing more than a dozen quality d&b twelves as Helen T, setting up her own London studio and adopting the name Angel Farringdon for garage and breakbeat productions. Sherry from The Rood Project had EPs on Symphony Sounds and Whitehouse, which was followed by the huge oceanic jungle tune *Thunder*—massive for Randall at AWOL. DJ Dazee was also involved with Bristol's Ruffneck Ting crew, and DJed at lots of raves like Dreamscape, Helter Skelter, World Dance. And so on.

MC Tali, during her time with Full Cycle, would get abuse from male posters on forums, the forerunners to Twitter trolls. 'They say horrible things about me, sexual things,' she told *DJ Mag* in 2003. 'These are just people who either wanna do me or be me. They can't have either, so they hate. That's my attitude, that's their problem.

'People feel represented in the industry when they see themselves represented,' she continued. 'The scene is vastly run by women, which is all very well but the fans want to see themselves represented on stage as well. We need our brothers to help speak out, and the people who put on events in the industry to think about how they can create a more diverse culture.'

Despite being one of the few successful women DJs in d&b at the time, Storm got involved in the Feline night at Herbal in Shoreditch in 2004—a night featuring all female DJs. It was started by DJs Alley Cat (originally from San Francisco), Miss Pink, and Tasha, with Lady MC and Chickaboo on mic duties, and the initial idea was to have back-to-back sets with established (male) DJs—to show how these women DJs could hold their own alongside their more established temporary DJ partner. But after Storm and Flight and Mantra got involved, the collective decided they didn't need the guys.

The night took off, although some had the attitude that a 'girls' night' wasn't as credible as a 'mens' night'. 'It's a double-edged sword—when you do an all-female night, it puts some people off,' says Miss Pink. 'It wasn't about being exclusively women, it was just saying, Look, we're pretty good at what we do.'

Renegade Hardware gave Feline a room at some of their London parties, and the collective went on to do Feline nights in cities like Milan, Budapest, Berlin, and Graz in Austria throughout most of the 2000s, as well as monthly at Herbal. 'It started from us booking ourselves to do a night, to promoters going, Well, they've got their own night,' says Miss Pink. 'You can't win. In some ways the b2b thing was better, 'cause it was inclusive. It wasn't a battle, although I think I did pretty well against Shy FX.'

Now, there are literally hundreds of women d&b DJs worldwide. Feline was important for its time, and remains so, helping to pave the way for EQ50 and far better representation of women as DJs and producers—and not just 'behind the scenes'.

### RENEGADE MEDIA

Jungle got very little press during the first half of the 90s; and, when it did, reviews invariably tended to focus on the near-mythical presence of crack or guns. There was the odd positive piece in style mags such as *The Face* or *i-D*, or dance titles like *Mixmag* and *DJ Mag* (with the reviews of Alex C in the latter particularly on-point), although they tended predominantly to focus on the core sounds of house and techno as the 4/4 dance scene bloomed in the UK. Rave mags were the exception, and one—*Atmosphere*—documented a lot of early pioneers and parties.

*Atmosphere* had patchy distribution, leading a Bristol promoter named Colin Steven—who co-ran Ruffneck Ting—to start his own title in 1994. 'I didn't DJ or make music, but I wanted to make more of a contribution than just being a promoter,' he recalls. 'As we never got *Atmosphere* in Bristol, I just wanted to cover the southwest on the back of our Ruffneck Ting flyer and tape-distribution network.'

*Knowledge* was born, and it grew to become a vital part of the movement. *Knowledge*—or *Kmag*, as it later became known—foregrounded drum & bass completely. It had junglists on the cover, and it soon started including covermount CDs with every issue. By the end of the 90s, it was hosting its own Drum & Bass Awards—the forerunner to the annual d&b award shows that still take place to this day.

*Generator* magazine was the first of the dance mags to give jungle/drum & bass a special edition—running a twenty-five-page special in September 1995 that profiled 'Who's Who In Jungle' in alphabetical order. It was only really after the breakthrough of Goldie's *Timeless*, and the London midweek nights like Speed and Movement, that d&b started getting more mainstream coverage in music mags, including weekly inkies *NME* and *Melody Maker*. Labels starting to employ PRs undoubtedly helped, too.

After a few years of positive coverage from the mid-90s onwards, the odd article would declare drum & bass dead at various points: when UK garage boomed during the darker techstep era, and similarly when dubstep exploded towards the end of the 2000s. The scene's solid foundations and ability to mutate to survive, and the fact that there were invariably d&b headz writing for most dance mags, ensured that coverage was generally favourable, even in some of its perceived leaner periods.

*Atmosphere* disappeared and reappeared under a variety of stewardships over the years, with Ray Keith even taking it on (as *ATM*) in the late 2000s. *Knowledge*, meanwhile, finally called it a day in 2014, with editor Colin Steven moving on to set up Velocity Press to publish music books.

'There were quite a few challenges over the years, but one of the main ones was the politics,' Colin remembers. 'As we were actually part of the drum & bass scene, it really hurt producers when we gave them a bad review or made any type of mistake with our coverage of them. We often got complaints, and I remember one time a famous producer/DJ called me and was on the verge of tears because of a bad record review! Getting the balance of criticism right was tricky. We didn't want to be controversial, as we relied on the scene for advertising, and we probably played it a bit safe with the criticism. However, I remember one time reading a thread on the Dogs On Acid forum and it said *Knowledge* only gives good record reviews, which hurt. You can't win!'

Like plenty of clubbers, some music journalists had a drum & bass honeymoon before sidestepping into other genres or cultures as they climbed the greasy pole. The scene essentially created its own media. Drum & Bass Arena, which operated digitally from the off, and then UKF have ensured that plenty of drum & bass coverage remains online to help keep the scene buoyant.

# 16 Stateside And Worldwide: D&B Goes Global

What began as a London-centric sound and scene spread rapidly through the 90s, not just across Britain but overseas too. America was first, and heading west across the Atlantic was a logical progression for jungle, as many of its core components had been born in the USA.

New York City, the place that produced Frankie Bones and helped bridge breakbeats and house, had several important clubs and DJs that pushed hardcore and jungle from practically the beginning. As the city that created hip-hop, the break was in its DNA already, but the club night NASA, helmed by British ex-pat DB and residents like Soulslinger, took it in a futuristic electronic direction.

DB was a fixture on London's club circuit in the 80s, and a resident at the Limelight club on Shaftesbury Avenue. When he blagged some gigs at New York club Mars with DJ partner Tommy D, he fell in love with the city, and he would return to play residencies at other hot venues like Palladium, Red Zone, and MK.

In 1989, he was convinced to relocate to New York by a friend, and he started to put on his own events with a distinct UK flavour. 'We threw a little party, renting a photographic studio above McDonald's on Sixth Avenue, and we called it Deep,' DB says. 'I'd already done a Deep in London at Hippodrome, and it was all the records that were hot in the UK that people couldn't hear here, like Soul II Soul—very English-centric. There were definitely house records too that were bigger in the UK than they'd ever been here. We did two or three parties for people we knew, and we thought we needed something else. So we teamed up with these other people, Frankie Jackson's Soul Kitchen. The musical format for Deep was hip-hop, house, and Hendrix.'

The club night was a success, drawing two thousand people each Saturday night, but it closed after a gun was fired outside the venue and fights broke out inside. Soon, DB would launch another event, Orange, where among the house and baggy indie-dance of The Stone Roses and Primal Scream, he began to tentatively play the new sound emerging in the UK at the time.

'Hardcore was starting to become a huge thing,' he says, 'and I wanted to play that. First I tried it at Deep, and that was horrible, but even at Orange, 50 per cent of the dancefloor would just leave. I knew that it wasn't going to work with the New York crowd then, and the older NY crowd was not having it—it didn't connect with them. The English people that were there, a lot of them were expats who wanted an English mentality and English music. But some were just here visiting so they were up for it, they knew what was going on back home, and as soon as they heard a Prodigy riff they would scream. That would energise the people who didn't know what it was.'

DB got more and more into the nascent UK genre, loving its fusion of the sounds he'd been playing for years. 'It was British producers who were into hip-hop who were also into techno, and they smashed those things together. The producers I knew, the guys that were on Moving Shadow, they were all definitely hip-hop heads.'

He launched yet another club night, Brilliant, where the sound switched avowedly towards the hardcore vibe. 'It was a straight-up copy of a British rave night,' he says. 'Moby was the first DJ to play with me, and then other locals who were inspired by what was happening.'

The night came to an end after only a few months, but when DB threw an AIDS benefit with Lifebeat, for a friend who was dying of the illness, he was approached by a lighting engineer, Scotty, who told him about an amazing venue that was available.

'He came to me and said, I've been offered this venue called the Shelter, do you want to do a party there? I knew of the Shelter, because [house DJ] Timmy Regisford was doing his Fridays there, it was an amazing venue. So we went, and the guy who owned the venue, Charles, a lovely dude, said, Yeah why don't you take on Fridays? It was a no-alcohol venue, which was an interesting challenge. Raving had definitely started, so it was kind of like, if you couched a club night as if it was a rave, where there was no alcohol and it was going all night till the morning...we teamed up with another kid from Long Island who had been putting on parties there, and my partner recruited a bunch of kids to help promote it.'

The night was named NASA, and after a lot of promotion—ten thousand flyers were distributed all over New York and as far afield as Washington DC—it swiftly became the hottest ticket in town. With a soundtrack that veered between breakbeat hardcore, early jungle, and techno—played by DB but also residents like Carlos Soulslinger and the late Jason Jinx—and running Friday night till nine in the morning, it had a very different crowd to the other New York clubs.

'Even in the second week I could tell something was going on,' DB says. 'First of all, there was no one there over twenty. All my older English friends didn't even want to come—it was too young. This was going to be their club, their thing. I was fine with that, I was going to do the music, not make this my social hangout, to make sure this could be the most cutting-edge event that New York had ever had. After a few weeks, we started to get an international rep.'

Part of the allure lay also in the reputation of the Shelter itself, with its exceptional Dave Soto soundsystem and legendary status in NYC's rich lineage of clubs. 'We had Laurent Garnier, Sven Väth—big names that were dying to play, 'cause they heard it was the shit. Some of that was because the Shelter had a reputation for being this amazing venue. It had a Sound Factory-type thing— part of that comes from the Paradise Garage kind of lineage. It was the alcohol-free, gay, black, purist musical form that those venues had. It had inherited some of that cachet.'

NASA had a rep as a wild place, where the young crowd were frequently off their heads, raving till dawn. 'After six weeks it suddenly took off, where it became scary to me,' DB says. 'I thought there was going to be a death in there. It was so young, so over-the-top energy-wise. You would find kids lying in the corner and I would go and get the security. They'd be fine—they'd just passed out from whatever. Thank God there was never a real tragedy. But it was definitely stressful to me, as I was so much older than everybody else, and by this time I was also drug-free. I wasn't partying, I was just working—it was my job.'

NASA was year zero for jungle in the USA, the place where many clubbers were first exposed to the sound. 'It was the birthplace for a lot of Americans where they discovered hardcore/jungle, but it was still pretty across the board. There were two kids, On-E and Jason Jinx, who were purely junglists—they'd play only that music—but I was still mixing it up. I'd play things like Jaydee's *Plastic Dreams*—that was my opening tune for a few weeks. Nobody else had it in New York—that was a NASA record. It's breaky, but I wouldn't call it hardcore. A lot of those R&S tunes were NASA tunes, because I was able to get them before anybody else had them, and we broke a lot of those records for New York, maybe the rest of the States.'

One of the residents, Carlos Soulslinger, was another important instigator for jungle/drum & bass in the USA. Originally from São Paulo, Brazil, he became a DJ in 1985 and travelled frequently to New York and London. In the latter city, he was exposed to acid house and rare groove, and acts like Adamski and Barrie K Sharpe, before moving to NY with his then-partner, Claudia Rey, in '89. Together, they started Liquid Sky, a one-stop-shop rave emporium that offered fashion and UK-centric records under one roof.

'We were into the UK vibe, so when we opened Liquid Sky, it was the first DJ/rave apparel meeting point in New York City,' Soulslinger says. 'People didn't know what rave was—they'd come inside the store and laugh.'

With his taste for the burgeoning British hardcore and jungle sound, Soulslinger was a perfect fit as resident at NASA, and the rave vibe of the club, he reckons, made sense in a country that had already had a countercultural revolution. 'With rave, there is a background of Woodstock here—there is a background of hippies, one love, this whole old/new concept,' he says. 'But this was the first generation where it became almost mainstream for the kids to have all the hair colours, piercings, tattoos. There was a big explosion of fashion.'

What Soulslinger would play at NASA was influenced not just by European artists but also New York's own musical melting pot. As well as A Guy Called Gerald's pioneering jungle material, he was also enraptured by the dub, house, and ragga productions of the city's Bobby Konders. 'I listened to a lot of Bobby Konders, which was like reggae, dub. I always loved him, used to go to his reggae parties, and I was very influenced by the basslines, which I tried to imitate in the jungle scene. Everybody from the UK and Belgium and Holland, there was a whole hardcore movement coming out.'

By '94, Soulslinger was obsessed with drum & bass, prompting him to start the first American label dedicated to the sound, Jungle Sky. 'When they found this format of half tempo, double tempo, that was 160bpm, I was like, *Wow, this is the universal music! This sums up everything, this is the new jazz, this is incredible.* I quit house, techno, I was like, *This is the thing.*' The imprint became an outlet for his own productions, with tunes such as *Ethiopia, Liquid Jungle Sky,* and *Abducted* some of the very first jungle tracks made on American shores.

That same year, he went to London and teamed up with Dave Stone of the SOUR label, going into a studio to finish some of his tracks and collaborate with MC Det, vocalist Elizabeth Troy, and T Power. 'Reese Gilmore was an engineer at the time, and we remixed and reproduced all my early jungle,' he says. 'Then I brought the whole SOUR crew with Shy FX to New York for the first time. It was in November of '94—everything is history. Meanwhile, Rob Playford went to Miami in late '93, '94—parallel to us here in New York, while I was bringing the SOUR crew, the Moving Shadow crew went to Florida. Jungle and breakbeat were happening so much here by then.'

In particular, Soulslinger's track *Abducted* was a credible US interpretation of the jungle sound, with its warping synth sub, MC chat, Reese moodiness, and micro-chopped breaks, while in subsequent years his label became an outlet for lush Stateside d&b from Jason Jinx, Kingsize, and DJ Wally/Pish Posh (the latter also released on Mo' Wax). Cultivating a distinctive American sound, Jungle Sky nonetheless drew criticism from some who saw it as sacrilegious to the original style.

'We had a severe critic at [US music magazine] *XLR8R*, who said, This is not jungle. I said, Look, either we can make the same template as everybody, or we can interpret within our scene. I was doing my interpretation through American lenses. Since the very beginning I started going faster than the jungle in the UK, which I was criticised for: *You play too fast*. But later the whole scene in America followed me, and started playing faster. My scene was accepting, so we kept going. We did very good for the time, we had a distribution deal via EMI. We were a small label, but we were rolling with big guys. We were everywhere we were supposed to be, at CMJ. We worked the US very well, from '94 till '99.'

After NASA, DB's enduring love affair with the jungle genre encouraged him to try a new venture. Alongside his A&R work for Profile Records, and curating compilations for the US market such as *Best Of Techno* (the first of its kind in the States), he decided to open a drum & bass record shop with his friend DJ Dara called Breakbeat Science—another first for the whole of the USA. Having already worked at the famous Eight Ball record store, and starting Temple Records underneath Liquid Sky, DB and his fellow DJ thought it was time for a dedicated space for the genre.

'Both of us were losing interest with everything except jungle, so we started fantasising whether an all-jungle shop would work,' he says. 'Every bit of advice we were given was, *Absolutely not, that is the worst idea*, but we had a silent killer as a partner. Paul Morris wanted to be involved. He owned a booking agency called AM Only, and I made him my partner. It was a three-way partnership. Paul is a very clever businessman, and he helped us build a business, even though he was never really around—he just stopped us doing stupid things. After a couple of months we took on a fourth partner, Sean Shooter, and Sean pushed Breakbeat Science to become a label with Dara, and I helped with the aesthetic, getting a lot of designers to do T-shirts. At one point we were doing a hundred grand a year in apparel. It became like ground zero for jungle in America—by '97, it became essential for any visiting Brit who was into that world to come visit us. We had the wall of Polaroids of who's who in the jungle scene.'

Drum & bass began a phase of popularity in America that would reach far beyond New York. As the genre hit its zenith of hype and fame in Britain, it was creating a sizeable impact in the States too. 'There was a short-lived flavour of the month moment,' DB says. 'With Roni Size Reprazent's *New Forms*, in '97, that was the few months when it was suddenly like, *This could go mainstream*. MTV was playing that video [*Brown Paper Bag*], which seemed so strange to us. We'd always been the poor relation of the dance family, the shitty room at the rave, and then suddenly it felt like there were raves that were giving as much space to the jungle room as to the other rooms. Sometimes it was a purely d&b rave. That was a whole new thing. The girls were starting to come to events.'

While rave culture on the West Coast and in the Midwest of the USA was well-established, it was musically somewhat different, driven by hard techno or the psychedelic breakbeats of the San Francisco scene, and collectives like Hardkiss or the Wicked Crew. Drum & bass, though, began to thrive in pockets, with raves thrown by Pasquale Rotella's Insomniac (now a massive American events company) incorporating d&b.

Producers started to crop up in less expected parts of the country, too. The most high-profile of these was Dieselboy (Damian Higgins), from Pittsburgh, Pennsylvania, who made his vinyl debut in '95 on a collaborative single with Bristol producers Tech Itch. *The Scythe* was a blend of sub-aqua chords and hard-stepping beats and bass, in line with the rough-edged style of the era. In '99, Dieselboy dropped his solo debut, *The Descent*, its clanking metallic snares, flatulent bass emissions, and *Mentasm* stabs sounding perfectly attuned to the

Steel City nickname of his industrial hometown. Quickly becoming the most recognisable international name in American d&b, Dieselboy would go on to release singles on a host of labels and launch his own Human Imprint stable. Also from Pittsburgh, trans DJ and producer 1.8.7 (Jordana LeSesne) made some of the best American drum & bass in the late 90s. Her 1997 EP *When Worlds Collide 1* for Jungle Sky showed her versatility, moving from punishingly tough Amen drops and synth splurges to rival Doc Scott on *Defcon 1* to the mellow jazz of *Blue Shift*, and she went on to make over fifty tracks that have been acclaimed by everyone from *Rolling Stone* magazine to *Mixmag*.

In Los Angeles, Hive (Michael Petrie) established a name for himself as a DJ, producer, and label boss of Violence Recordings. In a high-profile instance of the reach of American d&b, his track *Ultrasonic Sound* would feature in blockbuster sci-fi film *The Matrix*. He was also embraced by the UK scene, going on to put out EPs on C.I.A., True Playaz, and Metalheadz.

Given its appreciation for bass, California became something of a d&b hub, also producing the respected artist Gridlok, who has put out a steady stream of strong singles through the 2000s. A dedicated advocate of d&b since the mid-90s, DJ Noir is a Los Angeles-based selector who also runs the international Juke Bounce Werk collective, seeking to join the dots between Chicago footwork and various styles at 160bpm.

Seattle, Washington, is one of the strongest spots in America for the music, with artists like underground specialist Homemade Weapons and the trio of Quadrant, Kid Hops & Iris based there. Meanwhile, Atlanta, Georgia—best known for its southern hip-hop, R&B, and trap sound—is the home of one of the most visible American drum & bass acts today, Evol Intent, whose neurofunk-driven beats and label dovetails with the appetite for dubstep Stateside.

### TRUE POTENTIAL

It's notable that drum & bass has had peaks and troughs of success in America, and hubs around the country, while never quite catching fire in the same way that its slower musical cousin, dubstep, has done. Perhaps the slower tempo is more adaptable to American tastes and the ingrained love of hip-hop there, though superstar electronic artists like Skrillex have sought to draw a link between the related genres, making and playing drum & bass alongside his more typical dubstep sounds.

'In America, it hasn't reached a scratch of the potential of the sound or the artists,' Soulslinger says. 'I really believe that it can be our time. It's already big in festivals in America, and it's getting mainstream right now. Now there's another phenomenon too—pop and rock artists are incorporating drum & bass. My daughter, who is eighteen, sent me a track by Grimes, she said, Dad, you should remix this, and I said, It's already drum & bass! So the pop people, in the same way that hip-hop incorporated the house, and the trap, they stole from the rave scene—that's what is happening with drum & bass. The whole of America, from pop, from hardcore, they listened to drum & bass and were already influenced by the style.'

Another reason why drum & bass could gain more traction in America is the way in which geography has become less important. Whereas in the past the genre was viewed as very much UK-centric—and often considered inauthentic if not produced by the gatekeepers of the style—now, in the age of interconnectivity and genre-less taste, a new generation is more open to drum & bass from anywhere.

'There's definitely some very talented US producers now, and previously,' says DB. 'I think the thing that is different now is that the lock on where the music comes from has changed. People in the UK are more open to the fact that if it's not from London it might still be good, whereas it used to be very challenging for anyone outside that. Now there's been enough examples of amazing tunes coming from all over the place.'

Now that DJs and producers are more willing to experiment with style and tempo, d&b co-exists with other forms of dance music, often in the same set. One of the most adventurous artists to emerge from the US d&b scene is Denver's Sinistarr (Jeremy Howard), originally from Detroit. Residues of that city's electro and techno permeate his sound, in addition to the tempo-adjacent footwork that emanates from the nearby city of Chicago. In this, his is an authentically American sound, but it draws also from the speedy breakbeats and bass of the UK to create a very modern hybrid beloved of genre-merging DJs like Sherelle (Sinistarr released the debut EP on her and Naina's Hooversound label in 2020).

Sinistarr first discovered drum & bass by listening to the radio in Detroit. Though pirate radio is highly illegal in the USA, local stations are able to play pretty much what they want, including a high-speed hybrid dance sound that occasionally incorporated jungle. 'We called anything faster than your standard house and techno tempo ghettotech—which became the genre, ultimately— and had DJs on the R&B/hip-hop (also read: black-owned) radio stations mix those all together on weekend radio shows,' Sinistarr says.

In 2001, while in high school, Sinistarr heard a compilation of classic jungle tracks and was thrilled by the speed and fusion of sounds. 'It captivated me completely—it was the same R&B and dancehall, rap, jazz, and such I grew up listening to, but with these breaks I heard on Detroit radio, at the same tempos,' he says. 'It was only later I found out about the actual (mind-blowing) connections between London and Detroit, and that really helped me dive deeper in and ultimately make my own mark in the scene as a creator. I felt like drum & bass and jungle was a sound that I found on my own and related into my life, rather than joining the crowd of whatever was popular at the time, and it still feels that way today whenever I find new songs and sounds.'

When he first visited Denver in 2011, Sinistarr connected with the local Recon crew, participating as the small d&b scene in the city began to expand. 'Recon is one of the main drum & bass crews out here; they have been active since 2004, and I have been a resident DJ with them since 2012, travelling back and forth before ultimately moving here in 2019. Along with the scene, who we were booking to come to Denver went up in profile exponentially. They definitely saw way more d&b artists come through the city [mainly via Recon founder Maggie Despise] than Detroit ever did, and that instantly drew me in. Couple that with the rise of dubstep, and dance music overall in the States around that time, and it has been a continuous growth.'

As he became established as a drum & bass artist, Sinistarr looked to build contacts with other producers around the USA. 'My first forays into d&b were basically finding out who was Stateside, and I had a few local people that were spinning different styles of it,' he says, listing Ronin Selecta, MD! (RIP), Submorphics, SPKTRM, and Ojibiwa (RIP). 'I knew about the Breakbeat Science crew in New York at the time I started producing, so I already had people to send things to.'

Sinistarr's productions move between beat patterns and tempos in a playful and fluid fashion, sometimes veering closer to the nebulous 'club music' sound that has arisen from DJs who play across the board genre-wise (but with a strong focus on bass). His collaboration with Detroit electro maverick DJ Stingray,

2016's *Untitled*, manages to occupy a disorienting inter-zone between speedy arpeggio basslines and drums that skittered between d&b and dubstep; the more recent *Emo* cranks up electro to high speed, demonstrating its kinship with d&b, while throwing in both gorgeous chords and a steely technical edge.

In combining various aspects of his country's rich dance music culture with UK sounds, it feels as if Sinistarr has hit upon something that could only have emanated from America, but he reckons it's simply a natural corollary from the music he grew up with. 'I think that I just pull from the territory I come from, which is mainly focused on Detroit and Chicago,' he says, 'and being American as an addition to that, rather than brand everything as a new form—it just happened to be American, from Detroit, and so on. The States are so massive, so it would be tricky to set any one style as the example when so many producers come from so many different regional musical influences, spread across so many places, that are all wildly interchangeable—and anyone new as a producer could come about daily.'

As to whether jungle/drum & bass could ever break through to the mainstream in America, Sinistarr shares the optimism of Soulslinger, believing that there's already evidence it has a growing audience. 'Today, d&b is definitely more favoured than it used to be. Granted, it still has a way to go here—you'll hear EDM DJs play edits in their sets, house and techno DJs not too soon after. Crews like Recon and Stamina in San Francisco, my other residency, are really good at bringing fresh and at-the-moment talent to Stateside audiences, and there are a whole set of new, young, internet-savvy producers making their own lanes for themselves to grow and shape their path through all the new distribution and streaming services that have popped up since the dawn of YouTube.'

The birthplace of Stateside d&b, New York, remains an outpost of junglist goodness today, with artists like fusioneer Kush Jones (part of DJ Noir's Juke Bounce Werk collective), Adred (who released the album *KIM* on Metalheadz), and Dave Owen flying the flag for the style in the city. The Konkrete Jungle club night, which started in '94, ran until 2019, and is on a hiatus at the time of writing. DB runs the Thursday night party Secret Art Of Science at Brooklyn's lauded venue Public Records, and Adred has hosted the Natural Selection party since 2011. Liondub's label, Liondub International, has been going since 2008.

## WORLDWIDE

North America, of course, is not the only country to have resonated to the heavy bass frequencies of the genre. Further south, in Brazil, artists like DJ Marky, Patife, S.P.Y., and Bungle have forged their own style of d&b, merging elements of their country's samba, bossa nova, and funk with sunny breakbeats and basslines (see chapter 19).

In Japan, the most famous d&b export is Tokyo's Makoto. With releases on Good Looking, Liquid V, Hospital, and Creative Source, and a discography stretching back to 1998, Makoto Shimizu is a firmly embedded staple in the worldwide scene, known for his soulful and immaculate production. Better known for his pioneering house music, Soichi Terada also ventured into the d&b domain with the *Sumo Jungle* EPs; and DJ Kentaro, DMC World turntable champion in 2002, is known for his ferocious drum & bass mixes and productions like *North South East West*.

Singapore, meanwhile, has clubs such as the famous Zouk, which gave a platform to drum & bass as early as '96, with residents Zul and Ramesh playing the emerging techstep of the era. The city state would become an early hotspot for the sound in Asia, with clubs Area 22 and Insomnia catering to small but dedicated crowds. In 2005, Home Club opened there with a special focus on the genre.

'Drum & bass was a part of Home Club's DNA, as we felt that the spirit of the music fit like a glove to our objective, which was no bullshit, no pretence,' co-owner Kelvin Tan told *Vice*. Kiat, one of the residents of the club's +65 night, became the first Singaporean artist to release on Metalheadz: the track *Feeder*, with its abstract bleeps and crisp, stepping beat giving him an international rep and leading to further appearances on Soul:r, Hospital, and Function among others.

In South Africa, there are several artists who've made an indentation on the world stage, with SFR and Counterstrike two DJ and production acts who've had international recognition. Even further afield, New Zealand has a share of d&b producers who've had a major impact globally. Production duo Concord Dawn have released on Function, Metalheadz, and their own Uprising label; MC Tali had a high-profile debut album on Full Cycle, featuring production from Bristol's big dogs; Shapeshfter, Tokyo Prose, and The Upbeats are just three more of the country's key names.

Aside from the UK, Europe has the healthiest drum & bass scene. The Netherlands, in particular, has given rise to a plethora of renowned producers: there's neurofunk pioneers Black Sun Empire, Metalheadz technician Lenzman, and Martyn, who, in addition to his dubstep and techno, has produced a fair amount of d&b. Noisia, though, are arguably the biggest European export in d&b. Causing a big stir with their technical, sound design-savvy production style, the influential trio have had a considerable influence on what drives many dancefloors today. Since they started producing, they have sought to stand out from the crowd by honing a distinct audio signature, created by painstakingly crafting the futuristic tones that populate their tracks.

'We were super adamant that we wanted to make every sound ourselves,' says Tijs of the trio. 'We were also aware that if we were going to make a difference, it was there. You can't make a difference using other people's sounds.' Noisia split in 2020 after two decades together.

Jungle/drum & bass remained a close-knit scene for most of the 90s. It wasn't that you had to come from London or at least be from the UK—but there was perhaps an unconscious bias that made it important. One DJ/producer who'd found it hard to break into the scene was Teebee, from Norway. A DJ since 1990, he'd fallen in love with drum & bass by the mid-90s but couldn't really get a look in at first.

'On one occasion I was turned down trying to hand my DATs to a couple of big DJs who stated that I was not from the UK,' he recalls. 'My English was far from perfect at the time, and I'm pretty sure eighteen-year-old me did look extremely out of place.' With no drum & bass on the radio in Norway, no internet, and no club scene to speak of, Teebee had to phone up UK record shops and get them to play new releases down the phone to him so that he could order some. They'd still take two or three months to come through. 'The best of times, no joke!' he smiles now. 'Hard, but rewarding.'

A less determined person might have given up after a few years of rejection. It was only after a lot of hard work that he secured releases on Moving Shadow offshoot Audio Couture, and then Paul Arnold's Certificate 18. Just after the millennium, he won 'Best International Producer' at the *Knowledge* awards, 'although even that came with controversy, as we were not deemed fit or good enough to compete with domestic talent'.

Teebee ended up moving to live in the UK to be closer to the heart of the scene. He started up his own label, Subtitles; important for nurturing neuro talent over the years, it was to provide an early outlet for Noisia, Break, and Ulterior Motive. 'It wasn't until much later that I truly felt accepted,' he says. 'It's an ongoing thing for me, the constant fight to feel like you both contribute the right way and respect the music. I care too much about it all if I'm honest, but it comes from a place of love, so I'll roll with it.'

Since hooking up with Calyx and signing to Ram, Teebee has become a significant player—although he says he still doesn't feel totally accepted. 'Or maybe I don't want to feel accepted, but that is probably no one's fault but my own insecurities and the pressure I put on myself,' he says. 'I have always had my back against the wall in a sense, and I'm OK with that. It drives me forward. I love this culture too much to let my personal issues get in the way of my life's biggest passion and love.'

Though it's generally thought of as a house nation when it comes to dance music, France has a dedicated scene too, with DJs such as Elisa Do Brasil and producers such as Redeyes, Dirtyphonics, and Visages all making power moves in the country. In Italy, the Delta9 label has rapidly gained a name for its d&b output, while the festival Sunandbass, which takes place on the Italian island of Sardinia, is a summer go-to destination for drum & bass fans internationally.

'After the first one, we wanted to stop doing it, because we were exhausted and had to deal with an infrastructure that was not really ready for what we were doing,' says Sunandbass organiser Delekat. 'We were just a couple of students doing this, but we had such great feedback with people saying we had to do it again. Everyone was speaking very positively about it and telling their friends. We have the best ingredients: sunshine, so you are already in a good, positive mood during the day; good music to activate you, the catalyst for a good time. Combined with the landscape and surroundings there, it's the perfect ingredient. It's about bringing the community together. Everybody is there together, we don't have a VIP area, everyone is on holiday.'

More than simply a d&b-themed island vacation, Sunandbass and events of its ilk have helped to galvanise the scene and keep its artists motivated. 'It got my flame back on,'cause I was away for a while,' Brazilian d&b artist Patife says. 'Sunandbass was an injection of inspiration and love—all these people from very many places all going crazy for the same music on this tiny little island.'

Speaking of festivals, Croatia hosts Hospitality On The Beach at the Garden,

Tisno—one of a growing number of continental d&b getaways—and the long-running Outlook also stuffs plenty of d&b onto its line-ups. Meanwhile, Let It Roll in Prague, in the Czech Republic, grew out of club events in the early 2000s to become drum & bass's biggest standalone event, growing into an impeccably organised, thirty-thousand-capacity festival by the end of the 2010s, and attracting d&b headz from right across Europe.

The drum & bass scenes, DJs, and producers scattered across the world together comprise a synaptic network, united in their aim to further the cause. What started out being made in bedrooms and played at DIY raves has become internationally recognised and widely appreciated, despite the disapproval of the mainstream. Proving resilient to genre fads and kept alive by its passionate supporters, d&b is now a global phenomenon. And, in America, it looks as if there's room for even greater recognition and the world's biggest audience—provided that the genre's pioneers there can maintain its integrity in the face of market interests.

'I feel it is on its way to becoming a more normalised sound as dance music gets bigger here in the United States,' Sinistarr says. 'As long as we have the right people and faces in place as the new generation builds itself up, I think the movement to a wider audience could really work in our favour, in helping us build a bigger and well-educated, well-versed scene.'

# 17 This Is A Threshold: The Techstep Age

'The whole intelligent drum & bass thing bugged me quite badly,' says DJ, producer, engineer and label owner Optical (real name: Matt Quinn). 'That music was never meant to be like that—all smoothed out. It was supposed to be the opposite. To me drum & bass was a punk kind of thing, you know?'

By 1996, drum & bass had already been through multiple changes. Many within the scene had dabbled with the tranquilising tones of ambient and jazz, giving the genre more exposure in music magazines and newspapers. Though the likes of LTJ Bukem and Fabio had been expanding drum & bass with their more melodic DJ sets and releases via the Good Looking and Creative Source labels—and the best ambient d&b tracks were embraced by many DJs—some producers took it as an opportunity to plane away the rough edges of jungle.

There was a massive backlash to this repackaging, though, and Optical was one of many ready for something new. 'That sound to me was middle-of-the-road, and I can't stand anything that's middle-of-the-road,' he says.

Optical grew up in London and caught the dance music bug in 1988, during the acid-house Summer of Love. While living in a series of squats in the capital, he learned to DJ and went to raves thrown by traveller collectives like Spiral Tribe, sometimes playing the warm-up set at their free parties, including the famous Castlemorton. He got a job at a record distributor, Great Asset, on Gray's Inn Road, initially just making tea and sandwiches.

'They had a studio, and they released things like Smart E's' *Sesame's Treat*, and all those kinds of big rave tunes. That company was really well off at that time, so they decided to build a new studio. In return for me helping, they gave me a job in the end. They also said, Do you want to start your own record label? Come up with the idea, do the drawings and designs, make the music in the studio and then we'll release it for you. That was the way I got into it, but I was DJing for quite a long time before that.'

Optical honed his skills as an engineer and producer, eventually working on a different track each day, five or six days a week. He got hooked on the breakbeat sound, snapping up the earliest jungle releases on Limited Edition Records by the likes of Potential Badboy. On the flipside, he was making techno under the name Fly By Wire and had a techno label, Blame Technology, while engineering records by big house stars such as Adamski and Bam Bam. He engineered the *Lovers Rock Mix* of the classic Leviticus jungle track *Burial*, worked on Billy Bunter happy hardcore track *Let It Lift You*, and delivered his own remix of the proto-jungle gem *Durban Poison* by Babylon Timewarp, under the name Little Mat.

After a few years, he got bored of working on other people's sounds, and decided to start making his own beats. 'I was more focused on other people's music until '96, which was when I went, Do you know what, I'm wasting my time producing for other people, I could be producing some money for myself, making my career better. It got to '96, and I was like, I'm dropping the techno thing all together. Drum & bass was becoming the one.'

At this point, Optical knew he wanted to make something different, that was neither the wafty atmospheres of 'intelligent', nor the Amen-snare avalanches that were consuming the jungle scene. 'In '95, it was just an Amen-chopping nightmare—everywhere you went, there were ten thousand Amen snares,' he says. 'I was operating a laser sometimes when I didn't have any music work at Laserdrome in Peckham, so I was always constantly getting battered by Dr S Gachet, and ten thousand Amens!'

His first record under the Optical name, *No Time* on Celluloid Records, had splintered breaks but rode a clipped, unusual rhythm that you could easily imagine with a four-to-the-floor beat. The B-side, *THX* had cascading Rhodes keys, but gave way to science fiction sound design and swung out, cleverly cut-up drums. Sonically distinct, it was one of the records that indicated a new sound was waiting in the wings.

## SHADOW BOXING

Elsewhere, there were other rumblings. Coventry's Doc Scott, who had made tearing early darkcore beats on Reinforced and since become part of the

Metalheadz elite team, had released the prescient *Drumz 95*, remixing it under his Nasty Habits alias. Composed of stop/start beats that were simultaneously clipped but rock solid, with an intensity like being pummelled by an industrial drop hammer, this remix of *Drumz 95* was sparse in the extreme, a titanium rhythmic exoskeleton around which curl shivery green mists of sound design, adding to the oppressive atmosphere. The same year, Scott dropped the similar but even heavier *Shadow Boxing*. Drawing from the same pool of old kung-fu movie samples as the Wu-Tang Clan (who had recently had a seismic impact on hip-hop), and simplifying the drums further to a stentorian snap, the beats were accompanied by the most evil sequence of Reese bass notes imaginable. A wilful march towards apocalypse, phasing in and out of earshot, it was like something the Skynet computer from the *Terminator* films would play victoriously, once it had wiped out all humanity.

Though sharing the basic rhythmic structure of drum & bass, this new style largely stripped out the organic features of the original model, such as its reggae and funk samples, replacing them with a steely techno pulse. Around the same time, the No U-Turn label, helmed by Nico (Nicholas Sykes), was also beginning to shift in a more metallic direction. Though No U-Turn had started out in '92—and from its second release was focused on jungle tunes like the head-spinning roughness of Ed Rush's *Bludclot Artattack* and DJ Gunshot's bass-warping *Soundboy*—by '96 it had zeroed in on a novel, dark sound. Combining hard-stepping drum breaks—mostly doing away with the rapid-fire edits of the recent past—with gangsta rap samples and nightmarishly oppressive synth basslines, the music No U-Turn and its cohort of producers were making was evidence of the musical sea change in drum & bass. Tracks made by Ed Rush (real name: Ben Settle) at the time became more and more clipped, bristling with barely contained tension and heavier electronic atmospheres. Rush, along with Nico, had worked on an earlier track for the label Emotif that sowed the seeds for the techstep sound. In its original form, T Power & MK Ultra's *Mutant Jazz* was one of the best ambient drum & bass tracks of its era, though it was the DJ Trace remix that would detonate dancefloors and alter the course of the genre forevermore.

Together in the No U-Turn studio, Trace, Ed Rush, and Nico extracted the ethereal synth horn of the source material, soldering together head-cracking beats with genetically mutated bass to create something that had an enormous impact on both DJs and other d&b producers. The trio made the revolutionary track using an Akai S-1000 sampler, a Drawmer compressor, Roland D50 digital synth, and what Trace calls 'a great pair of ragga bass bins of Nico's that really gave us that dub feel'.

'I had this idea about switching two classic breaks together that would work against each other to create a groove,' Trace continues. 'I chose the Paris and Apache breaks, and they seemed to work well. The samples of T Power's original track were not really doing it, so I decided to reverse the piano riff, and this is what created that spooky intro sound that became the essence of the track. When we added in 808 bass and a distorted Reese bass, it felt natural. I don't think we had any idea of what exactly was to follow. It turned out to be what we know today as techstep, a name I came up with at the time.'

Drawing inspiration from the bass on Ray Keith's Renegade track *Terrorist* (rather than the original Kevin Saunderson tune as Reese, *Just Need Another Chance*), the No U-Turn crew had unwittingly stumbled upon a new path: 'This was the vibe for everything that ended up becoming the No U-Turn signature sound. We just added distortion—a lot of it.'

By 1996, Ed Rush had zeroed in on a murky, heavy sound, dropping tunes such as the neck-snapping *Mothership* solo, and, with Nico, *Sector 3*—a cavernous zone of surgically engineered Apache drum snips and oppressive techno vibes. Showcased on the debut No U-Turn compilation, *Torque*—which depicted a futuristic killer robot on its cover—it was clear the label had a style all of its own.

Not to be outdone, Metalheadz—having already released one of the pioneering records of the new style, *Drumz 95*—issued the killer *Metropolis* by Adam F. Though he was still best known for the sublime, Bob James-sampling ambient d&b of *Circles*, *Metropolis* was evidence that Adam F could wild out with the best of them. Starting with a discomfiting synth pad, it drops into tumbling breaks and evil Reese warps, its additional drum layers bringing a sinister funk to the sometimes stiff techstep domain.

Grooverider was also at the forefront of techstep, releasing a multitude of club bombs on his Prototype label, including a futuristic track by Dillinja (as Cybotron), *Threshold*, replete with soaring pads and rib-shattering sub-bass; and the angry, almost heavy metal bass noises of Boymerang's *Still* (an alias of post-rock pioneer Graham Sutton, part of the band Bark Psychosis). Best of all was Grooverider's own track as Codename John, *Warned*, with its trippy acid bleeps and chattering techstep breaks. Ray Keith, meanwhile, released a lot of high-quality techstep through his Penny Black imprint, with tunes like Twisted Anger's *Five O'Clock* tapping into the malevolent synth bass and lacerating beats that had become a hallmark of the sound.

There quickly developed a schism between those who wanted to stick to rigid drum patterns—the kick-snare beat introduced by Alex Reece's *Pulp Fiction*, which quickly became the dominant rhythm in d&b—and those who wanted to take the rhythmic twists of jungle to new places. Ed Rush and Optical had been introduced by Dom & Roland (Dominic Angas), and, when they met again at dubplate cutting studio Music House, they realised they shared a musical vision. The two DJ/producers recognised that there needed to be groove as well as menace in this new techstep sound, and they began to produce tracks together, starting the new label Virus to release them.

'When we started to do Virus, we wanted to have a dance element but not be crazy edits all the time,' Optical says. 'Going for a really solid beat, with a bit of shuffle and swing in it. Techstep was very two-step, they wiped out all the rhythmic parts of it, which was a reaction against that Amen over-chopping thing. It was like, *Let's go to the opposite end of the scale and have none of that snare-gun rattling thing*. But after a while as a DJ, you realise it's not that great on the dancefloor really, it's a bit tired. We didn't want to go back all the way to crazy edits again, so I think that's where the more funk break element came into it.'

Already well respected in the scene, the duo quickly made incursions into DJ sets and record bags with their hybrid style, evidenced by the crisply produced beats and interlocking bass bloops of tracks like *Medicine*, or their track for V Recordings, *Funktion*. Optical came to the techno aspect of the new sound as an expert, having made techno tracks and released them on his label in the past. Though he had grown tired of that genre's lack of rhythmic sophistication, he remained fascinated by its exploration of sound design, and he wanted to apply that same obsession to his d&b material with Ed Rush.

'I was always really fascinated in the sound part of techno—not the drum part,' Optical says. 'I thought the drums were preordained simplicity, so you never got to work on that very heavily, you stuck in the four-to-the-floor, some hats and a clap or whatever. But it was the sounds that were really interesting from a production point of view. I knew there was no crossover between the two things at the time, so when we started to make those records, I knew there was a gap in the market. There was room for a new thing to come along, but obviously you don't start off something and say, This is exactly how we're going to make this thing. There's a lot of experimenting.'

One of the reasons why Ed Rush & Optical stood apart was their use of hardware synthesisers, compressors, and effects units. While most drum & bass at that point was sample-based, the duo would go to great lengths to get the right sound, playing in live analogue synths before re-cutting the audio in a sampler. This gave them a truly techno edge, and it made their basslines and riffs buzz with life.

'It was all hardware. There was very little interaction with computers in those days,' Optical says. 'The computer was in the room to trigger off the MIDI signals to everything. It was super-basic, all the programming work was in the outboard boxes. To get our production super-tight, I always sampled the synths, so I could lock them into one consistent sound and level. Then you get the filter section from the sampler, where you can add even more layers of modulation. You can have more texture and depth that way.'

Just as punk dispensed with the bloated prog excesses of 1970s rock dinosaurs, Ed Rush & Optical saw a punk component to the music they were making, sweeping away the 'tasteful' ambient d&b and replacing it with something direct, driven, and sonically distorted. They emulated certain punk rock techniques too, driving their basslines through guitar stomp boxes and distortion pedals to get the monstrous effect they were known for. This was another consequence of Optical's engineering work for diverse artists across the genre spectrum.

'I had to work in a rock studio for a few months, and I was taught about amping guitars and stomp-box pedals and all that stuff,' he says. 'So I tried to bring that into what we were doing. As it turned out, that was great fun to work on. Instead of just sitting at a computer and staring at the screen, you're jumping around and twiddling things, moving a lot, like a real instrument kind of thing. We used to have to spend a day just making a few bass sounds, before we made the song. It was quite involved, there was wiring, you had to physically record into a DAT and then resample and do all this stuff. In a way, the less you have to play with, the more you can be creative.'

One of the pioneers of the techstep sound, Doc Scott, was a fan of hardcore punk/metallers Henry Rollins and Biohazard at the time, and drew a specific link between the guitar-heavy sound and this new iteration of d&b. 'Me and

Grooverider were listening to a Source Direct track, *Black Rose*, and we were going, This is like punk,' he told *Melody Maker*. 'Obviously it sounds different, but it's bringing that same kind of energy.'

The techstep sound brought some producers back into the scene as they saw the new creative possibilities within its beat structures and musical ideas. Jonny L, famed for his hardcore classic *Hurt You So*, had begun making atmospheric jungle and d&b, releasing a series of EPs that delved into Detroit techno and ambient influences. In 1997, though, he delivered the titanium juggernaut of *Piper*, a heartless, ice-cold creation on which, over a pulse of snare fuzz and hi-hats like rattling chains, there hovers swirling sound design like something out of a sci-fi horror flick. It sounded like being trapped in an airlock, with a rampaging xenomorph on your trail, and inspired music journalist Simon Reynolds to coin a new genre name, 'neurofunk', to describe its intense, introverted sound.

'Depending on the time of year, my surroundings or mood, I switch from melodic sounds to dissonant techno,' Jonny L says. 'Around 1997, I was in the latter mode. In terms of the music, clubs like Blue Note, DJs like Fabio & Grooverider, Bryan Gee, labels like Metalheadz and 31, were all synchronising at the crest of a big d&b wave. In the studio, analogue technology was peaking too; computers and samplers were powerful enough to practically make any sound or noise you could imagine, and boundaries were open. It was the right time to experiment. I wrote the album *Sawtooth* and the single *Piper* in this period.'

Though in some ways techstep had a seditious punk-rock energy, in other ways, it was more prog in its deep studio focus and emphasis on sound design. This was music as scientific audio research: splicing, experimenting, crafting with surgical rigour, testing sonic hypotheses.

'People have said *Piper* was an important tune within the evolution of d&b: at the time of making it, all I knew was that I really meant it, it was serious,' Jonny L has said. 'I really wanted to make *Piper* because I had been watching the film *Apollo 13*, thinking how similar it sometimes feels in the studio. Like an astronaut, there's no outside light, no concept of time, no distractions, locked in the studio with three days' worth of food and drink and flashing lights from the equipment, ready to explore the vast empty space of sound. I was trying to push boundaries, and loving the process of creating and writing.'

What techstep brought into being was a reduced, skeletal rhythmic style. Though it had many of the elements of the past (darkcore's sinister sound, breakbeat snippets, intense sub-bass), there was a steelier focus here, injecting a premillennial dread where there was once a more human quality to the music. In its transitional stage it was sometimes christened 'hardstep', but as the style ossified into something distinct, many began to call it techstep instead. The 1996 Emotif compilation *Techsteppin—A Journey Into Experimental Bass* was an early touchstone of the subgenre, featuring tracks by Doc Scott, Grooverider, Skyscraper (Trace and Nico), Ed Rush, and lesser-known purveyors such as Newcastle duo Elementz Of Noize. Grooverider's label compilation *The Prototype Years* also provided a vital techstep primer. In 1997, Grooverider's foreboding *Jeep* remix of Björk's *Bachelorette*, with its acid squidging bass, metallic stepping beat, and orca FX, showed that those outside the scene were still paying attention.

### RENEGADE HARDWARE TO BAD COMPANY

As a reaction to both the gentler ambient sound and also the success of the genre ushered in by albums from Goldie and Roni Size, the resolutely underground techstep became the dominant sound of drum & bass towards the late 90s. At a time when TV ad jingles with soft-focus jungle breaks had become all too prevalent, Trouble On Vinyl, a label run by Clayton Hines and Mark Hill, launched a deadly new offshoot. Renegade Hardware became known as one of the fiercest exponents of the techstep sound. Future Forces (an early collaboration by dBridge and Maldini) released the slamming *Dead By Dawn* through the label, while other studio sensei like Dom & Roland and Genotype were at the screw-faced forefront. Renegade Hardware went on to host arguably the defining club event of the techstep era, which ran for eleven years. The label's night at the End started in 1997 and attracted big crowds, with resident DJs Loxy and Ink renowned for pushing the most futuristic beats in their sets.

In 1998, perhaps the biggest stars of the techstep sound released their first single—a tune that instantly became a drum & bass club staple and remains a favourite to this day. Bad Company were the scene's first 'supergroup'. DJ Fresh (Dan Stein), dBridge (Darren White), Jason Maldini, and Michael 'Vegas' Wojcicki had worked together in various permutations before uniting as one, and the first track they made together and released—*The Nine* in 1998—blew them up, with its neck-snapping kick-snare beat, quick percussion changes, and positively demonic, abyssal bass.

'*The Nine* is probably the biggest tune we did,' dBridge says. 'That was the first release. It was weird in some senses, because around that time dubplate culture was very much a thing. No one picked up on it, and it wasn't until we gave it out on promo on white label and we'd already committed to releasing this record, and we were into it, then people said, What's this? In some ways it bucked the trend of the time. The scene tended to fragment and come back together but, from jump-up to techstep, both sides were into it. It kicked off this whole momentum.'

The big bastard beats and heavy, burbling Reese in the intro to *The Nine* were enough alone to ignite any dance, but then—every thirty-two bars—comes a scything, decapitating, primordial bassline to square off the frenetic dance mania. Relentless punchy beats and effervescent hi-hats ensured that when a DJ such as Andy C got hold of it in the mix, *The Nine* could take on a life of its own.

'It's just a wicked DJ tool really,' Vegas modestly told Drum & Bass Arena in 2014, revealing that Fresh and Maldini had made the track in one day— illustrating the prolific way these young producers used to work at the time.

Bad Company astutely put out *The Nine* as the first release on their own label, BC Recordings, and soon earned Grooverider's seal of approval with a release on Prototype—the dark, clattering monster *The Pulse*. 'I never expected us to blow up like we did,' dBridge told *Knowledge* at the time. 'I suppose we were like a breath of fresh air really, something that the scene needed.'

BC rapidly became one of the scene's biggest draws, pulverising parties wherever they played and in whichever combination. 'We just wanted to infuse some energy,' Fresh said to *Knowledge* at the time. 'We always used to talk about bringing back the hardcore, and although everyone's now taken that literally, it always meant just recapturing the energy of hardcore. At the end of the day I suppose we've established our own sound in the scene, which is a hard thing to do.'

When they started out, dBridge says, 'Dan [Fresh] borrowed some money from a mate of his and spent it on speakers, and we pooled our equipment, what we had, together into a studio. We spent a summer there writing [debut album] *Inside The Machine*, pretty much.'

In the studio, Bad Company aimed to capture a febrile liveliness—a similar kind to that which Optical had captured in his recordings with Ed Rush. 'I had a connection with Nico and No U-Turn, and he taught me a lot in terms of production,' dBridge says. 'For me, it was about seeing what you could do by building tracks live. We were doing mute mixes, letting the DAT machine play and recording volume fades and effects splashes. It felt really raw and quite punk in some ways, and that's what I was really into, catching a vibe and running with it. That's what I liked about it, especially with the early No U-Turn and stuff on Prototype.'

Bad Company's debut album, *Inside The Machine*, is a testament to the devastating power of techstep. Tracks like *Silicon Dawn* pulse with dark energy, dropping from beatific science fiction atmospheres into surgical drum cuts and evil bass that lurked like a leviathan. Meanwhile, the grisly *Oxygen (Drilla Killa)* has evil techno sequences and a head-banging forward drive that marked it as utterly separate to what had come in the genre before. Most of all, Bad Company were determined to create a signature sound—and, fired up by the possibilities of techstep, they let their imaginations run wild.

'It felt like these worlds were being created outside of just finding a really sick sample and putting a break on it, as it had been in the past,' dBridge says. 'I think as well, what I liked was that these techstep artists were finding their sound. You knew a Dillinja record, you knew a Photek record, a Full Cycle record. We were trying to do the same thing with Bad Company, which was trying to create our own sound, uniquely us. All of those things excited us.'

The group would go on to be highly successful, putting out a sequence of four albums until 2002 (they reformed in 2018 with a fifth, *Ice Station Zero*) and numerous singles. All four members would go on to be solo artists, most notably Fresh and dBridge. But as the 2000s rolled around, there were stirrings elsewhere in the d&b scene that suggested the dark techstep sound wouldn't dominate for much longer: V Recordings released the *Brasil EP* compilation in 2001, helping to return a warmer, soulful touch to drum & bass; Fabio's Creative Source label settled on a new groove he dubbed 'liquid funk'; and club nights like Swerve (with Fabio at the helm as resident) were starting to becoming popular.

'Dan was getting to a stage where he wanted to explore other things,' dBridge says, 'and I was getting more into going down to Swerve. Stuff Calibre was doing was connecting with me.' Though the dark groove continued in the underground, it was now time for something different.

# 18 Parallel Universes: Other Genres Influenced By D&B

The close, protective nature of early/mid-90s drum & bass was important for it to establish strong foundations. Its initial insularity did, however, unwittingly have reverberations in other genres of electronic music. Seduced by drum & bass's futurism, many producers from other genres wanted to get involved, but they invariably found it hard to break into the close-knit, London-dominated, dubplate-driven scene. A spin-off effect of this natural protectionism was other scenes using some of the production techniques developed by drum & bass producers in their own subgenres of electronic music. Drum & bass can therefore be said to have influenced most other electronic music genres—whether by co-option, ostracism, opposition, or fusion—both sonically and socially.

While jungle grew out of the dark side of hardcore rave, the 'happier' side of the music—populated by bouncy piano chords, breakbeats, and uplifting, anthemic (usually female) vocals—became known as happy hardcore. This was proliferated by DJs like Slipmatt, Sy, Seduction, Dougal, and Billy 'Daniel' Bunter, and it would often make up the second room at big raves like Dreamscape, Helter Skelter, and Raindance. With jungle considered too moody by some, happy hardcore continued to boom, in pockets, for the rest of the 90s, thanks to its own hardcore followers and compilation CDs like the *Bonkers* series on React, among others. Venerated Radio 1 DJ John Peel was a champion of the sound at one stage.

While still somewhat interconnected and friendly, this early 90s 'split' of happy hardcore and jungle was easy to observe. Other divergences were considerably more nuanced.

Carl Cox was one of the biggest DJs in the rave scene by the early 90s. He'd started out as a mobile DJ in his teens before acquiring his own soundsystem, which he'd lend out to illegal party organisers—so long as he got a set at the rave too. An early DJ at Shoom, he made his name by playing off three vinyl decks at raves to showcase his amazing skills on the turntables.

Fabio remembers Cox approaching him behind the decks at a Dreamscape rave they were both playing at in the early 90s. 'Groove just played this brand new tune and Carl came up to me and said, I can't do this no more, I don't know one tune Groove's playing. I was like, What do you mean? and he went, What are those tunes? I can't get 'em no more, Fab, I don't know what these tunes are. Groove just went in and smashed it, and Carl just sat down there in disbelief. He kept coming to me and going, What's this tune? He went, I'm not getting no dubs, I'm gonna have to start playing something else. And that's the reason. We were running that whole dubplate thing, getting the tunes first.'

While continuing to play breakbeat-derived tunes in his sets as the 90s progressed, Cox went on to plough his own furrow—playing a major part in building a global techno movement over the next twenty-five years, while acting as an ambassador for the electronic music scene as it dominated the twenty-first century's second decade, post-EDM. The next time Fabio saw Coxy play was in Miami, twenty years later, by which time he was one of the biggest DJs in the world.

Other techno DJs with a love for drum & bass include Nastia, who has played the odd d&b set at festivals; and Laurent Garnier, who played at Movement in London once, would often end on d&b during his all-night marathon sets at The End and elsewhere, and did a memorable back-to-back set with DJ Marky at Brazil's Skolbeats Festival in 2007.

At Rage, when jungle was germinating, Fabio & Grooverider would play all manner of Belgian brutalism, jungle tekno, and so on. The *Mentasm* stab from the Joey Beltram/Mundo Muzique tune was appropriated for a number of breakbeat hardcore tunes, and while Fab & Groove used to play quite a bit of techno before it got 'too mental and more towards gabber'—gabber being the ridiculously fast Dutch sound that even attracted a small, ugly, neo-Nazi vibe at times—some sounds from techno were fused into early jungle effortlessly. The Jumpin' & Pumpin' label didn't name its influential compilation series *Jungle Tekno* (1992–95) for nothing. Noise Factory's *Jungle Techno* on Ibiza Records in 1991 was the impetus the label needed to boss the jungle tekno sound for the next couple of years.

Kevin Saunderson, the most prolific of the trio of black guys dubbed the

Belleville Three techno originators from Detroit, had made a track in 1988 called *Just Want Another Chance* under the alias Reese. A twinkling, late-night groover, it was dominated by an incredible, deep-burrowing bassline that sounds like the subterranean rumblings from deepest Hades. Made on his Casio CZ-5000 synth by detuning a couple of saw waves so that they engaged in phase cancellation with one another, this Reese bass 'sound would be used on 1,001 other jungle and drum & bass tunes—almost as often as the Apache, Amen, and Think breaks. From Ray Keith's *Terrorist* throwdown as Renegade to DJ Trace's tech-steppy *Mutant Jazz* rewrite, Alex Reece's landmark *Pulp Fiction* to Boymerang's peerless *Still* on Prototype, the Reese bass showed how jungle/drum & bass wasn't afraid to heavily lean on other genres itself in the beginning. As the 90s progressed, however, techno and drum & bass maintained their own parallel universes.

By squeezing out the ragga in the mid-90s, some d&b producers and DJs were effectively saying that they wished to communicate the message or mood in their tunes sonically rather than verbally. This was pretty much what trip-hop—instrumental hip-hop—did initially, although the sound soon became synonymous with Bristol acts Massive Attack, Portishead, and Tricky, who all used vocals, before DJ Shadow's *Endtroducing* took intricate sampling to new heights.

Club sounds, though, needed more energy. The post-rave blunted downbeat of trip-hop was fine to be played in chill-out rooms, but these spaces started dwindling at club events in favour of the more beats-derived sounds emanating from room two or three—funk, soul, Balearic, phreakbeat, et cetera. It soon became inadequate to put the dusky sounds of Portishead in the same category as the embryonic chemical beats of what Tom Rowland and Ed Simons were doing with their Naked Under Leather club night in Manchester and on their early tunes like *Song To The Siren* and *Chemical Beats* under the name The Dust Brothers.

Accentuating block-rocking beats, acid sounds, and an anything-goes approach to sampling, what this duo—who quickly changed their name to the Chemical Brothers—were doing dovetailed with tracks like *Their Law* from The Prodigy's pivotal 1994 album *Music For The Jilted Generation*, Josh Wink's 303-snaking breakbeat power-driver *Higher State Of Consciousness*, and the back end of the Weatherall/Mondays/Primal Scream/Flowered Up indie-dance scene. The Chemical Brothers were soon installed at the weekly Heavenly

Social night, where mayhem and wild abandon ruled. Trip-hop remained the preserve of the blunted dubs of Mo'Wax and the weirder beats of Ninja Tune, with acts like Funki Porcini, DJ Vadim, and Ninja bosses Coldcut themselves. This new wilder style, with records on Skint and Wall Of Sound and others, was dubbed 'amyl-house' for a short while before it all got lumped in under the umbrella term 'big beat'.

A young DJ who would go on to play a key role in the big beat scene, Jon Carter saw jungle as the next logical step after hardcore. 'It was great to find the influence of soundsystem culture and the use of space in the music, stripping out the synth riffs and more bass-driven, with sampled 808 basslines taking the lead, and more intensive creativity with breakbeats—stripping away the Day-Glo colours and fairy wings,' he says. 'Like a pupa/chrysalis/butterfly evolution in reverse. It was heavy as fuck, it seriously rolled, and it blew your mind all over again. What's not to love?'

Carter worked at the No U-Turn studio with Nico, Ed Rush, and Trace, among others, 'with a lot of chopped up Amen and Apache break productions and, again, heavy on the 808. This was just as the sound was evolving, getting further stripped-down, with the kick-drum becoming much more defined and driving.'

Spending most Sundays at Metalheadz at the Blue Note, 'getting lost in the sound', it was only natural that he'd introduce the sound into his eclectic DJ sets. 'I was always drawn by reggae influences, and bass, breaks, and bleeps,' he says. 'I'd have two record boxes with about 220 tunes, starting at the front of one box at around 70/80bpm, arranged in tempo, through to early jungle and drum & bass at the back of the second box—basically twice the tempo of the start of the set. But that's part of the beauty of it—drum & bass works nodding on the half-step or full pelt. High energy, bass-heavy, pure dance. The progression in a set through these tempos was so important to me—bringing the energy up, and never really letting the crowd know what to expect as it got more and more intense.'

As it flourished, big beat took from the forensic science of drum & bass time-stretching techniques to make DJ-friendly tools with drum-roll crescendos, plus assorted sirens and hip-hop or movie samples. It even, sometimes, used guitars. It was hedonism with a pick 'n' mix, rock'n'roll attitude—another extension of the acid house legacy to bring in beats that weren't simply 4/4.

Big beat drew a lot of indie kids into dance music: after seeing a band, many wouldn't want to go home at 11pm, so they would go on to a club night. By the end of the evening at a big beat event—alongside tracks by Lo-Fi Allstars or Junkie XL or whoever—you might hear something new on Urban Takeover, like Aphrodite & Micky Finn's *Bad Ass* or their zippy *No Diggity* bootleg, or DJ Zinc's anthemic makeover of The Fugees' *Ready Or Not*, or the updated remix of Zinc's *Super Sharp Shooter*.

When Jon Carter released *Live At The Social Vol. 2* in 1996—brimming with Ragga Twins and Shut Up & Dance cuts, and Top Cat and Ini Kamoze a cappellas, all presented in an accessible way—it was hugely influential on the wider dance scene. Reinventing himself as the ultimate showman DJ, Norman Cook as Fatboy Slim then took big beat to the next level. But that's another story.

Likewise with Essex electro-punks The Prodigy, whose huge late-90s tracks such as *Firestarter* and *Breathe* got played in many different indie-disco emporiums. The Prodigy may have come from the rave scene—indeed, their first ever gig was at the Labyrinth night at the Four Aces in Dalston, a rave den of iniquity—but they very much ploughed their own furrow after the release of their first album, *Experience*. (In fact, on the 'expanded' version of *Experience*, they even subtitled a dark remix of their rave hit *Charly* the 'Trip Into Drum & Bass Version'.) Even though they knew people like Hype from the hardcore rave days, they were never sucked into becoming part of the drum & bass scene—or any scene, for that matter. Going down the live-band route and playing big shows and festivals, they became a huge act on their own terms.

Not a million miles apart from some d&b, The Prodigy allowed Pendulum— then on the cusp of exploding with *Hold Your Colour*—to remix *Voodoo People* in 2005, while a track like *The Big Gun Down* from the 2013 album *Invaders Must Die*, for instance, hits around 160bpm and could quite easily have been by someone like Krust. The Prodigy remained separate from drum & bass throughout, but they certainly turned more than a few people onto breakbeat-driven music over the years. When Keith Flint tragically died in 2019, Goldie was among the first to lead tributes from the music world.

### LIVE SETS TO NU-SKOOL BREAKS

Finding that they'd kick ass on the live stage, other festival-friendly bands such as Dreadzone and Dub Pistols introduced d&b-tempo breakbeats into their sets as the sound endured. 'After receiving a remix of one of our tunes as drum & bass, we decided to play that version live,' says Dub Pistols main man Barry Ashworth, whose DJ sets today often include lots of dub-wise d&b tunes. 'The energy that that brought to our live sets was immense. A lot of the dub records we were making, it seemed to make sense to double-time them, and it threw a whole different energy into it all and lit up the live shows—took them to the next level.'

Drum & bass had its own live bands from the off: Reprazent, Kosheen, Breakbeat Era, and, as the 2000s went on, Pendulum, Chase & Status, Noisia, London Elektricity, Dr Meaker, and Rudimental, among others. In 1996, Omni Trio said, 'To me, live is when Fabio, Grooverider, or Randall are playing out in a hall', but most of these exhilarating combos happily proved there was space for live performance too.

Growing out of an east London community music project, Asian Dub Foundation were one of the first 'drum & bass bands'. Operating on the margins of the scene and brilliantly combining junglist riddims with South Asian samples and a punk rock attitude, ADF released their early material on Nation Records, the label run by Aki Nawaz from militant beat-mongers Fun-Da-Mental.

After building up a big following in Europe, ADF signed to London Records and saw their album *Rafi's Revenge* nominated for the Mercury Music Prize in '98, the year after Reprazent's win. Around this time, a movement that came to be known as the Asian Underground was evolving, centred around Talvin Singh's Anokha night at the Blue Note—every Monday, the night after Metalheadz. Joi, State Of Bengal, TJ Rehmi, Badmarsh & Shri, and others came to the fore during the late 90s, all employing polyrhythmic pressure in part of their sound, and when Singh himself released his debut album, *OK*—fusing junglist riddims with tabla and classical Indian stylings—it scooped the Mercury in 1999.

Movement at Bar Rumba on London's Shaftesbury Avenue was one of drum & bass's most important nights. Jointly set up by the Bulldozer half-brothers Oliver and Edo and the team behind SOUR—Sound Of the Underground Records, the label behind Shy FX's *Original Nuttah*, as well as d&b's first MC album, 1996's *Freeform Reality* by MC Det—its sister label, Emotif, was primarily concerned with drum & bass from '95 onwards. Its other offshoot, Botchit & Scarper, inhabited more of a beatsy domain. Botchit artist Darin McFadyen, who became FreQ Nasty, used to do the lights at Movement, and cohorts T Power and B.L.I.M. released on both Emotif and Botchit. Recording in a tiny basement near the bottom of Kingsland Road, between a kebab shop and a taxi kiosk, Thursday nights became the night for the crew to hang down at Movement to check all the new d&b missives.

When Rennie Pilgrem—a veteran from the hardcore rave scene as part of Rhythm Section—wanted to start a breakbeat night in London, Bar Rumba seemed like the perfect spot. Teaming up with DJs Adam Freeland and Tayo Popoola—who both had day jobs as music PRs initially—they started the Friction night on a Friday to push what they called 'nu-skool breaks', which came in around the 130bpm mark. Rennie had been making and releasing breakbeat music on his TCR label since the early 90s, but he was now spearheading this new sound. Finding that they didn't have quite enough records to last a whole night, at their early breaks nights the Friction residents would often play drum & bass twelves from Full Cycle or sister imprint Dope Dragon at 33rpm.

B.L.I.M.'s 1997 remix of Raw Deal's *Headless Horseman Rides Again* on Botchit & Scarper was one of the template-setters for the sound nu-skool breaks, while Botchit stalwart FreQ Nasty was one of the scene's earliest and— with his high dreadlocks—most striking-looking stars.

At a tempo more comparable to house, these breaks grew exponentially after 2000 thanks to trailblazers like Stanton Warriors and the Plump DJs (until it crashed under the weight of too many bootlegs in about 2007), and they attracted a number of 'refugees' from drum & bass. Carl Hovland from Renegade Hardware act Usual Suspects (of *Killer Bees* fame) became 2 Sinners with Klaus 'Heavyweight' Hill. Aquasky, who'd released on Moving Shadow, Reinforced, and Good Looking, among others, became big fish in this new breakbeat pond. The Autobots duo had their grounding in d&b. Ed Solo—who'd worked with Dave Stone from Emotif/SOUR as Click & Cycle, and with Brockie when launching his Undiluted label—went on to be a linchpin breaks producer with Deekline, Against The Grain label boss Skool Of Thought, JFB, Krafty Kuts, and more. Krafty, The Freestylers, and others would often throw down drum & bass tunes towards the end of their sets in a similar way to the big-beat jocks. Meanwhile, d&b acts Sam Binga (as Baobinga) and Beat Assassins, who originally contained Joe 'Wooz' Lenzie from Sigma, both started out as breakbeat producers.

DJ Tamsin, a former resident at Roast and Orange who'd made several classic jungle tunes, started to make this slower breakbeat sound with the group Breakneck. For her, it was an exciting new twist on the formula. 'We needed something fresh to inspire us again, so taking the break down to the 130s was easy, and the jungle vibes were back!' she says. 'It was the early 90s tempo, but with improved tech available. There was some really great music made in that period. I remember DJing breaks sets and dropping in d&b on 33. It's a great tempo to be experimental.'

Beyond the demands of the dancefloor, drum & bass was influencing the more experimental reaches of electronic music, too. Aphex Twin (Cornwall's Richard D James), who had become renowned as much for downtempo classics like *Selected Ambient Works Vol. 1* and *2* and hectic acid-rave like *Digeridoo*, began to offer his own outlandish version of d&b in the mid-90s. *To Cure A Weakling Child* from his *Richard D James* album matched strange and optimistic synth melodies with the polyrhythmic splintered breaks of jungle, sending the beats through over-the-top sound-effects chains until they're torn apart. *Come To Daddy* was an even more extreme take, with its descending distorted guitar riff, chopped-up beat, and disturbing vocal. The atmosphere of horror wasn't entirely serious of course, and instead Aphex Twin seemed to be using d&b as just another intriguing tone to add to his odd and always playful palette.

Squarepusher might be seen as a purveyor of left-field electronics now, but many of his early works were more in line with jungle/drum & bass. Chelmsford-based Tom Jenkinson's track *Squarepusher Theme*, which emerged on Aphex Twin's Rephlex label, is composed of jazzy, sunlit bass guitar runs and intricately chopped breaks, sounding like Jaco Pastorius jamming with LTJ Bukem. 'I was into that Krome & Time EP, *The Licence*, then,' he told *DJ Magazine*. 'That was a big favourite, and then Splash *Babylon*, an epoch-defining track, that one, I reckon. Marvellous Cain's *Dub Plate Style*, that's another obvious one, and slightly older stuff like Bizzy B, Brain Records, *7 Minutes Of Madness.*'

The micro-drum sutures of these edit-heavy jungle tracks became a strong feature of Squarepusher's work, but perhaps due to the close-knit nature of the jungle world, his records, and those of others experimenting on the genre's fringes, were sidelined by the scene's gatekeepers. Most Squarepusher tracks, except perhaps the freaky garage cut *My Red Hot Car*, were too weird to play to a regular dancefloor anyway, and impossible to beat-mix.

'I certainly wasn't received with welcoming arms into that fraternity, which is kind of a shame,' he says. 'I felt I had something to contribute, some energy to bring to that world. Actually, the scene of drum & bass producers and DJs kind of kept it at arm's length. Luke [Vibert's] Plug records were a really big influence on what I was doing at the time, for certain. I actually remember going into a drum & bass record shop, very excited 'cause I'd heard *Plug 2* on the radio, and I said, I'm gonna go and buy it. I popped into Black Market as I thought they'd be all over it, and they'd never heard it. That little moment played out in the responses I got myself, and I remember asking other people about the record and they'd never heard of it. To my mind that's a fantastic example of innovation within the area we think of as drum & bass. It fell on deaf ears, it seemed, at least partly, in that fraternity, which is a shame. I dare say similar things happened to my stuff. But you've only got so much time to listen to records. I don't blame anyone; it's just, like, fair play.'

Luke Vibert was another artist who started out in the IDM/electronics world and made a series of excellent jungle tracks, as collected on the album *Drum 'n' Bass For Papa*, and provided incredible remixes of tunes like 2 Player's *Extreme Possibilities* under his Wagon Christ moniker, the latter moving from dusty trip-hop into hyperactive breaks and back. And Mike Paradinas, aka μ-Ziq, made a mark with his own jungle-influenced tracks, before releasing material by Remarc, Bizzy B, Criminal Minds, and Equinox on his Planet μ label.

Whereas some artists in the left-field electronic/braindance scene were content to hijack jungle beats and attach them to their strange synthscapes, others didn't feel that the microscopic edits of the sound were rhythmically extreme enough. A new breed of producer arose in the late 90s who turned breakbeats into metallic blurs of noise, stripping away the funk in favour of experimental weirdness. Artists like Venetian Snares, Shitmat, Kid 606, DJ Scotch Egg, and Soundmurderer blended over-the-top Amens with the sounds of modems disintegrating; a super-niche and nerdy micro-genre, breakcore (or drill & bass), was born.

### JUNGLE INTO HOUSE

It wasn't just European DJ/producers who wanted a piece of drum & bass action. New York house music pioneer Todd Terry—who'd essentially patented hip-house a decade previously, via his work on The Jungle Brothers' *I'll House You*—was so sold on the sound that he released a whole album of raw drum & bass, *Resolutions*, in 1999. Lead track *Blackout* could easily be an Urban Takeover jam, while *Yo* is a jazzy joint not unlike a Wax Doctor or DJ Pulse cut. Jazz skits sit alongside militant jungle-rap missive *I'm God*, with religion-debunking rhymes by MC Essential, while *Whatcha Know* features local NYC legend Cash Money applying more breakbeat pressure. Terry—by now referred to as Todd The God by some house-music aficionados—put the big room, electro-tinged *Let It Ride* on the B-side of the *Blackout* twelve, and even gained some MTV play from the accompanying video.

Put together in less than a month, Todd's album drew more attention to drum & bass Stateside—a house-music legend allying himself with d&b was pretty significant, after all—but *Resolutions* didn't garner the adoration and acclaim that Terry might've anticipated or even deserved. The science of breakbeat production had come on so much in five years that it was dismissed by some UK junglists as somewhat of a pastiche, although Todd did play a well-received DJ gig at Movement in London and earned the approval of some of the scene's inner sanctum.

'Todd Terry made *Blackout*, and he smashed it, but he didn't follow up,' believes Grooverider. 'I don't know any producers who have come into drum & bass from outside and smashed it.'

Barclay Crenshaw was another US house guy who fell in love with drum & bass. He started DJing the music but would find that at the house parties where he was playing in the late 90s, d&b tracks were too moody, and it would only be guys dancing. So he switched to house music, but when he started making Claude VonStroke records a decade later for his new label, Dirtybird—alongside Justin Martin, another drum & bass fiend—they ensured that a bassline sensibility was often present in their tracks. This bass house sound would come to dominate US floors by the latter part of the 2010s—and owed a sizeable debt to drum & bass. Other house DJs—from Eats Everything to Enzo Siragusa from FUSE—have also professed their influence from and love of drum & bass, bringing its sensibilities into their productions and even playing the odd drum & bass set when permitted.

### ARMAND VAN HELDEN

Another US house-music legend whose keen ears were pricked by 90s breakbeat science was Armand Van Helden. A fan of hardcore from when he was a hip-hop kid living in Boston, Armand became house music's remixer du jour after moving to New York at the start of the decade. After hearing Goldie's *Inner City Life* and other drum & bass tunes on the radio, he had a bash at making some d&b of his own—but he didn't think any of it was good enough to release.

'I also had it in my head that no Americans made drum & bass, and the ones that did, nobody in the UK paid attention to,' he says. 'The UK dominated that genre. If you were from anywhere outside in the world, you couldn't make it, 'cause you weren't in the scene, you didn't have the dubplates, you didn't have a DJ to pass it to and support you. They had enough people doing it, and they shut the doors on it. It sounds crazy, but if you were a fan and you were on the outside, it was a disaster trying to become a success in that genre. It would never happen. It was locked off 100 percent.'

Armand took a different path, and in the process he unwittingly propelled a new subgenre of electronic music in the mid-90s with a series of remixes. 'Instead of me trying to make drum & bass, and trying to appease the British, I thought, *Why don't I just go ahead and take all of the drum & bass elements except for the drums?* So I put them on house drums. That was my idea—if I can't get it that way, maybe I can do it in reverse?'

After using a souped-up bass part in his remix of Tori Amos's *Professional Widow*, he now adopted more drum & bass architecture for his overhaul of Belgian producer C.J. Bolland's *Sugar Is Sweeter*. Techniques such as time-stretched vocals, chopped-up beats, bassline sensibilities, and a stop-the-beats 'drop' were new to house music, and Armand even called his C.J. Bolland overhaul *Armand's Drum & Bass Mix*. 'This was the one where people were like, *Wait a minute, you're mixing drum & bass with house, this is crazy.*'

When Armand roughed up *Spin Spin Sugar* by UK indie band Sneaker Pimps and UK act Double 99 sampled his *Sugar Is Sweeter* remix for *RIP Groove*, he stoked the fires of a new electronic music subgenre germinating in London—speed garage. 'I made those tunes because the UK was a shut door,' he says. 'I was a fan of drum & bass music, but I couldn't find any other way to incorporate that architecture and those sounds into my music.'

A raft of skippy garage tracks with junglist tendencies followed, pitched-up and rewound on pirates with some added MC pressure, and at after-hours parties on Sundays in south London. These sessions had begun in 1994 at the Elephant & Castle pub on the roundabout of the same name, just down the road from the embryonic super-club Ministry Of Sound, after its flagship Rulin' house night kicked out at 6am. Soon moving to the larger Frog & Nightgown on the Old Kent Road, DJs like Matt 'Jam' Lamont, Dominic Spreadlove, and Norris 'Da

Boss' Windross would keep the area's restless post-club crowd going by pitching up US garage imports by Todd Edwards, the Armand Van Helden remixes, and, soon, homegrown tunes by Tuff Jam, Dem 2, and Grant Nelson. By the time Twice As Nice started in 1997, at the Colosseum in Vauxhall—where Movement would later hold a monthly night—a new scene was starting to coalesce.

First released in 1997, *Gunman* by 187 Lockdown was typical of a speed-garage anthem: depth-charged Reese bass, chirruping Amen break, time-stretching, micro rave-tics, gunshots, rewind sounds, a 'come selecta' exclamation from an unknown MC, and the sped-up watch chimes from soundtrack composer Ennio Morricone's *Carillon*, as used in the final duel in the 1960s Clint Eastwood spaghetti western *For A Few Dollars More*. (Hilariously, *Gunman* was then used for an Albert Square face-off between Pat Butcher and Mo Harris in popular BBC soap *EastEnders* a few years later.) It was essentially 'jungle-house'.

Speed garage drew a fair amount of disaffected junglists to its bling-tastic, champagne-popping club nights—specifically a more affluent, mature black crowd who felt techstep-derived drum & bass had become too dark and joyless. Some DJs and producers carved a new niche in this genre. Mikee B—one third of scene leaders the Dreem Teem, alongside Timmi Magic and DJ Spoony—was originally in breakbeat hardcore act Top Buzz. Original junglist Dr S Gachet got involved under his Johnny Biscuit moniker, and so on. Following the trajectory of Kelly G's remix of Tina Moore's *Never Gonna Let You Go*, a sub-strain developed—via tracks like Dem 2 *Destiny*—that consisted of a non-4/4, offbeat 'two-step' sound.

M.J. Cole, the in-house engineer at SOUR in its early days in the Kingsland Road basement, rose to become one of its chief hit-makers, songs like *Sincere* owing more to smooth, soulful R&B than any ragga tendencies. Jonny L moonlighted on a tune with Posh Spice and Dane Bowers from Another Level under his True Steppers moniker, nearly scoring a UK no. 1 with *Out Of Your Mind* in 2000. As radio-friendly UK garage tracks catapulted into the pop charts—*Sweet Like Chocolate* by Shanks & Bigfoot, Sweet Female Attitude's *Flowers*, Craig David and Artful Dodger and so on—elements of the media had begun pronouncing drum & bass dead. In truth, though, UKG and d&b co-existed and cross-pollinated throughout this millennial period—Jumpin Jack Frost would play at Twice As Nice, for instance.

In the clubs, the likes of DJ E-Z would mix up the soulful stuff with darker, more bassline-heavy bits by Wookie or DJ Narrows, or DJ Zinc's infectious instrumental *138 Trek*, with its bouncy burbling bassline, which crashed into the UK Top 30 based largely on vinyl sales. After *138 Trek* came a slew of 138bpm Bingo Beats DJ tools—some by Zinc himself under the name Jammin—for dark garage and nu-skool breaks spinners.

### DUBSTEP AND GRIME

Zinc was also coincidentally a crucial link to another London-born subgenre that developed in the 2000s and quickly went global. Zinc's long-term partner, Sarah Lockhart (aka Soulja), initially started the garage promo company Ammunition Promotions before co-founding a label, Tempa, and a corresponding club night—the hugely influential FWD>>—just after the millennium. The first Tempa release, *Let's Dance*, had clear jungle influences in its bassline and off-kilter breaks, and as garage veered back underground after its glitz and glam limelight period, more and more DJs and producers started pairing the skippy offbeat with panoramic, dub-infused aural soundscapes, warping the accompanying bass into abstraction.

FWD>>, situated at small basement club Plastic People on Curtain Road in Shoreditch, started germinating a new London sound that contained neither the flash of UKG or the freneticism of d&b—although it drew on elements of both. Accentuating bass-heavy sounds and stripped-down beats, this dub two-step sound started to be known as dubstep. One of FWD>>'s residents, a teenager known as DJ Hatcha, also worked at the Big Apple record shop in Croydon—a commuter town just south of London—where he met shop regulars like Mala and Coki (Digital Mystikz); Sarah Lockhart's brother Daniel, aka Youngsta; and other aspiring young producers such as Skream and Benga, who would all give him their new tunes. Zinc, Hype, and Grooverider would regularly pass through Big Apple, while Bailey worked there for a while too.

As the nascent dubstep scene coalesced, Hatcha was able to play this new hybrid sound down at FWD>>, collaborate with the likes of Kode9 and Benny Ill, and round up choice cuts on Tempa's hugely important *Dubstep Allstars Vol. 1* mix compilation, which he recorded in one take in 2004. Hatcha also had a show on Rinse, the pirate station that had initially started out playing mainly jungle before switching to garage in the late 90s. Rinse was managed by Uncle Dugs for quite a while, but when Sarah Lockhart became involved in 2004, the process to become a legal station accelerated, and it finally secured its permanent licence in 2011.

After releases on Big Apple's in-house label, Skream put out the haunting milestone *Midnight Request Line* on Tempa, closely followed by Benga's cooing *Night* (with Coki), and dubstep rapidly took off internationally due to assorted associated factors—largely aided by the internet. Dubstep provided a reset for electronic music that kept growing faster and faster, and it definitely influenced the Autonomic sound, pioneered by dBridge—one-quarter of the Bad Company powerhouse—and Instra:mental.

Burial, who would later work with Goldie, was the master of aural sound-sculpting in dubstep—soundtracking inner-city angst. Talking to cultural theorist Mark Fisher in 2007, he said, 'I love R&B and vocals, but I like hearing things that are true to the UK, like drum & bass and dubstep. Once you've heard that underground music in your life, other stuff just sounds like a fucking advert—imported.'

This street-real, dub-infused side of dubstep got its own brand of jump-up—tear-out dubstep—before the 'brostep' brigade began to proliferate. A derogatory genre term alluding to the fact that a load of 'cultureless frat boys' or 'bros'—were taking over, brostep largely did for dubstep by the end of the 2010s. US producer Skrillex—himself originally a drum & bass fan—took bassline abstraction to incredulous wobble-lengths with productions like *Scary Monsters & Nice Sprites*. Brostep face-melted with EDM; lacking the foundational strength of drum & bass, which had built up through more traditional networks in the 1990s, before the internet was in common use, it saw some of its leading producers start dissing dubstep and quitting it for pastures new.

'Skream and Benga should've been like us two in dubstep,' believes Grooverider. 'They had the Radio 1 show, they had all the promotional tools—they should've stayed in dubstep rather than talking about moombahton and disco and loads of other shit.'

'Dubstep people were really proud of its Croydon roots—and then they all just dissed it,' adds Fabio.

'Through the good times and the bad, we've always represented our music,' continues Groove. 'We ain't turned around and said we're gonna do some garage shit or a dubstep thing. We could've quite easily stepped over many a time. But we're not frauds, you know what I'm saying?'

'More than other genres, drum & bass is a way of life to people,' says Fabio. 'I was really upset about dubstep though, man,' concludes Grooverider. 'It's a British thing, and I always try to support British music. I can't believe how these so-called big DJs dissed their own music, 'cause a lot of it is born out of drum & bass at the end of the day.'

The aforementioned Rinse had been operating as a pirate since 1994, set up by Geeneus (then known as DJ Gee), Slimzee, and pals, and initially it wanted to rival Kool FM as the go-to jungle pirate. For its opening weekend, Geeneus had given a show to local east London guys Darren Joseph—who had started calling himself DJ Target—and his mate Kylea. Target had decided to become a DJ after attending an outdoor Kool FM event in Hackney while still at school. He did work experience at Moving Shadow in the mid-90s, when Goldie took him under his wing, and his young crew started going to as many jungle raves as they could get into—Roast, Jungle Fever, Voodoo Magic, and so on.

Kylea initially called himself DJ Wildchild, but he soon discovered that there was a DJ on Kool FM with the same name (Emma Wild) already embedded in the scene. He quickly came up with a new one—Wiley—and the crew began making a name for themselves on Rinse, with Wiley and others MCing. 'Jungle had done something to inner-city youths all over the country that no genre had up until this point,' DJ Target says in his book *Grime Kids*. 'It was UK. It was raw. It was organic. People could relate, and we finally had MCs speaking in their local accent instead of mimicking American slang and lyrics, as well as music that was completely original, yet fused cultures we had all grown up on.'

Despite garnering a following, the crew weren't really getting gigs in the drum & bass scene, so they decided to get into production as well. It was pretty rudimentary at first, compared to most jungle/drum & bass producers' work. When UK garage came along, they started going to those raves and playing more of that sound on their Rinse shows. MCs came more to the fore, and Pay As You Go Cartel coalesced alongside other crews in other parts of London like So Solid, Heartless, and then Wiley's Roll Deep entourage. Roll Deep included a young kid called Dylan, who Wiley had brought in. A couple of years previously, he'd been blagging jungle vinyl from DJ Target; he then started producing his own tracks, which led to him being signed by XL Recordings.

When Dizzee Rascal's *Boy In Da Corner* won the Mercury in 2003, it heralded a new London-born genre—grime—whose foundations had been laid by jungle/drum & bass and then UK garage. Wiley had been crucial in its explosion via the 'eski' sound (derived from his pivotal instrumental tune *Eskimo*), and a whole load of cross-pollinating hustle, and soon a whole raft of grime acts would start making their mark: Skepta and JME from Boy Better Know (who also had a show on Rinse), Lethal Bizzle, Kano, More Fire Crew, and then later crossover acts like Tinchy Stryder and Tinie Tempah. And then some tall fella called Stormzy...

Like drill, grime was, and still is, more of a vocal thing, but both can trace significant roots back to drum & bass—the first truly independent, homegrown black British music. Yet while MCs in drum & bass often play second fiddle to the DJs, in terms of billing and payment, grime MCs were front and centre. In his book *Inner City Pressure: The Story Of Grime*, Dan Hancox points out grime's deep connection to its musical forerunner: 'Deep in its spirit, jungle is grime's true antecedent. Its aesthetics—a hard, scowling dark side that is counterpointed by ludic, transcendent expressions of joy—were essential to the mutation of UK garage as it became grime.'

# 19 Shake Ur Body: Liquid Funk, Brazilian Beats, And Beyond

After the seminal Speed night came to an end, Fabio started up Swerve in the late 90s as a continuation. Kicking off at the Velvet Rooms on Charing Cross Road on a Wednesday night, before moving to The End, also in central London, Swerve was a crucial incubator for the strain of the music that would ultimately become known as 'liquid'.

By the mid-90s, Roni Size wasn't the only one making jazzy jungle. Independently, labels like Moving Shadow and Reinforced had been moving that way with some of their releases, often taking their original artists with them on this odyssey. Peshay, aka Paul Pesce, was one such artist. After making some dark material for Reinforced in 1992, he hooked up with LTJ Bukem for *19.5*, which lifted a strings 'n' keys opening from Salsoul funksters The Jammers and a snippet of vocal by Rowetta from the Happy Mondays. He'd soon release *Piano Tune*, also on Bukem's Good Looking—a deadly track built around a simple, descending set of mournful minor chord keys, before Amen and Think breaks launch it into the cosmos. The AA-side ripped India's ecstatic, gospel-like vocal from Strictly Rhythm house anthem *Love & Happiness* by River Ocean, creating an achingly soulful twilight mood.

Showing that he had several strings to his bow, Peshay was also snared by Goldie for the menacing *Predator* on Metalheadz, and then James Lavelle's Mo' Wax put out his jazzy swinger *Miles From Home*—an early Swerve classic. He then signed to Island Blue, a subsidiary of Universal, where he was A&Red by Ross Allen, a DJ pal of Gilles Peterson.

Peshay was only one of scores of producers dabbling with jazzy jungle. Subject 13, aka Dave Stewart and Roy Bleau, had also made darkside hardcore initially before turning to a more soulful sound, their sax-tastic *Good Guys, Bad Guys* being a prime example. (Subject 13 were also notable for their organisation of under-eighteen raves, where they generally played the harder side of the music. 'You've got to give back to the community,' they note in the booklet that accompanies the 1997 *Breakbeat Science 2* compilation on Volume. 'If you can help to get kids on the right path at an early stage, then all the better. We enjoy it. These are the adults of the future, the adults of tomorrow.')

Via their Vibez Recordings stamp, Subject 13 put out early material by the likes of Intense and Big Bud, who also showed up on Bukem's Good Looking and Fabio's Creative Source. Fabio started up the latter label in 1995, with the fluttery, oceanic, flute-tickled steppa *Heaven* by Carlito, and it played a pivotal part in the development of the liquid sound. Fabio's midweek Swerve nights were a place for him to test out tunes and play what he liked, and it served as a focal meeting point for the London scene in the same way that the weekly Movement night at Bar Rumba did the following night.

Grooverider was resident at Metalheadz on a Sunday, and he would later start his own night, Grace at Herbal, at the Shoreditch end of Kingsland Road. Via his Prototype label, he mostly fed into the darker sound, but both he and Fabio would guest at each other's nights and play everything—all styles of drum & bass, across the board. This didn't stop Fabio being typecast as 'Mr Jazzy' at one point, though ...

'Yeah, thanks for bringing that up!' he laughs. 'I went through a phase where a lot of the tunes I played were kind of jazzy, but it doesn't mean don't send me nothing else, 'cause I love everything. Sometimes in music there's little ways you go for a while, and my little thing for a while was the jazzy thing.'

In 2000, Fabio put out the *Liquid Funk* compilation on Creative Source—a landmark release that included acts like Carlito, Intense, Hidden Agenda, Subject 13, Fellowship, Big Bud, Primary Motive, and Peshay. The more musical form now had an all-encompassing name—liquid funk, or liquid for short. Fabio continued to play the sound at Swerve, and his approachability helped foment the expansion of the subgenre. 'When Danny Byrd first arrived, I remember introducing him to Fabio at Swerve, and Fabio going, Oh, you're Danny Byrd, you're the man,' says Chris Goss, Hospital Records' managing director. 'It blew his mind. He'd only been making music for a couple of years, and he'd only had a couple of records out.'

### THE BRAZILIAN EFFECT—MARKY, SUNSHINE UPLANDS, SHY FX

In the run-up to 2000, drum & bass remained the most futuristic, innovative UK-derived music around. It had exploded into the mainstream via Roni Size and Reprazent's Mercury win, experienced the earthquake of the breakthrough of Goldie, and more, but for every mainstream breakthrough, there's often an opposite reaction—a desire by some to return underground. Restore order. Regroup.

The dark sound was the natural antidote to a brush with commercialism—Renegade Hardware, Hardleaders, Ray Keith's Dread, Techstep, and No U-Turn. Techstep chimed with the overarching mood among much of the nation's youth. It's hard to imagine now, in this post-COVID-19 world, but in the late 90s there was considerable paranoia about computer glitches bringing about the end of the world. Apocalyptic predictions about the Millennium Bug were debated in ganja-filled studios, and even though a Labour government had sailed in on a crest of optimism in May 1997, the overarching, prevailing wind switched somewhat back towards the dark side as the new century dawned.

The science behind crafting a tune became ever more intricate, as sci-fi soundtracks—past and future—were thrown into the mix. Some producers were simply reflecting the code of the streets, but the effect of this raft of dark tunes dominating floors once again was to frighten some people away from the drum & bass dances—chiefly women. 'There was definitely more interesting stuff going on outside the scene at that point,' believes Marc Royal, aka T Power. 'It got very utilitarian, chased all the women out. The scene really needed the women to come back—it was a sausage party.'

Many of the parties still banged, but some increasingly seemed like a load of sweaty blokes with their tops off, moshing as if they were at a heavy-metal gig. Simultaneously, the rise of UK garage—with its happy positivity—took some of the shine off drum & bass's futurism. A new dawn was brewing, though, especially when the end of the century didn't signal that the party was over. Instead, a new portal opened up, significantly influenced by one man and his uplifting, infectious energy.

Brazilian-born Marco Antonio da Silva was a hip-hop kid as a teen, and hip-house was his gateway into São Paulo's fledgling dance music scene. 'I just followed the transition from acid house to techno, to hardcore rave to jungle tekno, into jungle and drum & bass,' he says. 'When I first heard jungle I thought, *Wow, this is strange and different, but interesting.* Nobody was playing it in Brazil, so I ordered around ten or twenty records from a store in Miami—it was so hard to get records from the UK. So I just had the records from the big labels—Suburban Base, Moving Shadow, and Reinforced.'

Marky built up a little collection to start playing out in Brazilian clubs, and he dreamt about visiting London to see his heroes. He saved up some money and made the voyage in 1997, along with DJ Patife. 'At first, I really wanted to see DJ Hype—he was just a complete DJ—he put turntablism into a DJ set,' he says. 'I went to True Playaz at The End, saw DJs like Zinc, Mampi Swift, and Brockie play too. Andy C played the last set.'

The d&b scenesters he met on this trip were friendly enough, but only up to a point, and Marky returned to São Paulo to carry on DJing alongside pals such as Wagner (aka Patife) and Xerxes (XRS), turning Brazilian electronic music fiends onto drum & bass.

Thursdays in London in the late 90s were all about Movement. Edo van Duijn and his half-brother, Oliver Brown, were part of the Movement crew, along with V Recordings boss Bryan Gee and the Botchit/SOUR gang—Dave Stone, Vini Medley, Martin Love, and co. The next time Patife visited London, in the autumn of 1998, he brought with him a videotape of a d&b night the guys had put on in São Paulo. 'There were a thousand people on the dancefloor, singing the basslines and the choruses of jungle tunes,' says Patife.

'It had footage of Patife playing to a thousand people at the legendary Arena club in São Paulo,' remembers Oliver Brown, 'and Marky to five thousand at Toco Dance Club—with amazing, almost synchronised dancing of the whole crowd to go with it.'

The Brazilians had called their own night in São Paulo 'Movement', but they wanted to do more of an official tie-in. Oliver and Edo took Patife to Bryan Gee's office in Brixton, and within two minutes of playing him the videotape, Bryan was dancing around exclaiming that he wanted to go to Brazil. The team decided to scope it out.

Edo's dad had had a series of jobs in South America. Working a day job as a subeditor for *Minx* magazine in London at the time, he was tasked to write an article on plastic surgery in Bogotá, the capital of Colombia, so he stopped off in São Paulo on the way back and dropped by Marky and Patife's Movement night at Lov.e to investigate whether to officially lend the Movement brand name to it. After experiencing the crowd's passion and fervour, Edo called up Bryan, completely enthused: 'You need to get your arse over here—it is running' is how Bryan remembers the conversation with Edo going. They hastily arranged a night for Bryan to play in São Paulo.

'When I got into the club, Lov.e, I was like, *This is Bar Rumba in Brazil—serious ting.* The place was buzzing,' Bryan remembers.

Usually, it's the visiting international DJs who get the acclaim, but a tall, skinny resident DJ called Marky was rocking the joint. 'I see some guy called Marky going crazy on the decks, and I'm thinking, *Shit, I've got work to do here, I'm gonna have to dig deep.* He had the skills, and he was smiling! Drum & bass DJs didn't smile back then—we was all moody and serious.

'He was smiling and waving and looking happy, and the crowd was feeding off his energy,' Bryan continues. 'He smashed the place. I was so impressed that I thought, *We've got to bring this guy back to the UK, everybody's got to see this guy.* DJ Hype was the furthest I'd seen with the scratching and stuff, but Marky took it to another level, and he was having fun with it. It blew my mind.'

The Movement crew brought Marky over to play at Bar Rumba, and then Mass in Brixton at a V Recordings night. The immediate impact he had was phenomenal. After watching the Brazilian's hyper-energetic, skill-laden Brixton set, *Melody Maker* reported, 'Other junglists are going to have to up their game.'

Oliver and Edo immediately took on managing Marky from London; Edo moved to São Paulo; and a corridor effectively opened up between the two cities—a cultural exchange—that would lead to a steady flow of UK d&b DJs playing Brazil at clubs and festivals, and Marky injecting his unique positivity into the UK scene. 'When I'm DJing, I always want to show people how much I love the music—my passion for the music,' he says. 'When I started playing in the UK, other DJs were like, *Woah* [makes moody face], and wouldn't even dance in the DJ booth. I tried standing still but I can't—I need to move.'

As the Brazilians started getting their act together, production-wise, Bryan Gee had the foresight to recognise this new horizon for the sound and A&R the tracks on *The Brasil EP*, which came out on his label, V Recordings, in 2001. Marky did a DJ-friendly remix of a recent track by samba-funk multi-instrumentalist Max De Castro, *Samba Raro*, but it was DJ Patife who stole the show with *Sambassim*. Beginning with some slow, *batucada* percussion before Brazilian singer Fernanda Porto enters the fray with the sultry *joie de vivre* of an Astrud Gilberto, *Sambassim* displays an incredible lightness of production touch—ably demonstrating that you don't need big booming beats or bass for a drum & bass tune to fly. Fernanda Porto even mentions 'drum & bass' in the song, which was an added bonus. *Sambassim* unwittingly gave birth to 'drum & bossa', and it further opened up a fifth column for d&b: Latin/samba vibes.

Brazil's homegrown samba scene also provided inspiration for a Marky original with producer XRS, who he'd known since the hardcore days. One day, when the pair were trying to make a drum & bass tune that would fit in with the sound of various London producers, they felt that their flow wasn't running. Marky drove home and went through some records to bring back to the studio to sample. One of these was a seven-inch disc that belonged to his dad—*Carolina Carol Bela* by Toquinho & Jorge Ben. 'My dad used to play lots of stuff like this when me and my sisters were kids,' Marky recalls.

Cutting up bits of samba/bossa legend Jorge Ben's tropical, flamenco-sounding guitar and time-stretching the odd warm note, they finished the track in a few hours on rudimentary equipment—a PC, a couple of keyboards, and a Yamaha mixing desk. 'It's basically a five- or six-channel tune—very simple. It doesn't have to be all about mixdowns and heavy sounds,' says Marky. 'Sometimes it's more about the vibe and to make people happy, and some people forget about that. In all styles of music, not just in drum & bass.'

'We did think we had something special when we finished it, but then you almost always do when you finish a track, otherwise you'd just put it in the trash,' Marky adds, philosophically. 'I don't think we understood quite how much impact it would have long-term, though—and how it might change our lives.'

When Marky got home after finishing this track with XRS, his mum was still doing housework—washing clothes. He thus gave the track the working title *LK* ('liquid kitchen'), and it stuck. It was an instrumental at first, apart from a muted bit of vocal sample towards the end that the guys put in as an homage to the original artists.

Marky played *LK* in his sets while touring the UK with Bryan Gee before heading back home to Brazil. Soon, *LK* had been cut to dubplate by a few key DJs, and the vibe started to build. 'The next time I came to the UK, everywhere I went, I was getting asked to play a track called *It's The Way*,' he says, 'and I had no idea what tune that was. I was touring with [MC] Darrison at the time. Then I would play the *LK* instrumental, and everyone was saying, That's the track!'

Stamina MC had been improvising lyrics over *LK* whenever anyone played it down at Movement (hence the reference to 'the Movement crew' in the finished version), adding an extra layer to the track. 'When the whole crowd started singing Stamina's freestyle lyrics, we immediately got him into the studio to record his vocals,' says Marky.

Stamina recorded his vocals in London and got them sent over to Marky, who layered them over the *LK* instrumental live at his next party. When this went off, he took the a cappella CD back to the studio with XRS, and they mastered the vocal onto the instrumental. Before they knew it, BBC Radio 1 had picked up on it, and *LK* smashed into the UK Top 20 in the middle of the summer of 2002.

'We were really surprised—we never thought it could be that big,' says Marky. 'We were just two kids from São Paulo, so playing big shows in the UK was already a major thing, without getting into the Top 20.'

The guys even went on *Top Of The Pops*, the long-running TV chart show. 'That was weird, but really cool!' chuckles Marky. 'It was great to do and experience, and I'm glad to be able to say that I have performed on the show. The dancers were all a bit last-minute, and just made it a bit surreal.' With Marky scratching live on the TV show, Stamina gave a commanding vocal performance, and the song cemented its place as one of the sounds of the summer of 2002.

'I made tracks better than *LK* which didn't have the same success,' says Marky. 'But we made an anthem—not many people get to do that. Roni Size made *Brown Paper Bag*, Goldie did *Inner City Life*, Shy FX made *Shake Ur Body…*'

### SHY FX & T POWER

After tracks such as *Police State* and excursions into ambient and breakbeat, Marc Royal, aka T Power, hooked up with his old SOUR Records buddy Andre Williams, aka Shy FX, just before 2000 to pool equipment resources for a studio in Whitechapel. With Marc working days and Andre doing nights, there was a natural overlap, and they inevitably started working on tunes together.

'Andre had this massive backlog of ideas, some in very simple forms, like eight-bar loops, and we started going through all of these,' Marc recalls. 'I said, You've got vocals on these? and he said, Oh, yeah, that's from a recording session. I couldn't believe it! I was in between projects, so I said, Why don't we try and get these things fixed up? You'd need a major record deal for these—it was full-on vocals.'

A singer called Dianne Joseph, from late-90s all-female British R&B trio Truce, was recording in another studio in the block, and the guys enlisted her for a vocal—initially in return for a remix. 'The rhythm track was already there in place for *Shake Ur Body*, and she came in, listened to it, and wrote the top line in, like, ten minutes,' Marc remembers. 'Did the verses, then she was gone two hours later. Suddenly we were left with this tune, and were like, *What the fuck do we do with this?*

'We finished it up, and started sending it out to people,' T Power continues. 'They didn't want the vocal on there at all, saying, You need to chop it up and turn it down. And we were like, You really need to try to fit this into your set, because the scene needs this right now.'

Shy had released the tropical, superfly *Bambaata* in 1998, but since then had sat on the rest of the tracks in his studio—finished or not. 'You have to wait until the time is right,' he told *DJ Mag* at the time. 'The scene was far too dark until recently. How do you tell when the time is right? You just feel it. I DJ every week—you can tell things from that.'

The right scene DJs started caning *Shake Ur Body* in 2001, and Shy eventually put it out on his own Ebony Recordings. After being played on BBC Radio 1—by Jo Whiley—offers from major labels flooded in. The guys went with EMI offshoot Positiva in the end—it probably helped that XL co-founder Nick Halkes was involved in setting up Positiva, and was someone who clearly knew his onions.

'For us, it wasn't about huge amounts of money,' said T Power at the *Shake Ur Body* video shoot. 'Obviously that's part of the story, but it had to be someone who was going to understand that it had to be done correctly. There's no need to water the product down when it's already smashing it up on the underground. It had to be done on those terms, and Positiva were quite happy to let us have final say on everything.'

Marc was quite strident about getting 'proper urban music' into the mainstream charts on the artists' own terms. 'It can be done without having it watered down, you can have people see real music that's well grounded, rather than majors just reeling off another piece of commercial shit,' he told *DJ Mag*. 'Drum & bass definitely got angsty towards the end of last century. But going through that has maybe made people look at things a bit different. Or maybe it's just a cyclic thing, it goes round in circles.

'We weren't even sure that it'd work at the time. The drum & bass scene was still changing, it was still quite dark, the whole liquid funk thing was just starting to really get going. Now it's in full flow, it's accepted that that's the way it's going again,' he continued. 'Everyone's opened their eyes, people are experimenting more with the music. It'll push everything forward, it'll allow producers to be more creative again rather than worrying, *God, what if such and such doesn't play it?* It's healthy for the scene.'

The guys baulked at the time about appearing on *Top Of The Pops*, but they agreed to make a video for *Shake Ur Body*. Positiva tendered for some treatments, and they opted for one choreographed by a woman named Anisha that they would only have to make a small cameo in. A film crew and a large dance troupe decamped to the Engine House Thames Water Station near Staines, west of London, for the shoot one fresh February day in 2002. Full of huge piston engines and pipes, the English Heritage-listed building had a definite nautical feel inside—scenes from the *Titanic* movie had been filmed there a few years previously.

As if to underline the authenticity of the operation, a load of significant drum & bass playas showed up for cameos in the video: Adam F, Andy C, Skibadee, Mampi Swift, Brockie, Carl Collins from Hardleaders and other friends and associates hung out on the balcony, while a posse of sassy breakdancers threw shapes on the lit-up, chequered dancefloor.

With its jazzy intro a sped-up sample of Cal Tjader's 1965 lounge-soul track *Leyte*—some likened it to the theme from the HBO series *Sex & The City*— *Shake Ur Body* oozed positivity, sass, and a waist-winding groove. It smashed into the UK Top 10 in April 2002, peaking at no. 7. This was drum & bass permeating the mainstream on its own terms again.

'Anyone from the circuit will know that it's smashed it up everywhere for the past few months,' Shy told *DJ Mag* at the time. 'All the DJs and everyone have all been in it for a while, they've all seen [drum & bass] blow up and go back underground again, and right now we've got a scene that's running by itself. It doesn't need majors or magazines, it's more than healthy enough to cope independently.'

Shy FX and T Power went on to have other big tracks together following *Shake Ur Body*, such as ruffneck breakbeat-funk jam *Don't Wanna Know* with Di and Skibadee—another UK Top 20 record—and the flamenco-fabulous *Feelin'*

*U* with Kele Le Roc after signing to London Records offshoot ffrr. Drum & bass had hit the sunshine uplands again, but the pair certainly weren't that keen on the attention that mainstream success brought. 'It felt really weird,' says Marc. 'I am not cut out for that level of attention. It was very discomforting for me. I'm not wired for that world, I'm way better at being tucked away in the studio and getting on with it. When it completely blew up and we were doing TV stuff, you'd go to Oxford Street and people were doing double-takes. You'd go into Virgin Megastore and you had everybody staring at you. It was like, *We need to get out of here, let's get a cab back to the studio*.

'People that excel in that world with that kind of attention, like the Lady Gagas, Taylor Swifts, have to be wired in a very specific way to be able to deal with it,' he continues. 'It fucks your head up.'

## UPLIFTING SOUND

*Shake Ur Body* and *LK* were arguably the two most important records of this immediate postmillennial era, but it's too simplistic to pinpoint just a couple of tracks amid a wealth of uplifting tunes. The sassy *Ultra Obscene* by Breakbeat Era—Roni Size and DJ Die's project with Bristol singer Leonie Laws—had actually come out in 1999, along with the album of the same name, and a tapestry of other tracks were peppered around this apex. J Majik's house-y *Love Is Not A Game* with soul diva Kathy Brown came out on fledgling house imprint Defected, while Zinc's superb slab of spy mania, *Casino Royale*, was another notable 2001 cut. Meanwhile, Shimon & Andy C's huge, fun-time, party-rockin' track *Body Rock* entered the UK Top 40 from vinyl sales alone in January 2002.

Manchester duo Future Cut had released on Renegade Hardware and Trouble On Vinyl offshoot Renegade Recordings in the late 90s, and just after the millennium teamed up with a young local Mancunian MC called Jenna Gibbons, aka Jenna G, to form Un-Cut. One of their first tracks together, *Midnight*—with its jazzy intro, giant disco stabs, and full vocal—shifted a stack of white labels in 2001 (partly thanks to a tougher, rollin' overhaul by Marcus Intalex & ST Files), and earned them major publishing and record deals. On the release of their debut album in 2002, *The Un-Calculated Some*, on WEA, *Midnight* was re-released and punctured the UK Top 30. Hot on its heels, D. Kay & Epsilon recruited Stamina MC for their feelgood party-tune *Barcelona* in 2003.

What was significant about all of these tracks is that they came from the scene itself, via the traditional routes of dubplates and promos to DJs—from the grassroots, rather than manufactured in the mainstream. And it was as if the Brazilian influence had greenlit a lighter mood on many drum & bass dancefloors.

Marky says he's been told lots of times that he was instrumental in ushering in a more positive vibe to postmillennial drum & bass. 'I think it was just bringing people around to realising that bass-heavy music didn't need to be dark and gloomy,' he says. 'It can be light and funky, but still have the same effect. Still today I love to dance to tracks that have a lot of harmonies mixed in with the basslines.'

Marky had brought out a mix CD, *The Brazilian Job*, on Movement's in-house label in 2001, and it remains one of the biggest-selling d&b comps to this day. It kicks off with the *LK* instrumental—pre-*Stamina* vocal—before breezing through Carlito & Addiction's *Supergrass*, Marcus Intalex & ST Files' *Nightfall*, the Total Science remix of London Elektricity's *My Dreams*, and Un-Cut's *Midnight* hit. It was a snapshot of a typical Marky DJ set, moving through the shades; building a set by playing things of beauty as well as kick-ass missives by Bad Company, Shimon, and Origin Unknown (Andy C and Ant Miles), plus J Majik's overhaul of the whirling hype-house hit *Spaced Invader* by Hatiras; then there's a Future Cut and an Ed Rush & Optical dark segment, before the tone lightens again.

Scratching, messing with the EQs, cutting and pasting, picking up the CDJ and scratching behind his head, Hendrix-style—Marky is a *proper* DJ. Jigging up and down like a jack-in-the-box, his whole body moving to the rhythm, his feel for the music is infectious. When he DJs, it's like he's been infected with the sounds—hot-wired.

Marky did things with drum & bass tracks on the decks that few other DJs would do. Only really DJ Hype and latterly thrice DMC champ DJ Craze from the USA—a new convert to the sound who Marky ended up doing some shows with—would perform expert turntablist tricks in their sets on a par with Marky. As younger decknicians like JFB and Jaguar Skills would later demonstrate, drum & bass lent itself well to mixology too.

After mixing a covermount CD for a summer issue of *DJ Mag* in 2002, which turned out to be the biggest seller of the year, Marky appeared on the cover of the magazine the following year—an accolade that made the national newspapers back in Brazil. He went on to host Marky & Friends parties at festivals like Skolbeats and clubs like Fabric, and slotted into the growing international touring circuit.

'The Brazilian thing was good for drum & bass,' says Bryan Gee. 'It opened up the doors to a whole new audience of people—the Latin sound and all that. And it made DJs have fun when they were playing—Marky brought that to the table. Drum & bass was a serious place before that. It was us and them. He made it cool to smile and be happy, not like you're some cheesy guy. And the music had so much soul.'

## TAKE ME TO THE HOSPITAL

Hospital's rise coincided with the boom in popularity of the liquid sound. Chris Goss had hooked up with Tony Colman in the early 90s, originally to help him run the Tongue N Groove label, which was primarily a vehicle for Tony's jazzy street soul band, Izit. When the band folded as the acid-jazz world shifted its culture from live music to downbeat trip-hop, they shelved the Tongue N Groove label and started making their own producer-based music at their Red Corner Door studio in Barons Court, London.

Chris and Tony both lived in Tottenham at the time, where jungle pirates and record shops were prevalent. 'Jungle and that soundsystem culture was such a big part of local life, such an exciting soundtrack,' says Chris. 'Even though it was much harder to make drum & bass, it felt more exciting and current—it had a real edge to it. I love house music, but—and I don't want this to come out the wrong way—it's almost a bit too easy, it's four-to-the-floor. When you really get into chopping up drum breaks and making tunes at 158bpm, as it was then, it was this whole other universe. Programming, texture, bottom end, sound design— there was so much to it, it just felt like a world of possibilities to us, really.'

The guys were attracted to the jazzy drum & bass sound of 1995–96, but they wanted to push it further. 'We thought, *Fuck it, let's sample James Last, Roy Budd, or classic British soundtrack composers*. And we did. Those first handfuls of records we ended up calling loungecore—we were into that lush, warm, slightly cheesy, easy listening sound. Also, we knew that other producers would never go and sample those records.'

Most people in drum & bass totally ignored the first few records on the nascent Hospital label, as London Elektricity and other pseudonyms. It wasn't until the label's seventh release that they started to find their feet, as jazzy sidewinder *Song In The Key Of Life* received plays by Fabio and Doc Scott. By 1999, LE had released their debut album, *Pull The Plug*, and the support for that enabled Hospital to start putting out music by other people, too. 'We had a licensing deal with Sony, which was a crucial thing for us,' remembers Chris. 'Sony had their own department in Japan just to release drum & bass. They signed up Good Looking, V, Full Cycle, Vibez, and Hospital. We were blessed. They started with these compilations involving all of us.'

Landslide and Danny Byrd were the first two external Hospital artists, soon followed by a young guy named Lincoln Barrett from Wales. His first two releases as High Contrast were ignored by most, but then came funky discoid number *Make It Tonight* in 2001, soon followed by a majestically symphonic *Return Of Forever*. In July 2004, when Radio 1 unveiled a new DJ from Dublin, Ireland, who went by the name Annie Mac, the first record she played on the station was *Racing Green*, a widescreen, galloping release by High Contrast that truly blew him up. Annie Mac's wholehearted embrace of drum & bass would considerably help the more radio-friendly side of the genre in the years that followed.

Chris stepped down from London Elektricity in 2001 to concentrate on running Hospital, while Tony continued LE as a solo project. Soon, he'd revisited his live band roots for the touring London Elektricity live show, touring extensively between 2003–05 with jazz singer Liane Carroll and MC Wrec on vocals, Landslide on keys, and the seemingly multi-tentacled Jungle Drummer on live drums. (Colman would later reimagine London Elektricity as a pioneering, multi-instrumental big band in 2016, after his kids had grown up.) Hospital also started its Hospitality night at Herbal in Shoreditch, a small club that became a bit of an east London drum & bass Mecca—Chris Inperspective's Technicality, Grooverider's Grace, the Therapy Sessions, and the all-female Feline crew all held regular, mostly monthly sessions there. The guys started doing Hospitality in other cities like Cardiff, Bristol, Norwich, and Berlin, as well as teaming up with the Detonate promoters in Nottingham, Digital's drum & bass specialists in Newcastle, and so on.

'Herbal was always packed, but we knew we had to do something to make a bigger impression—and that we'd have to hire a venue ourselves,' says Chris. 'We've always wanted to do things a bit differently, so when it came to doing a big club, we thought, *Let's try to find somewhere where no one else is doing a drum & bass rave*. And Heaven is where it all started, with Rage. It's also one of

Europe's biggest gay clubs, and there's a certain strength in going somewhere that can be even more inclusive. It felt like the perfect space.'

Herbal was a small, three-storey space with a maximum capacity of four hundred, so moving into this eighteen-hundred-capacity iconic central London club felt like a leap of faith. They needn't have worried, though; the first Hospitality at Heaven—featuring Andy C, LTJ Bukem, Bryan Gee, and the Hospital roster—had queues around the block. 'This was a huge turning point for us,' believes Chris. 'Literally in one night, things had changed. We put our flag in the sand.'

Hospitality ran at Heaven for three-and-a-half years before Heaven was sold, leaving them temporarily venue-less. 'That was when our events crystallised, when people took us seriously as more than just a label,' says Chris. 'It was massive for us.' The next logical step up turned out to be the five-thousand-capacity Brixton Academy, 'another venue so rich in our city's musical heritage. It just seemed like another crazy step to take, so why not?'

They also did Hospitality at Fabric's short-lived sister club, Matter, in Greenwich, while the label grew alongside the events brand. In 2006, they launched a sublabel, Med School, with a release by Brazilian drum & bass dude S.P.Y. They signed Logistics, Cyantific, Nu:Tone, and then, in 2010, a kid from Belgium, Boris Daenen, who called himself Netsky. His first smooth liquid release, *Moving With You*, immediately made an impact, and he started releasing albums; a bit further down the line, he would become somewhat of a pop drum & bass EDM superstar.

Hospital worked with High Contrast, Netsky, and the Austrian duo Camo & Krooked for a number of years before they all moved on. They were all quite different artists. 'The relationship between an artist and a label is first of all about trust,' says Chris, on losing their three biggest acts around 2016. 'And a healthy, creative environment in which to collaborate. With all three artists we nailed that, over different lengths of time. All three, at different times, got to a point where they said, I wanna go and do something else.'

After four albums with Hospital, High Contrast signed to 3Beat; Netsky inked a major-label deal with Sony; and Camo & Krooked jumped to drum & bass rivals Ram—but they all parted on amicable terms. High Contrast continued to play Hospitality shows, while Netsky returned to the label in 2020 for a drum & bass record. 'Boris will always feel like family to us,' says Chris.

'We can continue positive, productive working relationships with artists like this, even if they're not signed.'

The next risky venture by Hospital was to stage the UK's first drum & bass festival, Hospitality In The Park, in Finsbury Park in north London on Saturday, September 24, 2016. A multi-tent, daytime event, it attempted to cater for all the flavours of drum & bass—not just the Hospital sound. 'It was moving into the culture and phenomenon of daytime events,' Chris says. They also did daytime events at Studio 338 in London, repeating and selling out the London festival in subsequent years and trialling a couple of festivals in Croatia, at the much-used Garden Place, Tisno—Hospitality On The Beach. (These events, like everybody else's, were then cruelly curtailed by COVID-19.)

The Hospital team weren't the only ones to amplify their recorded output by running events—arguably the greatest marketing tool for releases of all. V Recordings had always run its Planet V nights, and after the label's success with Marky, Bryan Gee kickstarted another sub-label—the fairly self-explanatory Liquid V. An early release was by Calibre, whom Fabio had discovered just before 2000.

Belfast lad Dominick Martin had his first single as Calibre, *Last Man On Earth*, on short-lived Irish d&b label Quadrophonic, before Fabio snapped him up for a two-track release. In one sense archetypal jazzy jungle, there was a particular lightness of touch to the production on *Mystic* that gave it widescreen appeal, way beyond the dance. A synthesised jazz bass tone, airy strings, and ambient washes transport the listener to a distant shore at low tide—this was proper transcendent, cinematic material. It's no wonder Fabio took Calibre under his wing, acting as a kind of mentor and releasing his debut album, *Musique Concrete*, on Creative Source in 2001.

Among a scene of blabbermouths—often by necessity—Calibre let his music do the talking. He rarely does interviews, doesn't use social media, and has never allowed his productions to be remixed. 'I'll always remember one of the earliest trips I took down to Music House,' he told *DJ Mag* in an interview years later. 'Randall came up to me, kissed me, and told me I was blessed.'

The duality in a typical Calibre production is typified by his first outing on Soul:r, the label run by perhaps his spiritual peer at the time, Marcus Intalex. On *Fire & Water* (2001), individualistic drum programming and a wobble-board bassline are offset by snippets of the 1975 reggae track *Miss Wire Waist* by Carl

Malcolm. The title line to the lover's rock paean to 'the slim girl dem'—which led to Carl Malcolm following it up with *Fattie Bum Bum*—is put through Calibre's mangle, leading to a distorted, echoing, otherworldly effect, rendering the track uplifting yet mournful.

The same phrase could be said to characterise much of Calibre's catalogue moving forward—and much of the liquid genre, too, in a sense. Not needlessly joyful or crassly happy-clappy, but not gloomy and depressing either, by taking bits of jazz's street-real melancholia or soul's romantic beauty this strand of drum & bass was able to keep its street cred—and flourish for many years to follow.

Growing up in Northern Ireland, Calibre couldn't not be affected by the tensions between Nationalist and Unionist communities that often spilled over into violence, until the 1998 Good Friday agreement led to a truce. 'Where I was coming from had a lot to do with where I wanted to go, because I was traumatised from growing up in Belfast,' he said in 2013. 'Technical knowledge gives you some understanding of how your craft develops, but being a human being, it's important to understand that's a part of it as much as anything. This is where I was coming from, and for me, it was an escape from my background.

'I think it affected me as a person, and art is something that comes out of that,' he continued. 'It doesn't have to relate to that thing, it just has to come from it. That's the impetus, it's the thing that presses the buttons, it's the thing that makes me want to go out there and find some sense in the world. I don't really like to talk about Northern Ireland—who I am and where I come from definitely has something to do with the music, but I don't think it inspired me to do it.'

Super-prolific, Calibre set up his own signature label in 2003—literally, Signature Records—to give himself complete control of his output. The Latin-tinged *Peso* and Bob Marley-sampling *My Chances* kicked things off, while his collaboration with fellow liquid pioneer High Contrast, *Mr Majestic*, drew heavily on Horace Andy's *Money, The Root Of All Evil*—the roots righteousness of dub being frequently in the mix for some so-called liquid tunes.

As Calibre started DJing internationally more, he started working with vocalists like DRS for *Timeout*, and Diane Charlemagne—the achingly soulful voice of *Inner City Life*—on the beatific *Bullets*. It's well documented, meanwhile, that his era-defining 2005 album, *Second Sun*, including its radiant title track, was written at the peak of his alcoholism.

'I used to write tunes on all types of substances, and drink was one of them,' the recovered alcoholic, who's been dry since 2010, told *DJ Mag* in 2018. For quite a while, Calibre helped Marcus Intalex run Soul:r, and the two became great friends, playing back-to-back sessions at Sunandbass and producing together on occasion, including the smooth roller *Run Away* in 2014, featuring MC Fox from Manchester.

A true treasure of the scene, Calibre is now sixteen artist albums deep. He's explored plenty of other music genres, releasing on labels such as Craig Richards's The Nothing Special, Mala's Deep Medi, and Shy FX's Digital Soundboy, as well as collecting the set of drum & bass stalwarts like 31, Critical, Exit, Commercial Suicide, C.I.A., and so on.

'There are only really two kings of this music,' says Goldie in *Drum & Bass: The Movement*. 'Two poles, if you like. Dillinja, and Calibre. At both ends of that spectrum. Everything in between is us.'

Fabio may have created the lane for liquid to flow into, but he and Grooverider have always played a broad spectrum of drum & bass. 'That's why I've always tried to stay out of those little traps,' Fabio says, explaining how he sidestepped the lazy 'Mr Jazzy' tag. 'You fall into those little traps, you're not coming out of it. So it's best to know that we play drum & bass—and that's it. It's a global thing. We can go anywhere and play this shit, and it's all good.

'I don't look at a jump-up track and think, *Oh, this is jump-up, I'm not gonna play it*,' Fabio continues. 'I'd never think that, 'cause I just think, *This is a drum & bass track*—I really do. I might hear something from Calibre and something from Hazard and love the tracks equally.'

'It doesn't stop there; from that side of things, who broke Fred V & Grafix?' says Grooverider. 'Camo & Krooked? I played their tune before anybody else. When I think about Hospital Records, a lot of their artists is down to me.'

'You'd more likely think it was me, yeah,' says Fabio. 'There were things on our [Radio 1] radio show that you probably wouldn't associate with me and Groove that we brought through as well. You gotta remember, we're drum & bass—we brought this to the table. You can't pigeonhole us, 'cause we can play anything within drum & bass. I know everything that's going on, and I will play accordingly. That's what it's about.'

# 20 Breakbeat Chaos: Adam F, Fresh, Pendulum, And D&B's Brush With The Mainstream

Like a lot of young junglists in their formative years, Adam Fenton was a hip-hop kid before he got into hardcore and then drum & bass. Self-taught on an abandoned piano as a kid (his dad was 70s glam-rocker Alvin Stardust, although his parents split up when he was young and he hardly saw his dad as a child), he started releasing tunes in 1994 on Moving Shadow sub-label Section 5, run out of a record shop on the Kings Road, and the record-shop-affiliated Lucky Spin.

Reflecting some of his musical influences, tracks like *Circles*—with its 'Check, check, check' snippet and jazz-funk sample—and the superfly daisy-age *F-Jam* with MC Conrad initially took him down a jazzy jungle route, but then he started hanging out at Metalheadz on a Sunday night, as well as Speed on a Wednesday. 'Just being in that dark, intense atmosphere and energy was so exciting ... and unpredictable,' he recalled of Metalheadz years later. 'With *Metropolis*, I remember coming home from the club and just having to make that track. I was in this intense, dark, and futuristic place in my mind, and that's where all the sounds and elements came from to put that one together.'

*Metropolis* is all about tension. Following a dramatic opening chord, there's *Bladerunner*-style fuzzy interference for near enough a whole minute before any beats come in. The gaseous interference continues over a matrix of sci-fi clangs, incisive jabs, and skippy snare, until a guttural bass precedes the Sensurround drop. It was debuted at Metalheadz, blind, by Grooverider. 'It was such an honour for me when it was played in the club,' Adam reflected later. 'I went over to Grooverider and gave him the dubplate. As he'd heard *Circles* already, he just took the record out and played it. He hadn't even heard it! That was ultimate respect back then.'

Predictably, *Metropolis* destroyed the Blue Note dancefloor, and Goldie snapped up the tune for 'Headz. Soon, as part of the major-label gold rush,

Adam had signed to Positiva/EMI, and the resulting album, *Colours*, which he toured with a live band, remains one of drum & bass's strongest, in terms of musicality and production values.

Still feeding back into the scene, he gave *Brand New Funk* to V Recordings in '98. Repeating the trick of building tension with nearly a minute of eerie, beatless atmosphere, this massive funk jam cemented Adam F's name at the heart of the scene. It meant he could do what he wanted from this point—which he duly did.

Reigniting his love of hip-hop, he passed some beats to LL Cool J for the title track of the rapper's no. 1 album *G.O.A.T.*, then hooked up with Redman for a track that set the tone for Adam F's own *KAOS*. 'After I'd come up with the initial concept, I was going through a load of orchestral CDs and film scores,' he explained to *DJ Mag*'s Tim Irwin in early 2002. 'Then I went into the studio and wrote some music with that kind of feel. I recorded a crazy intro with a big orchestra and choir, and because I was thinking of Redman for the first track, I got them to sing his name. The direction of my tracks is always inspired by a mad intro, and that one went on to inspire the whole album.'

Redman flipped when he heard the intro. After all, it was like having a whole orchestra and choir devoted to bigging you up in the style of Carl Orff's 1935 epic *O Fortuna*, otherwise known in the UK as music from the Old Spice aftershave advert. It became the basis of *Smash Sumthin*, a UK Top 10 hit, and led to US hip-hop heavyweights like M.O.P, Guru from Gang Starr, De La Soul, Pharoahe Monch, Capone-N-Noreaga, and Lil' Mo guesting on the resulting *Kaos: The Anti-Acoustic Warfare* album, as well as dancehall don Beenie Man. The singles all went Top 50, and Adam then asked assorted junglists—Roni Size, Origin Unknown, Dillinja, Ray Keith, Mampi Swift, Bad Company, John B, High Contrast, Hype & Pascal, J Majik, and more—to remix tracks for *Drum & Bass Warfare*, which came out on his own Kaos Recordings in late 2002.

Back in London, Adam had struck up a friendship with DJ Fresh from Bad Company, who'd just launched his own Breakbeat Punk label as an offshoot from BC Recordings. The two decided to merge their labels, initially for their own productions (including their 2004 collaboration *When The Sun Goes Down*), although this changed when they signed Pendulum. By halfway through the 2000s, they were putting out tunes by Chase & Status and Drumsound & Bassline Smith, and Fresh had his debut album, *Escape From Planet Monday*, out on Breakbeat Kaos in 2006. Opener *Nervous* owes a definite debt to Pendulum's rockist tendencies, but elsewhere, *X Project* is more influenced by electroclash; *The Pink Panther* is experimental zithering around; and the singles *Submarines* and *All That Jazz* with MC Darrison (emo and jazzy respectively) demonstrated how Fresh was starting to push margins.

While Adam F was breaking into acting, appearing in Brit flicks *The Heavy* (with Vinnie Jones) and *Cuckoo* (with Richard E. Grant), Fresh continued exploring different styles. With vocals from Stamina and Koko, *Hypercaine* was unashamedly accessible, and it made BBC Radio 1's daytime playlist; the follow-up, *Gold Dust*—featuring Ms Dynamite—had a similar pop sensibility. *Lassitude*, a collaboration with up-and-coming scene talent at the time, Sigma, also broke the UK Top 100, with the *Kryptonite* album rounding up these singles in 2010 and becoming his most commercial release to date. There was only one way Fresh's trajectory was heading.

Almost since its inception as the UK's first super-club in 1993, Ministry Of Sound had released compilation CDs and signed a swathe of one-off big underground dance singles, and steered them to international chart success, via sub-labels like Data and Rulin'. By the end of the 2000s, the company had started signing and developing artists in the traditional record label sense. Ministry was big and well-organised; they knew how to get records away, and they effectively had the muscle of a major while still being independent. The label's first signing was pop rapper Example; they also signed DJ Fresh, and later Wretch 32, among others.

Fresh's first single under his new deal featured powerful vocals by Sian Evans from live drum & bass act Kosheen: 'It's gonna get, it's gonna get, it's gonna get louder,' they soar. 'We're gonna get, we're gonna get, we're gonna get stronger … You can't tame this energy inside.'

Riding off the back of its use in a Lucozade TV advert, *Louder* shot straight into the UK charts at no. 1, selling 140,000 copies—more than double its nearest rival, according to the Official Charts Company—and knocking US pop singer Jason Derulo's *Don't Wanna Go Home* off the top spot. But *Louder* wasn't a drum & bass track—it was dubstep. It was essentially capitalising on the big-room dubstep sound that was being flirted with by drum & bass acts Chase & Status and Nero, who had remixed Fresh's *Hypercaine* in 2009, and the output of Magnetic Man—Skream, Benga, and Artwork's short-lived dubstep 'supergroup'—and Skrillex's *Scary Monsters & Nice Sprites*. About two-and-a-half minutes into the radio edit, though, the beats on *Louder* do escalate to drum & bass tempo, as if foreshadowing what was soon to follow. Fresh also went out on tour under the banner FRESH/LIVE.

A few months later, in February 2012, Fresh released his next single, *Hot Right Now*, featuring a then-unknown Albanian-English singer named Rita Ora, who was just twenty-one at the time. This also rocketed to no. 1 in the UK charts, making it drum & bass's first UK chart-topper. A milestone.

While *Hot Right Now* didn't exactly rise out of the drum & bass DJ underground in the way that Shy FX & T Power's *Shake Ur Body* had, remixes by Camo & Krooked and Zed Bias fed the clubs. Fresh followed it up with Top 10 singles like electro-bass cut *The Power*, featuring Dizzee Rascal, and an electro/reggae/hip-hop collaboration with Diplo, *Earthquake*, before releasing the no. 3 smash *Dibby Dibby Sound*—a moombahton carnival anthem that updated Jay Fay's *Dibby Dibby* (which in turn sampled the Rebel MC & Tenor Fly track from 1991) and also featured Ms Dynamite again. Fresh was clearly now doing whatever the hell he liked.

As 2014 moved into 2015, Fresh released further radio-friendly dance-pop singles with Ellie Goulding and Ella Eyre, before calling on his old mucker, Adam F, to make *Believer*. Clearly intended as a nod to d&b's roots, the track was built with an Amen-lite break, Baby D keys, and a Reese bassline, accompanying an uncredited Yola Carter diva vocal. Daytime radio was evidently not quite ready for more of a jungle missive, and the single stiffed at no. 58.

## PENDULUM

By 2000, Bad Company had enough material for a couple of albums, *Digital Nation* and *Inside The Machine*, and set up their own website to help promote themselves. As was common with many of these new-fangled 'websites' at the time, the site had a community forum, which quickly took on a life of its own. The Dogs On Acid phenomenon was born.

An increasingly disparate scene needed meeting-point hubs, and the Y2K networking version of Music House or Movement or Swerve saw them move onto the web. AOL Instant Messenger (AIM) allowed producers to share tracks online, so that a DJ in another city or country wouldn't have to wait for a physical manifestation of a new tune to be placed into their hands—they could download a track made that day and burn it to CD, even though dubplates and vinyl remained the preferred medium for drum & bass for a few more years. Similarly, chat rooms and message boards were revolutionising communication many years before the Facebook monolith came along. Dogs On Acid (DOA) and Drum & Bass Arena soon became the go-to message boards for the scene; forum members could vibe off a new tune, speculate about track IDs, arrange meet-ups, and even ask for production tips and find that lots of d&b producers—even well-known ones—were often only too willing to share their knowledge with others.

Initially running their burgeoning mini-empire out of Fresh's spare room in north London, Bad Company were one of drum & bass' biggest names by 2002. The handy thing about there being four of them was that they could go off and DJ in two pairs, if they wanted, and be involved in different projects at the same time.

It was at a Bad Company show in Perth, Australia—with Fresh and Maldini on the decks—that heavy-metal band members Gareth McGrillen and Rob Swire first experienced the full power of a drum & bass set. 'It was definitely the first time I couldn't breathe because of the amount of bass coming out of the system,' Swire told *DJ Mag* a few years later. 'The energy was unreal.'

'The first time I heard drum & bass, it was the kind of drum & bass that I like,' said Gaz McGrillen in 2008. 'We weren't really into the jungle thing. We got into it late and when we heard it, it was kind of dark and twisted, and really aggressive and energetic. I think that's the same as rock and metal and punk.'

Swire and McGrillen met local d&b DJ Paul Harding, aka El Hornet, who himself had been a drummer in a punk band in Perth, and the trio decided to try to make some drum & bass music together. Pretty much the first thing they produced was *Vault*: a revving, growly beast that subconsciously built on the marauding Bad Company sound. 'We weren't worried about which DJs might play it or who would sign it—they weren't considerations,' Gaz told *DJ Mag* in 2007. 'We just wanted to smash up clubs in Perth.'

It did more than just that, though. They passed the track to fellow Antipodeans Concord Dawn, and soon—via clandestine DJ networks—Ed Rush was opening his sets with it, Andy C was all over it, and Doc Scott had signed it for his 31 Recordings imprint. By the end of 2002, they were flying over to London to pick up the award for 'Best Track' at the *Knowledge* Drum & Bass Awards, welcomed as the latest international newcomers to make their mark.

Having been somewhat isolated in Perth on Australia's west coast, they jumped at the chance when Fresh offered them free accommodation for a few months in his London flat. 'Again, there was no game plan,' said Rob. 'Paul was keen to come over to get DJ work, and we decided that if we could get enough shows to pass between us and survive, then we could build things from there. At that point we still didn't really have a clue.'

What aided Pendulum considerably was *Another Planet*, which sampled in its first drop the otherworldly—and mildly distorted—commanding voice of renowned Hollywood actor Richard Burton, narrating *The Red Weed* section (after Earth has succumbed to the Martians) from the middle of Jeff Lynne's apocalyptic, epic sci-fi score to *War Of The Worlds*. With its zany, processed synth top line vying for attention—almost call-and-response style—with the buzzsaw bass, it was bonkers and bananas jump-up that slayed it on the dancefloor.

Fresh and Adam F snapped up *Another Planet* for Breakbeat Kaos and helped propel it into the UK Top 50 on vinyl sales alone. What's more, it pricked the ears of previously rockist radio DJs like Zane Lowe and Mary Anne-Hobbs at BBC Radio 1, and Eddy Temple-Morris at indie station XFM.

The next Pendulum release was a collaboration with UK breaks duo The Freestylers, with Fresh getting in on the studio action as well. The menacing *Tarantula* brought ragga chatter Tenor Fly, a long-term Freestylers cohort, along for the ride, while the freewheeling pogo cut *Fasten Your Seatbelts* offset a bit of soundboy dancehall chat with a tear-out/jump-up sensibility. By the time *Slam* was ready to be unleashed on an unsuspecting public, the groundwork had been well and truly laid.

*Slam* was supplemented by a genius video featuring a chubby businessman dancing topless to the track around Soho. Taking his shirt off and tying his tie around his head, he attracts quite a crowd when wobbling to the tune outside an Oxford Street shoe shop, and also outside the Black Market record shop on D'Arblay Street after he sets down his portable CD player. Nicky Blackmarket comes out of the shop halfway through the video to give the dancer a perplexed look and then a bottle of water, mirroring the friendly response seen at thousands of raves over the years when a seemingly out-of-place character first gets into the vibe and is welcomed by the rave cognoscenti. The video also recalls Spike Jonze's shoot for *Praise You* by Fatboy Slim, which featured a weird dance troupe cavorting around a shopping mall and was also a big MTV hit.

Smashing into the UK Top 40, *Slam* set up Pendulum nicely for the *Hold*

*Your Colour* LP, which punctured the Top 30 in mid-2005. The title track may have included some rock riffing from Rob, but, on the whole, the guys thought they weren't really being influenced by their rock/metal backgrounds. 'Everyone was saying they could hear it in our sound,' said Rob. 'Adam F, Fresh...everyone was pointing to this rock attitude in our tracks, but we just didn't see it.'

'Once we had really come to grips with the fact that our strongest influence had come from our rock/metal backgrounds, that was it,' added Gaz. 'We just took off with a new direction.'

Liam Howlett from The Prodigy hand-picked Pendulum to remix his band's bewitching rave anthem *Voodoo People* for the hits package *Their Law*, and they responded with an electronic punk-rock blitzkrieg that soared into the UK Top 20 on its own. 'Pendulum are the first beat-makers since Liam Howlett to properly integrate the aggression and energy of rock & roll,' said Radio 1's Zane Lowe at the time.

The band were attracting fans from well beyond the traditional junglist spectrum—in 2008, Gaz mentioned 'emo-screamo kids and punk kids and skaters', as well as indie kids and metal types, coming to their shows. Pendulum were recruiting a whole swathe of rock fans to the drum & bass cause, but they were also moving further away from d&b themselves. They fell out with Breakbeat Kaos over the reissue of a compilation from 2004 that they weren't informed about or happy with—Rob posted on Dogs On Acid in March 2006 to state that the band didn't endorse the repackaged *Jungle Sound Gold* release— and ended up signing to major label Warner Bros and recruiting a full band.

By the time it came to release their next album, El Hornet had left the production nucleus to concentrate on DJing, and Pendulum had begun writing tracks with instruments—more like a traditional rock band. *In Silico* was named with a nod to grunge band Nirvana's last album, *In Utero*, from fifteen years earlier. 'That meant born of the womb; *In Silico* means born of silicon, born of synthetics,' Gaz explained to *DJ Mag*'s Allan McGrath in a 2007 cover feature. When McGrath suggested that it meant synthetic powered rock, Gaz concurred: 'We want to properly bring together both worlds. We were hearing the same power—the same energy levels in both; but we wanted it to be real from both angles, and not mashed together in a way that they don't make sense.'

On forums such as Dogs On Acid, the more 'rock' Pendulum became, the more frequently they were being slagged off by jungle purists. Snarky comments from keyboard warriors would suggest that Pendulum had ruined drum & bass, which on one occasion prompted a reply from Rob Swire that many interpreted as a diss of the whole drum & bass scene. On November 30, 2007, he made his final post on DOA: 'To everyone in the scene I pissed off with that "stale pig shit" comment—you took it the wrong way (or I wrote it the wrong way),' he said. 'It was aimed at some people on DOA that claimed "we killed drum and bass"—and I was trying to say that ANY genre (not just dnb) that can be toppled by one artist alone…probably deserves to die. For example, even Miles Davis couldn't have toppled jazz.'

He went on to suggest, 'My only real problem with dnb … is the insular thinking that sometimes pollutes every electronic scene. When people don't look outside their given genre/scene for musical inspiration, things tend to get boring and tired very quickly. The music goes in circles, repeating itself … the amount of fans never changes, new people aren't attracted to the scene to give it fresh input and shit gets stale very quickly. All the drum n bass I have really liked since I got into it sounded like it took inspiration from different places.' He signed off with a 'fuck you' to the haters.

Although cut from the same cloth as *Slam*, Pendulum's next single, *Granite*, was noticeably more of a synthetic rock song. Goldie declared in a filmed interview backstage at Turbulence in Newcastle in April 2008 that it was 'shit' and accused Pendulum of turning their backs on the scene that broke them, as a result of the Dogs On Acid furore. Addressing the band directly on camera, he said, 'I've never heard an interview where you mentioned where you came from—and you came from drum & bass.' (They later made peace, however.)

The band's next single, *Propane Nightmares*, sounded more like a symphonic nu-metal anthem with heavy drums, and it cracked the UK Top 10. The *In Silico* album came out in mid-2008 and peaked at no. 2 in the UK album charts. The band went on to have another successful album, *Immersion*, and singles such as *Watercolour*, which also made the Top 10. Several years of endless touring followed, including a spell supporting nu-metallers Linkin Park, before, around 2011, Swire and McGrillen morphed into Knife Party. The new duo mined more of an electro-house/dubstep furrow, and they ended up becoming a big EDM act. Pendulum did return as a live act in 2017, but the buzz was never quite the same. Though they were never everybody's cup of tea, they remain the most successful drum & bass-derived live act to date.

**TAKE WHAT?**

Sigma—aka Cam Edwards and Joe Lenzie—were just one of scores of d&b acts beavering away in the underground for years to scratch a living. In 2014, a bootleg they did of the Kanye West/Charlie Wilson track *Bound 2* got picked up by radio, and it was propelled to no. 1 after they had it re-sung and signed to 3 Beat, a commercially leaning indie label that had grown out of a record shop in Liverpool.

Not long afterwards, they had another no. 1, *Changing* featuring Paloma Faith; further hits followed with Labrinth and Rita Ora, who had first shot to prominence on Fresh's chart-topper *Hot Right Now* three years earlier. Their record company had engineered these high-profile collaborations, but the next one was a step too far for many in the drum & bass scene. It was with the ultimate British pop act of the last thirty years, Take That.

'Gary Barlow's team were keen to do it, and he's an incredibly talented songwriter and musician,' Sigma said in justification. 'For us to be offered to work with someone who's got that legacy and those skills, it was a no-brainer.

'We're always aware of our music being a gateway,' they continued. 'We know we have a responsibility to introduce electronic music to a generation who will be able to go out to clubs and festivals in the near future. That's important for any genre. You need those big tunes to be played on the radio, so the next generation are aware there is an electronic music culture and decide to investigate it.'

The likes of Bryan Gee, Digital, London Elektricity, and Sam Binga were generally supportive towards Sigma for trying something new, and about the possible role of *Cry* as a 'gateway' into the scene. Grooverider had previously termed *Changing* with Paloma Faith a gateway tune but warned in *DJ Mag*, 'If you're doing that chart thing, then do not forget the side of the scene that made you. Don't forget your roots! You made some proper, proper tunes back in the day. Don't stop making them now you're smashing it in the charts.'

Others, such as Mantra, Rockwell, and Marcus Intalex, were more dismissive of the collaboration in the same magazine. 'In my mind it's not drum & bass, just pop music with a drum & bass skeleton,' said Marcus Intalex. 'It also breeds a generation of people who think that drum & bass is just the commercial crap they hear on the radio.'

Most dismissive of all was Goldie. 'Don't drag him [Barlow] or drum & bass into this fucking gentrified mess,' he said, before pointing out that Future Cut

kept their pop production as a separate alias, and that others who had big hits—
like Chase & Status, Fresh, and Shy FX—continued to make groundbreaking
underground music. 'Where's the polarity and variety?' Goldie scoffed. 'This is
the problem with the gentrified side of drum & bass: when you sign up with
that major label and you get that big cheque and they're making those decisions
for you, then you sign away any right to say anything about the genre and the
underground. Music becomes ugly when things get simplified and formulated
and watered down.'

Goldie went on to liken such commercial cheese to McDonald's, before
saying, 'This type of music does not represent d&b anymore ... there's no space
for this shit in our dances. ... Our music is built on oppression. The best stuff is
made when you feel everyone is against you and you're mad as fuck. We all know
when you [Sigma] can make those types of records, when you're being honest
with yourselves. Remember: a truthful idea will always last in the honesty of
time. And that's all I want to hear and see from everyone involved in drum &
bass; honesty, integrity, and a dutifulness and respect to where you've come from.
We can take the genre to some crazy places, but if you're not giving back then
you ain't coming back to the underground, boys.'

Unlike most Take That singles—and indeed, Sigma's previous few singles,
since hitting the pop charts—*Cry* was a comparative flop, failing to make the
Top 20 in the UK.

# 21 Mutation And Evolution: From Autonomic To Half-Time, Footwork To Neurofunk

Towards the end of the 2000s, there seemed to be few new innovations in drum & bass. The heavy and dark sound offered nothing particularly fresh, while the sunshine rays of liquid d&b continued in much the same vein as before. It took the efforts and ideas of an artist who'd already been involved with every permutation of the genre—abetted by a loose collective of co-conspirators—to open a path to somewhere new.

Darren White, best known for his work as dBridge and as part of the group Bad Company, had become tired of both bombast and smoothed out sounds, and, as both a producer and the boss of the Exit label, he was eager to create a different type of d&b. He had grown up in the Worcestershire spa town of Malvern listening to 80s synth-pop on the radio, before getting into the indie rock of Chapterhouse and The Stone Roses. He then had his mind blown by hardcore at the famous (and nearby) Castlemorton rave. 'I was lucky enough to be at Castlemorton,' he says. 'That was literally just around the corner from where I lived. We knew the area; we knew ways in and out that the police didn't. So that really sealed it for me in terms of underground dance music.'

dBridge had already absorbed many sides of music when he became hooked on the early jungle sound, which he investigated further after moving to London in 1992. Inspired by events at Peckham Laserdrome, Desert Storm in Lee Valley, Roast at Turnmills, and the Moving Shadow label, he started making music as The Sewage Monsters with his brother Steve (known today as Steve Spacek).

'We used Cubase on an Atari ST, an Akai S950, a Yamaha SY22 keyboard, and a pair of Yamaha NS10s. It was my brother's setup, pretty basic. Back then, sampling each other was rife—it was quite lawless in some ways. You'd hear a tune with a break on it, and, before you know it, everyone's sampled that break or a riff or whatever. We didn't have a deck then, so some of the tunes we were sampling off cassette, off the radio.'

After this first foray into production, dBridge connected with GMC Blood, and together they became The Dubb Hustlers. In the background was the continuous rhythmic bustle of pirate radio. 'It was something you felt part of. The pirate radios, you were either into Rush FM or Kool FM—there was always a slight north/south divide. Another one was Shockin. I was a Rush FM guy. We knew some people who were doing parties, the Desert Storm ones. It was probably through getting more involved in making the music that I felt a part of the scene. It was coming out of everybody's cars in the summer. The amount of pirate radio stations was ridiculous; the legal stations were jockeying for space more than anything. It was something that all your mates were into, something you could all connect with. Coming from Malvern as well, which is quite a small village in comparison to London, and suddenly being a part of this burgeoning, massive scene—it felt natural to me, and there were people who DJed in the crew, MCs in the crew, and I knew I wanted to produce. That was my connection with all of that.'

After hooking up with Lennie De Ice's Armshouse Crew, dBridge played PAs at Desert Storm and built up a solid discography of roughneck jungle and early hardstep tracks. EPs on Trouble On Vinyl, Screwface, and Phat Trax followed, before he went on to join gnarly super-group Bad Company (whose exploits are detailed elsewhere). After a few years, though, he had grown disillusioned with the slamming sound they'd made their own. At Swerve, he became excited by liquid funk—the soulful d&b sound typified by the likes of Calibre that was bubbling under at that time. In parallel, he was intrigued by the wonky hip-hop being made by Detroit's J Dilla and other producers, and started to make his own version of it alongside his brother, Spacek.

'I helped out on the Spacek *Vintage Hi Tek* album he did for !K7,' dBridge says. 'It felt like me going out on my own, rather than with all them lot [Bad Company], and discovering this whole other side to me. It was always there, but I was connecting with it. It was something I needed to do for my own sanity, I think.'

He launched the Exit label in 2003 as an outlet for more forward-thinking d&b, releasing his own material and like-minded beats by Break, Calibre, and Goldie (under his Rufige Kru guise). Remaining active on the scene, he collaborated again with Vegas in 2004, resulting in the classic *True Romance*, which surfaced on Metalheadz Platinum. Then, around 2006, dBridge became excited by something he considered to be a novel fusion of ideas and styles.

'I was starting to get booked down at Swerve, and then I heard *Naked Zoo* on Soul:r, which Marcus Intalex had put out, this Instra:mental release, and it just blew my mind, like, *What is this and who are these guys?* I just knew I had to get in touch with them, just to get some more music.'

Part of a Soul:r compilation, *DAT:MUSIC*, that also included tracks by fellow futurists Martyn, Klute, and Seba, the stripped-bare cyborg minimalism of *Naked Zoo* had a touch of Detroit and a touch of soul; and, though recognisable as d&b in its beat structure, it sounded somehow new. Its sonorous analogue bass, writhing this way and that, had something alive about it that caught dBridge's ear. 'Me and Instra:mental just got talking and, finding out that we had similar tastes, they invited me down to the studio.'

The duo of Damon Kirkham and Alex Green had already released some significant singles as Instra:mental alongside Source Direct in the early 2000s, but their sound had undergone a remarkable metamorphosis by the time dBridge met them. The Exit label boss was used to doing everything 'inside the box' with software and eschewed analogue gear, so when he visited Instra:mental's studio, he was surprised to see that they were hardware heads.

'I was coming from being in Bad Company, and we were on the cutting edge. We were getting away from hardware. Then going down to Instra:mental's studio and suddenly seeing all this synth hardware, I started thinking, *Hang on a minute, I've got that, I've got that,* and suddenly realising, *Where is my equipment?* And realising that was part of it as well.'

What Instra:mental created around this time sounded like nothing else in the genre. *Photograph*, with its melancholy 1980s mauve-tinted synth smear, found sounds, and barely there rhythmic pulse, is a collision between the dramatic soundtracks of Tangerine Dream or Vangelis, electro, and d&b; *Sakura*, an ode to the Japanese cherry blossom season, is on a cyberpunk *Ghost In The Shell* flex, its tumbling taiko drums propelling the melodic synth majesty forward in a fusion of ancient and modern, history and future. This sound appealed hugely to dBridge, who had also grown up influenced by synth-pop, *Blade Runner*, John Carpenter, and electro.

The three producers began to influence each other's output, and they started to collaborate, too, jamming out tracks in the studio more like a band than a typical electronic music producer. 'Damon was messing around on the keyboard, Boddika [Green] would be doing something on the boards, and the studio was set up in such a way that we could all do our own things,' dBridge says. 'We connected musically, the equipment made a difference, and it was realising we had those similarities, especially with the 80s stuff, the chord progressions, the mood. Just the emotiveness of certain things. Damon was really into Drexciya, Aphex Twin, Squarepusher, things like that. We found that there was that commonality between all of us.'

What all three began to make was nothing short of revolutionary in sound. Their debut track together, *Wonder Where*, released in 2009 on Instra:mental's Nonplus label, mixes a lush neo-soul vocal from dBridge with a monstrously distended Reese bass that simmers beneath the surface, and rhythms that seem to slip between hip-hop tempo and rapid-fire drum & bass. Surrounded by wisps of synth and intricate melodic detail, it's emotionally direct yet seething with contained aggression—a masterpiece of restraint that worked as a futuristic torch song and a dancefloor drop-down equally well.

The flipside was even more surprising: *No Future* has a dancehall kick-drum pulse that flickers into distinctive stepping percussion, and a chilling spoken-vocal that intones, in a plummy newsreader voice, 'Lies, confusion, government control, crime, money, panic, terror. London—no future.' Minimalistic, with just a techno bass tone glowing neon in the darkness, this new sound had more in common with the dubstep of the era, and in fact, what Instra:mental and dBridge were making would prove a vital link between underground dance scenes and genres.

All active DJs in clubs around the UK and beyond, the trio decided to join forces and start a mix series. The Autonomic podcast was born: a place where they could showcase their fresh soundtrack-influenced, synth-heavy sound, the work of like-minded producers, and music that had influenced them, from Detroit electro to ambient and weird hip-hop.

'Me and Damon sat down and said we should do a podcast, 'cause that was around the time that they were seen to be popular. Once we started it, we realised there were other people out there who all had similar tastes as well, and they started sending us music.'

## THE AUTONOMIC SOUND

At the end of the 2000s, dubstep was the pre-eminent underground genre, and it was mutating. The Autonomic sound dBridge and Instra:mental were making seemed to have an affinity with the work of dubstep producers like Skream or Mala; there was a similar emphasis on space and bass. 'Obviously dubstep had blown up, but there were all these people on the fringes of it, like Scuba sending us stuff, Ramadanman [now Pearson Sound] sending us stuff,' says dBridge. 'I've got some old Joy Orbison and James Blake stuff—they were connecting to us via the podcast as well.'

Other artists began to release music in the Autonomic mode. ASC tapped into the minimalistic rhythmic pulse of the genre with the atmospheric bass, half-time drums, and bleeps of *Porcelain*; Consequence emitted the brooding beat science of *Live For Never* on Exit. Skream, on hiatus from Rinse/Tempa, made the techno sequences and rapid 808s of *Minimalistix*. What all the music shared was an openness to electronic experimentation, and a looser interpretation of rhythm. Though for the most part maintaining the 170bpm tempo of drum & bass, stripping away all but the bare minimum of drums gave these records a sense of space that was absent elsewhere in the genre. As a result, it often felt as if this music was half the speed—which made it more malleable and mixable with other styles.

In an article for *Fact* magazine, producer Sam Binga told Laurent Fintoni that Autonomic 'opened up the links and influences between and behind musical genres'. Drum & bass, which many felt had been stuck in a rhythmic rut, unable to move beyond its conventional structure, was suddenly free of its style shackles, and it could once again become as experimental and innovative as it had been before.

The Autonomic sound would remain popular for the next few years, with dBridge, Instra:mental, and other DJs in tune with this deeper style hosting Room 3 at London's Fabric. 'That always amazes me that we pretty much did a world tour off the back of a podcast,' dBridge says. 'I thought that was pretty impressive. I liked the way we just kept it to twelve episodes rather than overdoing it. Off the back of that, we were doing these cool nights at Fabric, getting some amazing people coming down. James Blake, Jimmy Edgar, Shackleton, all these people that we were really into, playing at our night.'

It got the trio their own entry in the club's long-running mix series, too: *FabricLive 50*, released in early 2010, found the three DJs mixing their new productions with material by UK electronic whiz Actress, Hessle Audio boss Pearson Sound, and dubstep man Distance, in addition to tracks from seasoned drum & bass producers such as Genotype, Loxy, and Alix Perez, who'd been excited by the freshness of the Autonomic approach. Along with the compilation *Mosaic* on Exit Records, it's probably the most complete showcase of the sound outside of the podcast series, and it's also indicative of how Autonomic could exist in between a variety of different music scenes, sometimes binding them together or suggesting new hybrids.

Autonomic had effectively run its course as a subgenre a few years after the *FabricLive* CD was released. Fed up with receiving formulaic material that tried too hard to conform to its structures, Instra:mental and dBridge decided to move on. 'With music, once you get onto something, some people try to reverse-engineer it, thinking, *It's this, these chord progressions*, they try to do a paint-by-numbers version of it,' dBridge says. 'For a while, we were getting sent stuff and it was like, *ugh*.'

But Autonomic's legacy has been far more enduring. Its pluralistic attitude to mixing styles together—no doubt aided by the internet and ease of access to music—has persisted in club culture. DJs now are far more likely to blend a variety of tracks rather than just relentless kicks and snares, and the synth-heavy, atmospheric feel that dBridge and Instra:mental brought in can be heard in everything from Ivy Lab to Sinistarr. Though Instra:mental moved closer to techno afterwards, with Boddika becoming a successful 4/4 DJ, dBridge has maintained an experimental forward-looking perspective at his Exit Records label. In his eyes, Autonomic's spirit never really died: 'Autonomic was never meant to be a genre, but it somehow ended up one. It still feels pretty unresolved, and it's still where I'm at musically.'

### HALF-TIME

The half-time tempo suggested by Instra:mental's productions—where the beat still moves at a rapid pace but the rhythm is stretched out to create the sensation of wading through treacle—has become a potent weapon in drum & bass. The Autonomic bunch were not the first to have the idea, though their stylistic fusions, arriving at a time when many forms of dance music were merging, became immediately appealing to artists who wanted to experiment with beat structures.

Before them, producers like Amit had hit upon a style with all the menace and motion of d&b, but with the speed seemingly slowed right down. Amit's *MK Ultra*, released on Klute's Commercial Suicide label in 2005, has a thudding kick-drum and hissing hats that progress at heartbeat tempo, and an evil, elephantine synth bass that moves at double the speed. It was one of the first tracks to be described as half-time—a nebulous term that takes in many tracks and artists that blend dub, hip-hop, and jungle, sometimes with the Chicago-born genre/dance style, footwork.

Amit Kamboj had a varied musical diet growing up, featuring everything from dub and hip-hop to Indian film soundtracks and punk. When he got an Amiga in 1989, he learned to code, and he simultaneously got interested in making music on the computer using a Master Sound sampler and MED sequencer. Honing his sound from loops and samples, influenced by hardcore and then jungle, he worked hard at creating a production style. Though he put out tracks under a few names, such as Quartex and Tronic, it was as Amit that he really made his mark. Starting to experiment with the half-time style as early as 1999, he drew inspiration from his love of dub as well as more esoteric influences when he made the style-defining *MK Ultra*.

'Though *MK Ultra* wasn't my first half-time track, it did gain wide attention,' he says. 'It was born out of a love of early hardcore tracks, political brainwashing techniques, Paul Verhoeven, and King Tubby. At that point I wasn't concerned whether it was drum & bass or not, I was more focused on developing my own sound. It definitely helped attract a wider audience to my music, and presented me with some incredible opportunities, including the chance to support Sonic Youth in Holland and to work alongside Bill Laswell.'

Amit became renowned in the drum & bass community for his singular half-time sound, which peppered his productions alongside more structurally conventional takes on jungle. For him, the exciting thing about producing beats in this style was being able to mess with time and move between different beats and tempos fluidly. 'Moving between bpms gives you a great degree of freedom and exposes you to other genres and territories,' Amit says. 'By moving between bpms, you not only discover new possibilities but also learn how to solve new problems, such as mixdowns, arrangement flow, and sound design. You can then cross-pollinate this newfound knowledge throughout your future productions, thus making you a better all-round producer.'

Though artists like Amit or Instra:mental helped to lay the foundations, the unique conditions of the late-2000s club scene made the half-time style appealing too. At the same time, the wonky hip-hop emanating from LA and Detroit, typified by the synth-laden creations of Flying Lotus, Samiyam, and Dabrye, was dovetailing with the work of artists who had experimented with dubstep and grime in the UK, from Zomby to Joker.

Om Unit (real name: Jim Coles), a Bristol-based producer originally from Berkshire via London, had already made a variety of different genres up to the point when he began to fashion a distinctive form of d&b bearing the fingerprints of all these influences. His 2012 album *Aeolian* on Civil Music contains gems like *Ulysses*: deceptively chilled dubstep tracks with basslines that speed off at double time, even as the slow kick-snare beats threaten to accelerate at high speed but never do.

Coles had started out making jungle in 1994 while he was still a teenager, getting his musical education from tape packs and record-buying trips to Hard Edge in Maidenhead (home of Shoebox Recordings), and the famous rave hub Basement Records in Reading. 'At that time I was living in a little village where there was nothing going on,' he says. 'The sounds from the big city were the in-thing. I got swept away with it. I was lucky having a computer at home, and a friend of mine showed me some simple software. That's where I got started.'

As well as making instrumental hip-hop beats as 2Tall, Coles got hooked on the dubstep sound when he went to London club nights DMZ and FWD>>. Having made a variety of beats and genres around the beginning of the 2010s, he eventually had the idea to combine all these ideas in one place.

When the online music store Boomkat reviewed *Aeolian*, they used the term 'slow fast' to describe it. 'I liked that idea—slow on the bottom, fast on the top,' Coles says. 'It's not a deep thing, it's just like half-time drumming. As a kid, I was a drummer. The idea that you have this hip-hop groove on the bottom, people have been doing it for years, Amit was doing it years ago. People like Justice and Deep Blue were doing experiments in the 90s, even.'

Though he wasn't the first to do it, Om Unit's disruption of the temporal structure of drum & bass made a significant impact. Via releases on forward-thinking d&b labels Metalheadz and Exit, he cultivated a reputation for his experiments with rhythm, and rather than being ostracised for deconstructing the genre to such an extent, he has been embraced by the scene.

'Metalheadz and Goldie were super-welcoming; people like Digital I got to remix; I got to DJ with Doc Scott and remix *Shadowboxing*, I got to remix *Space Funk* with DLR and Mako, and with Sam Binga, Alix Perez, Ivy Lab, Richie Brains, there's been this whole [half-time] conversation, which I've been honoured to be a part of. It's my personal journey, I've done all these chapters. The most awesome thing about it was being able to be an outsider casting a different light on things that may have inspired people. It feels like I've contributed something to that culture.'

His tune with Sam Binga, *Small Victories*, was like a 1980s synth-funk soundtrack, with rapid-fire hi-hats but a plodding snare drum, while releases on Om Unit's own label Cosmic Bridge literally acted as a conduit between genres and specialised in music allied to grime and dubstep, but with a deep connection to d&b too. Artists like Moresounds, Kromestar, J:Kenzo, and DJ Madd stretched out their dubstep creations on Cosmic Bridge, operating in a post-genre interzone that was as dizzying on the dancefloor as it was delirious fun.

### FOOTWORK HYBRIDS

Loosely connected to half-time's temporal displacement is the genre of Chicago footwork, born in the Midwest US city's Southside and named after a specific, speedy form of street dance. Productions by local artists RP Boo and Traxman shifted the kick-drums of house into an avalanche of speedy hits that suited the rapid-fire acrobatics of the dancers. Sitting around 160bpm, with its stripped-back sensibility, repetition, and reliance on rap and soul samples, footwork shares a lot with drum & bass, and it has inspired UK artists to incorporate the sound into their productions. Om Unit's Philip D Kick alias is just one example; his remix of Remarc's jungle classic *R.I.P.* fused the Amen breaks and ragga snippets of the original with half-time rhythms and kinetic kick drums. 'What got me about the Chicago footwork thing, though, was this tension between the different rhythm layers,' he says. 'I definitely wanted to explore that.'

After touring the UK and Europe and releasing music via Planet Mu's seminal early footwork compilation *Bangs & Works*, the genre's pioneers—among them the late DJ Rashad, and DJ Spinn—began to incorporate snippets of jungle samples and breakbeats that they'd heard in clubs, starting a transatlantic exchange of ideas and influences. DJ Rashad's *Let It Go*, for instance, has breakbeats snapping on the offbeat as in jungle, the classic old rave vocal 'Let it go', and lush pads, but the speedy kick-drums of footwork remain.

'We did a co-interview, me and Rashad, back in 2013, and he said Kode9 totally hooked him up with folders of jungle samples,' Om Unit says. 'I know Machinedrum gave him tons of sample packs, like *Jungle Warfare*. I think *Let It Go* was a result of him being given these samples. It's an example of what can happen when people choose to connect cultures.'

Everyone from Bristol's Addison Groove, with his *Footcrab* track, to Texas producer Wheez-Ie got in on the act of dabbling with footwork, while Om Unit and Fracture incorporated the footwork flavour into the output of their labels. 'What I like about the footwork style is the rawness and the lack of over-production,' Fracture says. 'The fact that it's all intended to be danced to.'

### A WAY FORWARD

For some DJs, the dubstep era from the late 2000s to the early 2010s was a great palate cleanser. With its different rhythmic ideas and lack of rules, it seemed as exciting to some as the first flashes of innovation in hardcore and jungle. Crucially, dubstep and the mutations that sprang from it offered a way forward.

Fracture (Charlie Fieber), a DJ and producer who first came to fame in the early 2000s working with studio partner Neptune (Nelson Bayomy)— releasing tracks on Danny Breaks' Droppin' Science label, Inperspective, and Med School—was ready for something different when dubstep came to fruition. In 2007, he released *The Phonecall*, a dark and disturbing dubstep piece, heavy with sub but littered with subtle jungle samples and a skippy, almost garage beat. It showed another side of the producer, who viewed the new sound as another means of expression.

'That early era of dubstep was great,' Fracture says. 'It interested me in the same way as the early hardcore stuff. I concentrated on jungle/d&b, as that's what really spoke to me at a young age, but really, as a listener and lover of music, I am constantly listening to what's new and searching for different stuff.'

This experiment in genre would go on to influence the direction of Astrophonica, the label he set up with Neptune. Soon gaining renown as an outlet for experimental but still club-wrecking drum & bass, the imprint has become a home for artists pushing at the boundaries. Moresounds' *Blood*, released in 2013, moves to a stately dancehall beat, ragga samples, and heavy sub, but periodically drops into swung-out jungle breaks, accelerating in dual tempo at 80/160bpm. Fracture, Sam Binga & Rider Shafique's *She Want It Ruff* was a more explicit nod to dancehall, but again with little breakbeat drum fills that remind you that you are still in the drum & bass area. Released on Exit in 2014, Fracture's *Loving Touch* uses the half-time trick to astonishingly potent effect, its plodding dubstep beat accompanied by speedy 808 bass booms, skippy breaks, and a classic house vocal, drawing a link between house music's golden age and a new era of dance. On paper, it sounded incongruous, but with Fracture's expert production, the idea works incredibly well, offering another example of his deft alchemical abilities.

'I've definitely always had a fascination with being on the edge of new sounds and styles,' Fracture says. 'There's a certain feeling of total unknown chaos at that point, where people are making stuff quickly and no one quite knows what to call it. That's when the best records of any style of underground music are made. Before they get labelled as something. I crave that ground.'

Another production duo, based in Manchester, would mint a bona fide half-time anthem to sit alongside the tempo-trashing productions and labels of Fracture and Om Unit. Dub Phizix and Skeptical's 2011 release *Marka*, featuring Strategy, also moves to a dancehall pulse, the rapper's double-time ragga chat coasting effortlessly over the menacing slow electronics beneath. A massive club tune, *Marka* was more dubstep or grime than anything else, illustrating just how much the bass-heavy subgenres of dance music had begun to commingle.

Half-time's connection with hip-hop is impossible to discount. Artists from the USA who've made a variety of genres, but who count drum & bass and rap as core ingredients in their material, have made significant contributions to half-time. Machinedrum's albums and singles on Planet Mu and Ninja Tune have occupied the murky nebulous area where bass-heavy styles collide. His tune *Don't 1 2 Lose U* mixes rapid-fire techno synth stabs with a woozy beat that seems to tantalisingly slip out of time, hovering between dimensions. Its hip-hop lope makes sense, considering his Stateside location.

Meanwhile, Eprom, a long-time stealthy operator on LA's hip-hop-leaning beat scene, made tunes that merged half-time, dubstep, and wobbly bass—like *Pipe Dream*—with a rap rhythm sensibility. Ivy Lab, a London group that was originally the trio of Halogenix, Stray, and Sabre, started off as drum & bass producers, but they have since minted their 20/20 LDN label to put out slower beats that still radiate the references of their past. Tracks such as *Shamrock* contain hoover synths that suggested an acquaintance with jungle history, slotting them into a wonky hip-hop template. 'We just happened to start working together at a time when we were really into a certain style of drum & bass,' Stray told *XLR8R*. 'The shift to focus on more hip-hop or half-time material was actually a shift back to our roots.'

'That's a British mentality,' Sabre also said. 'We describe our music as taking British basslines and mixing them with American drum-machine electronica.'

With Om Unit, Ivy Lab, Fracture, Machinedrum, and many more artists contributing, half-time has become an established part of the make-up of drum & bass, and its tempo slippage has made the club a more unpredictable and exciting place to be for dancers. And, with half-time almost a genre of its own now, Amit is happy that his experimentation has contributed to its emergence. 'Once you define something and give it a name, it can quite easily become trendy and fashionable—something I never wanted,' he says. 'Looking back at it now in context, I can see the benefit of it having its own defined name. Since I began developing half-time all those years ago, it has gone on to inspire so many younger producers, and this brings me a lot of pride.'

### NEUROFUNK

Emerging concurrently with the half-time and Autonomic sounds was another subgenre that had arguably the most dominant role on drum & bass dancefloors in the 2010s. The term 'neurofunk' was originally coined by music journalist Simon Reynolds to describe hyper-detailed, dark beats with a strong emphasis on sound design—the kind being made by artists like Jonny L or Ed Rush & Optical in the late 90s—but it was later adopted to mean any d&b with an industrial edge and malevolent energy.

Neurofunk sprang from the techstep sound at the end of the 90s and the start of the 2000s. Representing a refinement of the ideas first expressed by the likes of Bad Company, this subgenre in the hands of a new wave of producers became a minimalist, dark club sound, where the most machine-like, metallic textures, digital timbres and evilest bass tones were highly prized. It's the sound that first inspired Noisia, and their technical, futuristic and studio pristine sound.

Excessively digital, neurofunk was the antithesis to the sampled breakbeats and organic reggae snippets of jungle's past: a computerised sound with pristine razor-sharp drums and bloated, distorted basslines that belch mechanically like some monstrous cyborg toad. Characterised by the productions of Phace, Misanthrop, Black Sun Empire, and Mefjus, this was the ultimate refinement of studio technique; a robotic, dark sound that has proven dynamite in d&b clubs and beyond—though one that would sometimes be viewed less favourably by jungle's keepers of the flame.

One of neurofunk's biggest acts, Noisia, became a massive festival draw, luring fans in with their searing synth bass and crunching drops. Meanwhile, some of the biggest DJs in the scene today, from Andy C to Friction, continue to release neurofunk on their labels and play it in their sets. Raw, direct, and tough, and loaded with punk energy, it's a youthful sound typified by the productions of artists like Current Value.

'Matrix and Fierce, Ed Rush & Optical, Stakka & Skynet, Cause 4 Concern, Konflict, Ram Trilogy, Bad Company's *Inside The Machine* and *Digital Nation*— we'd listen to those so much,' says Tijs of Noisia. For him, neurofunk is a loaded term that conjures up negative as well as positive connotations. 'I grew up with it—that term was there before Noisia,' he says. 'There was a website that had it, but it was actually funky stuff. What is now called neurofunk is the really hard Eatbrain, Methlab kind of sound. For me, that isn't neurofunk, it's the old Matrix records and the old Ed Rush & Optical records. But nobody uses that definition anymore. Neurofunk, that tech sci-fi thing, it can hold things back a little.'

Bringing highly atmospheric elements and polyrhythmic energy to their productions, Noisia elevated the technical style into something more than mere club fodder, mixing their dancefloor tracks with cinematic interludes on albums such as 2016's *Outer Edges*. 'We've always done super loud, angry stuff, but also done really deep stuff,' Tijs says. 'Without the mix of both, there's no balance. A lot of drum & bass I hear is just very much on the eighth notes, and then I'm like, *This is boring*. If it's just really good sound in a boring grid, it doesn't excite me. There has to be something rhythmic in there that triggers me, or it has to be more of a mood, a cinematic world that you go into. We've done both.'

Konflict's *Messiah*—first released in 2000 on Renegade Hardware's *Essential Rewindz* compilation—symbolises the real beginning of neurofunk, with its jittery drums, percussion changes, dark atmosphere and manic energy. It has since become a template. In an article about the subgenre for UKF, Current Value described its magnetism: 'To me it is the most boundary-pushing, and in terms of producing, the most challenging kind of electronic dance music—in regards to sound design, as well as rhythmical structures and time signatures.'

This style of drum & bass is a long way from the early days of production, when artists would tend to use a hardware sampler and tracker software in tandem, and celebrate gritty, lo-fi sounds. Instead, the ultimate goal of neurofunk is the sound quality and clean production made possible by today's digital audio workstations.

## JUMP-UP

A form dedicated entirely to the dancefloor, jump-up has its roots in the direct and club-ready hardstep sound, which was born in the second half of the 90s and refined in the early 2000s by producers like Clipz and Twisted Individual. Like hardstep, it favours rolling linear beats, making a feature of digital, bright, and melodic synth basslines that are like catnip to clubbers. Newer artists like Serum, Upgrade, and Voltage have popularised the style, with tunes like Turno's massive *The Invaderz* becoming huge underground hits.

In an article for *DJ Mag*, Majistrate told Dave Jenkins about jump-up's dancefloor appeal. 'It is all about the hooks,' he said. 'Kids now—even in Belgium, where the leading sound has been pretty harsh and aggressive for years—are buying into the hooks. People want something to sing along to. It might be a vocal or the melody of the bass pattern. People don't want to hear new tunes dropped in every ten seconds. They want something a bit more than that.'

Though it's sometimes derided by those who favour a darker sound or more breakbeat-driven styles, jump-up is a form of drum & bass that powers the sets of many of the biggest DJs in the scene, and it is especially popular with d&b's new generation of clubbers. Like EDM, it's a gateway drug for many new d&b converts. 'It's an opportunity to be silly and to jump around like an idiot and not stand at the back scratching your beard at how a snare is made,' Upgrade said in the same article.

## MUTATIONS

These various subgenres are just a sample of the many ways jungle/drum & bass has morphed into different shapes over its lifespan. The music continues to mutate now, even in these uncertain, post-COVID times. Artists like Sherelle, Sinistarr, and Itoa incorporate it into productions and sets that focus more on tempo than specific genre, zeroing in on and panning out from breakbeat rhythms, and seeing them as part of a wider dance/electronic rhythmic narrative. Jungle's resilience has come in part from its flexibility and ability to adapt but always retain some semblance of form.

# 22 The Next Wave: Shogun Audio, Critical Music

Record labels are pillars of jungle/drum & bass culture. Certain imprints have driven the development and evolution of the genre in a similarly important way to pirate radio, dubplates, raves, and reggae. Think of Metalheadz, Good Looking, Exit, or Renegade Hardware, and there's an instant recall of the sound, aesthetic, approach. They inspire cult followings and become brands, with their adherents pledging blind loyalty to their output, secure in the knowledge it will be strong.

In the 2000s, two labels in particular would become influential in shaping today's d&b sound. Based in Brighton, Shogun Audio, run by Friction and K-Tee, has been a launchpad for many of the next generation of d&b talent. Standout producers like Spectrasoul, Alix Perez, Rockwell, and Icicle all got their start on the label, which has balanced many different flavours of drum & bass while championing those who dare to think differently. Meanwhile, in London, Kasra's Critical Music label has gone from DIY beginnings to become a highly influential force, releasing everything from the techy sound-design vibes of Mefjus to the grime-infused beats of Sam Binga & Rider Shafique.

Growing up in Brighton, Friction (real name: Ed Keeley) loved dance music, but he couldn't get into many clubs or raves as a teenager. He'd embark on regular pilgrimages to London, failing to convince his mates to join him: 'We'd all get tape packs and flyers, but no one would go to a rave unless there was an under-eighteens one on in Brighton or whatever. I was the one who was taking it that step further: *I'm going to London tonight, who wants to come?* No one! That was when I was branching off and going to these clubs, really seeing and believing—hearing big Moving Shadow tunes and falling in love with the music from there. I would get on the train on my own even if I didn't know anyone, just so I could be part of that music. I sacrificed parts of my youth for it, but I don't regret it.'

One place Friction could get into was Peckham's Laserdrome, a vital early jungle proving ground. He was captivated immediately. 'Randall was a resident, Dr S Gachet was a resident—everyone would play down there. It was the heads' club,' he says. 'I really liked Gachet's style, 'cause he'd play these big tunes—they were jungly but they had an atmosphere to them, and then they'd drop into these big shock out Amens. I loved that music and I loved Randall's mixing, because he'd roll out, stay in the mix for ages. Hearing two tunes together and staying in the mix and creating a key change or emotion out of two tunes together—it was like, *This is what I want to do.*'

Jungle became an obsession for Friction, and he threw himself into becoming a DJ. In the early 2000s, he started to have some success with his early productions, with True Playaz, 31 Records, and Renegade Hardware releasing his singles. Offered to sign exclusively to a few labels, Friction decided instead to go the independent route and set up his own imprint. From the beginning, it would be an outlet for not just his tracks, but for artists across the musical spectrum. 'I wanted to do it differently to what else was out there,' he says, 'and I wanted to start a label that was releasing drum & bass tunes with no directive.'

Initially releasing singles with a broad musical remit by respected artists like Spirit, Klute, and Noisia, Shogun Audio began to crystallise its sound when Friction signed and pushed a new generation of artists with a similar mindset. 'I found and nurtured people like Alix Perez, Spectrasoul, and Icicle, taking them from up-and-coming artists. Dave from Spectrasoul was assisting me with the label and he started to make tunes with another guy, Jack. That was how Spectrasoul started. It's like a movement started without us even realising it. A sound and everything just happened, and it was all happening so naturally.'

Releasing music that sat somewhere between soulful and futuristic, metallic and tuneful, Shogun—ably aided by Friction's business partner Keir Tyrer, who used to record for Ram and Hardware as K-Tee—quickly got a reputation for its own style. While not exactly a subgenre, this blend of liquid funk and techy production became a late-2000s signifier for drum & bass. Soon, Shogun had its own night at London's much-missed club The End. Releases like Alix Perez's *Down The Line* featuring the dub-dunked vocals of MC Fats, had brisk beats, warm synths, and rough distorted bass; Icicle's *Spartan* took the sound design and cosmic atmospheres of techno and soldered them to a steely d&b exoskeleton.

'This whole style, we discovered it by accident, but it was this aggressive, soulful sound,' Friction says. 'We had something that no one else had, and we were in at The End. That's the way we kept it.'

Shogun Audio really hit its stride in the next decade. Friction started hosting his own show on Radio 1 in 2012, and the label put out startling and original tracks like Rockwell's electro-techno hybrid *Detroit* and the cyborg R&B of *Light In The Dark* by Spectrasoul and Terri Walker.

When signing tracks, the label boss has always been driven by one factor. 'I think the music has to be based on—how does this feel when I listen to it? Yes, it needs to be produced to a certain level, and that's my second point. Is the production good enough, is the kick punching through? Is the snare cutting through, can I feel that bottom end to the track. But that has to come second. If that comes first, then you've got the order wrong. It should always be about the music.'

Kasra had quite a different introduction to music: through hardcore punk, noise music, and the DIY tape scene. Kasra Mowlavi grew up in London, the child of an Iranian dad and an Irish mum, and gravitated towards the sound of distorted guitars. 'I was into alternative guitar music. I used to listen religiously to John Peel, who obviously didn't just play that kind of music—it was everything else in between, too.'

At school, some of his friends were into the same stuff as him, while the others liked dance music—something he was initially very resistant to. 'At first I discounted it,' he says. 'When you're young—it's different now—you're stubborn, and you're in camps who are quite particular about how you feel about music, you'd wear it as a badge of honour. I was like, *That's not real music, it's made on a computer.*'

However, as time went on, he heard more and more sounds he enjoyed, and started to recognise a similarity between the fiercely independent ethos of the records and artists he loved, and the way that dance producers and labels would operate. 'I saw there was quite a synergy in the message that was behind the music, the driving force behind it. It was very much that underground spirit. You make a record, press it up, and you get it out there. There was no grand plan, no desire to have commercial success. And there was a similarity between people making a racket in a garage in northwest America and people making some noise on their computer in east London. So I found it normal when I realised that there was a similar feeling behind it.'

Kasra had his ears opened to drum & bass one night at The End, with Storm and Loxy playing. From there, there was no turning back. 'It was like, *Woah, what the fuck is this?* It felt like the future. Hearing it in a club environment was unlike anything I'd ever heard before. There was a certain degree of experimentation that there still is today in drum & bass that was really interesting to me, and the energy, the tone and the mood.'

As he delved into the scene, he recognised another similarity between the limited-edition tapes or vinyl pressings he'd bought in the past, and the dubplate culture that drove d&b clubs and pirate radio for so long. 'You had to really hunt out these things,' he says. 'Some of the records I've got came out in editions of 150. Granted, not that many people wanted them, because they were particularly noisy, but you had to be really on the ball to get them. You couldn't just click online and buy, you had to be on mailing lists for shops. With the dubplate thing, if you want to hear that tune again, you had to hope that when it came out, you found it. Or you'd have to go and see that DJ or hope that at some point, someone would play it on the radio. But the energy you had to put in was really quite high. There was something really exciting about that.'

Kasra began to go to Metalheadz at Limelight and Swerve at the Velvet Rooms, hearing DJs like Flight, Fabio, and Marcus Intalex, and connecting with heads in the scene. Throwing himself into DJing and production, he started the Critical Music label in 2002, putting out tunes by established artists Breakage, Calibre, and Bungle in the early days. In the 2010s, the label began to forge a more distinct identity with its roster, releasing records by Enei, Sabre, Ivy Lab, and Mefjus. For every frosty, metallic track, there was a more soulful or ragga-influenced counterpart, or an excursion into hybrid beats. Dub Phizix's 2012 tune *Never Been* took a dancehall beat and added layers of speedy percussion, MC Fox giving the half-time track a restrained ragga respray before little drops into splintered Amen breaks, while on Mefjus's *Suicide Bassline*, frightmare synths shatter like glass before a pummelling distorted techno sub. The uniting factor was avoiding retro nostalgia—pushing the sound forward in a subtle way that could still connect with the dancefloor.

'I want to be seen as a label that puts out interesting music, that pushes forward and tries to do some different things,' Kasra says. 'Not standing still or trying to replicate the past. Seeing what can be done within the bpm range of where we operate. Not that we're crazy experimentalists, I don't think that's necessarily true, but I'd like to think of every release as bringing something interesting to the table, showcasing a lot of the different stuff that can be done within the genre. There's the half-time stuff that the Ivy Lab guys are doing, and the harder edge of things that Mefjus does, for instance.'

Building up a following as one of the strongest new-school labels in drum & bass, over time Critical Music has become larger than the sum of its parts, evolving beyond what its creator could have first imagined. 'I'm a massive fan of a guy called Ian MacKaye who runs Dischord Records, a punk label out of Washington, DC,' Kasra says. 'He was in a band called Fugazi. I was listening to an interview with him, and he said that a label is like a living organism with moving parts and people, responsibilities; that really resonated with me.'

'Critical Music is completely different to when I started it off. You guide it as much as you can, but there's certain things we put out now that I never thought we'd put out. I never thought we'd do a dancehall record, but we did; I never thought we'd be doing some of the best-selling records in the scene. You obviously aspire to that stuff. It does take on a bit of its own life because it's not just mine, it's the artists' as well. It's really important to me that when they want to do something, we can provide them the platform.'

The focus and drive of Friction and Kasra, and their labels, is reflective of the independent ethos of jungle/drum & bass as a whole. With their music mostly shunned by the mainstream industry and ignored by the press (beyond a few artists), people within the scene have been forced to do things themselves— and from this determination has arisen a collective strength. Drum & bass has thrived because of its independence; away from the glare of the spotlight, it's been able to develop as a resilient, ever-evolving form.

'In a way, it's good for us,' Kasra says. 'It's a scene that exists in the shadows. We're not influenced by trends. You see these DJs blow up and they're playing all these big techno parties, and then the next year it's like, *Oh, that guy is not really doing that anymore because everyone has moved on to something else now.* We just get on with our thing. Drum & bass is a music that is really hard to make, technically you have to be really skilled to make good drum & bass, I think most people would agree with that. It's a lot of work. The audiences and fees are nothing compared with what you might get in house and techno. But people really love it, they really care, they're really passionate. That makes it a really exciting, vibrant scene. I always compare it to heavy metal. Heavy metal is not really cool, and it doesn't get on the radio. But it will sell tickets, because the people care about it and they go to the parties. They go to the club nights and the gigs. There's an identity that comes with it. I think that's really important, because it makes the scene thrive.'

# 23 The Jungle Resurgence: Breakbeats, Basslines, And Hybrids

In the last few years, jungle has undergone a creative resurgence spurred on by an influx of new producers, seasoned heads who recognise a renewed interest in the genre, great club nights (prior to the pandemic), and a plethora of small independent record labels that cater to a passionate fan-base. Jungle and drum & bass have never gone away, of course—but a new generation is discovering the sound, and fresh ideas are again filtering into the scene.

On one side, the music is more commercially viable than ever. DJ Fresh, once known for being part of Bad Company and underground hits, reached no. 1 in the UK charts with tunes *Hot Right Now* and *Louder*. Crossover act Sigma collaborated with 'boy band' Take That. Andy C, the boss of Ram Records and a highly respected DJ from the earliest days of hardcore and jungle, sold out Wembley Arena and played there all night—the first person to do so at the enormous venue.

Up until COVID-19 struck, the underground was bubbling. Jump-up drum & bass, powered by punk-like energy, raucous synth bassline hooks, and new breed producers like Turno, Upgrade, and Serum, had a strong youth following. Festivals like Let It Roll in the Czech Republic, Sunandbass in Sardinia, and Hospitality In The Park in the UK were attracting capacity crowds.

Some of the most exciting developments in the scene have come from a revived appreciation for the original jungle sound, with more producers experimenting with chopped-up breakbeats and heavy dub basslines, sometimes injecting new influences and sounds. Record labels such as Ako Beatz, Skeleton, 7th Storey Projects, Green Bay Wax, Rua Sound, Repertoire, Myor, Western Lore, and many more have cultivated loyal customer bases, with vinyl releases sold direct through Bandcamp. Many incredibly talented producers have sprung up, such as Tim Reaper, Shiken Hanzo, Dead Man's Chest, Djinn, Decibella, and Coco Bryce, mindful of jungle's musical heritage but determined to put their own signature stamp on it.

A central peg of this platform is the club night Rupture. Based at Corsica Studios in Elephant & Castle, south London, the event has helped to galvanise the modern jungle scene, inviting both new school DJs like Forest Drive West and scene legends such as Paul Ibiza to command packed dancefloors, playing an uncompromising mix of rolling breaks and all sounds across the musical spectrum. Run by British-Punjabi Indra Khera (Mantra) and black British David Henry (Double O), the club has a booking policy that is inclusive to women and people of colour. Rupture's dancefloor reflects this mix of ethnicity and gender, standing in opposition to the 'whitewashing' that has blighted other areas of the scene (see next chapter). The club night also has an attendant record label—another primary source for the best new jungle beats.

### MANTRA & DOUBLE O

Like so many others, Mantra discovered dance music through an elder sibling. She idolised her older brother, who went out raving and frequently had Kool FM on at home in London. Though her first musical love was actually UK garage, she got swept up in club culture; and, when she discovered drum & bass properly, there was no going back.

'My mum let me go to a rave when I was fourteen, which was the worst mistake of her life!' Mantra says. 'Me and my mate begged our parents, like, *I promise, you let us go to this one rave, we'll never ask you again until we're eighteen.* Of course we had our fake IDs and managed to get in, and we were shell-shocked— we just couldn't believe the power of it. The music, the feeling, being totally immersed in it. My brother was militant: you could go to the loo and nothing else, stay by his side. When I was fifteen, I started going to my first d&b things, in about '99, 2000. I got into the Bad Company, Ed Rush, No U-Turn sound.'

Deciding she wanted to DJ herself at sixteen, Mantra didn't have to look far to get hold of decks. Her dad was setting up a Punjabi radio station in Southall, and he already had a pair of Technics. Later, while attending music college in Islington, she made a new friend who would help to solidify her appreciation for classic jungle.

'I met my best mate, Panka—she had moved over from Hungary, and I think at this point I would have been about twenty-one or something. Already we were going to Herbal a lot—Bassbin and Technicality. Panka was wearing a Bassbin jumper one day, and me, being all bolshy, I said, What you know about Bassbin? And she said, My boyfriend's Equinox, and I was like, Oh, shame! Through her, I met Marlon, and it was through her that we started properly digging for records. I'd go to second-hand shops, but I didn't really know what to look for. I'd just go for tune names and end up with a load of shit, basically. But me and Panka would go shopping every week and call Marlon up. She was the big catalyst and driving force in introducing me to all that Source Direct, breakbeat-driven style of jungle.'

Double O got into rave culture at the start of the 90s. Originally from Doncaster, he was a breakdancer before falling in love with house and techno. With Sheffield nearby, he was heavily influenced by Warp Records and the bleep sound, visiting the city to hear Winston Hazel DJ, while concurrently soaking up Detroit techno rhythms. He started to DJ at the legendary Doncaster Warehouse venue—'a big old-school rave place, for a small town we used to have a lot of people from London, Nottingham, Sheffield'—preferring the 4/4 sound to the more garish hardcore style prevalent at the time. Soon, though, he began gravitating to the jungle sound.

'Around late '92, '93, I started buying more jungle,' Double O says. 'Then it was Ibiza Records, early Reinforced, you started hearing the odd bassline coming into tunes, more of a dub influence. Then my ears pricked up, 'cause my brother was in a reggae soundsystem, so he was always playing and buying records. When I started hearing samples from these tunes he had, I was like, *OK*. It started to change. Saying that, there were some Detroit tunes that were doing that as well. But the UK had more of the thing with the hip-hop breaks. So it was when I started to hear the basslines come into hardcore that I started thinking, *This is getting more interesting now*, and it slowly evolved.'

After moving to London, he met Mantra, and in the early 2000s they'd go raving to the aforementioned Bassbin club night, Technicality, and Metalheadz— the only events where they could hear the rolling breaks and basslines of original jungle. 'I stopped making music from around '98 until 2003—I was in a weird place,' says Double O. 'I'd turn the radio on and all I'd hear was jump-up. It was only when I had met Indi, Equinox, and Panka, that's when I went to Technicality and realised people were still making the breaks, still chopping.'

'Everything was centred around Herbal back then—they had, like, four drum & bass nights a week that we would go to,' Mantra says. 'Hospitality started there, Bassbin and Technicality were the main ones, and we were working for SRD, the distribution company, pulling and packing records. Quite a lot of record labels would come through there, so we would get an allowance of a few records a week.'

While appreciating the techstep sound they'd hear at Renegade Hardware's event at The End, Mantra and Double O were frustrated that there weren't enough club nights playing the music they liked, so they decided to try starting their own. 'We thought we could bring a slightly different angle,' Mantra says. 'I felt like we could have a slightly broader palette of music if you like, than just being breakbeat or techy stuff.'

'There wasn't enough going on,' adds Double O, 'so we thought, *Let's start our own thing*. We bit off more than we could chew, starting at Dingwalls in Camden. Quite a big venue for our first night, but that was the beginning of something we wanted to do. It was like, *Let's stick at it and develop our own night.*'

When it started, in 2006, Rupture took a while to get going. As one of the few outposts for jungle at the time, the event was viewed with bemusement by some naysayers. 'I remember flyering outside clubs and people looking and saying, Who are they? and throwing flyers in your face,' Double O says. 'They wanted to hear jump-up, which I'm not dissing, but that's not what we wanted to hear.'

In time, though, Rupture built a reputation for its dedicated crowd, great line-ups and atmosphere. Older heads would increasingly mingle with a new influx of ravers, helping to kickstart a refreshed jungle sound. 'Once you're serious about what you want to do, and you build something, people will come,' says Double O. 'Once you really believe and have a passion, there's someone who will believe in what you're doing—if you're passionate about it, if you're willing to stick with something. To start with, it was a lot of the older heads, and then the younger ones started getting into it. The friendlier attitude as well, it's a totally different atmosphere.'

Sampled breakbeats in drum & bass were scarce on dancefloors for some years, but they have gradually come back into vogue. As a younger audience has connected with sampled drums for the first time, they've put their own spin on jungle. At the same time, established artists like Paul Woolford, in his Special Request guise, have helped popularise breaks and jungle within the techno scene, while artists such as Denham Audio or Mani Festo have brought a slower 140bpm style to popular consciousness.

'Sometimes things have a snowball effect—you've got people like Special Request, these huge superstar DJs who are playing a lot of jungle, which can open things up to huge audiences,' Mantra says. 'Things can pick up momentum. There is definitely a bit of a buzz around it now, which is wicked, because with the raves, you get young people coming and that's what you need. It's like, young people, fresh perspectives, approaching jungle from a different place—that's what makes it exciting.'

Among the most exciting new-school jungle producers is Sully. When he started out, Jack Stevens was producing two-step garage and dubstep-adjacent beats, but in recent years, he's focused on jungle. Though tunes like *Soundboy Don't Push Your Luck* shred Amens and roll out Reese bass with the best of them, recent track *Swandive* mixes horizon-chasing sci-fi synths with melodic drum glissandos that sound like a cascade of pots and pans, in the best possible way. Tim Reaper (real name: Ed Alloh) is another producer who has gained deserved acclaim recently, putting out a dizzying run of releases on many labels. While he's a precise beat surgeon, he's mixed his blizzards of Amens with excursions into 4/4 jungle tekno and melodic, emotional synth work, as on his epic remixes of Special Request on Hooversound.

### SHERELLE

Within today's jungle/d&b scene, there's a certain degree of nostalgia for the golden early-to-mid-90s style, and a fascination with it among the younger audience. But those rolling breakbeats also materialise in other, more novel ways in the sets of the most adventurous artists. Sherelle is one of the most innovative DJs in this regard: her sets on Reprezent radio, NTS, and, recently, Radio 1—not to mention at plenty of clubs and festivals—have attracted a large fan-base, thanks to her futuristic hybrid approach. Merging jungle old and new with Chicago footwork and flecks of techno and dubstep, her speedy 160bpm style is at once unconstrained by genre while also steeped in heritage and history. As likely to play something by Lemon D or Dillinja as she is a brand-new track by Sinistarr from her label Hooversound, Sherelle has found a signature style that is proving influential on the most progressive artists in the scene.

When she was growing up, Sherelle's mum and sister were her biggest influencers, putting her on to R&B, hip-hop, and reggae. 'From day dot, I was able to get into all kinds of different music, especially from the black experience,' she says. But she also encountered jungle super early in her life, and it made an impression—even then. 'I was in the car with my mum, sister, and uncle, and pirate radio was on. It's the first time I heard *Renegade Snares*. I must have been about three. I was moving house, so it was 1997. I didn't know it was called that until I played *Grand Theft Auto* many years later.'

It was through video-game soundtracks that she initially discovered jungle and drum & bass, coming across the Omni Trio/Foul Play classic and also the latter's *Finest Illusion* on *GTA*, before later hearing tunes by DJ Marky and Artificial Intelligence on football game *FIFA Street 2*. As she got heavily into music, she would download all kinds of things via the P2P program Limewire, investigating the complete catalogues of artists both familiar and obscure.

'The computer broke down loads of times, 'cause I was downloading mass amounts of music and getting lots of viruses to cram onto my iPod Classic,' she says. 'With my generation, there isn't just one genre that pins us down. Back in the 90s, people listened to just jungle or drum & bass. They were known for a particular scene and that was it, whereas our generation, there are so many examples and things that we can look to that essentially, someone like myself or others can put that into a mix.'

As Sherelle grew fascinated by jungle, she discovered another sound that would have a profound effect on her future: footwork. Stumbling upon a DJ Nate tune offered as a free download on a now-defunct website, she was bowled over by this strange genre. She didn't know what it was called at the time, but she began to investigate. She listened to a mix that the American artist Machinedrum made for *Mixmag*, and she was surprised to hear him blend jungle and footwork together. But it was the late DJ Rashad and his footwork-jungle crossover tracks like *Let It Go* that made all the elements fall into place.

'All of a sudden, all these experiences I'd had, Rashad made it all make sense,' Sherelle shares. 'All these songs that I'd been interested in and loved from day dot, but didn't know what it was called, and then he came along. I saw the Boiler Room set he did for Ray-Ban alongside DJ Manny and DJ Spinn, and it's been that kind of journey from there. Honing a lot of my past experiences and running with it. I was on Reprezent radio at the time, being like, *No one plays footwork and jungle, maybe that could be my niche?* Mixing two genres together at the same bpm. There's a lot of tracks that if you put them together, it's a mind-blowing, snare-filled, drum-filled explosion.'

Since then, Sherelle has honed a deadly and ferocious style as expertly mixed as it is sonically devastating. The various musical styles that she mixes all have one vital aspect in common: their lineage in the history of black music.

'As an English person inclined to play music of black origin and experience, I immediately got what footwork was and what jungle was,' she says. 'Jungle, the way it came up and was created, was mostly via young black males and females. It was their experience from their parents, especially ragga jungle. There was a similar kind of crossover link with footwork—again, it's about the black experience. For example, in a DJ Rashad tune, the samples are primarily coming from soul or old-school hip-hop tracks. I saw the connection between the two, therefore it made sense to put them together.'

While some have lumped in the music Sherelle plays under the nebulous and vague term 160—referring to its tempo—she points out that such a non-definition has potential pitfalls. Instead, emphasising the history and origins of what she includes in her sets is imperative. 'I want to make sure that the next generation coming through know where the music has come from,' Sherelle says. 'There's been a topic recently about the definition of 160. It's something I'm known for and have championed in the past. A good friend of mine based in the USA, DJ Noir, who runs an amazing collective called Juke Bounce Werk, was talking about the erasure of black culture, when you use the catch-all term of 160. That's something I don't want to contribute to, at all.

'I am drawn to this music because it's naturally my generation's experiences,' Sherelle continues. 'Jungle, the origins of d&b, to footwork—all this is integral and important to me, to make sure people do know the origins. DJ Noir has a point, in saying a lot of people are not necessarily going to know the history behind it, to really understand where the music has come from. I think preserving music of black origin is key to the success and progression of electronic music today. Although Black Lives Matter has been in many different forms over the years, I'm glad that because of that movement, people are now researching what their music is about and being more appreciative of black and POC labels.'

Sherelle runs the Hooversound label with fellow DJ and friend Naina. Having released several futuristic EPs from genre-meshing artists Hyroglifics and Sinistarr, and then achieving a coup by pulling in a Special Request/Tim

Reaper collaborative EP, it's their ambition to build a label that is instantly identifiable when you hear one of its releases—in a similar way to Metalheadz, for instance. Unconstrained by tempo or genre, Hooversound will be more about celebrating the unconventional.

'The label is basically to serve as a place for people to go and find something different from the club music we have today,' she says. 'Hopefully, when you hear a set and you hear a Hooversound song, you know it's Hooversound straight away because of the fact it's quite wonky or different from everyone else's tune. Something to have gun fingers to and explode and swear and push your friend and lose it to, basically. To fuck up the current ecosystem is pretty much what we would like to do, and in turn become a really big dance label where people go to find amazing music.'

# 24 Outro: Fallen Soldiers, Whitewashing, Gender Equality, And Changes

## FALLEN SOLDIERS

At the boutique Shindig festival in Somerset on May 24, 2017, Sunday afternoon is set up for a drum & bass extravaganza. Bukem, Marky, and Fab & Groove are playing out the day, but news filters through during Bukem's set of the fall of another true drum & bass soldier: Marcus Intalex.

When the stalwart scene DJs in attendance hear about Marcus's death they are absolutely gutted, but they elect to play on anyway. Marky drops an unreleased collaboration he did with Marcus for the first time, and he actually weeps at the decks at one point as memories of his great friend come flooding back through his music. Fabio, following on, plays pretty much a total Marcus Intalex appreciation set. Taking advantage of having thousands of drum & bass tracks at his fingertips on his USBs, he draws deep, rolling out Marcus's *Nightfall* with ST Files just as night falls. It's emotional.

The drum & bass scene has always looked after its own, and it pulls together at times of need and loss. Goldie spent time with Marcus's mum up in Manchester in the run-up to his funeral, while Hype wanted someone to do a Marcus tribute mix on his radio show, so he called up Randall—who absolutely delivered.

The not-for-profit Marcus Intalex Music Foundation (MIMF) was set up in the aftermath of his passing, with patrons including Goldie and long-term Manchester DJ Dave Haslam. 'One of Marcus's greatest passions was to encourage and guide aspiring music talent, as well as pass on the knowledge he himself acquired over the course of his long-standing and successful career,' the MIMF blurb reads. 'His importance to the Manchester music scene cannot be overstated, and as an extension of that, the Marcus Intalex Music Foundation aims to continue working in this spirit. From workshops and studio sessions, to seminars and events; we will host and facilitate a series of programming for people to explore, learn and immerse themselves in everything we love about music and the people we admire.'

Early events at venues such as Gorilla and Band On The Wall were headlined by Goldie and Marky, with Marx XTC and Paul Taylor—both friends from Marcus's time at Burnley club Angels back in the day—helming DJ workshops for up-and-coming DJs in the Manchester area.

In January 2018, another DJ/producer pioneer, Tango—who'd released on Formation, Creative Wax, and Moving Shadow—suddenly passed away. And in August of the same year, another soldier left the planet: Spirit, who had released on Metalheadz, Commercial Suicide, Shogun Audio, V Recordings, and Dispatch. Tributes were paid to both by all the UK scene's main players.

May 2019 saw many of the scene's original pioneers come together for a special tribute show at Village Underground in Shoreditch in memory of Kemistry, twenty years after the tragic passing of the drum & bass angel.

### WHITEWASHING

In its frenzied first few years, drum & bass was a truly multiracial scene. It may have attracted a whole new swathe of white people during its crossover period, but many of its originators remained embedded in its fabric, drum & bass for life.

In the mid-90s, d&b was still a subculture of independent labels and record shops—an in-person network of producers, DJs, promoters, and enthusiasts. The scene's members operated on the fringes, frequenting raves where a lot of illegal drugs were consumed, smoking weed (copiously, in some cases), surviving through stealth, grafting. A lot of the early pioneers were true rebels—living for the parties, the pirates, the next big tune, the buzz of creating a fresh new universe. They were outlaws, not toeing the line, vibing off each other, hurtling towards the twenty-first century with a bag of records and a street-real attitude. It was fanatics chopping up breaks; sampling jazz, funk, reggae, techno, or whatever else took a producer's fancy; spitting out rollers for the dances.

It might not be immediately clear, but the majority of the people interviewed for or profiled in this book are black or mixed race. And some of the other important black contributors to the scene's early days have been almost forgotten, or have had to go back to day jobs. Names like Sky Joose, Anthill Mob, Cool Hand Flex, Mike De Underground, Trigga, DJ Dextrous, Teebone, Rude Boy Keith, Uncle 22, Nigel Doyle, Prizna, Errol Simms, Chatta B, Carl

Collins from Hardleaders and more would also have appeared in this book if there were another two volumes or so.

Foundational artists and DJs—black and white—have battled on like soldiers, embracing new technologies like social media and in-the-box digital music-production and DJing techniques. They've been the true renegades who have built this worldwide drum & bass community—initially a distillation of the black British experience, with inner-city joy and rage and community and good times at its heart.

In the mid-90s, it was everyone together: you were judged by the content of your character and the quality of your tunes. When everyone was jumbled up in a glorious, multicultural melting pot, nobody needed to emphasise d&b's blackness—it was just there, significantly prominent, indisputably inseparable from the whole music genre. The music's 'blackness' made it cool for white kids, but a unity of experience shared by working-class white and black kids in inner-city areas propelled it forward.

With black people so central to jungle/drum & bass, surely this was the one music genre that couldn't be 'whitewashed'. Or could it?

Other music scenes have been whitewashed over the years—jazz, rhythm & blues, disco, funk, even the house and techno subgenres of electronic music. But nobody back then could have foreseen that drum & bass would ever be in danger of going down the same route.

'In a lot of cases, when this music becomes mainstream, it becomes disassociated from black experience and black context,' believes cultural critic Lisa Tomlinson, a lecturer and professor at the University of the West Indies in Jamaica. 'We talk about cultural appropriation...we reduce it to just borrowing, or sampling, another reductionist term. *Borrowing* or *sampling* sound like nice words, because they sound like an equal exchange. But there's a power dynamic embedded in that borrowing.'

Early adopters and creators have had their work, their ideas, appropriated and assimilated in most music forms over the years. Knowing your history is vital to every fan of any style of music. Just as The Beatles and the Stones frequently acknowledged their debt to Little Richard and Chuck Berry, so individual drum & bass artists who've made it big almost always tip their hats to some of the black pioneers of the music. Most people in drum & bass consistently emphasise the importance of history; many in the scene know all about and acknowledge the architects, but there are repeatedly new d&b converts, and some of those, who may have been brought in by the neurofunk explosion in Europe or the post-EDM boom in the USA, may only see a succession of white producers and DJs in their clubs or festivals. In some respects there has been an evident disconnect from the black roots of drum & bass (and most of the music it has sampled), and what the scene looks like today. This underlines the need for constant education as to the origins of jungle/drum & bass and the crucial importance of its black pioneers and continuing artists.

The online group Drum & Bass Against Racism (DABAR) was formed in the late 2010s as a discussion group. Amid the growing trend of post-Brexit racism in the UK and the wider world, it was set up as a forum for like-minded headz to talk about these issues in a positive way.

'A lot of people are hesitant to challenge racism because they may not have the confidence or experience to discuss it,' DABAR founder Grant Porter told UKF's Dave Jenkins. 'Getting to grips with the language and ideas surrounding white privilege and white supremacy is not easy. Many artists are warned about what they say now, because too much politics can alienate your fan-base. Some people feel they can't even say racism is wrong because they fear they'll get challenged.' DABAR actively promotes anti-racism—not just challenging blatantly racist statements or acts, but spotlighting unconscious bias and entitlement.

## 2020

The drum & bass scene, born out of jungle and the inner-city blues, was flourishing as it entered its fourth decade. Fab & Groove had just staged Return To Rage, a memorable one-off night at Heaven with many of the DJs from its original heyday—Frost, Bryan Gee, Storm, Kenny Ken, DJ Ron, Ray Keith, et cetera—representing. 'Drum & bass is the healthiest it's ever been,' said Fabio, as we turned the corner into 2020.

The youthful sound of jump-up was thriving, thanks to Voltage, Serum, and Bou & Dutta; half-time had grown into its own distinct shape, with artists such as Ivy Lab, Fracture, Alix Perez, and Om Unit; the classic breakbeat and sub-bass-led jungle sound was having a moment, thanks to artists like Tim Reaper and Coco Bryce; and there were more women producers and DJs than ever before, with Sherelle, Djinn, Decibella, Mantra, and others getting the true sound out there. Many of the legends of the scene were enjoying revitalised

DJing careers, like Digital, J Majik, and Storm, while genre champions like DJ Hype or Kenny Ken have continued to represent from the beginning.

Who could've predicted what a clusterfuck 2020 itself would prove to be when, in March, the worldwide Coronavirus lockdown turned everything on its head. Then, in May, came the revitalised Black Lives Matter movement.

As the reality of the pandemic dawned in March 2020, all music events in the UK and most other countries immediately ceased. Not just drum & bass but the whole of the electronic music scene was shut down. Some drum & bass DJs, such as Frost, Zinc, Marky, and Doc Scott, started doing live streams from home. The scene sat it out, waiting for the virus to clear.

On May 25, in the early weeks of the pandemic, Drum & Bass Arena released its documentary *Drum & Bass—The Movement*, which was framed to cover the history of drum & bass music from 1996 to 2016. But using D&B Arena's birth in the mid-90s as the starting point had an unfortunate by-product, in that it omitted some of the music's early black pioneers, as an increasing parade of white dudes in black T-shirts explained d&b's more recent developments. Drum & Bass Arena has always represented the full spectrum of the scene admirably, and there is no question that its staff or output was ever racist—the opposite, in fact. But they did receive a barrage of criticism. 'I'm shocked at how much history has become reframed/rewritten/reworked,' *State Of Bass* author Martin James said when he viewed the doc. 'Junglism is black culture. There are white guests in the house of junglism who respect black histories. This film pays no respect.'

To be fair, acts like Noisia, Pendulum, Chase & Status, and Sub Focus have taken drum & bass stadium-sized in the post-millennial internet age, and the shift into the digital era has meant that these big acts have dominated computer screens and Spotify playlists. But it's skewed the balance: with a large number of white artists getting top billing, the make-up of d&b audiences too has changed. It should never be forgotten that drum & bass IS black music. It came from black culture.

To have racists in any drum & bass scene in the 2020s is not only abhorrent but ludicrous. Yet even in 2020, there were a few sad racists showing their ignorance. Doc Scott had to ban some of them from the chat while doing his DNBvid broadcasts in the middle of the year, while DJ Zinc's posting of a 'Black Lives Matter' sign on his Facebook page in the summer of 2020, shortly after the killing of George Floyd by police officers in Minneapolis on May 28, led a string of his followers to type 'All Lives Matter' in a sad display of ignorant whataboutery. One US d&b fan posted in response, 'Over here in America the racists love that ALM bullshit, it's not a good look for the land that gave us jungle.' Zinc subsequently posted a photo of a young black girl holding up a sign explaining the BLM ethos, yet still the All Lives Matter posts continued. ('We never said "Only Black Lives Matter". We know "All Lives Matter". We just need your help with #BlackLivesMatter, for black lives are in danger,' the sign reads.)

In early June, on what was dubbed #BlackOutTuesday, many in the music industry were united in posting black squares on their social channels in solidarity with the BLM movement, and promising to look at change and diversity within the industry. This campaign was admirable in many respects, but it also triggered a number of things. The BLM-related protests made the d&b scene look at itself for perceived 'whitewashing', and led companies to check their practices.

A lot of labels in drum & bass were set up by an enterprising DJ/producer or two in the hurly-burly of the 1990s, and as they've gone into the digital age, they've had to adapt to professional practices. Hospital Records, the biggest d&b label, was one of the music companies that posted a black square on #BlackOutTuesday. Chris Inperspective had left Hospital a few months earlier, and he started calling out the brand in a string of Facebook videos for allegedly having only white remixers on a remix compilation for reggae label Jet Star— and for not having many black artists on its roster.

After taking stock following a social-media shitstorm, Hospital, to its credit, responded proactively and posted a new pledge for black representation on the label, as well as initiating a twelve-month development scheme for a black artist. Its website-cum-shop now has a prominent 'Equality & Inclusion' tab on its front page, outlining the various pledges. 'These actions are the start of our commitment to contribute to a more equal and inclusive drum & bass community that is more reflective of its origins,' the Hospital team says. 'In turn, we trust these changes will lead to more diversity in our artist roster and event line-ups.'

Around the same time, in a Twitter discussion on the black origins of music genres, Dutch producer Dkay—of *Barcelona* fame—spoke in such a patronising way to Cleveland Watkiss, now an MBE, that he effectively cancelled himself. 'Maybe watch some docs or read a book,' he said, in response to Cleveland's question about why most engineers in the jazz era were white. 'Btw, I've been making you money for fifteen years, as I can see in my royalty statements, hope you enjoy it.'

In August of 2020, US junglist stalwart AK1200 tweeted, 'Almost all of my biggest influences as a DJ were black DJs.' He referenced Randall, Fabio, Grooverider, Brockie, Frost, and DJ SS from the drum & bass scene, plus Carl Cox and Miami bass dude Magic Mike from his home state of Florida. 'Before this moment, though, I've never once categorised them as black DJs and I should never have to again,' AK1200 continued.

'Why would you?' tweeted Grooverider in reply. 'And you should never have to.'

'Never,' Frost agreed.

That was exactly the point. In the early days, it was everybody together—the rave scene had seen to that. Often, working-class black and white youth had grown up in the same areas, gone to the same schools, hung out together—this was multiracial Britain at work. While there was undeniably the sense of a black brotherhood of sorts—a strength amid a community that still experienced overt or covert racism from the wider outside world—drum & bass was anything but a closed shop.

DJ Flight, who was inspired to start DJing by the early hardcore and jungle scene, finds the mostly white club crowds she sees now disheartening, as she remembers the multicultural raves and nights she went to in the 90s. 'The way dance music has been moving over the last few years, it's becoming more and more whitewashed, and people aren't really remembering the roots of it,' she says. 'If there was no soundsystem culture brought to the UK, then most of these genres wouldn't have taken off or developed how they have.

'I'd like to see more of a mix in crowds again,' she continues. 'Sometimes I get depressed—I look at photos of events and it's mostly white men. I didn't get into it for this reason. I don't want to sound bitter or anything, but one of the main reasons I fell in love with it was because it was so mixed and felt so open, and anyone could do anything. Now it feels like it's very narrow.'

DJ, producer, and label owner Chris Inperspective shares this assessment. As the man behind the seminal Technicality club night and a long-time supporter of the deeper sound in drum & bass, he co-founded the Black Junglist Alliance (BJA) in the aftermath of his spat with Hospital Records.

'Now, drum & bass is so white, you've got kids going, *Well, what have black people got to do with drum & bass?*' he says. 'That to me is because the picture that labels and promoters keep painting is a white, homogenised picture. You have people saying it can't be that whitewashed. Yeah, it is, because when you look at the club crowds, we aren't there.'

Equinox reckons that part of the power of jungle/drum & bass in the past was its ability to build bridges between people, but he sees a quite different scene today. 'The crowd is not mixed anymore, and the people's names that are up in lights now, you don't see many young black producers or any ethnicity out there, like it was back in the days,' he says. 'That makes me sad, because I liked the fact that rave music brought various people together. Different classes, different backgrounds and races. The thing about hardcore and jungle and rave culture in general is it brought a lot of different people together regardless of their colour, their beliefs and stuff. That needs to be done again.'

There are positive strides being made towards more inclusivity and representation of black and non-white artists in the scene. One of those is the club night Rupture, run by Mantra and Double O. It has been widely praised for its great atmosphere and diverse line-ups—and the mix of races and genders in the talent booked for the night is reflected in how mixed the crowd is, too.

'The reason why Rupture have a huge audience that is very diverse is because they're pushing loads of different faces, they're booking black people all the time and you've got a woman and a black guy that run it, so therefore the audience is different,' Chris Inperspective says. 'It's about who's at the top. If the people at the top are black or of colour, then the audience will be black or of colour, too.'

It's something Chris is putting into practice with the Black Junglist Alliance, which aims to build a network of black and non-white artists in the scene across the world, and showcase the integral black roots of the genre. 'It's to create a bit of unity,' he says. 'We want to continue that. We've set up a YouTube channel to try to get some more black representation in drum & bass, to do it in a stylised way. Black Junglist Alliance is to do with ownership and inclusion. We need to get that back again. We're going to ensure future generations have the opportunity.

'There's a lot of black organisations in many industries, and there's a reason for that: because we've been marginalised on a societal scale,' he continues. 'So it's political. We're not the Black Panthers, or the Black Avengers (our unofficial title), but we are certainly gonna be making sure that ownership and inclusion of people of colour is the primary concern within jungle and drum & bass.'

## EQ50

In the last few years, another problem that has been highlighted is the lack of women DJs, producers, and label owners in the drum & bass scene. Though pioneers like Kemistry & Storm, DJ Rap, and Tamsin were there from the start, comparatively few women artists have broken through since the start of the 90s, and d&b has remained, like other areas of music, a male-dominated area. A growing number of female producers and DJs have sought to redress this considerable imbalance lately, with Sherelle, Decibella, Djinn, Kyrist, Mollie Collins, and more all representing via their DJ sets or heavyweight tracks.

Dismayed by the dominance of males on club line-ups and in label discographies, DJ Flight, Mantra, Sweetpea, MC Chickaboo, Alley Cat, and Jenna G set up the EQ50 mentorship programme, which aims to match aspiring women artists with leading labels and offers them the tools they need to succeed in the industry.

'In 2018, I tallied up how many women had played for Hospital, Metalheadz, Critical, and Rupture in a year,' Mantra says. 'I was so shocked by how few—we're talking one to three percent of their line-ups were women. Rupture wasn't great, but stood at seventeen percent. I posted these findings online, and it seemed to have quite a big impact. Off the back of this, Red Bull got in touch and asked me to curate a Normal Not Novelty evening at their studios—an evening of music workshops and Q&As for women. The night was wicked, and there was such a great energy. A few of us started emailing about possible next steps, and slowly the idea was formed that we should start our own collective aimed at promoting diversity within drum & bass. It's been a slow and steady process, as we're all very mindful of making sure we do things in the right way.'

With EQ50 involved, it is clear that there are now more opportunities for women to succeed in d&b. 'Our mentorship has just started, and already Ram and Shogun Audio have signed tunes from their mentees,' Mantra adds. Sure enough, Athena's liquid paean *Miss You* came out on Shogun at the start of 2021.

It's encouraging to see that, not only does drum & bass continue to be rhythmically and musically inventive—in 2021, via organisations like EQ50, Black Junglist Alliance, and DABAR, it's facing up to many of the issues that have impacted upon it. As the most resilient of genres, it will undoubtedly adapt, survive, and thrive, through this decade and many more.

# Afterword

As 2020 turned into 2021 and lockdowns continued, an outsider might've written off drum & bass as finished—along with much of the rest of the dance music scene. With clubs decimated and DJs out of work, it was going to take a while for the scene to get back to 2019 levels of thriving. But it seems clear that drum & bass has so many fans, so many people internationally invested in the culture and the music, that truly it will never die. It might take a bit of time to recover its full glory, but its time on pause could actually have made the scene stronger.

Most of those who have dealt in drum & bass for nearly three decades have been on considerable journeys in that time. Jumpin Jack Frost, following his drug burnout around the millennium, did lots of rehab therapy and, later on, self-reflection, when writing his autobiography, *Big Bad & Heavy*. 'I didn't originally plan to speak about my depression and my anxiety, but as I became more comfortable with the process of writing the book, it all came out,' he says. 'If you talk about it, you find you're not alone out there. A lot of people think that their mental health situation might be isolating, or they don't feel comfortable talking about it because there's stigmas attached to it. I was really uncomfortable about sharing things in my book originally; even before the book came out, I was quite anxious about how talking about my depression and anxiety would be received—I was nervous about how people would see me. But the reaction was really good—a lot of people said they took a lot of strength from my honesty, which made it all worth it.'

Now, Frost talks about mental health on music industry panels and has qualified as a mental-health first-aider; he hosts a monthly discussion podcast, *The Frost Report*, and at the time of writing planned to release both a new album and another book. 'My advice to any young people out there who are feeling anxious or depressed is: don't ever feel that you're alone,' he says. 'There are always people to talk to, there are many people out there who can help you right now. You're never alone. Being a man is being able to go out there and share your feelings.'

Goldie, meanwhile, is like a machine. He still practises yoga every day, and recently launched an activewear clothing brand, Yogangster—the dichotomy appealing to his sense of humour. Not that he's given up art and music, though— the opposite, in fact. He's still on absolute missions with both, opening an art gallery in Bangkok called Aurum, painting more than at any time since he was a teenager, and producing lots of multi-genre music with James Davidson as Subjective—a project that deliberately isn't pure drum & bass. As if to square the circle, he signed the third Subjective album with Pete Tong, the A&R guy who originally signed *Timeless* and is now heading up Three Six Zero Recordings.

Does all this activity mean he's neglected his pioneering Metalheadz label that's stayed true to the craft for over a quarter of a century? Not on your nelly! From Thailand, he still oversees the new breed of 'Headz talent making waves such as Phase from Belgium, London-based Grey Code, Gremlinz from Toronto, New York's Adred, and Blocks & Escher, whose *Something Blue* album was an electronica-augmented, emotive art-jungle masterpiece. Meanwhile, he's also looped in Nookie, one of the Reinforced originals back in the day, for a techno album and a drum & bass album to help keep the metal flowing.

Anyone who knew Frost and Goldie in the 90s could scarcely have predicted these outcomes, but they are victory stories for music—triumphant tales of how trauma and discrimination have been expressed and overcome through art. Of course, both can still throw down a heinous cutting-edge drum & bass DJ set when they want to—they still retain a renegade attitude amid the greater serenity in personal lives.

Hype, too, is another one who's calmed down. Over the course of the COVID-19 lockdowns, he made some life changes, including kicking his Playaz label back into gear. 'I have had time now to kind of reset myself, after being in that fast lane of the music game without taking any real time out for the last thirty-nine years,' he told *DJ Mag*. 'Being forced to stop was a blessing in disguise. I gave up smoking ganja, and that has changed me for the better.'

In late 2020, he began streaming DJ sets from his basement Playaz Dungeon studio, reflecting on his musical legacy and inviting guest DJs and MCs to throw down—and occasionally employing puppets. If you know, you know.

'The Playaz Dungeon is a mix of today's digital era and the older analogue era, with music spanning forty years and longer scattered about the place,' Hype says. 'It's meant to push and raise the standard of producers, DJs and MCs, including myself, while enjoying the vibe of actually hanging out and trying out styles and flavours, with artists being taken out of their comfort zones and challenged musically.'

Hype also started sporadically tweeting about his journey at the start of 2021. 'A lot of my old friends from that early era of my life are either mad, dead, or in prison,' he wrote. 'That was my destination too, if I had followed my original path. Music saved me from following a path of destruction in my teens, and now in 2021 it's saving me again thru this COVID craziness.' He is glad to have ended up in HMV rather than HMP.

Doc Scott also pulled himself through some dark times. After whizzing through the 1990s at a hundred miles per hour, by 2002 he was physically, mentally, and creatively drained. A scary path of self-destruction culminated in a breakdown around 2008. 'I needed help,' he told UKF's Dave Jenkins in 2018. 'I thought I could work it out myself, but I couldn't do it. I couldn't figure out what had gone wrong, so I broke down to my wife, and she called Goldie, who put me onto this group called the Hoffman Group.'

Goldie had been helped by this therapy process a few years previously. 'If you're struggling with things, whether it's substance issues or self-harming or suicidal thoughts, then you need to talk to people, because it's impossible to sort it out internally,' Doc Scott said. 'Therapy gives you the tools to deal with these things, and my week with the Hoffman Group was the toughest week I've had in my life. But had I not done it, I don't think I'd be here.' By the end of the decade, he was back at the top of his game, picking up awards for his DNBvid-19 live stream series of 2020 and smashing it with his label 31 Recordings.

With gigs cancelled for most of 2020 and a good part of 2021, other junglists ploughed new furrows too. Flight recorded a series of groundbreaking podcasts, interviewing Rasta poet Benjamin Zephaniah, radio DJ Jamz Supernova, former West Brom footballer Brendan Batson, and a host of others to collate their Windrush Stories. Sherelle landed a residency on BBC Radio 1 and secured a landmark release for her Hooversound label that featured Tim Reaper pairing with Special Request. Goldie carried on doing art and music and yoga, while entertaining everyone with comedy Instagram videos from Thailand. Fab & Groove helmed a 24-Hour Legends stream in aid of the Sickle Cell Society, running through their influences and calling in DJ pals Goldie, Zinc, Carl Cox, London Elektricity, and Benji B. Clayton from Renegade Hardware started talking about hosting a podcast interviewing many of the scene's founding soldiers.

With no club nights or festivals happening, the scene moved and adapted in perpetual motion. Metalheadz, Critical Music, V, 31, and Shogun Audio continue to have packed release schedules, while labels like Diffrent, The North Quarter, Hooversound, and 1985 Music are representing the new breed. Sales of drum & bass were up twenty percent on Beatport in 2020, despite there being no real-life gigs to play the tunes at, and there were three d&b no. 1s in the overall Beatport chart—by Serum (*Chop House*), Bou & Trigga (*Veteran VIP*), and the Phibes remix of Beat Assassins *Homegrown*. The site's curator, Yann Bonnet, thinks we've entered a new golden age for the sound. 'The historical artists and labels are still active, whilst, at the same time, a bunch of newcomers and new labels grew rapidly (in less than two years),' he told UKF. 'Moreover, the large spectrum of drum & bass and its subgenres allow a great diversity of production, making the genre more popular worldwide.'

### A REBEL SOUND

Drum & bass will morph, adapt, and steer its own ship to new beginnings over the coming years. It's come a long way already. A whole swathe of the acid-house generation have made jungle/drum & bass their career, their lifestyle, their sound of choice. The first black British electronic music genre, the rebel sound has led the way in sonic frontierism and has arguably given birth to more brain-warping futuristic sounds than any other recorded music genre. Its wealth of talented characters and next-level music events have made it one of the most tribal of music genres—once you're in it, you're truly *in* it.

It's this generation's jazz. It's been our punk. It's the UK's answer to hip-hop—a ravier, more sonic-obsessed sound—and has influenced every single electronic music genre since its inception in one way or another. In doing so, it has carved its own path, because the true rebels always walk alone anyway (as the EZ Rollers tune *Retro* would have it).

'I don't even know half the people in the scene anymore, but I do recognise all the heads who were there back in the day, who are still there—they are the backbone of the scene,' says Roni Size. 'It's spread out now, on a worldwide level. Now there are countries which have their own independent scenes. People thought, *What goes up must come down*, and it hasn't yet, and I think that's because of the energy of the music—nothing else has that, except maybe some thrash metal. I don't think it's going anywhere soon.'

'It's part of my fucking bloodline, man,' says Goldie.

Drum & bass forever, baby!

# Select Bibliography

*All Crews: Journeys Through Jungle/Drum & Bass Culture*, Brian Belle-Fortune
(Vision, 2004)

*Altered State: The Story Of Ecstasy Culture & Acid House*, Matthew Collin
(Serpent's Tail, 1997)

*Big Bad & Heavy*, Jumpin Jack Frost (Music Mondays, 2017)

*DIY Culture: Party & Protest In Nineties Britain*, edited by George McKay
(Verso, 1998)

*Energy Flash: A Journey Through Rave Music*, Simon Reynolds (Picador, 1998)

*Grime Kids: The Inside Story Of The Global Grime Takeover*, DJ Target
(Orion, 2018)

*Inner City Pressure: The Story Of Grime*, Dan Hancox (William Collins, 2019)

*Intelligent Woman*, DJ Rap (Music Mondays, 2018)

*Join The Future: Bleep Techno & The Birth Of British Bass Music*, Matt Anniss
(Velocity Press, 2019)

*More Brilliant Than The Sun: Adventures In Sonic Fiction*, Kodwo Eshun
(Verso, 1998)

*Nine Lives*, Goldie (Sceptre, 2002)

*Ocean Of Sound: Aether Talk, Ambient Sound And Imaginary Worlds*, David
Toop (Serpent's Tail, 2001)

*State Of Bass: Jungle—The Story So Far*, Martin James (Boxtree, 1997)

*The Rough Guide To Drum N' Bass*, Peter Shapiro (Rough Guides, 1999)

# Acknowledgements

Goldie, Andy C, DJ Flight, Jumpin Jack Frost, Bryan Gee, Roni Size, Fabio & Grooverider, DJ SS, Mark Archer, DJ Storm, 2 Bad Mice, Remarc, Mantra, Warlock, Flinty Badman of Ragga Twins, DJ Trace, Fracture, A Guy Called Gerald, Danny Briottet, DJ Krust, DJ Die, Jonny L, Ray Keith, Nicky Blackmarket, Danny Donnelly, DJ Rap, MC Det, DJ Ron, John Morrow of Foul Play, Omni Trio, Digital, DJ Tamsin, Miss Pink, Brian Belle-Fortune, General Levy, Mark XTC, Simon 'Bassline' Smith, L Double, Paul Arnold, Rob Smith of Smith & Mighty, Justice, T Power, Photek, Equinox, DJ Marky, Patife, Oliver Brown, Edu van Duijn, Chris Goss, Tony Colman, Keir Tyrer, DJ Paulette, Colin Steven, Reeves Gabrels, Teebee, Chris Inperspective, DB, Carlos Soulslinger, Sinistarr, Thijs de Vlieger of Noisia, Optical, dBridge, Amit, Om Unit, Friction, Kasra, Double O, Sherelle, Dieselboy, Dave Stone, Martin Love, Danny Shutdown, Doc Scott, Clayton Hines, Nico, Alex Banks, Hype, Zinc, Randall, LTJ Bukem, Gilles Peterson, Paul Woolford, Charlotte Devaney, Laurence Verfaillie, Jon Carter, Barry Ashworth, Terry Ryan, Jay Cunning, Klaus Hill, Todd Terry, Barclay Crenshaw, Armand Van Helden, MJ Cole, Josey Rebelle, Scott Bourne, Ben Hindle, Martin Brown, Ben Willmott, Alex Constantinides, Dave Jenkins, Martin Carvell and all at *DJ Mag*, Shino Parker, Jayne Winstanley, Kate Patrick, Joe Roberts, Sarah Ginn, Jamie Simonds, Chelone Wolf, Daniel Newman, Tristan O'Neil, Dave Swindells, Chris Dexta, Jimmy Mofo, Sherman, Martin James, Tim Barr, and Simon Reynolds. Sorry for anyone we missed out!

Ben Murphy would also like to thank Hannah for her encouragement and belief during the preparation and writing of this book; Mia and Mac for the motivation; Allan McGrath for his advice; and Jawbone Press for believing in this project.

Carl Loben would also like to thank Lou, Rudy and Jacob for the headspace during the writing of Renegade Snares; my dad; and Irvine Welsh for the kick up the backside.

# Index

# ALSO AVAILABLE IN PRINT AND EBOOK EDITIONS FROM JAWBONE PRESS